80-11

Penguin Education

Motivation

Second Edition

Edited by Dalbir Bindra
and Jane Stewart

Penguin Modern Psychology Readings

General Editor

B. M. Foss

Motivation

Second Edition

Edited by Dalbir Bindra and Jane Stewart

Penguin Books

Penguin Books Ltd, Harmondsworth,
Middlesex, England
Penguin Books Inc., 7110 Ambassador Road,
Baltimore, Md 21207, U.S.A.
Penguin Books Australia Ltd,
Ringwood, Victoria, Australia

First edition 1966
Reprinted 1966, 1968
Second edition 1971
This selection copyright © Dalbir Bindra and Jane Stewart, 1966, 1971
Introduction and notes copyright © Dalbir Bindra and
Jane Stewart, 1966, 1971

Made and printed in Great Britain by
Hazell Watson & Viney Ltd
Aylesbury, Bucks
Set in Monotype Times

Contents

Preface to the Second Edition

Though the problem of motivation has remained unchanged in its essential definition for over a hundred years, attempts to understand the problem have taken varied and changing forms. One of the most dramatic shifts in the direction of research took place during the past few years – after the preparation of the first edition of this book (1966). The new ideas and findings so greatly altered the overall research scene that it seemed desirable to us to bring together the old and new materials into a reorganized volume of selected Readings on motivation. Hence this second edition.

When we were preparing the first edition, research on motivation seemed to divide into two main areas: motivation proper and reinforcement. Under the heading of motivation psychologists studied the conditions, mainly internal, that instigate various types of goal-directed actions. The concept of reinforcement referred to the observation that certain types of stimulation have rewarding or punishing effects on behaviour, and thus may be used to alter the probability of occurrence of particular actions. What the recent theoretical and experimental developments have done is to indicate that the phenomena to which these two concepts, motivation and reinforcement, refer may arise from a common set of processes – that motivation and reinforcement may fundamentally be the same thing.

The view of motivational processes that is now emerging is this: any goal-directed action is instigated by a central motivational state, which itself is created by an interaction within the brain between the neural consequences of bodily organismic states ('drives') and neural consequences of environmental incentives ('reinforcers'). Changes in behaviour that have traditionally been produced by manipulating 'motivation' or 'reinforcement' are the outcomes of influences from both the bodily organismic states and the environmental incentive objects. This view provides a coherent and convenient framework for posing specific questions about motivational processes and for organizing the experimental work that is being done to answer them.

For the above reasons the present edition differs substantially from the first. In all, we have deleted twenty-four of the selections in the first edition and have added seventeen. Parts Five and Six of this edition are almost wholly new. The first two Parts, which provide the historical background of the current work, remain essentially the same in content and organization. The middle two Parts, Three and Four, retain some of the earlier selections, but they have been reorganized and expanded.

Introduction

In this volume we provide an account of the current state of psychological knowledge about motivation. The excerpts and articles reproduced here represent theoretical and experimental writings that deal with the fundamental problems in this area of psychology. The arrangement of selections is designed to indicate the historical roots of current developments and the probable direction of future progress.

Chapter headings in psychology – emotion, motivation, perception, learning, and the like – designate neither distinctly separate sets of behavioural phenomena nor unique psychological processes. An assumption basic to the work of psychologists is that there exist a few key processes which are responsible for all the variety of behaviour observed in nature. The same processes are assumed to produce behaviour we describe as 'emotional' (e.g. anger, fear, joy), 'motivational' (e.g. eating, maternal behaviour, drug addiction), 'perceptual' (e.g. estimating sizes, shapes and distances), 'learning' (e.g. response shaping, acquiring motor skills), and 'thinking' (e.g. problem solving, reasoning). Chapter headings do not clearly subdivide psychological knowledge; they serve merely as convenient guideposts indicating the current areas of search for the basic processes. Chapter headings change as our ideas about the nature of these processes change.

The beginning of the concept of motivation as a basic psychological process is difficult to trace. The term does not seem to have been used by psychologists trained in the Wundtian structuralist tradition. It crept into the writings of functionally minded psychologists in England and America in the 1880s. The term frequently appeared in chapters on voluntary action or will, midst discussions of desire, impulse, and intention. Sully in 1884 said that the desire that precedes an act and determines it is to be called 'its moving force, stimulus or motive'. 'A desire when chosen becomes a *motive*,' wrote Dewey (1886). These definitions indicate that motivation was considered to be an entity that impelled one to action of a particular type. The idea of motivation of impulsion to action toward particular goals, which had been implicit in the idea of instinct, was thus extended to voluntary action as well.

McDougall (1908) made this extension of the concept of motivation to 'voluntary behaviour' explicit by suggesting that instincts were the 'prime movers of all human activity'. Avoiding the metaphysical tone of McDougall's doctrine of instinct, Woodworth (1918) proposed the concept of *drive* to refer to 'the motives and springs of action' that arouse a particular type of action. Troland's *The Fundamentals of Human Motivation* (1928) provided a physiological interpretation of the roles of pleasure and pain in human actions and learning. Warden's research monograph, *Animal Motivation*, was published in 1931, and Tolman's *Purposive Behavior in Animals and Men* in 1932. Young brought together much of the early research and provided the first systematic account of the area in his *Motivation of Behavior* (1936). It was during this period, the 1930s, that 'motivation' gained acceptance as a fundamental psychological concept. Since that time textbook writers have viewed motivation as a major subdivision of psychological knowledge.

The questions about behaviour that initially led to the adoption of the motivation concept are evident in psychological discussions today. These questions concern primarily the *why* and *how* of behaviour – the instigation of action. Why are animals active at all? Given the existence of certain activities (e.g. eating, drinking) in the repertoire of an animal, why does it engage in these activities at certain times but not at others? Once initiated, why is an activity terminated? How do actions become goal-directed, enabling the animal to attain particular outcomes with responses that are not particular but highly variable? How are pleasure and pain related to motivational processes? Recognizing that animals tend to repeat activities that lead to certain consequences (rewards) and stop doing what leads to certain other consequences (punishments), what precisely is the role of such reinforcers in the instigation of action?

The excerpts and articles collected in this volume represent attempts by major investigators to answer the above questions. The period covered extends roughly from 1900 to 1970. The selections are collected in six Parts. The writings in the first four

Parts present and examine the four major ideas concerning the nature of motivational processes. The fifth Part presents the current attempts to integrate the various ideas and lines of experimental evidence into a unified account of motivation. The final Part deals with the problem of neurophysiological mechanisms of motivation. Brief editorial notes introduce each Part.

References

DEWEY, J. (1886), *Psychology*, Harper & Row.
McDOUGALL, W. (1908), *An Introduction to Social Psychology*, Methuen.
SULLY, J. (1884), *Outlines of Psychology*, Appleton-Century-Crofts.
TOLMAN, E. C. (1932), *Purposive Behavior in Animals and Men*, Appleton-Century-Crofts.
TROLAND, L. T. (1928), *The Fundamentals of Human Motivation*, Van Nostrand.
WARDEN, C. J. (1931), *Animal Motivation: Experimental Studies on the Albino Rat*, Columbia University Press.
WOODWORTH, R. S. (1918), *Dynamic Psychology*, Columbia University Press.
YOUNG, P. T. (1936), *Motivation of Behavior: The Fundamental Determinants of Human and Animal Activity*, Wiley.

Part One Motivation as Instinct

The ancient view held that instincts were the instigators of certain primitive animal actions, which were different from intelligent and voluntary actions characteristic of man. Since the turn of the twentieth century, several writers have developed this instinct view of motivation with reference to the scientific study of both animal and human behaviour. Perhaps the formulations that have influenced psychologists the most are those of McDougall, Freud, and two ethologists, Lorenz and Tinbergen. The common feature of all these formulations is that instinct, as a psychophysiological entity, consists of energy-generating and direction-guiding processes, which together produce *all* forms of behaviour, animal and human, primitive and intelligent. Energy determines the instigation of action and the directional processes determine the form of the action. The writers differ in the relative importance each gives to the energy and directional processes, and in the way these processes are thought to interact, as well as in their conceptions of the underlying mechanisms. Some excerpts from the writings of McDougall and Freud and from the early writings of Lorenz and Tinbergen are reproduced in the following pages. This is followed by a critique of instinct-energy models by Hinde and a more general examination of the place of the concept of instinct in today's psychology by Beach.

1 W. McDougall

On the Nature of Instinct

Excerpts from W. McDougall, *An Introduction to Social Psychology*, Methuen, 1908, chapter 2.

The human mind has certain innate or inherited tendencies which are the essential springs or motive powers of all thought and action, whether individual or collective, and are the bases from which the character and will of individuals and of nations are gradually developed under the guidance of the intellectual faculties. These primary innate tendencies have different relative strengths in the native constitutions of the individuals of different races, and they are favoured or checked in very different degrees by the very different social circumstances of men in different stages of culture; but they are probably common to the men of every race and of every age. [. . .]

In treating of the instincts of animals, writers have usually described them as innate tendencies to certain kinds of action, and Herbert Spencer's widely accepted definition of instinctive action as compound reflex action takes account only of the behaviour or movements to which instincts give rise. But instincts are more than innate tendencies or dispositions to certain kinds of movement. There is every reason to believe that even the most purely instinctive action is the outcome of a distinctly mental process, one which is incapable of being described in purely mechanical terms, because it is a psychophysical process, involving psychical as well as physical changes, and one which, like every other mental process, has, and can only be fully described in terms of, the three aspects of all mental process – the cognitive, the affective, and the conative aspects; that is to say, every instance of instinctive behaviour involves a knowing of some thing or object, a feeling in regard to it, and a striving towards or away from that object.

We cannot, of course, directly observe the threefold psychical aspect of the psychophysical process that issues in instinctive behaviour; but we are amply justified in assuming that it invariably accompanies the process in the nervous system of which the instinctive movements are the immediate result, a process which, being initiated on stimulation of some sense organ by the physical impressions received from the object, travels up the sensory nerves, traverses the brain, and descends as an orderly or coordinated stream of nervous impulses along efferent nerves to the appropriate groups of muscles and other executive organs. We are justified in assuming the cognitive aspect of the psychical process, because the nervous excitation seems to traverse those parts of the brain whose excitement involves the production of sensations or changes in the sensory content of consciousness; we are justified in assuming the affective aspect of the psychical process, because the creature exhibits unmistakable symptoms of feeling and emotional excitement; and, especially, we are justified in assuming the conative aspect of the psychical process, because all instinctive behaviour exhibits that unique mark of mental process, a persistent striving towards the natural end of the process. That is to say, the process, unlike any merely mechanical process, is not to be arrested by any sufficient mechanical obstacle, but is rather intensified by any such obstacle and only comes to an end either when its appropriate goal is achieved, or when some stronger incompatible tendency is excited, or when the creature is exhausted by its persistent efforts. [. . .]

An instinctive action, then, must not be regarded as simple or compound reflex action if by reflex action we mean, as is usually meant, a movement caused by a sense-stimulus and resulting from a sequence of merely physical processes in some nervous arc. Nevertheless, just as a reflex action implies the presence in the nervous system of the reflex nervous arc, so the instinctive action also implies some enduring nervous basis whose organization is inherited, an innate or inherited psycho-physical disposition, which, anatomically regarded, probably has the form of a compound system of sensori-motor arcs.

We may, then, define an instinct as an inherited or innate psycho-physical disposition which determines its possessor to perceive, and to pay attention to, objects of a certain class, to experience an emotional excitement of a particular quality upon perceiving such an object, and to act in regard to it in a particular manner, or, at least, to experience an impulse to such action.

It must further be noted that some instincts remain inexcitable except during the prevalence of some temporary bodily state, such as hunger. In these cases we must suppose that the bodily process or state determines the stimulation of sense-organs within the body, and that nervous currents ascending from these to the psycho-physical disposition maintain it in an excitable condition. [. . .]

Are, then, these instinctive impulses the only motive powers of the human mind to thought and action? What of pleasure and pain, which by so many of the older psychologists were held to be the only motives of human activity, the only objects or sources of desire and aversion?

In answer to the former question, it must be said that in the developed human mind there are springs of action of another class, namely, acquired habits of thought and action. An acquired mode of activity becomes by repetition habitual, and the more frequently it is repeated the more powerful becomes the habit as a source of impulse or motive power. Few habits can equal in this respect the principal instincts; and habits are in a sense derived from, and secondary to, instincts; for, in the absence of instincts, no thought and no action could ever be achieved or repeated, and so no habits of thought or action could be formed. Habits are formed only in the service of the instincts.

The answer to the second question is that pleasure and pain are not in themselves springs of action, but at the most of undirected movements; they serve rather to modify instinctive processes, pleasure tending to sustain and prolong any mode of action, pain to cut it short; under their prompting and guidance are effected those modifications and adaptations of the instinctive bodily movements which we have briefly considered above.

We may say, then, that directly or indirectly the instincts are the prime movers of all human activity; by the conative or impulsive force of some instinct (or of some habit derived from an instinct), every train of thought, however cold and passionless it may seem, is borne along towards its end, and every bodily activity is initiated and sustained. The instinctive impulses determine the ends of all activities and supply the driving power by which all mental activities are sustained; and all the complex intellectual apparatus of the most highly developed mind is but a means towards these ends, is but the instrument by which these impulses seek their satisfactions, while pleasure and pain do but serve to guide them in their choice of the means.

Take away these instinctive dispositions with their powerful impulses, and the organism would become incapable of activity of any kind; it would lie inert and motionless like a wonderful clockwork whose main-spring had been removed or a steam-engine whose fires had been drawn. These impulses are the mental forces that maintain and shape all the life of individuals and societies, and in them we are confronted with the central mystery of life and mind and will.

2 S. Freud

Source, Aim and Object of Instinctive Energy

Excerpt from S. Freud, 'Instincts and their vicissitudes' (1915), in
Collected Papers, Hogarth Press, 1925, volume 4, chapter 4.

If we apply ourselves to considering mental life from a biological
point of view, an 'instinct' appears to us as a borderland concept
between the mental and the physical, being both the mental
representative of the stimuli emanating from within the organism
and penetrating to the mind, and at the same time a measure of
the demand made upon the energy of the latter in consequence of
its connection with the body.

We are now in a position to discuss certain terms used in
reference to the concept of an instinct, for example, its impetus,
its aim, its object and its source.

By the *impetus* of an instinct we understand its motor element,
the amount of force or the measure of the demand upon energy
which it represents. The characteristic of impulsion is common to
all instincts, is in fact the very essence of them. Every instinct is
a form of activity; if we speak loosely of passive instincts, we can
only mean those whose aim is passive.

The *aim* of an instinct is in every instance satisfaction, which
can only be obtained by abolishing the condition of stimulation
in the source of the instinct. But although this remains invariably
the final goal of every instinct, there may yet be different ways
leading to the same goal, so that an instinct may be found to
have various nearer or intermediate aims, capable of combination
or interchange. Experience permits us also to speak of instincts
which are *inhibited in respect of their aim*, in cases where a certain
advance has been permitted in the direction of satisfaction and
then an inhibition or deflection has occurred. We may suppose
that even in such cases a partial satisfaction is achieved.

The *object* of an instinct is that in or through which it can
achieve its aim. It is the most variable thing about an instinct and

is not originally connected with it, but becomes attached to it only in consequence of being peculiarly fitted to provide satisfaction. The object is not necessarily an extraneous one: it my be part of the subject's own body. It may be changed any number of times in the course of the vicissitudes the instinct undergoes during life; a highly important part is played by this capacity for displacement in the instinct. It may happen that the same object may serve for the satisfaction of several instincts simultaneously, a phenomenon which Adler calls a 'confluence' of instincts. A particularly close attachment of the instinct to its object is distinguished by the term *fixation*: this frequently occurs in very early stages of the instinct's development and so puts an end to its mobility, through the vigorous resistance it sets up against detachment.

By the *source* of an instinct is meant that somatic process in an organ or part of the body from which there results a stimulus represented in mental life by an instinct. We do not know whether this process is regularly of a chemical nature or whether it may also correspond with the release of other, e.g. mechanical, forces. The study of the sources of instinct is outside the scope of psychology; although its source in the body is what gives the instinct its distinct and essential character, yet in mental life we know it merely by its aims. A more exact knowledge of the sources of instincts is not strictly necessary for purposes of psychological investigation; often the source may be with certainty inferred from the aims.

Are we to suppose that the different instincts which operate upon the mind but of which the origin is somatic are also distinguished by different qualities and act in the mental life in a manner qualitatively different? This supposition does not seem to be justified; we are much more likely to find the simpler assumption sufficient – namely, that the instincts are all qualitatively alike and owe the effect they produce only to the quantities of excitation accompanying them, or perhaps further to certain functions of this quantity. The difference in the mental effects produced by the different instincts may be traced to the difference in their sources. In any event, it is only in a later connection that we shall be able to make plain what the problem of the quality of instincts signifies.

Now what instincts and how many should be postulated? There is obviously a great opportunity here for arbitrary choice. No objection can be made to anyone's employing the concept of an instinct of play or of destruction, or that of a social instinct, when the subject demands it and the limitations of psychological analysis allow of it. Nevertheless, we should not neglect to ask whether such instinctual motives, which are in one direction so highly specialized, do not admit of further analysis in respect of their sources, so that only those primal instincts which are not to be resolved further could really lay claim to the name.

I have proposed that two groups of such primal instincts should be distinguished: the *self-preservative* or *ego*-instincts and the *sexual* instincts. But this proposition has not the weight of a necessary postulate, such as, for instance, our assumption about the biological 'purpose' in the mental apparatus; it is merely an auxiliary construction, to be retained only so long as it proves useful, and it will make little difference to the results of our work of description and classification if we replace it by another. The occasion for it arose in the course of the evolution of psychoanalysis, which was first employed upon the psycho-neuroses, actually upon the group designated transference neuroses (hysteria and obsessional neurosis); through them it became plain that at the root of all such affections there lies a conflict between the claims of sexuality and those of the ego. It is always possible that an exhaustive study of the other neurotic affections (especially of the narcissistic psychoneuroses, the schizophrenias) may oblige us to alter this formula and therewith to make a different classification of the primal instincts. But for the present we do not know what this new formula may be, nor have we met with any argument which seems likely to be prejudicial to the contrast between sexual and ego-instincts.

3 K. Lorenz

An Energy Model of Instinctive Actions

Excerpts from K. Lorenz, 'The comparative method in studying innate behaviour patterns', *Symposia of the Society for Experimental Biology*, Cambridge University Press, volume 4, 1950, pp. 221–68.

At the level of superficial observation the innate behaviour patterns in question appeared reflex-like in that they were set off by a sort of 'trigger-action' in a very specific stimulus situation. But on closer inspection it became apparent that these activities are, at bottom, to a very high degree independent from external stimulation. Captive animals, deprived of the normal object or releasing situation of an innate behaviour pattern, will persist in discharging the same sequences of movements at a very inadequate substitute object or situation. The longer the normal stimulation is withheld, the less necessary it becomes, in order to set off the reaction, to supply *all* of the stimuli pertaining to it. The longer the reaction does not go off, the finer the trigger that releases it seems to become set. In other words, the threshold of the stimulation necessary to release this type of innate reaction is not a constant, but is undergoing a continuous process of lowering, going on throughout the time during which the reaction is not released. This gradual lowering of threshold does, in a good many cases, actually reach the theoretically possible limit of zero, that is, the activity in question will finally go off *in vacuo*, with an effect somewhat suggestive of the explosion of a boiler whose safety valve fails to function. This occurrence has been termed 'Leerlaufreaktion' in German, vacuum reaction and explosion reaction. I would move the general acceptance of Armstrong's (1942) term 'energy accumulation activity' for reasons discussed later.

The consequences of the 'damming up' of a certain innate activity are, however, not confined to the threshold of the mechanism (whatever that mechanism may be) which releases the activity. It is not only a facilitation of the releasing process, not only an increase of passive excitability that takes place, but, quite on the contrary, an active and peculiar excitation. Any one of these particular innate behaviour patterns, however small and unimportant it may seem in itself, develops into an active source of excitation which influences the whole of the organism whenever it finds its outlet blocked. In this case, the undischarged activity becomes a *motive* in the literal and original sense of the word, derivated from *movere*, 'to move'. In the simplest and most primitive case the organism shows undirected, 'random' locomotion, *kineses* as we term it. In more highly differentiated types these kineses are interlaced with taxes orienting the organism's locomotion in space, or even with conditioned responses and all the most complicated and least analysed forms of animal and human behaviour, which, for lack of a better term, we are wont to describe as 'intelligent'. Though the activities thus elicited comprise the whole range of behaviour, from its simplest to its most complex form, they have one decisive character in common: they are all *purposive* in the sense which E. C. Tolman (1932) has given to this term, that is to say, they all tend to bring about, by *variable* movements, an *invariable* end or goal, and they go on until this goal is reached or the animal as a whole is exhausted. The invariable end or goal is represented by the releasing stimulus situation and, therewith, the discharge of the specific behaviour pattern that had been dammed up. The purposive behaviour striving for this discharge was called *appetitive* behaviour by Wallace Craig (1918); the behaviour pattern finally discharged was termed *consummatory action*.

The method of dual quantification

A very considerable percentage of all animal activities consists of the typical successive links of appetitive behaviour, attainment of a desired stimulus situation, to which an innate releasing mechanism responds and sets off the discharge of accumulated endogenous action. In the vast majority of cases where we find an organism responding specifically and without previous experience to certain stimulus situations, closer investigation will reveal one or other of the innumerable variations to this theme, always leading up in one way or the other to the final discharge of consummatory actions. What we can objectively observe is exclusively this discharge. But this discharge is dependent upon two absolutely heterogeneous causal factors: (1) the level attained by the accumulated action-specific energy at the moment and (2) the effectiveness of external stimulation. None of these two factors is directly accessible to our observation. Absolutely identical reactions can result, in one case, from an extremely low level of endogenous accumulation and strong stimulation, and, in the other, from a high level of accumulated action-specific energy and a very weak external stimulation, or even, in the case of explosion activity, from internal factors alone, external stimulation not taking any part in the activity at all. [. . .]

The practical way of proceeding in experiments of dual quantification is obvious, after what has already been said. Presenting the animal with a given stimulus situation and recording the intensity of its reaction presents us, as I have explained, with an equation containing two unknowns: we do not know how much of the intensity recorded is due to internal accumulation of action-specific energy and how much is due to external stimulation. The obvious thing to do is to let *maximal* stimulation impinge upon the organism immediately after the first experiment, in order to see how much specific energy is 'left'. This already gives us a definite notion about the *relative* effectiveness of the stimulation supplied in the first experiment. What we are doing is best illustrated in a hydro-mechanic model which, in spite of its extreme crudeness and simplicity is able to symbolize a surprising wealth of facts really encountered in the reactions of animals. In Figure 1 the tap supplying a constant flow of liquid represents the endogenous production of action-specific energy; the liquid accumulated in the reservoir represents the amount of this energy which is at the disposal of the organism at a given moment; the elevation attained by its upper level corresponds, at an inverse ratio, to the momentary threshold of the reaction. The cone-valve represents the releasing mechanism, the inhibitory function of the higher centres being symbolized by the spring. The scale-pan which is connected with the valve-shaft by a string acting over a pulley represents the perceptual sector of the releasing mechanism, the weight applied corresponds to the impinging stimulation. This arrangement is a good symbol of how the internal accumulation of action-specific energy and the external stimulation are both acting in the same direction, both tending to open the valve. It can also easily and obviously represent the occurrence of explosion activity. The activity itself is represented by the spout discharged from the jet. The intensity of the reaction is symbolized by the distance to which the jet springs, in other words, by the speed of the outflow. This automatically corresponds to the proven fact that the consumption of action-specific energy in the time unit is in direct proportion to the intensity of the reaction. The intensity of the reaction can be read on the scale. To this apparatus we can easily attach a gadget exactly symbolizing the way in which a sequence of different movement patterns belonging to one scale of action-specific excitation is activated. A row of little funnels attached below the gradation will meet the case where, with the attaining of a higher level of excitation, the activities corresponding to lower levels are discontinued (as, for instance, in the taking-to-wing ceremony of the greylag goose). It is, however,

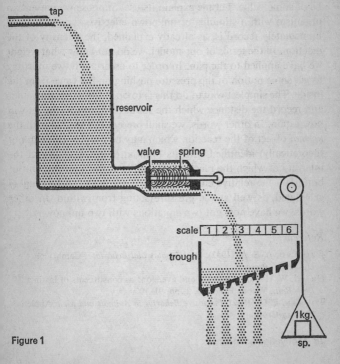

Figure 1

much more usual that the movements activated at the lowest levels of action-specific excitation are continued unceasingly all the while those corresponding to higher levels are discharged. We can symbolize this by fixing below the scale an oblong trough which has an oblique bottom perforated by a number of holes. The outflow from these holes then represents the intensity scale of a sequence of different activities, such as fin-spreading, gill-membrane expanding, etc. For reasons subsequently to be expounded, we have arranged the scale tray representing the receiving section of the innate releasing mechanism in such a manner as to let some of the ultimate flowing-out of liquid impinge on it in a diffuse way.

This contraption is, of course, still a very crude simplification of the real processes it is symbolizing, but experience has taught us that even the crudest simplisms often prove a valuable stimulus to investigation. As an instrument for the quantification of external and internal stimulation this model has already proved to be of some value. Let me explain its use. Suppose we present an organism with a stimulus of unknown effectiveness. All we can immediately record is, as already explained, the intensity of the reaction. In the terms of our model, we do not know what weight we have applied to the pan. In order to ascertain it, we must try to get some notion of the pressure pushing on the valve from the inside. The simplest way to do this is to open the valve altogether and record the distance which the spout delivered by the jet will now attain. In other words, we shall present our animal with the *normal* object of the reaction which may be roughly (though not theoretically) identified with its optimal object, and record the intensity of which the reaction is capable at the moment. Out of both data the relative effect of the first stimulus can be roughly calculated, as well as the pressure acting from within. In other words, we have now got two equations with two unknowns.

References

ARMSTRONG, E. A. (1942), *Bird Display and Behaviour*, Cambridge University Press.
CRAIG, W. (1918), 'Appetites and aversions as constituents of instincts', *Biol. Bull.*, Woods Hole, no. 2, pp. 91–107.
TOLMAN, E. C. (1932), *Purposive Behavior in Animals and Men*, Appleton-Century-Crofts.

4 N. Tinbergen

Hierarchical Organization of Instinctive Actions

Excerpts from N. Tinbergen, *The Study of Instinct*,
Oxford University Press, 1951, chapter 5.

These excerpts are reproduced here because of their historical interest and
influence. Tinbergen has revised his views since the publication of *The
Study of Instinct*. For his recent views see N. Tinbergen, 'On aims and
methods of ethology', *Zeitschrift für Tierpsychologie*, volume 20,
number 4, 1963, pp. 410–33.

Hierarchical organization

A closer study of differences in complexity leads us to the conclusion that the mechanisms underlying [instinctive] reactions
are arranged in a hierarchical system, in which we must distinguish
between various levels of integration.

The reproductive behaviour of the male stickleback may be
taken as an example.

In spring, the gradual increase in length of day brings the
males into a condition of increased reproductive motivation,
which drives them to migrate into shallow fresh water. Here, as
we have seen, a rise in temperature, together with a visual stimulus
situation received from a suitable territory, releases the reproductive pattern as a whole. The male settles on the territory, its
erythrophores expand, it reacts to strangers by fighting, and
starts to build a nest. Now, whereas both nest-building and
fighting depend on activation of the reproductive drive as a
whole, no observer can predict which one of the two patterns will
be shown at any given moment. Fighting, for instance, has to be
released by a specific stimulus, viz. 'red male intruding into the
territory'. Building is not released by this stimulus situation but
depends on other stimuli. Thus these two activities, though both
depend on activation of the reproductive drive as a whole, are
also dependent on additional (external) factors. The influence
of these latter factors is, however, restricted; they act upon
either fighting or building, not on the reproductive drive as a
whole.

Now the stimulus situation 'red male intruding', while releasing the fighting drive, does not determine which one of the five types of fighting will be shown. This is determined by additional, still more specific stimuli. For instance, when the stranger bites, the owner of the territory will bite in return; when the stranger threatens, the owner will threaten back; when the stranger flees, the owner will chase it; and so on.

Thus the effect of a stimulus situation on the animal may be of different kinds. The visual stimulus 'suitable territory' activates both fighting and nest-building; the visual stiuation 'red male in territory' is specific in releasing fighting, but it merely causes a general readiness to fight and does not determine the type of fighting. Which one of the five motor responses belonging to the fighting pattern will be shown depends on sign stimuli that are still more restricted in effect. The tactile stimulus 'male biting' releases one type of fighting, the visual stimulus 'male threatening' another type. The stimulus situations are not of an essentially different order in all these cases, but the results are. They belong to different levels of integration and, moreover, they are organized in a hierarchical system, like the staff organization of an army or of other human organizations. The facts (1) that at each of the levels an external stimulus can have a specific releasing influence and (2) that each reaction has its own motor pattern mean that there is a hierarchical system of IRMs (Innate Releasing Mechanisms). [. . .]

Appetitive behaviour and consummatory activity

The distinction between appetitive behaviour and consummatory act separates the behaviour as a whole into two components of entirely different character. The consummatory act is relatively simple; at its most complex, it is a chain of reactions, each of which may be a simultaneous combination of a taxis and a fixed pattern. But appetitive behaviour is a true purposive activity, offering all the problems of plasticity, adaptiveness, and of complex integration that baffle the scientist in his study of behaviour as a whole. Appetitive behaviour is a conglomerate of many elements of very different order, of reflexes, of simple patterns like locomotion, of conditioned reactions, of 'insight' behaviour, and so on. As a result it is a true challenge to objective science, and therefore the discrimination between appetitive behaviour and consummatory act is but a first step of our analysis.

A consideration of the relationships between appetitive behaviour and consummatory act is important for our understanding of the nature of striving in animals. It is often stressed that animals are striving towards the attainment of a certain end or goal. Lorenz has pointed out not only that purposiveness, the striving towards an end, is typical only of appetitive behaviour and not of consummatory actions, but also that the end of purposive behaviour is not the attainment of an object or a situation itself, but the performance of the consummatory action, which is attained as a consequence of the animal's arrival at an external situation which provides the special sign stimuli releasing the consummatory act. Even psychologists who have watched hundreds of rats running a maze rarely realize that, strictly speaking, it is not the litter or the food the animal is striving towards, but the performance itself of the maternal activities or eating.

Holzapfel (1940) has shown that there is one apparent exception to this rule: appetitive behaviour may also lead to rest or sleep. As I hope to show further below, this exception is only apparent, because rest and sleep are true consummatory actions, dependent on activation of a centre exactly as with other consummatory actions.

Whereas the consummatory act seems to be dependent on the centres of the lowest level of instinctive behaviour, appetitive behaviour may be activated by centres of all the levels above that of the consummatory act. As has been pointed out by Baerends (1941), appetitive behaviour by no means always leads directly to the performance of a consummatory act. For instance, the hunting of a peregrine falcon usually begins with relatively random roaming around its hunting territory, visiting and exploring many different places miles apart. This first phase of appetitive behaviour may lead to different ways of catching prey, each dependent on special stimulation by a potential prey. It is continued until such a special stimulus situation is found: a flock of teal executing flight manoeuvres, a sick gull swimming apart from the flock, or even a running mouse. Each of these situations may cause the falcon to abandon its 'random' searching. But what follows then is not yet a consummatory action, but appetitive behaviour of a new, more specialized and more restricted kind. The flock of teal releases a series of sham attacks serving to isolate one or a few individuals from the main body of the flock. Only after this is achieved, is the final swoop released, followed by capturing, killing, plucking, and eating, which is a relatively simple and stereotyped chain of consummatory acts. The sick gull may provoke the release of sham attacks tending to force it to fly up; if this fails the falcon may deftly pick it up from the water surface. A small mammal may release simple straightforward approach and subsequent capturing, etc. Thus we see that the generalized appetitive behaviour was continued until a special stimulus situation interrupted the random searching and released one of the several possible and more specific types of appetitive behaviour. This in its turn was continued until the changing stimulus situation released the swoop, a still more specific type of appetitive behaviour, and this finally led to the chain of consummatory acts.

Baerends (1941) came to the same conclusion in his analysis of the behaviour of the digger wasp *Ammophila campestris*, and probably the principle will be found to be generally applicable. It seems, therefore, that the centres of each level of the hierarchical system control a type of appetitive behaviour. This is more generalized in the higher levels and more restricted or more specialized in the lower levels. The transition from higher to lower, more specialized types of appetitive behaviour is brought about by special stimuli which alone are able to direct the impulses to one of the lower centres, or rather to allow them free passage to this lower centre. This stepwise descent of the activation from relatively higher to relatively lower centres eventually results in the stimulation of a centre or a series of centres of the level of the consummatory act, and here the impulse is finally used up.

This hypothesis of the mechanism of instinctive behaviour, though supported by relatively few and very fragmentary facts and still tentative therefore, seems to cover the reality better than any theory thus far advanced. Its concreteness gives it a high heuristic value, and it is to be hoped that continued research in the near future will follow these lines and fill in, change, and adapt the sketchy frame. [. . .]

Neurophysiological facts

It is of great importance for our understanding of instinctive behaviour as a whole to realize that the various instincts are not independent of each other. We have rejected the reflex hypothesis of behaviour and we have seen that each instinctive mechanism is constantly primed, that is to say, prepared to come into action. Such a system can only work because blocking mechanisms prevent the animal from performing continuous chaotic movements.

Now chaos is further prevented by another principle, viz. that of inhibition between centres of the same level. As a rule, an animal can scarcely do 'two things at a time'. Although there is a certain amount of synchronous activity of two instincts, this is only possible at low motivation, and, as a rule, the strong activation of instinctive behaviour of one kind prevents the functioning of another pattern. Thus an animal in which the sexual drive is strong is much less than normally susceptible to stimuli that normally release flight or eating. On the other hand, when flight is released, the thresholds of the reproductive and feeding activities are raised. The same relationship of mutual inhibition seems to exist between centres of lower levels. Intensive nest-building, for instance, renders the male stickleback much less susceptible than usual to stimuli normally releasing fighting, and vice versa. [. . .]

Another set of interrelations, though in itself perhaps not of primary importance in the organization of behaviour, has to be considered now: those revealed by the occurrence of 'displacement activity'. This phenomenon will be discussed in some detail, because it is not generally known and yet seems to be of great importance for our understanding of the neurophysiological background of instinct.

It has struck many observers that animals may, under certain circumstances, perform movements which do not belong to the motor pattern of the instinct that is activated at the moment of observation. For instance, fighting domestic cocks may suddenly pick at the ground, as if they were feeding. Fighting European starlings may vigorously preen their feathers. Courting birds of paradise wipe their bills now and then. Herring gulls, while engaged in deadly combat, may all at once pluck nesting material, etc. In all the observed instances the animal gives the impression of being very strongly motivated ('nervous'). Rand (1943) has called such movements 'irrelevant' movements. Makkink (1936) gave an implied interpretation by using the term 'sparking-over movements', suggesting that impulses are 'sparking over' on another 'track'. Kirkman (1937) used the term 'substitute activities' which I adopted in 1939 (Tinbergen, 1939). Later the term 'displacement activity' was proposed (Tinbergen and van Iersel, 1947; Armstrong, 1948), and this term will be used here.

The phenomenon has been clearly recognized and analysed independently by Kortlandt (1940) and by Tinbergen (1939, 1940). An examination of the conditions under which displacement activities usually occur led to the conclusion that, in all known cases, there is a surplus of motivation, the discharge of which through the normal paths is in some way prevented. The most usual situations are: (1) conflict of two strongly activated antagonistic drives; (2) strong motivation of a drive, usually the sexual drive, together with lack of external stimuli required for the release of the consummatory acts belonging to that drive.

The fact that a displacement activity is an expression, not of its 'own' drive (of autochthonous motivation as Kortlandt (1940) called it) but of a 'strange' drive (of allochthonous motivation), makes it possible for it to act as a signal to fellow members of the same species, provided it can be distinguished from the 'genuine' activity, activated by its 'own' drive. As a matter of fact, many displacement activities are different from their 'models' and do act as signals. Thus displacement digging in sticklebacks is actually understood by other sticklebacks as a threat (as an expression of the fighting drive); it is different from its 'model', true digging, in that the spines are erected.

References

ARMSTRONG, E. A. (1947), *Bird Display and Behaviour*, Cambridge University Press.
BAERENDS, G. P. (1941), 'Fortpflanzungsverhalten und Orientierung der Grabwespe Ammophila campestris', *Jur. Tijdschr. Entomol.*, vol. 84, pp. 68–275.

HOLZAPFEL, M. (1940), 'Triebbedingte Ruhezustände als Ziel von Appetenzverhalten', *Naturwiss*, vol. 28, pp. 273–80.

KIRKMAN, F. B. (1937), *Bird Behaviour*, London–Edinburgh.

KORTLANDT, A. (1940), 'Wechselwirkung zwischen Instinkten', *Arch. néerl. Zoöl*, vol. 4, pp. 442–520.

MAKKINK, G. F. (1936), 'An attempt at an ethogram of the European avocet (*Recurvirostra avosetta L.*) with ethological and psychological remarks', *Ardea*, vol. 25, pp. 1–60.

RAND, A. L. (1943), 'Some irrelevant behavior in birds', *Auk*, vol. 60, pp. 168–71.

TINBERGEN, N. (1939), 'The behavior of the Snow Bunting in spring', *Trans. Linn. Soc. N.Y.*, vol. 5.

TINBERGEN, N. (1940), 'Die Übersprungbewegung', *Zs. Tierpsychol.*, vol. 4, pp. 1–40.

TINBERGEN, N., and VAN IERSEL, J. J. A. (1947), '"Displacement reactions" in the three-spined stickleback', *Behav.*, vol. 1, pp. 56–63.

5 R. A. Hinde

Critique of Energy Models of Motivation

Abridged from R. A. Hinde, 'Energy models of motivation', *Symposia of the Society for Experimental Biology*, Cambridge University Press, volume 14, 1960, pp. 199–213.

Introduction

The problem of motivation is central to the understanding of behaviour. Why, in the absence of learning and fatigue, does the response to a constant stimulus change from time to time? To what is the apparent spontaneity of behaviour due? This paper is concerned with one type of model which has been developed to help answer such questions – namely that in which changes in the organism's activity are ascribed to changes in the quantity or distribution of an entity comparable to physical, chemical or electrical energy.

Such models have been developed by theoreticians with widely differing backgrounds, interests and aims, and the frameworks of ideas built round them diverge in many respects; but in each case the energy treatment of motivation is a central theme (Carthy, 1951; Kennedy, 1954). They have had a great influence on psychological thought, and although they are unlikely to continue to be useful, it is instructive to examine their nature, their achievements and their limitations.

The models

The four models or theories to be discussed here are those of Freud, McDougall, Lorenz and Tinbergen. They are only four of many in which energy concepts are used, but in them the energy analogy is made explicit in terms of a mechanical model, instead of being merely implied by a 'drive' variable which is supposed to energize behaviour. The models were designed to account for many features of behaviour in addition to the phenomena of motivation, and here it will be necessary to extract only those aspects relevant to the present theme.

In the psychoanalytic model (Freud, 1932, 1940) the id is pictured as a chaos of instinctive energies which are supposed to originate from some source of stimulation within the body. Their control is in the hands of the ego, which permits, postpones or denies their satisfaction. In this the ego may be dominated by the super-ego. The energy with which Freud was particularly concerned – the sexual energy or libido – is supposed not to require immediate discharge. It can be postponed, repressed, sublimated, and so on. The source of this energy lies in different erogenous zones as the individual develops, being successively oral, anal and phallic, and it is in relation to these changes that the individual develops his responses to the external world. The instinctual energy is supposed to undergo various vicissitudes, discussions of which often imply that it can be stored, or that it can flow like a fluid. It may become attached to objects represented by mental structures or processes (libidinal cathexes) and later withdrawn from them in a manner that Freud (1940) likened to protoplasmic pseudopodia: it has also been compared with an electric charge. Thus some of the characteristics of the energy depend on its quantitative distribution.

McDougall (1913) envisaged energy liberated on the afferent side of the nervous system, and held back by 'sluice gates'. If the stimuli necessary to open the gates are not forthcoming, the energy 'bubbles over' among the motor mechanisms to produce appetitive behaviour. On receipt of appropriate stimuli, one of the gates opens, and the afferent channels of this instinct become the principal outlet for all available free energy. Later (1923) he used a rather more complex analogy in which each instinct was pictured as a chamber in which gas is constantly liberated. The gas can escape via pipes leading to the executive organs when the appropriate lock(s) is opened. The gas is supposed to drive the motor mechanisms, just as an electric motor is driven by electrical energy.

The models of Lorenz and Tinbergen have much in common with McDougall's. Lorenz's 'reaction specific energy' was earlier (1937) thought of as a gas constantly being pumped into a container, and later (e.g. 1950) as a liquid in a reservoir. In the latter case it is supposed that the reservoir can discharge through a spring-loaded valve at the bottom. The valve is opened in part by the hydrostatic pressure in the reservoir, and in part by a weight on a scale pan which represents the external stimulus. As the reservoir discharges, the hydrostatic pressure on the valve decreases, and thus a greater weight is necessary to open the valve again.

Tinbergen (1951) pictured a hierarchy of nervous centres, each of which has the properties of a Lorenzian reservoir. Each centre can be loaded with 'motivational impulses' from a superordinated centre and/or other sources. Until the appropriate stimulus is given the outflow is blocked and the animal can show only appetitive behaviour; when the block is removed the impulses can flow into the subordinate centre or be discharged in action.

It is important to emphasize again that the theories of these authors have little in common except for the energy model of motivation – they were devised for different purposes, and the more recent authors have been at pains to emphasize their differences from the earlier ones. For instance, for McDougall the most important feature of instinct was the 'conative-affective core', while for Lorenz it was the stereotyped motor pattern. Furthermore, the models differ greatly in the precision with which they are defined. The Freudian model is a loose one: its flexibility is perhaps necessary in view of the great range of behavioural and mental phenomena it comprehends, but makes it very difficult to test. The other models are more tightly defined, but differ, as we shall see, in their supposed relations to the nervous system.

In spite of such differences, all these models share the idea of a substance, capable of energizing behaviour, held back in a container and subsequently released in action. In the discussion which follows, I shall be little concerned with the other details of the models, or with the ways in which the theories based on them differ. Furthermore, I shall disregard the niceties of terminology, lumping instinctual energy, psychophysical energy, action specific energy and motivational impulses together as, for present purposes, basically similar concepts.

Reality status of the models

Until recently, students of the more complex types of behaviour could get little help from physiology, and had to fashion their concepts without reference to the properties of the nervous system. Many, indeed, advocated this course from preference, either on grounds of expediency, suggesting that knowledge of the nervous system was still too primitive and might be misleading, or on principle, claiming that physiology and behaviour were distinct levels of discourse. At present the models and theories used in attempts to understand, explain or predict behaviour range from those whose nature is such that physiological data are irrelevant (Skinner, 1938) to those which consist of a forthright attempt to describe psychological data in physiological terms (Hebb, 1947, 1955). The former type may be applicable over a wide range of phenomena, but only at a limited range of analytical levels: the latter may point the way to analysis at lower levels, but their expectancy of life depends on their compatibility with the phenomena found there.

The originators of all the models discussed here regard them as having some relation to structures in the nervous system, but vary in the emphasis which they lay on this. Tinbergen, although freely emphasizing the hypothetical status of his model, clearly regards his 'centres' as neural structures, and his 'motivational impulses' as related to nerve impulses. He speaks of his hierarchical scheme as a 'graphic picture of the nervous mechanisms involved'. McDougall likewise regards the relationship between model and nervous system as a close one, for he localizes the 'sluice gates' in the optic thalamus. Lorenz, on the other hand, usually treated his model in an 'as if' fashion – he did not suggest that we should look for reservoirs in the body. He did, however, bring forward physiological evidence in its support – quoting, for instance, Sherrington's work (1906) on spinal contrast, and von Holst's (1936) work on endogenous rhythms in fishes; and he sometimes uses such terms as 'central nervous impulse flow' as a synonym for 'reaction specific energy'. His use of physiological evidence was, however, *post hoc* – the model was based on behavioural data and the physiological evidence came later.

Freud's model developed from physiology, in particular from a sensory-excitation–motor-discharge picture of nervous function, and its basic postulates are almost a direct translation of such ideas into psychological terms – excitation into mental energy, the discharges of excitation into pleasure, and so on (Peters, 1958). However, Freudian theory developed far beyond these primitive notions, and then bore little or no relation to physiology, even though the instincts were supposed to have an ultimately physiological source.

Thus two of these models (Tinbergen and McDougall) had explicitly physiological implications; that of Lorenz was usually used in an 'as if' fashion; and Freud's, although it had physiological roots, became divorced from any supposed structures or functions in the nervous system. However, as we shall see, all have been influenced by the covert introduction of existence postulates concerning the explanatory concepts used.

Difficulties and dangers

In the following paragraphs we shall consider some of the difficulties and dangers inherent in the use of an energy model of motivation. These arise in part from misunderstandings of the nature of the model, and in part from incompatibilities between the properties of the model and those of the original.

Confusion between behavioural energy and physical energy

We have already seen that behavioural energy, postulated to account for changes in activity, need share no properties with physical energy. Not only is there no necessary reason why it should be treated as an entity with any of the properties of physical energy, but the question of its convertibility into physical energy is a dangerous red herring. The way in which the properties of the model may be confused with those of the original have been discussed for Freudian theory by Meehl and MacCorquodale (1948). Concepts like libido or super-ego may be introduced initially as intervening variables without material properties, but such properties have a way of creeping into discussion without being made explicit. Thus Meehl and MacCorquodale point out that libido may be introduced as a term for the 'set of sexual needs' or 'basic strivings', but subsequently puzzling phenomena are explained in terms of properties of libido, such that it flows, is dammed up, converted, regresses to earlier channels, and so on. Such properties are introduced surreptitiously as occasion demands, and involve a transition from admissible intervening variables, which carry no existence postulates, to hypothetical constructs which require the existence of decidedly improbable entities and processes.

Such difficulties are especially likely to occur when a model which purports to be close to the original, like that of Tinbergen, develops out of an 'as if' model, like that of Lorenz. This case has been discussed elsewhere (Hinde, 1956). To quote but one example, ethologists have called behaviour patterns which appear out of their functional context 'displacement activities'. These activities usually appear when there is reason to think that one or more types of motivation are strong, but unable to find expression in action: instead, the animal shows a displacement activity, which seems to be irrelevant. Thus when a chaffinch has conflicting tendencies to approach and avoid a food dish, it may show preening behaviour. Such irrelevant activities were explained on the energy model by supposing that the thwarted energy 'sparked over' into the displacement activity – sparking over being a property of (electrical) energy which was imputed to the behavioural energy. This idea hindered an analytical study of the causal factors underlying displacement behaviour. Thus it has recently become apparent that many displacement activities are not so causally irrelevant as they appear to be, for those factors which elicit the behaviour in its normal functional context are also present when it appears as a displacement activity. For example, some displacement activities appear to be due to autonomic activity aroused as a consequence of fear-provoking stimuli or other aspects of the situation. The displacement activity may consist of the autonomic response itself (e.g. feather postures in birds) or of a somatic response to stimuli consequent upon autonomic activity (Andrew, 1956; Morris, 1956). In other cases the displacement behaviour consists of a response to factors continuously present, which was previously inhibited through the greater priority of the incompatible behaviour patterns which are in conflict (van Iersel and Bol, 1958; Rowell, 1959). Of course it remains possible that the intensity of the apparently irrelevant behaviour is influenced by factors not specific to it, including those associated with the conflicting tendencies (see also Hinde, 1959).

Similarly in psychoanalytic theory we find not only that within one category of instincts (e.g. sexual) the constituent instincts can change their aim, but also that 'they can replace one another – the energy of one instinct passing over to another' (Freud, 1940). Explanations of this type may be useful at a descriptive level, but are misleading as analysis proceeds.

The distinction between the accumulation and release of energy

In all energy models, the energy is supposed to build up and subsequently to be released in action. McDougall, Lorenz and Tinbergen, all of whom were influenced by Wallace Craig, compare the releasing stimulus to a key which opens a lock. This apparent dichotomy between releasing and motivating effects is a property of the model, and may not be relevant to the mechanisms underlying behaviour. Although many factors appear to have both a motivating and a releasing effect on the responses they affect – they appear both to cause an increase in responsiveness, and to elicit the response – this does not necessarily imply that two distinct processes are at work. For example, if a given input increased the probability of a certain pattern of neural firing, it might appear in behaviour both that the responsiveness was increased and that the behaviour was elicited.

This sort of difficulty is the more likely to arise, the more precisely the model is portrayed. Thus McDougall, who did not work out his model in such detail as Lorenz and Tinbergen, implied that motivation and release were in fact one process when he wrote: 'The evoking of the instinctive action, the opening of the door of the instinct on perception of its specific object, increases the urgency of the appetite.'

Implications about the cessation of activity

In all these theories, the cessation of activity is ascribed to the discharge of energy – the behavioural energy flows away as a consequence of performance. Influenced by the analogy with physical energy, Freud held that the main function of the nervous system is to reduce excitation to the lowest possible level. McDougall, Lorenz and Tinbergen imply a similar view, and the two latter emphasize that it is the performance of more or less stereotyped motor patterns which involve the discharge of the energy.

This view of the cessation of activities comes naturally from models in which the properties of physical energy are imputed to behavioural energy. It is, however, also supported by another type of argument, also involving a *non sequitur*. Much behaviour is related to an increase in stimulation. Therefore, it might be argued, all activity is due to an increase in stimulation, and cessation of activity is related to a decrease. On an energy model, stimulation may increase the energy, and thus a decrease in activity is related to a decrease in energy.

Such a view is incompatible with the data now available on two grounds. First, cessation of activity may be due to the animal encountering a 'goal' stimulus situation, and not to the performance of an activity. If this goal stimulus situation is encountered abnormally early, the behaviour which normally leads to it may not appear at all. McDougall recognized this, and indeed defined his instincts in terms of the goals which brought about a cessation of activity. This, however, made it necessary for him to be rather inconsistent about his energy model. While the energy was supposed to drive the motor mechanisms, it was apparently not consumed in action, but could flow back to other reservoirs or to the general source. The more precisely described Lorenz/Tinbergen models, on the other hand, do not allow for reduction in activity by consummatory stimuli: reduction in responsiveness occurs only through the discharge of energy in action. These models are misleading because they are too simple – energy flow is supposed to control not only what happens between stimulus and response, but also the drop in responsiveness when the response is given. In practice, these may be due to quite different aspects of the mechanisms underlying behaviour: for instance the energy model leaves no room for inhibition (Kennedy, 1954). Further, even if the cessation of activity is in some sense due to the performance, many different processes may be involved: the mechanism is not a unitary one, as the energy model implies (see below).

Secondly, if activity is due to the accumulation of energy and cessation to its discharge, the organisms should come to rest when the energy level is minimal. In fact, much behaviour serves the function of bringing the animal into conditions of increased stimulation. This has been shown dramatically with humans subjected to acute sensory deprivation – the experimental conditions are intolerable in spite of the considerable financial reward offered (Bexton, Heron and Scott, 1954). Energy theories are in difficulty over accounting for such 'reactions to deficit' (Lashley, 1938).

Unitary nature of explanation

In these energy models, each type of behaviour is related to the flow of energy. Increase in strength of the behaviour is due to an increased flow of energy, decrease to a diminished flow. The strength of behaviour is thus related to a single mechanism. It is, however, apparent that changes in responsiveness to a constant stimulus may be due to many different processes in the nervous system and in the body as a whole – for instance, the changes consequent upon performance may affect one response or many, may or may not be specific to the stimulus, and may have recovery periods varying from seconds to months. Energy models, by lumping together diverse processes which affect the strength of behaviour, can lead to an over-simplification of the mechanisms underlying it, and distract attention from the complexities of the behaviour itself. Similarly, energy models are in difficulty with the almost cyclic short-term waxing and waning of such activities as the response of chaffinches to owls, the song of many birds, and so on.

Kubie (1947) has emphasized this point with reference to the psychoanalytic model. Changes in behaviour are referred to quantitative changes in energy distribution, but in fact so many variables are involved (repression, displacement, substitution, etc.) that it is not justifiable to make easy guesses about what varied to produce a given state. Similar difficulties in relation to other models have been discussed by Hinde (1959).

Precht (1952) has elaborated the Lorenzian model to allow for some complication of this sort. Analysing the changes in strength of the hunting behaviour of spiders, he distinguishes between 'drive' which depends on deprivation, and 'excitory level', which is a function of non-release of the eating pattern. The distinction is an important one, but it may be doubted whether the elaborate hydraulic system which he produced is really an aid to further analysis.

Tinbergen's model translated the Lorenzian reservoir into nervous 'centres'. Changes in response strength are ascribed to the loading of these centres. Now for many types of behaviour it is indeed possible to identify *loci* in the diencephalon whose ablation leads to the disappearance of the behaviour, whose stimulation leads to its elicitation, and where hormones or solutions produce appropriate effects on behaviour. There is, however, no evidence that 'energy' is accumulated in such centres, nor that response strength depends solely on their state. Indeed the strength of any response depends on many structures, neural and non-neural, and there is no character-by-character correspondence between such postulated centres and any structure in the brain.

Although the greatest attraction of these energy models is their simplicity – a relatively simple mechanical model accounting for diverse properties of behaviour – there is a danger in this, for one property of the model may correspond to more than one character of the original. This difficulty has in fact arisen in many behaviour systems irrespective of whether they use an energy model of motivation. Thus a single drive variable is sometimes used not only with reference to changes in responsiveness to a constant stimulus, but also to spontaneity, temporal persistence of the effects of the stimuli, after-responses (i.e. the persistence of activities after the stimulus is removed), the temporal grouping of functionally related activities, and so on. As discussed elsewhere (Hinde, 1959), there is no *a priori* reason why these diverse characters of behaviour should depend on a single feature of the underlying mechanism: an over-simple model may hinder analysis.

Independence of activities

Another difficulty which arises from the use of energy models, though by no means peculiar to them, is due to the emphasis laid on the independence of different activities. Lorenz and Tinbergen (1938) write 'If ever we may say that only part of an organism is involved in a reaction, it may confidently be said of instinctive action.' Activities are interpreted as due to energies acting in specific structures, and not as responses of the organisms as a whole. Both types of attitude carry disadvantages, but an over-emphasis on the independence of activities leads to a neglect of, for instance, sensory, metabolic or temperamental factors which affect many activities.

R. A. Hinde 45

Is an energy concept necessary?

We have seen that these energy models will account for diverse properties of behaviour, but that they meet with serious difficulties when the behaviour is analysed more closely. They have also been strangely sterile in leading to bridgeheads with physiology. These shortcomings of energy models have been emphasized by a number of other writers (e.g. Kubie, 1947; Deutsch, 1953; Bowlby, 1958). Energy concepts are useful in descriptions of changes in behaviour, but are they necessary? Colby states that 'a dynamic psychology must conceive of psychic activities as the product of forces, and forces involve energy sums. It is thus quite necessary that metapsychology have some sort of energy theory'. Is this really so?

Kubie (1947) has pointed out that psychological phenomena are the product of an interplay of diverse factors. A rearrangement of these factors can alter the pattern of behaviour without any change in hypothetical stores of energy. Such a view is in harmony with the known facts about the functioning of the nervous system. The central nervous system is not normally inert, having to be prodded into activity by specific stimuli external to it. Rather it is in a state of continuous activity – a state supported primarily by the non-specific effects of stimuli acting through the brainstem reticular system. Factors such as stimuli and hormones which affect specific patterns of behaviour are to be thought of as controlling this activity, of increasing the probability of one pattern rather than another. Changes in strength or threshold can thus be thought of as changes in the probability of one pattern of activity rather than another, and not as changes in the level of energy in a specific neural mechanism. This involves some return to a 'telephone exchange' theory of behaviour, but with emphasis on the non-specific input necessary to keep the switch mechanism active, and with switches which are not all-or-none, but determine the probability of one pattern rather than another. Furthermore, switching does not depend solely on external stimuli, i.e. we are not concerned with a purely reflexological model. This is not the place to pursue this view further: it suffices to say that it seems possible and preferable to formulate behaviour theories in which concepts of energy, and of drives which energize behaviour, have no role.

References

ANDREW, R. J. (1956), 'Some remarks on conflict situations, with special reference to *Emberiza* spp', *Brit. J. Animal Behav.*, vol. 4, pp. 41–5.

BEXTON, W. H., HERON, W., and SCOTT, T. H. (1954), 'Effects of decreased variation in the sensory environment', *Canad. J. Psychol.*, vol. 8, pp. 70–6.

BOWLBY, J. (1958), 'The nature of the child's tie to his mother', *Internat. J. Psychoanal.*, vol. 39.

CARTHY, J. D. (1951), 'Instinct', *New Biol.*, vol. 10, pp. 95–105.

COLBY, K. M. (1955), *Energy and Structure in Psychoanalysis*, Ronald Press.

DEUTSCH, J. A. (1953), 'A new type of behaviour theory', *Brit. J. Psychol.*, vol. 44, pp. 304–17.

FREUD, S. (1932), *New Introductory Lectures on Psychoanalysis*, Hogarth Press, 1946.

FREUD, S. (1940), *An Outline of Psychoanalysis*. Hogarth Press, 1949.

HEBB, D. O. (1949), *The Organization of Behaviour*, Wiley.

HEBB, D. O. (1955), 'Drives and the CNS (Conceptual Nervous System)', *Psych. Rev.*, vol. 62, pp. 243–54.

HINDE, R. A. (1956), 'Ethological models and the concept of drive', *Brit J. philo. Sci.*, vol. 6, pp. 321–31.

HINDE, R. A. (1959), 'Unitary drives', *Animal Behav.*, vol. 7, pp. 130–41.

HOLST, E. VON (1936), 'Versuche zur Theorie der relativen Koordination', *Pflüg. Arch. ges. Physiol.*, vol. 237, pp. 93–121.

IERSEL, J. J. A. VAN, and BOL, A. C. (1958), 'Preening of two tern species: A study of displacement', *Behav.*, vol. 13, pp. 1–89.

KENNEDY, J. S. (1954), 'Is modern ethology objective?', *Brit. J. Animal Behav.*, vol. 2, pp. 12–19.

KUBIE, L. S. (1947), 'The fallacious use of quantitative concepts in dynamic psychology', *Psychoanalytic Q.*, vol. 16, pp. 507–18.

LASHLEY, K. S. (1938), 'Experimental analysis of instinctive behaviour', *Psychol. Rev.*, vol. 45, pp. 445–71.

LORENZ, K. (1937), 'Über die Bildung des Instinktbegriffes', *Naturwiss.* vol. 25, pp. 289–300, 307–18, 324–31.

LORENZ, K. (1950), 'The comparative method in studying innate behaviour patterns', *Sym. Soc. Exp. Biol.*, vol. 4, pp. 221–68.

LORENZ, K., and TINBERGEN, N. (1938), 'Taxis und Instinkthandlung in der Eirollbewegung der Graugans', *Z. Tierpsychol.*, vol. 2, pp. 1–29. Translated in C. H. Schiller, (ed.) (1957), *Instinctive Behaviour*, Methuen.

MCDOUGALL, W. (1913), 'The sources and direction of psychophysical energy', *Amer. J. Insanity*. Quoted in McDougall (1923).

MCDOUGALL, W. (1923), *An Outline of Psychology*, Methuen.

MEEHL, P. E., and MACCORQUODALE, K. (1948), 'On a distinction between hypothetical constructs and intervening variables', *Psych. Rev.*, vol. 55, pp. 95–107.

MORRIS, D. (1956), 'The feather postures of birds and the problem of the origin of social signals', *Behav.*, vol. 9, pp. 75–113.

PETERS, R. S. (1958), *The Concept of Motivation*, Routledge & Kegan Paul.

PRECHT, H. (1952), 'Über das angeborene Verhalten von Tieren: Versuche an Springspinnen', *Z. Tierpsychol.*, vol. 9, pp. 207–30.

ROWELL, C. H. F. (1959), 'The occurrence of grooming in the behaviour of chaffinches in approach-avoidance conflict situations, and its bearing on the concept of 'displacement activity', Ph. D. Thesis, Cambridge.

SHERRINGTON, C. S. (1906), *Integrative Action of the Nervous System*, Scribner.

SKINNER, B. F. (1938), *The Behavior of Organisms*, Appleton-Century-Crofts.

TINBERGEN, N. (1951), *The Study of Instinct*, Oxford University Press.

6 F. A. Beach

The Descent of Instinct

F. A. Beach, 'The descent of instinct', *Psychological Review*, volume 62, 1955, pp. 401–10.

The delusion is extraordinary by which we thus exalt language above nature . . . making language the expositor of nature, instead of making nature the expositor of language.
Alexander Brian Johnson: *A Treatise on Language.*

The basic ideas underlying a concept of instinct probably are older than recorded history. At any rate they are clearly set forth in the Greek literature of 2,500 years ago. They have been controversial ideas and they remain so today. Nevertheless, the instinct concept has survived in almost complete absence of empirical validation. One aim of the present article is to analyse the reasons for the remarkable vitality of a concept which has stood without objective test for at least two millennia. A second objective is to evaluate the concept as it relates to a science of behavior.

Origins in philosophy and theology

The concept of instinct evolved in relation to the broad problems of human destiny, of Man's place in nature, and his position in this world and the next. From the beginning, instinct has been defined and discussed in terms of its relation to reason and, less directly, to the human soul.

During the fourth century BC the Greek philosopher Heraclitus declared that there had been two types of creation. Men and gods were the products of rational creation, whereas irrational brutes comprised a separate category of living creatures. Heraclitus added the observation that only gods and men possess souls. The close relation between rational powers and possession of a soul has been reaffirmed time and again during the ensuing 2,500 years. Heraclitus did not advance the concept of instinct but he laid the groundwork for its development.

Stoic philosophers of the first century AD held that men and gods belong to one natural community, since they are rational beings. All animals were specifically excluded since they are not creatures of reason and even their most complex behavior takes place 'without reflection', to use the words of Seneca. This stoical taxonomy was both flattering and convenient since, according to the tenets of this school, members of the natural community were forbidden to harm or enslave other members.

It is significant that neither Heraclitus nor the Stoics based their conclusions upon objective evidence. Their premises concerning the psychology of animals were not derived from empirical observation; they were demanded by assumption of the philosophical position that animals lack a rational soul.

Aristotle, who was more of an observer than a philosopher, was of a different mind. In *Historia Animalium* Man is placed at the top of Scala Natura (directly above the Indian elephant), and is accorded superior intellectual powers, but none qualitatively distinct from those of other species.

In the thirteenth century Albertus Magnus composed *De Animalibus*, based chiefly upon the writings of Aristotle but modifying the Aristotelian position where necessary to conform to Scholastic theology. Albertus removed Man from the natural scale, holding that he is unique in possessing the gift of reason and an immortal soul. Animals, lacking reason, 'are directed by their natural instinct and therefore cannot act freely'.   –

St Thomas Aquinas, student of Albertus, supported his teacher's distinction between men and animals. Animals possess only the sensitive soul described by Aristotle. The human embryo is similarly endowed, but the rational soul is divinely implanted in the fetus at some time before birth.[1] The behavior of man therefore depends upon reason, whereas all animals are governed by instinct. Like the Stoic philosophers, the Scholastics were unconcerned with factual evidence. Their emphasis upon instinctive control of animal behavior was dictated by a need of the theological system, and in this frame of reference instinct was a useful concept.

Roughly four centuries after the time of St Thomas Aquinas,

1. It is not irrelevant to point out that weighty disputation concerning the exact age at which the soul enters the fetus retarded the advancement of embryological knowledge during its seventeenth century beginnings.

René Descartes and his followers aggressively restated the existence of a man-brute dichotomy. The bare facts of the Cartesian position are common knowledge, but for the purpose of the present argument it is important to ask why Descartes felt so strongly about the matter – felt compelled to hold up man as the Reasoner, at the same time insisting that all other living creatures are only flesh-and-blood machines. The explanation stands out in the following quotation:

After the error of atheism, there is nothing that leads weak minds further astray from the paths of virtue than the idea that the minds of other animals resemble our own, and that therefore we have no greater right to future life than have gnats and ants (René Descartes, *Passions of the Soul*).

From Albertus to Descartes the argument runs clear. The theological system posits a life after death. Hence the postulation of the soul. But mere possession of a soul is not enough. Each man must earn the right of his soul's salvation. This in turn depends upon reason, which man exercises in differentiating good from evil, behavior which is sinful from that which is not. An afterlife is man's unique prerogative; no animals share it. They have no souls and therefore no need to reason. But how are the complex and adaptive reactions of subhuman creatures to be explained if not by reason, foresight, volition? They are comfortably disposed of as products of instincts with which the Creator has endowed all dumb brutes.

That the thirteenth-century point of view persists today is shown by the following quotation:

In animals there are only instincts, but not in man. As St Thomas points out, there cannot be any deliberation in a subrational being (even though we may get the impression that there is). . . . Instincts in animals seem to operate according to the pattern of physical forces, where the stronger always prevails; for animals are utterly devoid of the freedom which characterizes man. . . . That is why when one studies human behavior one must rise above the purely animal pattern and concentrate upon those two faculties, intellect and will, which separate man from animal (Msgr Fulton J. Sheen, *Peace of Soul*).

To summarize what has been said thus far, it appears that the descent of the instinct concept can be traced from early philosophies which set man apart from the rest of the living world and sought for him some divine affinity. This was achieved by claiming for man alone the power of reason. By a process of elimination the behavior of animals was ascribed to their natural instincts. During the Middle Ages this dichotomous classification became a part of Church doctrine, with the result that possession of reason and of a soul were inextricably linked to the hope of eternal life. Prescientific concepts of instinct were not deduced from the facts of nature; they were necessitated by the demands of philosophical systems based upon supernatural conceptions of nature.

Early scientific usage

When biology emerged as a scientific discipline, there was a general tendency to adopt the prescientific point of view regarding instinct. Some exceptions occurred. For example, Erasmus Darwin's *Zoonomia* expressed the theory that all behavior is a product of experience, but this point of view was subsequently disavowed by the grandson of its sponsor. Charles Darwin made the concept of instinct one cornerstone of his theory of evolution by means of natural selection.

To bridge the gap of the Cartesian man–brute dichotomy, and thus to establish the evolution of mind as well as structure, Darwin and his disciples amassed two types of evidence. One type purported to prove the existence of human instincts; the other pertained to rational behavior in subhuman species. The idea of discontinuity in mental evolution was vigorously attacked, but the dichotomy between instinct and reason was never challenged.

The nineteenth-century literature on evolution shows plainly that the concept of instinctive behavior was accepted because it filled a need in the theoretical system, and not because its validity had been established by empirical test.

Contemporary psychologists such as Herbert Spencer were influenced by the evolutionary movement, and the idea of an instinctive basis for human psychology became popular. William James, in Volume 2 of his *Principles*, insisted that man has more instincts than any other mammal. McDougall's widely read *Social Psychology* listed human instincts of flight, repulsion, parental feeling, reproduction, self-abasement, etc. Woodworth, Thorndike, and other leaders agreed that much of human behavior is best understood as an expression of instinctive drives or needs.

One of the difficulties with such thinking is that it often leads to the nominal fallacy – the tendency to confuse naming with explaining. Some psychological writers were guilty of employing the instinct concept as an explanatory device, and the eventual result was a vigorous revolt against the use of instinct in any psychological theory.

The anti-instinct revolt

Dunlap (1919) was one opening gun in the battle, but the extreme protests came from the most radical Behaviorists as represented by Z. Y. Kuo (1924). For a while the word 'instinct' was anathema, but the revolt was abortive, and there were three principal reasons for its failure.

First, Kuo denied instinct but admitted the existence of unlearned 'units of reaction'. By this phrase he meant simple reflexes, but in using it he set up a dichotomy of learned and unlearned behavior which was fatal to his basic thesis. It merely shifted the debate to arguments as to the degree of complexity permissible in an unlearned response, or the proportion of a complex pattern that was instinctive. The second error consisted essentially of a return to the position taken by Erasmus Darwin at the close of the eighteenth century. Having averred that the only unlearned reactions consist of a few simple reflexes, the opponents of the instinct doctrine invoked learning to explain all other behavior. This forced them into untenable positions such as that of maintaining that pecking behavior of the newly-hatched chick is a product of head movements made by the embryo in the shell, or that the neo-natal infant's grasp reflex depends upon prenatal exercise of this response. The third loophole in the anti-instinct argument derived from a dualistic concept of the hereditary process. Admitting that genes can affect morphological characters and simultaneously denying that heredity influences behavior, opponents of instinct were hoist by their own petard. If the physical machinery for behavior develops under genetic control, then the behavior it mediates can scarcely be regarded as independent of inheritance.

It is important to note that this war over instinct was fought more with words and inferential reasoning than with behavioral evidence. It is true that a few individuals actually observed the behavior of newborn children or of animals, but most of the battles of the campaign were fought from the armchair in the study rather than from the laboratory.

Current thought in psychology

Although there are militant opponents of the instinct doctrine among present-day psychologists, it is undoubtedly correct to say that the concept of instincts as complex, unlearned patterns of behavior is generally accepted in clinical, social and experimental psychology. Among experimentalists, Lashley suggested that instinctive behavior is unlearned and differs from reflexes in that instincts depend on 'the pattern or organization of the stimulus', whereas reflexes are elicited by stimulation of localized groups of sensory endings (1938).

Carmichael (1947) expressed agreement with G. H. Parker's statement that human beings are 'about nine-tenths inborn, and one-tenth acquired'. Morgan (1947) studied food-hoarding behavior in rats, and concluded, 'since it comes out spontaneously without training, it is plainly instinctive'. The following quotation reveals that some modern psychologists not only embrace the concept of instinctive behavior, but consider it a useful explanatory device.

Of the theories of hoarding which have been advanced, the most reasonable one in terms of recent data is that the behavior is instinctive . . . (Waddell, 1951).

At least three serious criticisms can be leveled against current treatment of the problem of instinctive behavior. The first is that psychologists in general actually know very little about most of the behavior patterns which they confidently classify as instinctive. In his paper Lashley (1938) mentions the following fifteen examples:

1. Eating of Hydra by the Planarian, Microstoma.
2. Nest-building, cleaning of young and retrieving by the primiparous rat.
3. Restless running about of the mother rat deprived of her litter.
4. Homing of pigeons.

5. Web-weaving of spiders.
6. Migratory behavior of fishes.
7. Nest-building of birds, including several species.
8. Mating behavior of the female rat in estrus.
9. Dancing reactions of the honey-bee returning to the hive laden with nectar.
10. Visual reactions of rats reared in darkness.
11. Responses of the sooty tern to her nest and young.
12. Reactions of the seagull to artificial and normal eggs.
13. Sexual behavior of the male rat.
14. Mating responses in insects.
15. Mating responses in domestic hens.

It is a safe guess that most American psychologists have never observed any of these patterns of behavior. At a conservative estimate, less than half of the reactions listed have been subjected to even preliminary study by psychologically trained investigators. The significance of this criticism lies partly in the fact that those psychologists who *have* worked in the area of 'instinctive' behavior tend to be more critical of the instinct concept than are those who lack first-hand knowledge of the behavioral evidence.

Relevant to the criticism of unfamiliarity is the fact that the degree of assurance with which instincts are attributed to a given species is inversely related to the extent to which that species has been studied, particularly from the developmental point of view. Before the development of complex behavior in human infants had been carefully analysed, it was, as we have seen, a common practice to describe many human instincts. Longitudinal studies of behavior have reduced the 'unlearned' components to three or four simple responses not much more complex than reflexes (Dennis, 1941).

The second criticism is that despite prevailing ignorance about the behavior which is called instinctive, there is strong pressure toward premature categorization of the as yet unanalysed patterns of reaction. The history of biological taxonomy shows that the reliability of any classificatory system is a function of the validity of identification of individual specimens or even populations. Unless the systematist is thoroughly familiar with the characteristics of a given species, he cannot determine its proper relation to other groups. Similarly, until psychologists have carefully analysed the salient characteristics of a given pattern of behavior, they cannot meaningfully classify or compare it with other patterns.

The third criticism of current treatment of instinctive behavior has to do with the classificatory scheme which is in use. When all criteria which supposedly differentiate instinctive from acquired responses are critically evaluated, the only one which seems universally applicable is that instincts are unlearned (Munn, 1938). This forces psychology to deal with a two-class system, and such systems are particularly unmanageable when one class is defined solely in negative terms, that is, in terms of the absence of certain characteristics that define the other class. It is logically indefensible to categorize any behavior as unlearned unless the characteristics of learned behavior have been thoroughly explored and are well known. Even the most optimistic 'learning psychologist' would not claim that we have reached this point yet. At present, to prove that behavior is unlearned is equivalent to proving the null hypothesis.

Perhaps a more serious weakness in the present psychological handling of instinct lies in the assumption that a two-class system is adequate for the classification of complex behavior. The implication that all behavior must be determined by learning or by heredity, neither of which is more than partially understood, is entirely unjustified. The final form of any response is affected by a multiplicity of variables, only two of which are genetical and experiential factors. It is to the identification and analysis of all of these factors that psychology should address itself. When this task is properly conceived and executed there will be no need nor reason for ambiguous concepts of instinctive behavior.

Genes and behavior

Experimental investigation of relationships between genetical constitution and behavior was exemplified by the pioneering studies of Yerkes (1913), Tryon (1929), and Heron (1935). Interest in this area has recently increased, and a large number of investigations have been summarized by Hall (1951) who anticipates a new interdisciplinary science of psychogenetics.

As Hall points out, the psychologist interested in examining gene–behavior relations has several approaches to choose from.

He can compare the behavior of different inbred strains of animals currently available in the genetics laboratory. He can cross two strains and study the behavior of the hybrids. Selective breeding for particular behavioral traits is a well-established technique. The behavioral effects of induced mutations have as yet received very little attention but should be investigated.

It is known that selective breeding can alter the level of general activity (Rundquist, 1933), maze behavior (Heron, 1935), emotionality (Hall, 1938), and aggressiveness (Keeler and King, 1942) in the laboratory rat. Inbred strains of mice differ from one another in temperature preference (Herter, 1938), aggressiveness (Scott, 1942), and strength of 'exploratory drive' (Thompson, 1953).

Various breeds of dogs exhibit pronounced differences in behavioral characteristics. Some are highly emotional, unstable and restless; whereas others are phlegmatic and relatively inactive (Fuller and Scott, 1954). Special breeds have been created by selective mating to meet certain practical requirements. For example, some hunting dogs such as the foxhound are 'open trailers'. While following a fresh trail they vocalize in a characteristic fashion. Other dogs are 'mute trailers'. The F_1 hybrids of a cross between these types are always open trailers although the voice is often that of the mute trailing parent (Whitney, 1929).

Inbreeding of domestic chickens for high egg production has produced behavioral deficiencies of various kinds. Although hens of some lines are excellent layers, they have almost totally lost the normal tendency to brood the eggs once they have been laid (Hurst, 1925). The maternal behavior of sows of different inbred lines of swine is strikingly different. Females of one line are so aggressively protective of their young that they cannot be approached during the lactation period. Sows of a second genetical line possess such weak maternal interest that they frequently kill their litters by stepping or lying on the young (Hodgson, 1935).

Study of the effects of controlled breeding cast doubt upon the validity of any classificatory system which describes one type of behavior as genetically determined and another as experientially determined. For example, by manipulating the genotype it is possible to alter certain types of learning ability. As far as present evidence can show, the influence of genes on learning is as important as any genetical effect upon other behavior patterns commonly considered instinctive. There is no reason to assume that so-called instinctive reactions are more dependent upon heredity than noninstinctive responses; hence genetical determination is not a differentiating criterion.

The meaning of genetical determination

Behavior which is known to vary with the genotype is often incorrectly defined as 'genetically determined' behavior. Although we can show a correlation between certain genes and particular behavior patterns, this is of course no proof of a causal relationship. Many other genes and nongenic factors are always involved in such correlations. This point is nicely illustrated by a series of experiments on audiogenic seizures in mice.

Susceptibility to fatal seizures is high in some inbred strains and low in others (Hall, 1947). When a high-incidence and low-incidence strain are crossed, the susceptibility of the F_1 generation is intermediate between those of the parental strains. So far the evidence strongly supports the conclusion that seizure incidence is genetically determined. However, the incidence of seizures can be altered without changing the genetic constitution.

This is accomplished by modifying the prenatal environment. Fertilized eggs recovered from the tubes or uterus of a female of one strain and introduced into the uterus of a female of a different strain will sometimes implant normally and produce viable young. This has been done using seizure-susceptible females as donors and seizure-resistant females as hosts. Under such conditions the genetical characteristics of the young are unaltered, but their susceptibility to fatal seizures is lower than that of their own genetic strain and higher than that of the 'foster' mothers in whose uteri they developed (Ginsberg and Hovda, 1947).

Studies of this sort emphasize the important but often neglected fact that postnatal behavior is affected by factors acting upon the organism before birth. As Sontag has pointed out, this is true of human beings as well as lower species.

Fetal environment may play a part in determining characteristics of the physiological behavior of any newborn infant. We are too often inclined to neglect this source of modification of physiological potential. Too frequently we think of the individual as beginning life only at birth. Yet because it is during the period of intrauterine life that most of the cells of the vital organs are actually formed, it is during this period that 'environmental' factors such as nutrition, oxygen, mother's hormones, etc. are most important in modifying their characteristics (1950, p. 482).

Another fundamental principle illustrated by the results of transplanting fertilized ova is that the uniformity of behavior which characterizes highly inbred strains of animals cannot be ascribed solely to homozygosity, but depends as well upon *minimal variability of the prenatal environment*. More broadly conceived, this principle implies that behavioral similarities and differences observable at birth are in part a product of intrauterine effects.

If forced to relinquish the criterion of genetical control, proponents of the instinct doctrine fall back upon the criterion of the unlearned nature of instinctive acts. Now learning is a process occurring through time, and can only be studied by longitudinal analysis. If instinctive acts are unlearned, their developmental history must differ in some significant fashion from that of a learned response.

The ontogeny of behavior

No bit of behavior can ever be fully understood until its ontogenesis has been described. Had psychologists always recognized this fact, much of the fruitless debate about unlearned behavior could have been avoided.

Perhaps the most widely cited psychological experiment on development and instinctive behavior is that of Carmichael, who studied the swimming behavior of larval amphibians (1927). He reared embryos in a solution which paralyzed the striped muscles but permitted normal growth. Animals that were thus prevented from practicing the swimming response were nevertheless capable of normal swimming when placed in pure water. These findings are often offered as proof of the claim that swimming is instinctive. However, to demonstrate that practice is not essential for the appearance of a response is only the beginning of the analysis. This point is clearly illustrated by certain observations of insect behavior.

Gravid female moths, *Hyponomenta padella*, lay their eggs on the leaves of the hackberry plant and die shortly thereafter. The eggs hatch, the larvae eat the leaves and eventually become mature. Females of this new generation in turn select hackberry leaves on which to deposit their eggs. Another race of moths prefers apple leaves as an oviposition site. The difference between the two races has been perpetuated, generation after generation, for many centuries. It would appear to be the example par excellence of a genetically controlled behavior trait. But such an explanation is insufficient.

When eggs of the apple-preferring type are transferred to hackberry leaves, the larvae thrive on the new diet. Thirty per cent of the females developing from these larvae show a preference for hackberry leaves when it comes time for them to deposit their eggs (Imms, 1931).

The evidence is of course incomplete. Why only 30 per cent of the insects show a reversal of preference is not clear. It would be illuminating if the same experimental treatment could be repeated on several successive generations. Nevertheless it appears likely that the adult moth's choice of an oviposition site is influenced by the chemical composition of the food consumed during the larval period (Emerson, 1943). If this interpretation is correct, the data illustrate the fact that a complex behavior pattern may be 'unlearned' and still depend upon the individual's previous history.

Comparable examples can be found in the behavior of vertebrates. Stereotyped patterns of behavior appear with great regularity in successive generations under conditions in which practice plays no obvious role. Nonetheless such 'species-specific' responses may be dependent upon previous experience of the organism.

The maternal behavior of primiparous female rats reared in isolation is indistinguishable from that of multiparous individuals. Animals with no maternal experience build nests before the first litter is born, clean the young, eat the placenta, and retrieve scattered young to the nest (Beach, 1937). However, pregnant rats that have been reared in cages containing nothing that can be picked up and transported do not build nests when material is made available. They simply heap their young in a pile in a corner of the cage. Other females that have been reared under conditions preventing them from licking and grooming their own bodies fail to clean their young at the time of parturition (Riess, 1950).

There are undoubtedly many adaptive responses which appear *de novo* at the biologically appropriate time in the absence of preceding practice, but the possibility remains that component parts of a complex pattern have in fact been perfected in different contexts. Whether or not this is the case can only be determined by exhaustive analysis of the ontogeny of the behavior under examination. Nonetheless, to define behavior as 'unlearned' in the absence of such analysis is meaningless and misleading.

Summary and conclusions

The concept of instinctive behavior seems to have originated in antiquity in connection with attempts to define a clear-cut difference between man and all other animals. Human behavior was said to be governed by reasoning, and the behavior of animals to depend upon instinct. In his possession of the unique power of reason, man was elevated above all other creatures, and, incidentally, his use of them for his own purposes was thus morally justified.

Christian theologians adopted this point of view and averred that man was given the power of reason so that he could earn his own salvation. Similar privileges could not logically be accorded to lower animals. Therefore they were denied reason and their behavior was explained as a product of divinely implanted instincts. In both sacred and secular philosophies the concept of instinct served a practical purpose, although in no instance was there any attempt to validate it by examination of the empirical evidence.

The concept gained a central position in scientific thinking as a result of the Darwinian movement. Proponents of the evolutionary theory accepted uncritically the assumption that all behavior must be governed by instinct or by reasoning. Their aim was to demonstrate that animals can reason and that men possess instincts. The same dichotomy has persisted in experimental psychology. Attempts to eliminate the instinct concept were unsuccessful because those who made the attempt accepted the idea that all behavior is either acquired or inherited.

No such classification can ever be satisfactory. It rests upon exclusively negative definitions of one side of the dichotomy. It obscures the basic problems involved. It reflects an unnaturally narrow and naïve conception of factors shaping behavior.

To remedy the present confused situation it is necessary first to refrain from premature classification of those kinds of behavior that are currently defined as unlearned. Until they have been systematically analysed it will remain impossible to decide whether these numerous response patterns belong in one or a dozen different categories.

The analysis that is needed involves two types of approach. One rests upon determination of the relationships existing between genes and behavior. The other consists of studying the development of various behavior patterns in the individual, and determining the number and kinds of factors that normally control the final form of the response.

When these methods have been applied to the various types of behavior which today are called 'instinctive', the concept of instinct will disappear, to be replaced by scientifically valid and useful explanations.

References

BEACH, F. A. (1937), 'The neural basis of innate behavior, I. Effects of cortical lesions upon the maternal behavior pattern in the rat', *J. compar. Psychol.*, vol. 24, pp. 393–436.

CARMICHAEL, L. (1927), 'The development of behavior in vertebrates experimentally removed from the influence of external stimulation', *Psychol. Rev.*, vol. 34, pp. 34–47.

CARMICHAEL, L. (1947), 'The growth of sensory control of behavior before birth', *Psychol. Rev.*, vol. 54, pp. 316–24.

DENNIS, W. (1941), 'Infant development under conditions of restricted practice', *Genet. psychol. Monogr.*, vol. 23, pp. 143–89.

DUNLAP, K. (1919–20), 'Are there any instincts?', *J. abnorm. Psychol.*, vol. 14, pp. 35–50.

EMERSON, A. E. (1943), 'Ecology, evolution and society', *Amer. Nat.*, vol. 77, pp. 97–118.

FULLER, J. L., and SCOTT, J. P. (1954), 'Heredity and learning ability in infrahuman animals', *Eugenics Q.*, vol. 1, pp. 28–43.

GINSBURG, B. E., and HOVDA, R. B. (1947), 'On the physiology of gene controlled audiogenic seizures in mice', *Anat. Rec.*, vol. 99, pp. 65–6.

HALL, C. S. (1938), 'The inheritance of emotionality', *Sigma Xi Q.*, vol. 26, pp. 17–27.

HALL, C. S. (1947), 'Genetic differences in fatal audiogenic seizures between two inbred strains of house mice', *J. Hered.*, vol. 38, pp. 2–6.

HALL, C. S. (1951), 'The genetics of behavior', in S. S. Stevens (ed.), *Handbook of Experimental Psychology*, Wiley.

HERON, W. T. (1935), 'The inheritance of maze learning ability in rats', *J. comp. Psychol.*, vol. 19, pp. 77–89.

HERTER, K. (1938), 'Die Beziehungen zwischen Vorzugstemperatur und Hautbeschaffenheit bei Mausen', *Zool. Anz. Suppl.*, vol. 11, pp. 48–55.

HODGSON, R. E. (1935), 'An eight generation experiment in inbreeding swine', *J. Hered.*, vol. 26, pp. 209–17.

HURST, C. C. (1925), *Experiment in Genetics*, Cambridge University Press.

IMMS, A. D. (1931), *Recent Advances in Entymology*, Blakiston's Sons.

KEELER, C. E., and KING, H. D. (1942), 'Multiple effects of coat color genes in the Norway rat, with special reference to temperament and domestication', *J. compar. Psychol.*, vol. 34, pp. 241–50.

KUO, Z. Y. (1924), 'A psychology without heredity', *Psychol. Rev.*, vol. 31, pp. 427–51.

LASHLEY, K. S. (1938), 'Experimental analysis of instinctive behavior', *Psychol. Rev.*, vol. 45, pp. 445–71.

MORGAN, C. T. (1947), 'The hoarding instinct', *Psychol. Rev.*, vol. 54, pp. 335–41.

MUNN, N. (1938), *Psychological Development*, Houghton Mifflin.

RIESS, B. F. (1950), 'The isolation of factors of learning and native behavior in field and laboratory studies', *Ann. N. Y. Acad. Sci.*, vol. 51, pp. 1093–102.

RUNDQUIST, E. A. (1933), 'The inheritance of spontaneous activity in rats', *J. compar. Psychol.*, vol. 16, pp. 415–38.

SCOTT, J. P. (1942), 'Genetic differences in the social behavior of inbred strains of mice', *J. Hered.*, vol. 33, pp. 11–15.

SONLAG, L. W. (1950), 'The genetics of differences in psychosomatic patterns in childhood', *Amer. J. Orthopsychiat.*, vol. 20, pp. 479–89.

THOMPSON, W. R. (1953), 'The inheritance of behaviour: behavioural differences in fifteen mouse strains', *Canad. J. Psychol.*, vol. 7, pp. 145–55.

TRYON, R. C. (1929), 'Genetics of learning ability in rats', *Univ. Calif. Publ. Psychol.*, vol. 4, pp. 71–89.

WADDELL, D. (1951), 'Hoarding behavior in the golden hamster', *J. compar. physiol. Psychol.*, vol. 44, pp. 383–8.

WHITNEY, L. F. (1929), 'Heredity of trail barking propensity of dogs', *J. Hered.*, vol. 20, pp. 561–2.

YERKES, R. M. (1913), 'The heredity of savageness and wildness in rats', *J. animal Behav.*, vol. 3, pp. 286–96.

Part Two Motivation as Drive

The debate on the value of the concept of instinct as the explanation of motivational phenomena had barely started, when Woodworth (1918) introduced the concept of *drive* as an alternative to that of instinct. The drive concept arose from the observation that certain experimental manipulations, such as food deprivation and induction of estrus, increased the level of general activity and facilitated the occurrence of particular unlearned and learned responses (e.g. eating, maze running, copulating). The work of investigators interested in the role of internal bodily functions in relation to motivation (e.g. A. J. Carlson, W. B. Cannon, C. P. Richter, C. J. Warden) led to the conceptualization of a drive as a specific biological state arising from the physiological consequences of change in a certain visceral function. This peripheral or sensory feedback interpretation of drive was judged to be invalid by Lashley and Morgan, who emphasized central neural mechanisms as the basis of drive.

Hull incorporated the biological view of drive into his formal theory of behaviour. Essentially, his view was that there exist four biological or *primary* drives (hunger, thirst, sex and pain), which form the primary sources of action, response reinforcement, and the acquisition of new or secondary drives. Dollard and Miller developed the concepts of acquired or secondary drive and reinforcement to account for complex human behaviour. However, there remained many difficulties with the Hullian concept of biological or homeostatic drives as the primary sources of all actions. These shortcomings were pointed out by Harlow and Hebb, who argued that many motivational phenomena could not be accounted for in terms of homeostatic drives.

7 R. S. Woodworth

Mechanisms and Drive

Excerpt from R. S. Woodworth, *Dynamic Psychology*
Columbia University Press, 1918, chapter 2.

Once the point of view of a dynamic psychology is gained, two general problems come into sight, which may be named the problem of 'mechanism' and the problem of 'drive'. One is the problem, how we do a thing, and the other is the problem of what induces us to do it. Take the case of the pitcher in a baseball game. The problem of mechanism is the problem of how he aims, gauges distance and amount of curve, and coordinates his movements to produce the desired end. The problem of drive includes such questions as to why he is engaged in this exercise at all, why he pitches better on one day than on another, why he rouses himself more against one than against another batter, and many similar questions. It will be noticed that the mechanism questions are asked with 'How?' and the drive questions with 'Why?' Now science has come to regard the question 'Why?' with suspicion, and to substitute the question 'How?' since it has found that the answer to the question 'Why?' always calls for a further 'Why?' and that no stability or finality is reached in this direction, whereas the answer to the question 'How?' is always good as far as it is accurate, though, to be sure, it is seldom if ever complete. It may be true in our case, also, that the question of drive is reducible to a question of mechanism, but there is *prima facie* justification for making the distinction. Certainly the motives and springs of action of human life are of so much importance as to justify special attention to them.

This distinction between drive and mechanism may become clearer if we consider it in the case of a machine. The drive here is the power applied to make the mechanism go; the mechanism is made to go, and is relatively passive. Its passivity is, to be sure, only relative, since the material and structure of the mechanism determine the direction that shall be taken by the power applied. We might speak of the mechanism as reacting to the power applied and so producing the results. But the mechanism without the power is inactive, dead, lacking in disposable energy.

In some forms of mechanism, such as a loaded gun, stored energy is present, and the action of the drive is to liberate this stored energy, which then does the rest of the work. This sort of mechanism is rather similar to that of a living creature. The muscles contain stored energy, which is liberated by a stimulus reaching them, the stimulus that normally reaches them being the 'nerve impulse' coming along a motor nerve. The nerve drives the muscle. The nerve impulse coming out along a motor nerve originates in the discharge of stored energy in the nerve cells controlling this nerve; and these central cells are themselves excited to discharge by nerve impulses reaching them, perhaps from a sensory nerve. The sensory nerve drives the motor center, being itself driven by a stimulus reaching the sense organ from without. The whole reflex mechanism, consisting of sense organ, sensory nerve, center, motor nerve and muscle, can be thought of as a unit; and its drive is then the external stimulus.

If all behavior were of this simple reflex type, and consisted of direct responses to present stimuli, there would be no great significance in the distinction between drive and mechanism. The drive would simply be the external stimulus and the mechanism simply the whole organism. On the other hand, what we mean by a 'motive' is something internal, and the question thus arises whether we can work our way up from the drive as external stimulus to the drive as inner motive.

The first step is to notice the physiological facts of 'reinforcement' or 'facilitation' and of 'inhibition'. These mean, in neural terms, the coming together of different nerve impulses, with the result in some cases that one strengthens the other, and in some cases that one weakens or suppresses the other. Take the familiar 'knee-jerk' or 'patellar reflex' as an example. This involuntary movement of the lower leg, produced by some of the thigh muscles, can only be elicited by a blow on the tendon passing in front of the knee (or some equivalent, strictly local stimulus). But the force of the knee-jerk can be greatly altered by influences coming from other parts of the body. A sudden noise occurring an instant before the blow at the knee will decidedly reinforce the knee-jerk, while soft music may weaken it. Clenching the fist or gritting the teeth reinforces the knee-jerk. The drive operating the knee-jerk in such cases is not entirely the local stimulus, but other centers in the brain and spinal cord, being themselves aroused from outside, furnish drive for the center that is directly responsible for the movement. If one nerve center can thus furnish drive for another, there is some sense in speaking of drives.

Still, the conception of 'drive' would have little significance if the activity aroused in any center lasted only as long as the external stimulus acting upon it through a sensory nerve; for, taken as a whole, the organism would still be passive and simply responsive to the complex of external stimuli acting on it at any moment. It is therefore a very important fact, for our purpose, that a nerve center, aroused to activity, does not in all cases relapse into quiescence, after a momentary discharge. Its state of activity may outlast the stimulus that aroused it, and this residual activity in one center may act as drive to another center. Or, a center may be 'sub-excited' by an external stimulus that is not capable of arousing it to full discharge; and, while thus sub-excited, it may influence other centers, either by way of reinforcement or by way of inhibition. Thus, though the drive for nerve activity may be ultimately external at any one moment there are internal sources of influence furnishing drive to other parts of the system.

This relationship between two mechanisms, such that one, being partially excited, becomes the drive of another, is specially significant in the case of what have been called 'preparatory and consummatory reactions' (Sherrington). A consummatory reaction is one of direct value to the animal – one directly bringing satisfaction – such as eating or escaping from danger. The objective mark of a consummatory reaction is that it terminates a series of acts, and is followed by rest or perhaps by a shift to some new series. Introspectively, we know such reactions by the satisfaction and sense of finality that they bring. The preparatory reactions are only mediately of benefit to the organism, their value lying in the fact that they lead to, and make possible, a consummatory reaction. Objectively, the mark of a preparatory reaction is that it occurs as a preliminary stage in a series of acts leading up to a consummatory reaction. Consciously, a preparatory reaction is marked by a state of tension.

Preparatory reactions are of two kinds. We have, first, such reactions as looking and listening, which are readily evoked when the animal is in a passive or resting condition, and which consist in a coming to attention and instituting a condition of readiness for a yet undetermined stimulus that may arouse further response.

The other kind consists of reactions which are not evoked except when the mechanism for a consummatory reaction has been aroused and is in activity. A typical series of events is the following: a sound or light strikes the sense organ and arouses the appropriate attentive reaction; this permits a stimulus of significance to the animal to take effect – for example, the sight of prey, which arouses a trend towards the consummatory reaction of devouring it. But this consummatory reaction cannot at once take place; what does take place is the preparatory reaction of stalking or pursuing the prey. The series of preparatory reactions may be very complicated, and it is evidently driven by the trend towards the consummatory reaction. That there is a persistent inner tendency towards the consummatory reaction is seen when, for instance, a hunting dog loses the trail; if he were simply carried along from one detail of the hunting process to another by a succession of stimuli calling out simple reflexes, he would cease hunting as soon as the trail ceased or follow it back again; whereas what he does is to explore about, seeking the trail, as we say. This seeking, not being evoked by any external stimulus (but rather by the absence of an external stimulus), must be driven by some internal force; and the circumstances make it clear that the inner drive is directed towards the capture of the prey.

The dog's behavior is to be interpreted as follows: the mechanism for a consummatory reaction, having been set into activity by a suitable stimulus, acts as a drive operating other mechanisms which give the preparatory reactions. Each preparatory reaction may be a response in part to some external stimulus, but it is facilitated by the drive towards the consummatory reaction. Not only are some reactions thus facilitated, but others which in other circumstances would be evoked by external stimuli are inhibited. The dog on the trail does not stop to pass the time of day with another dog met on the way; he is too busy. When an animal or man is too busy or too much in a hurry to respond to stimuli that usually get responses from him, he is being driven by some internal tendency.

'Drive' as we have thus been led to conceive of it in the simpler sort of case, is not essentially distinct from 'mechanism'. The drive is a mechanism already aroused and thus in a position to furnish stimulation to other mechanisms. Any mechanism might be a drive. But it is the mechanisms directed towards consummatory reactions – whether of the simpler sort seen in animals or of the more complex sort exemplified by human desires and motives – that are most likely to act as drives. Some mechanisms act at once and relapse into quiet, while others can only bring their action to completion by first arousing other mechanisms. But there is no absolute distinction, and it will be well to bear in mind the possibility that any mechanism may be under certain circumstances the source of stimulation that arouses other mechanisms to activity.

The inadequacy of either the consciousness or the behavior psychology, in their narrower formulations at least, is that they fail to consider questions like these. Their advantage as against a dynamic psychology is that they are closer to observable phenomena. Behavior we can observe, consciousness we can observe with some difficulty, but the inner dynamics of the mental processes must be inferred rather than observed. Even so, psychology is in no worse case than the other sciences. They all seek to understand what goes on below the surface of things, to form conceptions of the inner workings of things that square with the known facts and make possible the prediction of what will occur under given conditions. A dynamic psychology must utilize the observations of consciousness and behavior as indications of the 'workings of the mind'; and that, in spite of formal definitions to the contrary, is what psychologists have been attempting to accomplish since the beginning.

8 K. S. Lashley

Drive as Facilitation of Specific Neural Mechanisms

Excerpt from K. S. Lashley, 'Experimental analysis of instinctive behavior', *Psychological Review*, volume 45, 1938, pp. 445–71.

Most of the current theories concerning the nature of primitive drives have been derived by analogy with the hunger mechanism and assume some continued visceral activity, comparable to the contractions of the empty stomach, as the source of masses of excitation whose irradiation in the nervous system increases the general responsiveness of the animal. This analogy has certainly been overworked, especially as it is by no means assured that hunger motivation is itself synonymous with the hunger pangs. The work of Richter (1927) and Wada (1922) shows a correlation between rhythmic bodily activities and hunger contractions, but the activities of the animal under hunger motivation are not rhythmic. The rat in the maze does not stop running between hunger pangs. Even for hunger motivation we must assume, I believe, some source of continued excitation which is no more than activated by the hunger contractions.

When the theories of motivation by somatic sensory facilitation were developed, there was little evidence that activity could be sustained within the central nervous system. The maintenance of tension or activity through some form of circular reflex was more in accord with the conception that all excitation must pass over immediately into motor response, as first formulated by Dewey (1896). The recent demonstration of recurrent nervous circuits, perhaps capable of indefinite reverberation, by the anatomic and physiologic studies of Lorente de Nò, relieves us from the necessity of finding a peripheral mechanism to account for the maintenance of activity or for the dynamic tensions which are implied by the phenomena of motivation. The studies of the sexual and maternal motivation strongly suggest a central nervous mechanism which is merely rendered excitable by hormone action. What this means is that the seeking activities or reactions to a deficit, such as are measured by the obstruction method, are not a reaction to a continuous peripheral stimulus, such as is assumed in the evacuation theory, but are the expression of some central nervous activity or state.

The relation between the reactions to deficit and the excitability of the specific patterns of behavior is obscure. It is generally stated that the drive is first aroused, as by endocrine action, and that this, in turn, causes the appearance of the instinctive sensori-motor reactions. An increase in the excitability of sexual reactions is accepted as evidence for intensification of the drive. But the phenomenon actually observed is only a more ready excitation of specific responses. There is no need to postulate an extraneous drive to account for the fluctuations in the threshold of such reactions. The mechanism is present and under the influence of the hormone or of excitation by an adequate stimulus its excitability is increased.

Only in cases of reaction to a deficit is there any justification for introducing the notion of a drive as a source of facilitation. An increase in general activity or in exploratory behavior indicates an increased responsiveness to stimuli not obviously related to the specific sensori-motor patterns of the instinctive behavior. There is also inhibition of reactions to other stimuli, as when the chick removed from companions refuses to eat. This is a selective facilitation of activity and the facilitation originates with the organism. Does it call for the postulation of some source of energy apart from that of the specific sensori-motor patterns? The evidence indicates that the facilitation is probably independent of somatic stimulation and is of central nervous origin. Stimulation of an instinctive pattern will increase the intensity of the apparent drive. Thus sexual excitement in the male rat is aroused only by the very specific pattern of the female in heat, but once the animal is so excited, he will respond to less definite patterns of stimulation. The waning retrieving activity of the female is intensified by supplying her with a younger litter. Motivation of the hungry animal in the maze is really effective only after the maze has been associated with the getting of food. In these cases the apparent motivation seems to derive from a specific sensori-motor mechanism.

I suspect that all cases of motivation will turn out to be of this character; not a general drive or libido, or disturbance of the organic equilibrium, but a partial excitation of a very specific sensori-motor mechanism irradiating to affect other systems of reaction. In his *Dynamic Psychology* Woodworth (1918) suggested that habits might acquire dynamic functions, that a mechanism might become a drive, as he expressed the matter. I should carry this notion a step further and suggest that physiologically all drives are no more than expressions of the activity of specific mechanisms.

References

DEWEY, J. (1896), 'The reflex arc concept in psychology', *Psychol. Rev.*, vol. 3, pp. 357–70.

RICHTER, C. P. (1927), 'Animal behavior and internal drives', *Q. Rev. Biol.*, vol. 2, pp. 307–43.

WADA, T. (1922), 'An experimental study of hunger in its relation to activity', *Arch. Psychol.*, vol. 8, no. 57, pp. 1–65.

WOODWORTH, R. S. (1918), *Dynamic Psychology*, Columbia University Press.

9 C. T. Morgan

A Theory of Motivation

Excerpt from C. T. Morgan, *Physiological Psychology*, McGraw-Hill, 1943, chapter 22, pp. 458–65.

Survey of motivation

The discussion can begin with a survey of the problems and concepts of motivation. The general outline of the survey is as follows: motivation must be thought of in terms of patterns of nervous activity which arise not merely from receptor stimulation but also, and perhaps even more important, from the direct influences of chemical conditions in the blood. This pattern of nervous activity differs according to the factors giving rise to it, whether these are lack of food, water, or the presence of sex hormones. Each pattern of activity may produce more or less general activity, but also specific forms of behavior. In addition, the pattern involves the set or predisposition to perceive environmental stimuli in certain ways and to give certain responses to these stimuli. Such perceptions and responses may be said to be the goals of the motivated organism and contribute in part to the reduction of the pattern of nervous activity that, physiologically speaking, is the motive.

Motivation as a stimulus condition

The facts have already been presented in previous chapters [not included here] to show that motivation is not solely a matter of stimulation of receptors in some particular part of the body. Hunger, for example, is more than the result of gastric stimulation. Animals and human beings are impelled to eat in the absence of stomach contractions and, indeed, of a stomach; it is difficult, moreover, to argue that such desire for food exists only through learning. There is strong indication, indeed, that chemical conditions in the blood are more basic to hunger than gastric contractions and that these conditions lead both to central neural excitation and to gastric contractions. To clinch the argument are the well-established facts of specific hunger in which animals and human beings desire not food in general but particular kinds of food, and no one can argue that such selection is accomplished in terms of gastric stimulation.

Sexual drive, also, provides very striking proof of the non-stimulus basis of motivation. Various evidences of sexual drive can be seen in the absence of stimulation from the primary sexual organs; on the other hand, sexual drive clearly depends upon the presence of certain hormones in the blood, and it is quite probable that sexually motivated behavior is brought about by direct excitation of the nervous system. Similar arguments apply also to thirst-motivated behavior. It is necessary to formulate our conception of motivation, therefore, in terms broader than the doctrine of the reflex and of local stimulation of internal receptors.

Humoral motive factor

Without denying the fact that local stimulation can figure in motivated behavior, it must be argued first of all that one essential physiological factor in motivation is the chemical or humoral condition of the blood. We can call this the *humoral motive factor* (briefly, the h.m.f.). In the case of sexual drive, we know in part what the h.m.f. is, but in hunger we are still trying to identify it.

There are three possible ways, it appears, in which the h.m.f. may affect the brain.

1. The h.m.f. may affect the brain by direct stimulation. In this case, it is to be presumed, the nervous system differs somewhat in its various parts in respect of its reactions to factors in the internal environment; thus one h.m.f. may excite certain neural systems, and other h.m.f.'s. may excite other sets of neurons. The female sex hormones present a good example of this point, for experiments indicate that they directly excite centers of the brain stem and thereby bring out patterns of female sex behavior.

2. The h.m.f. may influence the nervous system by stimulation of internal receptors. A good example of this kind is the activation of carotid-sinus receptors by the carbon dioxide content of the blood. Whether or not there is such an influence in other kinds of motivation we do not yet know, but the possibility must not be excluded. Richter and Young, it will be recalled, have proposed to explain the phenomena of specific hunger by assuming that

bodily deficiencies affect the gustatory and olfactory receptors.
3. The h.m.f. may influence the brain by producing changes in
effectors which in turn excite receptors. The h.m.f. in hunger, for
example, probably causes contraction of gastric and intestinal
musculature, and because there are receptors in these muscles,
afferent excitations to the brain are produced. Similarly, the h.m.f.
may effect vasodilation in certain tissues and thereby excite
sensory fibers in the blood vessels. We do know that certain sex
hormones, for example, have a special affinity for influencing
sexually erogenous tissues, although cases of such an influence
figuring in motivation are not clearly established.

The central motive state

Next, although a nonphysiological psychologist may be perfectly
content to get along without referring to the nervous system, it is
quite clear that the nervous system is the locus of integration into
which motivating factors pour and from which patterns of
motivated behavior emerge. We might as well, then, recognize such
neural integrative activity and give it a name, the *central motive
state* (briefly, the c.m.s.).

The origin of the c.m.s. has already been indicated in referring
to the ways in which the h.m.f.'s may influence the nervous system.
In addition, too, the effect of stimuli arising from purely local
conditions, as in the emptying of the stomach which is in part the
cause of stomach motility, must be recognized.

The properties of the CMS

These may be derived from our general knowledge of motivated
behavior.

1. The c.m.s. appears to be partly self-perpetuating. That is to say,
there is some reverberatory activity in the neurons involved in the
c.m.s., such that neural activity, once it has been initiated, tends
to continue. In this respect the c.m.s. is no different from the c.e.s.
(central excitatory state) obtaining in reflex action and giving rise
to such phenomena as after-discharge, facilitation, and recruit-
ment. Lashley, among others, has pointed out, for example, that
although gastric contractions are distinctly periodic affairs, a rat
running a maze in search of food does not run in fits and starts
according to the contractions but shows a continuous and main-

tained motivation in search of food. Some of the reverberation maintaining the c.m.s. may be a purely central affair accounted for in terms of recurrent neural circuits; some of it, on the other hand, may be caused by circular, reflexive activity, i.e. the c.m.s. may lead to gastric contractions, to changes in the sexual organs, or the like, and these may, in turn, send in afferent stimulation which builds up the c.m.s.

2. In addition to reverberation, we must postulate three behavioral properties of the c.m.s. One of these is general activity. An increase in body activity goes along with the need for food and water and, in female animals, is dramatically correlated with sexual drive. Although some have argued that such activity arises from local tissue conditions associated with the drive in question, the facts may be interpreted as indicating that both local behavioral changes (e.g. stomach contractions) and general activity are the outcome of a c.m.s.

3. Another property of the c.m.s. is that it evokes specific forms of behavior. Gastric contractility may be considered as an example, although not the most important one. Much better are the various forms of 'heat' behavior seen in birds and in certain female mammals. The sexually excited male bird, for example, carries out patterns of strutting and vocalization. The female cat, as has already been described in detail, presents a special 'heat' posture, participates in treading, and gives other specific behavioral evidences, including its cries, of being in heat. These specific forms of behavior do not depend upon any especial environmental conditions and appear to be the expression of the c.m.s.

4. A further aspect of the c.m.s. is what may be called a *set* or potentiality for presenting various patterns of behavior when the appropriate stimulus conditions in the external environment are available. This is the priming property of the c.m.s. A hungry animal, for example, eats when food is in front of him, but does not exhibit the behavior involved in eating in the absence of food. The sexually excited female gives a 'receptive' behavioral reaction when mounted by a male; or conversely, the sexually motivated male mounts the receptive female when she is present but does not show mounting behavior in the absence of the female. Thus there are forms of behavior that depend not only upon the presence of

the c.m.s. but also upon external stimulus conditions, and in the absence of these, the c.m.s. can be said to prepare, prime, or set the organism for these forms of behavior when they become possible.

These three behavioral aspects of the c.m.s. – general activity, specific behavior and the readiness to perceive and react to stimulus situations in particular ways – are obviously intimately related to each other in such a way as to form an effective means of eventually remedying the condition which motivated the animal. In many ways, however, the priming aspect of the c.m.s. is its most important feature for the psychologist. It is this which makes motivated behavior appear so purposive, for it is the set to perceive and react in certain ways which defines the goal. The hungry animal, for example, 'wants' to eat, and its motivation is really as simple as that. The general activity is necessary and useful in enlarging the possibilities of finding food, but the set or readiness to eat is clearly what determines the habits learned in obtaining food.

Satiation

The question of what reduces motivation (c.m.s.), though probably not particularly relevant to the role of motivation in learning, is, nevertheless, of physiological interest. It is not, however, easy to answer, for there are at least four conceivable ways in which the c.m.s. might be eliminated.

1. The first is by eliminating the h.m.f. in the internal environment which gives rise, in cases where it operates, to the c.m.s. Thus if an animal lacks calcium, and this lack by influencing the brain causes calcium to be eaten, the eating would stop when enough calcium to eliminate the h.m.f. had been eaten, digested, and taken into the blood. This would be the simplest and most direct method of motive reduction, except that in view of the considerable time between eating materials and their utilization in the blood an animal would in this way always get more of the desired material than it actually needed. Moreover, the experimental facts indicate that although the h.m.f. may start the c.m.s., it does not finish it. Dogs with esophageal fistulas drink water in proportion to the amount they need, not until the water has gotten into the

blood-stream and offset what they need. Similarly, rats eat about as much sugar as they need within the first few minutes of eating and then turn, long before the sugar has been utilized, to other kinds of food. There are so many examples of this kind available that it is quite clear that in most cases motivation is reduced by mechanisms other than by the remedy of the condition which caused the motivated behavior.

2. Now there are several possible ways in which the c.m.s. might be reduced at least temporarily by factors other than elimination of the h.m.f. One is the liberation in the stomach or intestine of some hormone which 'signals' to the brain that the materials needed are on their way, so to speak, to the blood. In studies of gastric activity such materials have already been demonstrated; placing sugar in the small intestine, for example, causes gastric contractions to cease quite abruptly, and this result is known to be a humoral affair because it occurs in a denervated stomach. Water placed in the stomach, likewise, has been shown to allay thirst in a much shorter time than is required for the water to be absorbed into the blood and directly relieve the dehydrated condition; this effect, presumably, is a humoral one. Thus it is likely that one way of reducing motivation (c.m.s.) is by humoral messengers liberated into the blood to 'tell' the brain that relief is on the way.

3. Still a third possibility may be suggested, that the stimulation of receptors incident to behavior instigated by the c.m.s. may reduce the motivation. The taste of sugar, for which an animal is hungry, may, for example, reduce the motive to eat sugar. Or, in a somewhat more familiar example, the taste of water in the mouth may reduce thirst. Common experience indicates that in this latter case motivation is at least temporarily reduced. How general a mechanism this may be and by what neural means it operates, we do not know, but such sensory stimulation may be regarded as reducing the motivation in at least some instances.

4. The final possibility to be mentioned is that behavior resulting from the c.m.s. is motive reducing. Thus, in hunger, eating activity may reduce hunger. In thirst, too, the drinking of water, aside from its effect on the receptors of the mouth or in the gastrointestinal tract, may reduce the c.m.s. The experimental facts, indeed, indicate this conclusion for thirst, for in fistulated dogs

the amount of water drunk in a given period is directly proportional to the negative water load, whether or not this water goes into the organism and has any effect upon reducing the negative water load. It does not seem reasonable that this fact has anything to do with the excitation of buccal receptors, since a mouth that is wet is wet, and there can be no quantitative relation between amount of stimulation and the amount of drinking, which we know is proportional to negative water load. Thus it appears that the drinking behavior itself is satisfying.

A similar situation appears in the case of sexual behavior. Here there is no material to be taken into the body. Satisfaction of the motive (c.m.s.) takes place when a certain sequence of behavior has been completed, ending with the orgasm and the various behavioral components concerned in it. Thus, in this case, too, reduction of the c.m.s. is accomplished, it would appear, by prosecuting the specific behavior issuing from the motive state.

This point, it may be noted, is like that made earlier with respect to set. A motive primes the organism for behavior which, at least in part, satisfies the motive.

Emotional motivation

All that has just been said refers to motivated behavior arising from conditions within the organism: the depletion of food reserves, loss of water, and the accumulation of sex hormones. To refer to this class of motivations we may use the term *biogenic*, previously suggested as more adequate than the term *viscerogenic* which is frequently employed. With certain modifications, the analysis above may also apply to behavior which has an emotional motivation and, in the normal learning of animals and human beings, is as important, if not more important, than biogenic motivation. The principal difference, of course, is that in one case h.m.f.'s participate in producing the c.m.s., whereas in the other the c.m.s. is produced by some external stimulus, e.g. a noxious stimulus or some situation that the organism perceives as harmful.

The c.m.s., however, has the same general properties in emotion as in hunger.

1. It tends to persist, presumably through recurrent nervous circuits. We have seen that the reverberatory character of

emotional reactions is the outcome largely of cortical contributions to the emotional state, for animals without the cerebral cortex get over their emotion more quickly upon the withdrawal of the emotional stimulus than do normal animals.

2. The emotional state (c.m.s.) has relatively general patterns of behavior associated with it. Foremost of these is the general autonomic involvement. . . . Then, too, there tends to be general somatic activity, seen in the running of a scared animal or the restlessness of an angry or frightened animal.

3. There are also specific forms of behavior called out by emotional stimuli. The cat crouches, bares its teeth, and spits when presented with a dog. The startled organism executes special postural changes which have been described. These specific forms of behavior associated with emotional motivation are somewhat variable from time to time, but are nevertheless relatively fixed properties of the emotional motivation.

4. Finally, completing the parallel with biogenic motivation, central emotional states supply a set or preparation for reaction to stimulus situations. The cat faced with a dog not only displays certain special emotional reactions, but becomes primed for the whole series of reactions that are needed for fighting; these may be set off by the snarl or continuing approach of the dog. Illustrations of this sort could be multiplied but they are hardly needed; mere casual observation of human beings or animals in emotional situations will reveal that the organism is set or primed for a number of different reactions in addition to those being displayed at the moment.

The problem of how emotional states are reduced is somewhat simpler than that of biogenic c.m.s.'s. The principal factor, obviously, is the withdrawal of the stimulus situation that produces the emotional state. Even this is not entirely adequate, for the reverberatory property of emotion makes it outlast, sometimes for a considerable period, the presentation of the emotional stimulus.

The neural basis of the motive set

A word is in order about the neural basis of set, since the concept of set will become important in later discussion. Although the c.m.s. is certainly not to be regarded as localized in any particular part of the nervous system, it is perfectly legitimate to expect certain parts of the nervous system to be more concerned with one aspect of the motive state than with another. We have seen, for example, that fragments of emotional behavior are mediated by neural centers below the thalamus. The walking and running patterns, we know from a study of reflex behavior, are also organized at relatively low neural levels. Fragments of sexual behavior in animals also occur below the thalamic level.

The organization of the specific forms of behavior, however, seems generally to take place at the hypothalamic level. There have been localized the specific patterns of facial expression in emotion, and there have been found the specific forms of sexual behavior which issue directly from the c.m.s. Thus both the general and specific behavioral properties of motivating states appear to be organized at subcortical levels.

The other two properties of neural activity in motivation which have been enumerated, however, depend much more upon the cerebral cortex. The emotional reactions of the decorticate animal are much more easily elicited and subside much more quickly than do those of the normal animal. Moreover, the decorticate animal does not give evidence of perceiving the fuller implications of the motivating situation; thus, for example, although the decorticate dog snarls when its tail is pinched, it does not direct its emotional behavior toward the site of pinching, as the normal animal will do. In this case the emotional state does not bring in the set or preparation for reacting to the place of the pinch. Similarly, studies of the effects of cortical extirpation upon mating behavior show that in the absence of the cortex, or even a large part of it, the various perceptions normally associated with sexual drive are lacking. This holds even though the more specific and reflexive mating responses are not destroyed. A similar situation exists in the case of sleep, where, through the complex influences of the cerebral cortex, the normal polyphasic rhythm of infancy is transformed into the diurnal rhythm; but upon decortication, the animal relapses to its normal, more primitive, subcortically determined, polyphasic habits of sleep.

The conclusion, then, is this. The *set* aspect of motivation, i.e. the potentiality of perceiving various aspects of the external situation and reacting to them in an organized way, is dependent chiefly upon the cerebral cortex. Without the cortex, the motive state eventuates only in the immediate general and specific forms of behavior associated with the c.m.s., or humoral motivating influence giving rise to it; the more complex perceptions and organized responses which issue from the priming property of the c.m.s. are lacking.

10 C. L. Hull

Drive as an Intervening Variable in a Formal Behaviour System

Excerpts from C. L. Hull, *Principles of Behavior*, Appleton-Century-Crofts, 1943, chapters 5 and 14.

Drives are typical intervening variables

It is important to note in this connection that the general concept of drive (D) tends strongly to have the systematic status of an intervening variable, never directly observable. The need of food, ordinarily called hunger, produces a typical primary drive. Like all satisfactory intervening variables, the presence and the amount of the hunger drive are susceptible of a double determination on the basis of correlated events which are themselves directly observable. Specifically, the amount of the food need clearly increases with the number of hours elapsed since the last intake of food; here the amount of hunger drive (D) is a function of observable *antecedent* conditions, i.e. of the need which is measured by the number of hours of food privation. On the other hand, the amount of energy which will be expended by the organism in the securing of food varies largely with the intensity of hunger drive existent at the time; here the amount of 'hunger' is a function of observable events which are its *consequence*. As usual with unobservables, the determination of the exact quantitative functional relationship of the intervening variable to both the antecedent and the consequent conditions presents serious practical difficulties. This probably explains the paradox that despite the almost universal use of the concepts of need and drive, this characteristic functional relationship is not yet determined for any need.

Primary motivational concepts

At the outset it will be necessary to introduce two notions not previously discussed. These new concepts are analogous to that of habit strength ($_sH_R$) which is a logical construct conceived in the quantitative framework of a centigrade system.

The first of the two concepts is *strength of primary drive*; this is represented by the symbol D. The strength-of-drive scale is conceived to extend from a zero amount of primary motivation (complete satiation) to the maximum possible to a standard organism of a given species. In accordance with the centigrade principle this range of primary drive is divided into 100 equal parts or units. For convenience and ease of recall, this unit will be called the *mote*, a contraction of the word *motivation* with an added *e* to preserve normal pronunciation.

Because of the practical exigencies of exposition the second of the new concepts has already been utilized occasionally in the last few pages [not included here], where it has been referred to as the 'reaction tendency', a term in fairly general use though lacking in precision of meaning. For this informal expression we now substitute the more precise equivalent, *reaction-evocation potentiality*; or, more briefly, *reaction potential*. This will be represented by the symbol $_sE_R$. Like habit ($_sH_R$) and drive (D), reaction-evocation potential is also designed to be measured on a 100-point scale extending from a zero reaction tendency up to the physiological limit possible to a standard organism. The unit of reaction potentiality will be called the *wat*, a contraction of the name *Watson*.

It should be evident from the preceding paragraphs that D and $_sE_R$ are symbolic constructs in exactly the same sense as $_sH_R$, and that they share both the advantages and disadvantages of this status. The drive concept, for example, is proposed as a common denominator of all primary motivations, whether due to food privation, water privation, thermal deviations from the optimum, tissue injury, the action of sex hormones, or other causes. This means, of course, that drive will be a different function of the objective conditions associated with each primary motivation. For example, in the case of hunger the strength of the primary drive will probably be mainly a function of the number of hours of food privation, say; in the case of sex it will probably be mainly a function of the concentration of a particular sex hormone in the animal's blood; and so on. Stated formally,

$$D = f(h)$$
$$D = f(c)$$
$$D = \text{etc.},$$

where h represents the number of hours of food privation of the organism since satiation, and c represents the concentration of a particular hormone in the blood of the organism.

Turning now to the concept of reaction-evocation potentiality, we find, thanks to Perin's investigation (1942) that we are able at once to define $_SE_R$ as the product of a function of habit strength ($_SH_R$) multiplied by a function of the relevant drive (D). This multiplicative relationship is one of the greatest importance, because it is upon $_SE_R$ that the amount of action in its various forms presumably depends. It is clear, for example, that it is quite impossible to predict the vigor or persistence of a given type of action from a knowledge of either habit strength or drive strength alone; this can be predicted only from a knowledge of the product of the particular functions of $_SH_R$ and D respectively; in fact, this product constitutes the value which we are representing by the symbol $_SE_R$.

Summary and preliminary physiological interpretation of empirical findings

Having the more important concepts of the systematic approach of primary motivation before us, we proceed to the formulation of some empirical findings as related to motivation.

Most, if not all, primary needs appear to generate and throw into the blood stream more or less characteristic chemical substances, or else to withdraw a characteristic substance. These substances (or their absence) have a selective physiological effect on more or less restricted and characteristic portions of the body (e.g. the so-called 'hunger' contractions of the digestive tract) which serves to activate resident receptors. This receptor activation constitutes the drive stimulus, S_D. In the case of tissue injury this sequence seems to be reversed; here the energy producing the injury is the drive stimulus, and its action causes the release into the blood of adrenal secretion which appears to be the physiological motivating substance.

It seems likely, on the basis of various analogies, that, other things equal, the intensity of the drive stimulus would be some form of negatively accelerated increasing function of the concentration of the drive substance in the blood. However, for the sake of expository simplicity we shall assume in the present preliminary analysis that it is an increasing linear function.

The afferent discharges arising from the drive stimulus (S_D) become conditioned to reactions just the same as any other elements in stimulus compounds, except that they may be somewhat more potent in acquiring habit loadings than most stimulus elements or aggregates. Thus the drive stimulus may play a role in a conditioned stimulus compound substantially the same as that of any other stimulus element or aggregate. As a stimulus, S_D naturally manifests both qualitative and intensity primary stimulus generalization in common with other stimulus elements or aggregates in conditioned stimulus compounds.

It appears probable that when blood which contains certain chemical substances thrown into it as the result of states of need, or which lacks certain substances as the result of other states of need, bathes the neural structures which constitute the anatomical bases of habit ($_SH_R$), the conductivity of these structures is augmented through lowered resistance either in the central neural tissue or at the effector end of the connection, or both. The latter type of action is equivalent, of course, to a lowering of the reaction threshold and would presumably facilitate reaction to neural impulses reaching the effector from any source whatever. As Beach (1942) suggests, it is likely that the selective action of drives on particular effector organs in non-learned forms of behavior acts mainly in this manner. It must be noted at once, however, that sensitizing a habit structure does not mean that this alone is sufficient to evoke the reaction, any more than that caffeine or benzedrine alone will evoke reaction. Sensitization merely gives the relevant neural tissue, upon the occurrence of an adequate set of receptor discharges, an augmented facility in routing these impulses to the reactions previously conditioned to them or connected by native (inherited) growth processes. This implies to a certain extent the undifferentiated nature of drive in general, contained in Freud's concept of the 'libido'. However, it definitely does not presuppose the special dominance of any one drive, such as sex, over the other drives.

While all drives seem to be alike in their powers of sensitizing *acquired* receptor-effector connections, their capacity to call forth within the body of the organism characteristic and presumably distinctive drive stimuli gives each a considerable measure of distinctiveness and specificity in the determination of action which, in case of necessity, may be sharpened by the process of patterning to almost any extent that the reaction situation requires for adequate and consistent reinforcement. In this respect, the action of drive substances differs sharply from that of a pseudo-drive substance such as caffeine, which appears to produce nothing corresponding to a drive stimulus.

Postulate 1

The effective habit strength $(_S\bar{H}_R)$ is jointly a negative growth function of the strength of the habit at the point of reinforcement (S) and of the magnitude of the difference (d) on the continuum of that stimulus between the afferent impulses of s and s in units of discrimination thresholds (j.n.d.s); where d represents a qualitative difference, the slope of the gradient of the negative growth function is steeper than where it represents a quantitative difference.

Postulate 2

Associated with every drive (D) is a characteristic drive stimulus (S_D) whose intensity is an increasing monotonic function of the drive in question.

Postulate 3

Any effective habit strength $(_S\bar{H}_R)$ is sensitized into reaction potentiality $(_SE_R)$ by all primary drives active within an organism at a given time, the magnitude of this potentiality being a product obtained by multiplying an increasing function of $_SH_R$ by an increasing function of D.

From Postulates 1, 2, and 3 there may be derived the following corollary:

Major corollary

The amount of reaction potentiality $(_SE_R)$ in any given primary motivational situation is the product of (1) the effective habit strength $(s_1 + s_D\bar{H}_R)$ under the existing conditions of primary drive multiplied by (2) the quotient obtained from dividing the sum of the dominant value of the primary drive (D) plus the aggregate strength of all the non-dominant primary drives ($\dot{D}$) active at the time, by the sum of the same non-dominant drives plus the physiological drive maximum (M_D).

References

BEACH, F. A. (1942), 'Arousal, maintenance, and manifestation of sexual excitement in male animals', *Psychosom. Medicine*, vol. 4, pp. 173–98.

PERIN, C. T. (1942), 'Behavior potentiality as a joint function of the amount of training and the degree of hunger at the time of extinction' *J. exper. Psychol.*, vol. 30, pp. 93–113.

11 J. Dollard and N. E. Miller

Learned Drive and Learned Reinforcement[1]

Excerpts from J. Dollard and N. E. Miller, *Personality and Psychotherapy*, McGraw-Hill, 1950, chapter 5, pp. 62–8.

The helpless, naked, human infant is born with primary drives such as hunger, thirst and reactions to pain and cold. He does not have, however, many of the motives that distinguish the adult as a member of a particular tribe, nation, social class, occupation, or profession. Many extremely important drives, such as the desire for money, the ambition to become an artist or a scholar, and particular fears and guilts are learned during socialization.[2]

At present only a modest beginning has been made in the experimental study of learned drives and rewards. The work has a long way to go before it bridges completely the gap between the fundamental biological drives and the wonderfully complex web of socially learned motives that determine adult human behavior. The facts that have been learned, however, are extremely important for an understanding of normal and abnormal personality and of psychotherapy.

As Allport (1937) points out, the ability for drives to be acquired

1. For the experimental evidence supporting many of the conclusions given in this chapter, and the original, more detailed discussion of theory, see Miller (1950). Minor portions of this chapter are adapted from Miller and Dollard (1941).

2. It is entirely possible that the infant acquires a number of significant new drives (e.g. an increase in sexual motivation) as a physiological result of the process of maturation. But the extreme variability from society to society (Ford, 1949) and even among the social classes in our own society (Davis, 1948; and Warner *et al.*, 1949) is conclusive proof that many of the most important human motivations must be learned. It seems highly probable that other, more universal drives are also learned as the product of more universal conditions of human learning, such as the family. The presence of conditions favorable for the learning of such drives along with evidence that they can be modified by learning places the burden of proof on those who would claim that they are entirely the product of maturation.

is an exceedingly important factor in the development of the distinguishing characteristics of personality. No two people are exactly alike because each has learned different combinations of motives and values under the different conditions of life to which he has been exposed. Freudian theory contains many assumptions about how drives are changed by experience and how these changes affect the personality. Finally, an important part of what has often been called ego strength, or strength of character, is the ability of socially learned drives to compete with primary ones.

Fear as a learned drive and fear reduction as a reinforcement

Fear will be discussed first and in the most detail because it has been studied most thoroughly, provides the clearest examples of basic concepts, and is so important as a learned drive. When the source of fear is vague or obscured by repression, it is often called *anxiety*.

Rationale of experiments on animals. The basic facts and concepts can best be introduced by the discussion of a simple experiment on albino rats. In using the results from an experiment of this kind we are working on the hypothesis that people have all the learning capacities of rats so that any general phenomena of learning found in rats will also be found in people, although, of course, people may display additional phenomena not found in rats. Even though the facts must be verified at the human level, it is often easier to notice the operation of principles after they have been studied and isolated in simpler situations so that one knows exactly what to look for. Furthermore, in those cases in which it is impossible to use as rigorous experimental controls at the human level, our faith in what evidence can be gathered at that level will be increased if it is in line with the results of more carefully controlled experiments on other mammals.

Experiments verifying basic principles

In an experiment on albino rats, Miller (1948) used the apparatus illustrated in Figure 1. It consisted of two compartments, one black and one white, separated by a little door. Before beginning the experiment proper, he tested the animals in this apparatus and showed that they had no fear of either compartment. Then he gave the animals electric shocks in the white compartment and trained them to escape these shocks by running through the door (which was open) into the black compartment.

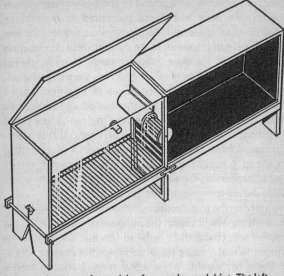

Figure 1 Apparatus for studying fear as a learned drive. The left compartment is painted white, the right one, black. In order to train the animals to fear the white compartment, a mild shock is administered through the floor of this compartment, which is a grid. During this training the experimenter, by pressing a button, causes the door between the compartments to drop open in front of the animal. In order to see whether the animal can learn a new habit when he is motivated by fear alone (without the primary drive of shock) the experimenter leaves the door closed and adjusts the apparatus so that the door drops when the animal performs the correct response, which is turning the wheel or pressing the bar as the case may be. An electric clock is automatically started when the animal is placed in the white compartment and stopped when the animal performs the correct response. (From Miller, 1948)

On later trials the electric shock was turned off so that the primary drive of pain was absent, but the animals still continued to run rapidly through the open door. When the door was closed so that they were confined in the white compartment, the rats showed obvious symptoms of fear such as urination, defecation, tenseness, and crouching. This fear must have been learned since it had not been present before the training with the electric shock.

Next, a test was made to see whether the fear would serve to motivate, and the escape from fear to reinforce, the learning of a new habit.[3] The animals were placed in the white compartment *without shock*, the door was closed but could be released by rotating a little wheel above it. Under these circumstances the fear motivated a variety of responses in the compartment: the animals stood up in front of the door, placed their paws on it, sniffed around the edges, bit the bars of the grid they were standing on, ran back and forth and gave other signs of agitation. In the course of this behavior they eventually touched and moved the wheel above the door. This caused the door to drop so they could run out of the fear-provoking white compartment. If this reduction in fear was a reinforcement, we would expect it to strengthen the response of turning the wheel. As Figure 2 shows, this is exactly what happened; the animals learned to move the wheel much faster during the series of test trials.

If escaping from the fear-producing white compartment was the reinforcement, we would expect the response to change when the reinforcement was changed. In order to test this, the conditions were changed so that turning the wheel would not open the door, but pressing a bar would. When wheel turning was no longer reinforced by escape from the fear-producing white compartment, this response was gradually extinguished, and variable, trial-and-error behavior reappeared. Figure 3 shows the disappearance of the response of turning the wheel during the trials in which it was not reinforced. At the same time, as Figure 4 shows, the new response, bar pressing, that allowed the animal to escape from the fear-producing white compartment, was learned.

In the foregoing experiment the fear was elicited by the cues in a specific place, the white compartment, and reduced by the removal of those cues when the animal escaped from that place. But it does not make any difference how the fear is elicited or reduced. For example, in another experiment a monkey was trained to fear a buzzer by pairing it with electric shock (Miller,

3. Mowrer (1939) was the first to state clearly the hypothesis that fear can serve as a drive and fear reduction as a reinforcement. Without working out the details, he suggested that this hypothesis should be applicable to the learning of neurotic behavior, superstitions, etc.

1950). Throughout this experiment the monkey remained in the same place, which was a special cage. It was found that any response that was followed by cessation of the fear-provoking

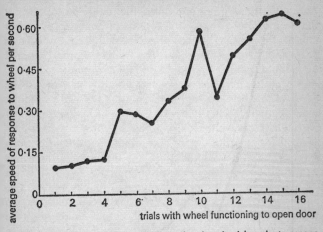

Figure 2 Learning the first new habit, turning the wheel, in order to escape from the fear-provoking cues in the white compartment. With mild pain produced by an electric shock as a primary drive, the animals have previously learned to fear the white compartment (see Figure 1) and to run out of it through an open door into the black compartment. Then they are given trials without any electric shock. During these trials they are presumably motivated by fear. The door is closed but can be opened by turning a little wheel. Under these conditions the animals learn to turn the wheel. The curve indicates their progressive increase in speed on successive trials. (From Miller, 1948)

buzzer would be strongly reinforced. For example, the monkey was taught to respond to the buzzer by immediately pulling a handle that turned it off.

The type of behavior that we have been describing is shown by people as well as by animals. A child who has not previously feared dogs learns to fear them after having been bitten, and this fear can motivate him to learn and perform a variety of new responses such as closing gates, climbing over fences, and avoiding certain streets. The clinical data to be discussed later will be full of many other examples.

Behavior puzzling when conditions of learning are unknown. In the preceding experiments the behavior is easy to understand because the white compartment and the buzzer are conspicuous external cues and the observer knows that they have been associ-

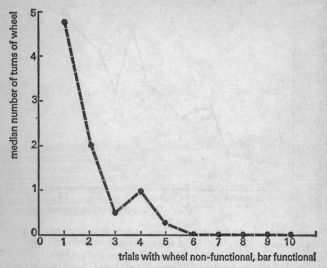

Figure 3 Unlearning the habit of turning the wheel when it fails to reduce the learned drive of fear. Conditions are changed so that turning the wheel no longer causes the door to drop open allowing the animal to escape from the fear-provoking cues in the white compartment. The animal can escape, however, by pressing a bar. The curve shows the progressive decrease in the amount of wheel turning during trials when it is no longer rewarded by a reduction in the strength of fear. (From Miller, 1948)

ated with pain produced by electric shocks. If the cues were more obscure or produced by internal thoughts or drives and the observer entered after the training with electric shock was completed, the behavior might be quite puzzling. In many examples of abnormal behavior it is only after time-consuming study that the therapist learns that certain cues are eliciting fear, exactly what these cues are, and why they are eliciting the fear.

To summarize, we say that fear is *learned* because it can be attached to previously neutral cues, such as those in the white compartment; we say that it is a *drive* because it can motivate, and its reduction can reinforce, the learning and performance of new responses, such as turning the wheel or pressing the bar. Therefore, we call the fear of a previously neutral cue a *learned drive*. [. . .]

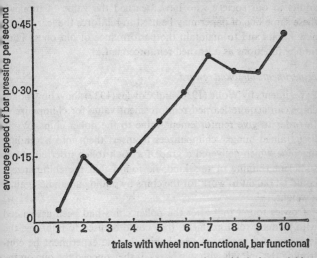

Figure 4 Learning a second new habit, bar pressing, with the learned drive of fear as a motivation. During further trials without shock, conditions are changed so that only pressing the bar will cause the door to drop open and allow the animals to escape from the fear-provoking cues in the white compartment. The curve shows the increase in speed in the performance of the second new habit, pressing the bar. (From Miller, 1948)

Learned reinforcement

Definitions of learned drive and learned reinforcement. When, as the result of learning, previously neutral cues gain the capacity to play the same functional role in the learning and performance of new responses as do primary drives, such as hunger and thirst, these cues are said to have *learned-drive value*.

When, as the result of learning, previously neutral cues gain the capacity to play the same functional role in the learning and performance of new responses as other reinforcements, such as food for the hungry animal or water for the thirsty one, they are described as *learned reinforcements*. They may also be called learned rewards or secondary reinforcements.

J. Dollard and N. E. Miller 97

Money is a common example of a learned reinforcement. To infants or to people who have not been subject to the influence of Western society, bits of paper with printing on them by the United States Treasury are relatively neutral cues. With most adults in our society who have 'learned the value of money', these same bits of paper may be used to reinforce the learning of new habits and to maintain the performance of old ones. Thus money functions as a learned reinforcement.

Experiments on token reward

Experiments by Wolfe (1936) and Cowles (1937) show how poker chips can acquire learned reinforcement value for chimpanzees. In order to give reinforcement value to the poker chips, Wolfe first trained hungry chimpanzees to insert them into a vending machine which delivered a grape for each token inserted. After sufficient training of this kind, he found that the chimpanzees could be taught to work for the chips by pulling a handle against a weight.

Cowles found that after the poker chips had been associated with primary reinforcement, they could be used to reinforce the learning of a variety of new habits. In one experiment he confronted the animals with two boxes. If they opened the one on the left they found a token; if they opened the one on the right they found nothing. Under these conditions they quickly learned to open the box on the left in spite of the fact that they were not allowed to exchange the tokens for food until after the end of the day's session. In other experiments the possible innate reward value of the token was controlled by giving the animal a token that had been associated with food if he performed the correct response and a different token that had been associated with the nondelivery of food if he performed the incorrect response. The learning of the correct response under these circumstances showed that the reinforcement value of the token depended upon its previous association with the primary reinforcement of eating food when hungry.

Learned rewards follow same laws as other habits. Other experiments on subjects ranging from chickens to children have shown that a variety of sounds and visual stimuli (and hence presumably any cue) can be made to function as a learned reinforcement by repeated, immediate association with primary reinforcement. In the experiments that have been done to date, the acquisition of learned reinforcement seems to follow exactly the same laws as the learning of any other habit. The learned reinforcement effect of the stimulus is strengthened by trials with primary reinforcement and extinguished by repeated nonreinforced trials.[4] According to the principle of the gradient of reinforcement, immediate associations between a cue and primary reinforcement are more effective in establishing learned reinforcement than are delayed ones. Learned reinforcement generalizes to other similar cues, but, with repeated primary reinforcement of one cue and nonreinforcement of another somewhat different one, a discrimination can be established. Learned reinforcements are more effective in the presence of a drive, and even the presence of an irrelevant drive (i.e., hunger for a learned reinforcement based on giving water to a thirsty animal) can increase their effectiveness somewhat. As with the performance of other responses, it is difficult to be certain whether or not their effectiveness is reduced all the way to zero in the absence of any drive.[5]

Reduce effects of delay. One of the important functions of learned reinforcement is to extend the effects of the gradient of reinforcement over longer intervals of delay between the performance of a response and its reinforcement by a primary reward.[6] Thus in Cowles' (1937) experiment the primary reward of food did not come until the end of the day's session. Learning was possible in

4. In adult human subjects many learned reinforcements seem to be exceedingly resistant to extinction, but some are readily extinguished. For example, in a completely uncontrolled inflation, the learned reinforcement value of money extinguishes. Presumably the resistance of learned reinforcement to extinction varies with the same conditions that affect the resistance of learned drives to extinction and presents the same problems in complex human situations involving interlocking hierarchies of learned drives and reinforcement.

5. According to a strict drive-reduction theory, their effectiveness would, of course, have to be zero in the absence of any drive to be reduced.

6. In fact, Spence (1947) has made a good case for the hypothesis that all the effects of delayed reinforcement are mediated in this way. If his hypothesis is correct, the gradient of reinforcement emerges as a deduction from two more fundamental principles: stimulus generalization and learned reinforcement.

spite of this delay because the chimpanzees received the poker chips as a learned reinforcement immediately after the selection of the correct box. Then later the learned-reinforcement value of the poker chips was maintained by immediate association with the primary reinforcement of food.

It is obvious that money functions in a similar fashion in our society. But this effect of learned reinforcement is not limited to one stimulus, such as money; after a child has learned to respond to promises, promises may be used in a similar way, provided the learned-reinforcement value of the promises is maintained by regular enough associations with primary reinforcement. After sufficient training, words that the child says to himself may function in the same way. As will be seen, this is a part of the mechanism of 'hope' and plays an important role in the response to remote goals.

Relationship between learned drive and learned reinforcement

In an experiment that we have already mentioned, albino rats were given an electric shock in the white compartment. In the learning process, they established not only a new drive (fear of the white compartment) but also a new reinforcement (escape from the white compartment). In this case it is clear that escape from the white compartment served as a reinforcement because it reduced the drive. Any cue that acquires the ability to stop the fear responses, and hence reduce the strong fear stimulus, will be expected to serve as a reinforcement for the frightened individual.

Conversely, when a child is being taught the value of money, not only is the money established as a learned reinforcement but also the need for money becomes a new drive. Similarly, after Wolfe (1936) had trained the chimpanzees to exchange poker chips for grapes, the sight of a poker chip out of reach in the work apparatus served as an *incentive* to motivate him to pull it in, and getting the poker chip served as a reinforcement for the response of pulling it in. The fact that the chimpanzees would refuse to work if they were given a free supply of poker chips suggests that getting the poker chips served to reduce their learned drive for them.

To a hungry infant, the sudden appearance of the mother with the bottle would be expected to function as a learned reinforcement; it also seems to soothe the infant and temporarily reduce crying and other signs of high drive. But if the bottle is not given to the child, its being near but not near enough eventually elicits responses that indicate increased drive. It is conceivable that in some cases in which the appearance of a rewarding object seems to produce an immediate increase in excitement, the foregoing sequence may occur so rapidly that an initial, temporary decrease in drive is not noted. On the other hand, it is entirely possible that the relationships we have been describing are not universal. For the purposes of this book it is enough to know that both learned drives and learned reinforcements can be established.

References

ALLPORT, G. W. (1937), *Personality*, Holt, Rinehart & Winston.
COWLES, J. T. (1937), 'Food tokens as incentives for learning by chimpanzees', *Compar. Psychol. Monogr.*, vol. 14, no. 5.
DAVIS, A. (1948), *Social Class Influences upon Learning: The Inglis Lecture, 1948*, Harvard University Press.
FORD, C. S. (1949), 'The arbitrary values of mankind', *Amer. Merc.*, vol. 68, no. 306, pp. 746–51.
MILLER, N. E. (1948), 'Studies of fear as an acquirable drive: 1. Fear as motivation and fear-reduction as reinforcement in the learning of new responses', *J. exper. Psychol.*, vol. 38, pp. 89–101.
MILLER, N. E. (1951), 'Learnable drives and rewards', in S. S. Stevens (ed.), *Handbook of Experimental Psychology*, Wiley.
MILLER, N. E., and DOLLARD, J. (1941), *Social Learning and Imitation*, Yale University Press.
MOWRER, O. H. (1939), 'A stimulus-response analysis of anxiety and its role as a reinforcing agent', *Psychol. Rev.*, vol. 46, pp. 553–66.
SPENCE, K. W. (1947), 'The role of secondary reinforcement in delayed reward learning', *Psychol. Rev.*, vol. 54, pp. 1–8.
WARNER, W. L. (1949), *Democracy in Jonesville*, Harper & Row.
WOLFE, J. B. (1936), 'Effectiveness of token rewards for chimpanzees' *Compar. Psychol. Monogr.*, vol. 12, no. 60.

12 H. F. Harlow

Mice, Monkeys, Men and Motives[1]

H. F. Harlow, 'Mice, monkeys, men and motives', *Psychological Review*, volume 60, number 1, 1953, pp. 23-32.

Many of psychology's theoretical growing pains – or, in modern terminology, conditioned anxieties – stem from the behavioral revolution of Watson. The new psychology intuitively disposed of instincts and painlessly disposed of hedonism. But having completed this St Bartholomew-type massacre, behavioristic motivation theory was left with an aching void, a nonhedonistic aching void, needless to say.

Before the advent of the Watsonian scourge the importance of external stimuli as motivating forces was well recognized. Psychologists will always remain indebted to Loeb's brilliant formulation of tropistic theory (1918), which emphasized, and probably over-emphasized, the powerful role of external stimulation as the primary motivating agency in animal behavior. Unfortunately, Loeb's premature efforts to reduce all behavior to overly simple mathematical formulation, his continuous acceptance of new tropistic constructs in an effort to account for any aberrant behavior not easily integrated into his original system, and his abortive attempt to encompass all behavior into a miniature theoretical system doubtless led many investigators to underestimate the value of his experimental contributions.

Thorndike (1911) was simultaneously giving proper emphasis to the role of external stimulation as a motivating force in learning and learned performances. Regrettably, these motivating processes were defined in terms of pain and pleasure, and it is probably best for us to dispense with such lax, ill-defined, subjective terms

1. This paper was presented 3 September 1951, as the presidential address of the Division of Experimental Psychology at the Chicago meetings of the American Psychological Association.

as pain, pleasure, anxiety, and frustration hypotheses – particularly in descriptive and theoretical rodentology.

Instinct theory, for all its terminological limitations, puts proper emphasis on the motivating power of external stimuli; for, as so brilliantly described by Watson in 1914, the instinctive response was elicited by 'serial stimulation', much of which was serial external stimulation.

The almost countless researches on tropisms and instincts might well have been expanded to form a solid and adequate motivational theory for psychology – a theory with a proper emphasis on the role of the external stimulus and an emphasis on the importance of incentives as opposed to internal drives per se.

It is somewhat difficult to understand how this vast and valuable literature was to become so completely obscured and how the importance of the external stimulus as a motivating agent was to become lost. Pain–pleasure theory was discarded because the terminology had subjective, philosophical implications. Instinct theory fell into disfavor because psychologists rejected the dichotomized heredity–environment controversy and, also, because the term 'instinct' had more than one meaning. Why tropistic theory disappeared remains a mystery, particularly inasmuch as most of the researches were carried out on subprimate animal forms.

Modern motivation theory apparently evolved from an overpopularization of certain experimental and theoretical materials. Jennings' demonstration (1906) that 'physiological state' played a role in determining the behavior of the lower animal was given exaggerated importance and emphasis, thereby relegating the role of external stimulation to a secondary position as a force in motivation. The outstanding work in the area of motivation between 1920 and 1930 related to visceral drives and drive cycles and was popularized by Richter's idealized theoretical paper (1927) and Cannon (1932).

When the self-conscious behavior theorists of the early thirties looked for a motivation theory to integrate with their developing learning constructs, it was only natural that they should choose the available tissue-tension hypotheses. Enthusiastically and uncritically the S–R theorists swallowed these theses whole. For fifteen years they have tried to digest them, and it is now time that these theses be subjected to critical examination, analysis and evaluation. We do not question that these theses have fertilized the field of learning, but we do question that the plants that have developed are those that will survive the test of time.

It is my belief that the theory which describes learning as dependent upon drive reduction is false, that internal drive as such is a variable of little importance to learning, and that this small importance steadily decreases as we ascend the phyletic scale and as we investigate learning problems of progressive complexity. Finally, it is my position that drive-reduction theory orients learning psychologists to attack problems of limited importance and to ignore the fields of research that might lead us in some foreseeable future time to evolve a theoretical psychology of learning that transcends any single species or order.

There can be no doubt that the single-celled organisms such as the amoeba and the paramecium are motivated to action both by external and internal stimuli. The motivation by external stimulation gives rise to heliotropisms, chemotropisms, and rheotropisms. The motivation by internal stimulation produces characteristic physiological states which have, in turn, been described as chemotropisms. From a phylogenetic point of view, moreover, neither type of motive appears to be more basic or more fundamental than the other. Both types are found in the simplest known animals and function in interactive, rather than in dominant-subordinate, roles.

Studies of fetal responses in animals from opossum to man give no evidence suggesting that the motivation of physiological states precedes that of external incentives. Tactual, thermal, and even auditory and visual stimuli elicit complex patterns of behavior in the fetal guinea pig, although this animal has a placental circulation which should guarantee against thirst or hunger (Carmichael, 1934). The newborn opossum climbs up the belly of the female and into the pouch, apparently in response to external cues; if visceral motives play any essential role, it is yet to be described (Langworthy, 1928). The human fetus responds to external tactual and nociceptive stimuli at a developmental period preceding demonstrated hunger or thirst motivation. Certainly, there is no experimental literature to indicate that internal drives are ontogenetically more basic than exteroceptive motivating agencies.

Tactual stimulation, particularly of the cheeks and lips, elicits mouth, head, and neck responses in the human neonate, and there are no data demonstrating that these responses are conditioned, or even dependent, upon physiological drive states. Hunger appears to lower the threshold for these responses to tactual stimuli. Indeed, the main role of the primary drive seems to be one of altering the threshold for precurrent responses. Differentiated sucking response patterns have been demonstrated to quantitatively varied thermal and chemical stimuli in the infant only hours of age (Jensen, 1932), and there is, again, no reason to believe that the differentiation could have resulted from antecedent tissue-tension reduction states. Taste and temperature sensations induced by the temperature and chemical composition of the liquids seem adequate to account for the responses.

There is neither phylogenetic nor ontogenetic evidence that drive states elicit more fundamental and basic response patterns than do external stimuli; nor is there basis for the belief that precurrent responses are more dependent upon consummatory responses than are consummatory responses dependent upon precurrent responses. There is no evidence that the differentiation of the innate precurrent responses is more greatly influenced by tissue-tension reduction than are the temporal ordering and intensity of consummatory responses influenced by conditions of external stimulation.

There are logical reasons why a drive-reduction theory of learning, a theory which emphasizes the role of internal, physiological-state motivation, is entirely untenable as a motivational theory of learning. The internal drives are cyclical and operate, certainly at any effective level of intensity, for only a brief fraction of any organism's waking life. The classical hunger drive physiologically defined ceases almost as soon as food – or non-food – is ingested. This, as far as we know, is the only case in which a single swallow portends anything of importance. The temporal brevity of operation of the internal drive states obviously offers a minimal opportunity for conditioning and a maximal opportunity for extinction. The human being, at least in the continental United States, may go for days or even years without ever experiencing true hunger or thirst. If his complex conditioned responses were dependent upon primary drive reduction, one would expect him to regress rapidly to a state of tuitional oblivion. There are, of course, certain recurrent physiological drive states that are maintained in the adult. But the studies of Kinsey (1948) indicate that in the case of one of these there is an inverse correlation between presumed drive strength and scope and breadth of learning, and in spite of the alleged reading habits of the American public, it is hard to believe that the other is our major source of intellectual support. Any assumption that derived drives or motives can account for learning in the absence of primary drive reduction puts an undue emphasis on the strength and permanence of derived drives, at least in subhuman animals. Experimental studies to date indicate that most derived drives (Miller, 1951) and second-order conditioned responses (Pavlov, 1927) rapidly extinguish when the rewards which theoretically reduce the primary drives are withheld. The additional hypothesis of functional autonomy of motives, which could bridge the gap, is yet to be demonstrated experimentally.

The condition of strong drive is inimical to all but very limited aspects of learning – the learning of ways to reduce the internal tension. The hungry child screams, closes his eyes, and is apparently oblivious to most of his environment. During this state he eliminates response to those aspects of his environment around which all his important learned behaviors will be based. The hungry child is a most incurious child, but after he has eaten and become thoroughly sated, his curiosity and all the learned responses associated with his curiosity take place. If this learning is conditioned to an internal drive state, we must assume it is the resultant of backward conditioning. If we wish to hypothesize that backward conditioning is dominant over forward conditioning in the infant, it might be possible to reconcile fact with S–R theory. It would appear, however, that alternative theoretical possibilities should be explored before the infantile backward conditioning hypothesis is accepted.

Observations and experiments on monkeys convinced us that there was as much evidence to indicate that a strong drive state inhibits learning as to indicate that it facilitates learning. It was the speaker's feeling that monkeys learned most efficiently if they were given food before testing, and as a result, the speaker routinely fed his subjects before every training session. The rhesus monkey is equipped with enormous cheek pouches, and consequently many subjects would begin the educational process with a rich store of incentives crammed into the buccal cavity. When the monkey made a correct response, it would add a raisin to the buccal storehouse and swallow a little previously munched food. Following an incorrect response, the monkey would also swallow a little stored food. Thus, both correct and incorrect responses invariably resulted in S–R theory drive reduction. It is obvious that under these conditions the monkey cannot learn, but the present speaker developed an understandable skepticism of this hypothesis when the monkeys stubbornly persisted in learning, learning rapidly, and learning problems of great complexity. Because food was continuously available in the monkey's mouth, an explanation in terms of differential fractional anticipatory goal responses did not appear attractive. It would seem that the Lord was simply unaware of drive-reduction learning theory when he created, or permitted the gradual evolution of, the rhesus monkey.

The langurs are monkeys that belong to the only family of primates with sacculated stomachs. There would appear to be no mechanism better designed than the sacculated stomach to induce automatically prolonged delay of reinforcement defined in terms of homeostatic drive reduction. Langurs should, therefore, learn with great difficulty. But a team of Wisconsin students has discovered that the langurs in the San Diego Zoo learn at a high level of monkey efficiency. There is, of course, the alternative explanation that the inhibition of hunger contractions in multiple stomachs is more reinforcing than the inhibition of hunger contractions in one. Perhaps the quantification of the gastric variable will open up great new vistas of research.

Actually, the anatomical variable of diversity of alimentary mechanisms is essentially uncorrelated with learning to food incentives by monkeys and suggests that learning efficiency is far better related to tensions in the brain than in the belly.

Experimental test bears out the fact that learning performance by the monkey is unrelated to the theoretical intensity of the hunger drive. Meyer (1951) tested rhesus monkeys on discrimination-learning problems under conditions of maintenance-food deprivation of 1·5, 18·5, and 22·5 hours and found no significant differences in learning or performance. Subsequently, he tested the same monkeys on discrimination-reversal learning following one, twenty-three, and forty-seven hours of maintenance-food deprivation and, again, found no significant differences in learning or in performance as measured by activity, direction of activity, or rate of responding. There was some evidence, not statistically significant, that the most famished subjects were a bit overeager and that intense drive exerted a mildly inhibitory effect on learning efficiency.

Meyer's data are in complete accord with those presented by Birch (1945), who tested six young chimpanzees after two, six, twelve, twenty-four, and forty-eight hours of food deprivation and found no significant differences in proficiency of performance on six patterned string problems. Observational evidence led Birch to conclude that intense food deprivation adversely affected problem solution because it led the chimpanzee to concentrate on the goal to the relative exclusion of the other factors.

It may be stated unequivocally that, regardless of any relationship that may be found for other animals, there are no data indicating that intensity of drive state and the presumably correlated amount of drive reduction are positively related to learning efficiency in primates.

In point of fact there is no reason to believe that the rodentological data will prove to differ significantly from those of monkey, chimpanzee, and man. Strassburger (1950) has recently demonstrated that differences in food deprivation from five hours to forty-seven hours do not differentially affect the habit strength of the bar-pressing response as measured by subsequent resistance to extinction. Recently, Sheffield and Roby (1950) have demonstrated learning in rats in the absence of primary drive reduction. Hungry rats learned to choose a maze path leading to a saccharin solution, a non-nutritive substance, in preference to a path leading to water. No study could better illustrate the predominant role of the external incentive-type stimulus on the learning function. These data suggest that, following the example of the monkey, even the rats are abandoning the sinking ship of reinforcement theory.

The effect of intensity of drive state on learning doubtless varies as we ascend the phyletic scale and certainly varies, probably to the point of almost complete reversal, as we pass from simple to complex problems, a point emphasized some years ago in a theoretical article by Maslow (1943). Intensity of nociceptive stimulation may be positively related to speed of formation of conditioned avoidance responses in the monkey, but the use of intense nociceptive stimulation prevents the monkey from solving any problem of moderate complexity. This fact is consistent with a principle that was formulated and demonstrated experimentally many years ago as the Yerkes-Dodson law (1908). There is, of course, no reference to the Yerkes-Dodson law by any drive-reduction theorist.

We do not mean to imply that drive state and drive-state reduction are unrelated to learning; we wish merely to emphasize that they are relatively unimportant variables. Our primary quarrel with drive-reduction theory is that it tends to focus more and more attention on problems of less and less importance. A strong case can be made for the proposition that the importance of the psychological problems studied during the last fifteen years has decreased as a negatively accelerated function approaching an asymptote of complete indifference. Nothing better illustrates this point than the kinds of apparatus currently used in 'learning' research. We have the single-unit T-maze, the straight runway, the double-compartment grill box, and the Skinner box. The single-unit T-maze is an ideal apparatus for studying the visual capacities of a nocturnal animal; the straight runway enables one to measure quantitatively the speed and rate of running from one dead end to another; the double-compartment grill box is without doubt the most efficient torture chamber which is still legal; and the Skinner box enables one to demonstrate discrimination learning in a greater number of trials than is required by any other method. But the apparatus, though inefficient, give rise to data which can be splendidly quantified. The kinds of learning problems which can be efficiently measured in these apparatus represent a challenge only to the decorticate animal. It is a constant source of bewilderment to me that the neobehaviorists who so frequently belittle physiological psychology should choose apparatus which, in effect, experimentally decorticate their subjects.

The Skinner box is a splendid apparatus for demonstrating that the rate of performance of a learned response is positively related to the period of food deprivation. We have confirmed this for the monkey by studying rate of response on a modified Skinner box following one, twenty-three, and forty-seven hours of food deprivation. Increasing length of food deprivation is clearly and positively related to increased rate of response. This functional relationship between drive states and responses does not hold, as we have already seen, for the monkey's behavior in discrimination learning or in acquisition of any more complex problem. The data, however, like rat data, are in complete accord with Crozier's (1929) finding that the acuteness of the radial angle of tropistic movements in the slug Limax is positively related to intensity of the photic stimulation. We believe there is generalization in this finding and we believe the generalization to be that the results from the investigation of simple behavior may be very informative about even simpler behavior but very seldom are they informative about behavior of greater complexity. I do not want to discourage anyone from the pursuit of the psychological Holy Grail by the use of the Skinner box, but as far as I am concerned, there will be no moaning of farewell when we have passed the pressing of the bar.

In the course of human events many psychologists have children, and these children always behave in accord with the theoretical position of their parents. For purposes of scientific objectivity the boys are always referred to as 'Johnny' and the girls as 'Mary'. For some eleven months I have been observing the behavior of Mary X. Perhaps the most striking characteristic of this particular primate has been the power and persistence of her curiosity-investigatory motives. At an early age Mary X demonstrated a positive valence to parental thygmotactic stimulation. My original interpretation of these tactual-thermal erotic responses as indicating parental affection was dissolved by the discovery that when Mary X was held in any position depriving her of visual exploration of the environment, she screamed; when held in a position favorable to visual exploration of the important environment, which did not include the parent, she responded positively. With the parent and position held constant and visual exploration denied by snapping off the electric light, the positive responses changed to negative, and they returned to positive when the light was again restored. This behavior was observed in Mary X, who, like any good Watson child, showed no 'innate fear of the dark'.

The frustrations of Mary X appeared to be in large part the results of physical inability to achieve curiosity-investigatory goals. In her second month, frustrations resulted from inability to hold up her head indefinitely while lying prone in her crib or on a mat and the consequent loss of visual curiosity goals. Each time she had to lower her head to rest, she cried lustily. At nine weeks attempts to explore (and destroy) objects anterior resulted in wriggling backward away from the lure and elicited violent negative responses. Once she negotiated forward locomotion, exploration set in, in earnest, and, much to her parents' frustration, shows no sign of diminishing.

Can anyone seriously believe that the insatiable curiosity-investigatory motivation of the child is a second-order or derived drive conditioned upon hunger or sex or any other internal drive? The S–R theorist and the Freudian psychoanalyst imply that such behaviors are based on primary drives. An informal survey of neobehaviorists who are also fathers (or mothers) reveals that all have observed the intensity and omnipresence of the curiosity-investigatory motive in their own children. None of them seriously believes that the behavior derives from a second-order drive. After describing their children's behavior, often with a surprising enthusiasm and frequently with the support of photographic records, they trudge off to their laboratories to study, under conditions of solitary confinement, the intellectual processes of rodents. Such attitudes, perfectly in keeping with drive-reduction theory, no doubt account for the fact that there are no experimental or even systematic observational studies of curiosity-investigatory-type external-incentive motives in children.

A key to the real learning theory of any animal species is knowledge of the nature and organization of the unlearned patterns of response. The differences in the intellectual capabilities of cockroach, rat, monkey, chimpanzee and man are as much a function of the differences in the inherent patterns of response and the differences in the inherent motivational forces as they are a function of sheer learning power. The differences in these inherent patterns of response and in the motivational forces will, I am certain, prove to be differential responsiveness to external stimulus patterns. Furthermore, I am certain that the variables which are of true, as opposed to psychophilosophical, importance are not constant from learning problem to learning problem even for the same animal order, and they are vastly diverse as we pass from one animal order to another.

Convinced that the key to human learning is not the conditioned response but, rather, motivation aroused by external stimuli, the speaker has initiated researches on curiosity-manipulation behavior as related to learning in monkeys (Davis, Settlage and Harlow, 1950; Harlow, 1950; Harlow, Harlow and Meyer, 1950). The justification for the use of monkeys is that we have more monkeys than children. Furthermore, the field is so unexplored that a systematic investigation anywhere in the phyletic scale should prove of methodological value. The rhesus monkey is actually a very incurious and nonmanipulative animal compared with the anthropoid apes, which are, in turn, very incurious nonmanipulative animals compared with man. It is certainly more than coincidence that the strength and range of curiosity-manipulative motivation and position within the primate order are closely related.

We have presented three studies which demonstrate that monkeys can and do learn to solve mechanical puzzles when no motivation is provided other than presence of the puzzle. Furthermore, we have presented data to show that once mastered, the sequence of manipulations involved in solving these puzzles is carried out relatively flawlessly and extremely persistently. We have presented what we believe is incontrovertible evidence against a second-order drive interpretation of this learning.

A fourth study was carried out recently by Gately at the Wisconsin laboratories. Gately directly compared the behavior of two groups of four monkeys presented with banks of four identical mechanical puzzles, each utilizing three restraining devices. All four food and puzzle-rewarded monkeys solved the four identical puzzles, and only one of the four monkeys motivated by curiosity alone solved all the puzzles. This one monkey, however, learned as rapidly and as efficiently as any of the food-rewarded monkeys. But I wish to stress an extremely important observation made by Gately and supported by quantitative records. When the food-rewarded monkeys had solved a puzzle, they abandoned it. When the nonfood-rewarded animals had solved the puzzle, they frequently continued their explorations and manipulations. Indeed, one reason for the nonfood-rewarded monkeys' failure to achieve the experimenter's concept of solution lay in the fact that the monkey became fixated in exploration and manipulation of limited puzzle or puzzle-device components. From this point of view, hunger-reduction incentives may be regarded as motivation-destroying, not motivation-supporting, agents.

Twenty years ago at the Vilas Park Zoo, in Madison, we observed an adult orangutan given two blocks of wood, one with a round hole, one with a square hole, and two plungers, one round and one square. Intellectual curiosity alone led it to work on these tasks, often for many minutes at a time, and to solve the problem of inserting the round plunger in both holes. The orangutan never solved the problem of inserting the square peg into the round hole, but inasmuch as it passed away with perforated ulcers a month after the problem was presented, we can honestly say that it died trying. And in defense of this orangutan, let it be stated that it died working on more complex problems than are investigated by most present-day learning theorists.

Schiller[2] has reported that chimpanzees solve multiple-box-stacking problems without benefit of food rewards, and he has presented observational evidence that the joining of sticks resulted from manipulative play responses.

The Cebus monkey has only one claim to intellectual fame – an ability to solve instrumental problems that rivals the much publicized ability of the anthropoid apes (Harlow, 1951; Klüver, 1933). It can be no accident that the Cebus monkey, inferior to the rhesus on conventional learning tasks, demonstrates far more spontaneous instrumental-manipulative responses than any old-world form. The complex, innate external-stimulus motives are variables doubtlessly as important as, or more important than, tissue tensions, stimulus generalization, excitatory potential, or secondary reinforcement. It is the oscillation of sticks, not cortical neurons, that enables the Cebus monkey to solve instrumental problems.

No matter how important may be the analysis of the curiosity-manipulative drives and the learning which is associated with them, we recognize the vast and infinite technical difficulties that are inherent in the attack on the solution of these problems – indeed, it may be many years before we can routinely order such experiments in terms of latin squares and factorial designs, the apparent *sine qua non* for publication in the *Journal of Experi-*

2. Personal communication.

mental Psychology and the *Journal of Comparative and Physiological Psychology*.

There is, however, another vast and important area of external-stimulus incentives important to learning which has been explored only superficially and which can, and should, be immediately and systematically attacked by rodentologists and primatologists alike. This is the area of food incentives – or, more broadly, visuo-chemo variables – approached from the point of view of their function as motivating agents *per se*. This function, as the speaker sees it, is primarily an affective one and only secondarily one of tissue-tension reduction. To dispel any fear of subjectivity, let us state that the affective tone of food incentives can probably be scaled by preference tests with an accuracy far exceeding any scaling of tissue tensions. Our illusion of the equal-step intervals of tissue tensions is the myth that length of the period of deprivation is precisely related to tissue-tension intensity, but the recent experiments by Koch and Daniel (1945) and Horenstein (1951) indicate that this is not true, thus beautifully confirming the physiological findings of thirty years ago.

Paired-comparison techniques with monkeys show beyond question that the primary incentive variables of both differential quantity and differential quality can be arranged on equal-step scales, and there is certainly no reason to believe that variation dependent upon subjects, time, or experience is greater than that dependent upon physiological hunger.

In defense of the rat and its protagonists, let it be stated that there are already many experiments on this lowly mammal which indicate that its curiosity-investigatory motives and responsiveness to incentive variables can be quantitatively measured and their significant relationship to learning demonstrated. The latent learning experiments of Buxton (1940), Haney (1931), Seward, Levy and Handlon (1950), and others have successfully utilized the exploratory drive of the rat. Keller (1941) and Zeaman and House (1950) have utilized the rat's inherent aversion to light, or negative heliotropistic tendencies, to induce learning. Flynn and Jerome (1952) have shown that the rat's avoidance of light is an external-incentive motivation that may be utilized to obtain the solution of complex learned performances. For many rats it is a strong and very persistent form of motivation. The importance of incentive variables in rats has been emphasized and re-emphasized by Young (1949), and the influence of incentive variables on rat learning has been demonstrated by Young (1949), Zeaman (1949), Crespi (1942) and others. I am not for one moment disparaging the value of the rat as a subject for psychological investigation; there is very little wrong with the rat that cannot be overcome by the education of the experimenters.

It may be argued that if we accept the theses of this paper, we shall be returning to an outmoded psychology of tropisms, instincts and hedonism. There is a great deal of truth to this charge Such an approach might be a regression were it not for the fact that psychology now has adequate techniques of methodology and analysis to attack quantifiably these important and neglected areas. If we are ever to have a comprehensive theoretical psychology, we must attack the problems whose solution offers hope of insight into human behavior, and it is my belief that if we face our problems honestly and without regard to, or fear of, difficulty, the theoretical psychology of the future will catch up with, and eventually even surpass, common sense.

References

BIRCH, H. C. (1945), 'The relation of previous experience to insightful problem solving', *J. compar. Psychol.*, vol. 39, pp. 15–22.

BUXTON, C. E. (1940), 'Latent learning and the goal gradient hypothesis' *Contr. psychol. Theor.*, vol. 2, no. 2.

CANNON, W. B. (1932), *The Wisdom of the Body*, Norton.

CARMICHAEL, L. (1934), 'An experimental study in the prenatal guinea-pig of the origin and development of reflexes and patterns of behavior in relation to the stimulation of specific receptor areas during the period of active fetal life', *Genet. Psychol. Monogr.*, vol. 16, pp. 337–491.

CRESPI, L. P. (1942), 'Quantitative variation of incentive and performance in the white rat', *Amer. J. Psychol.*, vol. 55, pp. 467–517.

CROZIER, W. J. (1929), 'The study of living organisms', in C. Murchison (ed.), *The Foundations of Experimental Psychology*, Clark University Press.

DAVIS, R. T., SETTLAGE, P. H., and HARLOW, H. F. (1950), 'Performance of normal and brain operated monkeys on mechanical puzzles with and without food incentives', *J. genet. Psychol.*, vol. 77, pp. 305–11.

FLYNN, J. P., and JEROME, E. A. (1952), 'Learning in an automatic multiple-choice box with light as an incentive', *J. compar. physiol. Psychol.*, vol 45, pp. 336–40.

HANEY, G. W. (1931), 'The effect of familiarity on maze performance of albino rats'. *Univer. Calif. Publ. Psychol.*, vol. 4, pp. 319–33.

HARLOW, H. F. (1950), 'Learning and satiation of response in intrinsically motivated complex puzzle performance by monkeys' *J. compar. physiol. Psychol.*, vol. 43, pp. 289–94.

HARLOW, H. F. (1951), 'Primate learning', in C. P. Stone (ed.), *Comparative Psychology*, Prentice-Hall, 3rd edn.

HARLOW, H. F., HARLOW, M. K., and MEYER, D. R. (1950), 'Learning motivated by a manipulation drive', *J. exper. Psychol.*, vol. 40, pp. 228–34.

HORENSTEIN, B. (1951), 'Performance of conditioned responses as a function of strength of hunger drive', *J. compar. physiol. Psychol.*, vol. 44, pp. 210–24.

JENNING, H. S. (1906), *Behavior of the Lower Organisms*, Columbia University Press.

JENSEN, K. (1932), 'Differential reactions to taste and temperature stimuli in newborn infants', *Genet. Psychol. Monogr.*, vol. 12, pp. 361–476.

KELLER, F. S. (1941), 'Light-aversion in the white rat', *Psychol. Rev.*, vol. 4, pp. 235–50.

KINSEY, A. C., POMEROY, W. B., and MARTIN, C. E. (1948), *Sexual Behavior in the Human Male*, W. B. Saunders.

KLÜVER, H. (1933), *Behavior Mechanisms in Monkeys*, University of Chicago Press.

KOCH, S., and DANIEL, W. J. (1945), 'The effect of satiation on the behavior mediated by a habit of maximum strength', *J. exper. Psychol.*, vol. 35, pp. 162–85.

LANGWORTHY, O. R. (1928), 'The behavior of pouch-young opossums correlated with the myelinization of tracts in the nervous system', *J. compar. Neurol.*, vol. 46, pp. 201–48.

LOEB, J. (1918), *Forced Movements, Tropisms and Animal Conduct*, Lippincott.

MASLOW, A. H. (1943), 'A theory of human motivation', *Psychol. Rev.*, vol. 50, pp. 370–96.

MEYER, D. R. (1951), 'Food deprivation and discrimination reversal learning by monkeys', *J. exper. Psychol.*, vol. 41, pp. 10–16.

MILLER, N. E. (1951), 'Learnable drives and rewards', in S. S. Stevens (ed.), *Handbook of Experimental Psychology*, Wiley.

PAVLOV, I. P. (1927), *Conditioned Reflexes*, Oxford University Press. Translated by G. V. Anrep.

RICHTER, C. P. (1927), 'Animal behavior and internal drives', *Q. Rev. Biol.*, vol. 2, pp. 307–43.

SEWARD, J. P., LEVY, N., and HANDLON, J. H. Jr (1950), 'Incidental learning in the rat', *J. compar. physiol. Psychol.*, vol. 43, pp. 240–51.

SHEFFIELD, F. D., and ROBY, T. B. (1950), 'Reward value of a non-nutrient sweet taste', *J. compar. physiol. Psychol.*, vol. 43, pp. 471–81.

STRASSBURGER, R. C. (1950), 'Resistance to extinction of a conditioned operant as related to drive level at reinforcement', *J. exper. Psychol.*, vol. 40, pp. 473–87.

THORNDIKE, E. L. (1911), *Animal Intelligence*, Macmillan Co.

WATSON, J. B. (1914), *Behavior: An Introduction to Comparative Psychology*, Holt, Rinehart & Winston.

YERKES, R. N., and DODSON, J. D. (1908), 'The relation of strength of stimulus to rapidity of habit formation', *J. compar. Neurol. Psychol.*, vol. 18, pp. 459–82.

YOUNG, P. T. (1949), 'Food-seeking drive, affective process, and learning' *Psychol. Rev.*, vol. 56, pp. 98–121.

ZEAMAN, D. (1949), 'Response latency as a function of amount of reinforcement', *J. exper. Psychol.*, vol. 39, pp. 466–83.

ZEAMAN, D., and HOUSE, B. J. (1950), 'Response latency at zero drive after varying numbers of reinforcements', *J. exper. Psychol.*, vol. 40, pp. 570–83.

13 D. O. Hebb

Drives and the CNS (Conceptual Nervous System)[1]

D. O. Hebb, 'Drives and the CNS (Conceptual Nervous System)'
Psychological Review, volume 62, 1955, pp. 243–54.

The problem of motivation of course lies close to the heart of the general problem of understanding behavior, yet it sometimes seems the least realistically treated topic in the literature. In great part, the difficulty concerns that c.n.s., or 'conceptual nervous system', which Skinner disavowed and from whose influence he and others have tried to escape. But the conceptual nervous system of 1930 was evidently like the gin that was being drunk about the same time; it was homemade and none too good, as Skinner pointed out, but it was also habit-forming; and the effort to escape has not really been successful. Prohibition is long past. If we *must* drink we can now get better liquor; likewise, the conceptual nervous system of 1930 is out of date and – if we must neurologize – let us use the best brand of neurology we can find.

Though I personally favor both alcohol and neurologizing, in moderation, the point here does not assume that either is a good thing. The point is that psychology is intoxicating itself with a worse brand than it need use. Many psychologists do not think in terms of neural anatomy; but merely adhering to certain classical frameworks shows the limiting effect of earlier neurologizing. Bergmann (1953) has recently said again that it is logically possible to escape the influence. This does not change the fact that, in practice, it has not been done.

Further, as I read Bergmann, I am not sure that he really thinks, deep down, that we should swear off neurologizing entirely, or

1. Presidential address, Division 3, at American Psychological Association, New York, September, 1954. The paper incorporates ideas worked out in discussion with fellow students at McGill, especially Dalbir Bindra and Peter Milner, as well as with Leo Postman at California, and it is a pleasure to record my great indebtedness to them.

at least that we should all do so. He has made a strong case for the functional similarity of intervening variable and hypothetical construct, implying that we are dealing more with differences of degree than of kind. The conclusion *I* draw is that both can properly appear in the same theory, using intervening variables to whatever extent is most profitable (as physics for example does), and conversely not being afraid to use some theoretical conception merely because it might become anatomically identifiable.

For many conceptions, at least, MacCorquodale and Meehl's (1948) distinction is relative, not absolute; and it must also be observed that physiological psychology makes free use of 'dispositional concepts' as well as 'existential' ones. Logically, this leaves room for some of us to make more use of explicitly physiological constructs than others, and still lets us stay in communication with one another. It also shows how one's views concerning motivation, for example, might be more influenced than one thinks by earlier physiological notions, since it means that an explicitly physiological conception might be restated in words that have – apparently – no physiological reference.

What I propose, therefore, is to look at motivation as it relates to the c.n.s. – or conceptual nervous system – of three different periods: as it was before 1930, as it was say ten years ago, and as it is today. I hope to persuade you that some of our current troubles with motivation are due to the c.n.s. of an earlier day, and ask that you look with an open mind at the implications of the current one. Today's physiology suggests new psychological ideas and I would like to persuade you that they make psychological sense no matter how they originated. They might even provide common ground – not necessarily agreement, but communication, something nearer to agreement – for people whose views at present may seem completely opposed. While writing this paper I found myself having to make a change in my own theoretical position, as you will see, and though you may not adopt the same position you may be willing to take another look at the evidence and consider its theoretical import anew.

Before going on it is just as well to be explicit about the use of the terms motivation and drive. 'Motivation' refers here in a rather general sense to the energizing of behavior, and especially to the sources of energy in a particular set of responses that keep them temporarily dominant over others and account for continuity and direction in behavior. 'Drive' is regarded as a more specific conception about the way in which this occurs: a hypothesis of motivation, which makes the energy a function of a special process distinct from those S–R or cognitive functions that are energized. In some contexts, therefore 'motivation' and 'drive' are interchangeable.

Motivation in the classical (pre-1930) CNS

The main line of descent of psychological theory, as I have recently tried to show (1953), is through associationism and the stimulus-response formulations. Characteristically, stimulus-response theory has treated the animal as more or less inactive unless subjected to special conditions of arousal. These conditions are first, hunger, pain, and sexual excitement; and secondly, stimulation that has become associated with one of these more primitive motivations.

Such views did not originate entirely in the early ideas of nervous function, but certainly were strengthened by them. Early studies of the nerve fiber seemed to show that the cell is inert until something happens to it from outside; therefore the same would be true of the collection of cells making up the nervous system. From this came the explicit theory of drives. The organism is thought of as like a machine, such as the automobile, in which the steering mechanism – that is, stimulus-response connections – is separate from the power source, or drive. There is, however, this difference: the organism may be endowed with three or more different power plants. Once you start listing separate ones, it is hard to avoid five: hunger, thirst, pain, maternal, and sex drives. By some theorists, these may each be given a low-level steering function also, and indirectly the steering function of drives is much increased by the law of effect. According to the law, habits – steering functions – are acquired only in conjunction with the operation of drives.

Now it is evident that an animal is often active and often learns when there is little or no drive activity of the kinds listed. This fact has been dealt with in two ways. One is to postulate additional drives – activity, exploratory, manipulatory, and so forth. The other is to postulate acquired or learned drives, which obtain their energy, so to speak, from association with primary drives.

It is important to see the difficulties to be met by this kind of formulation, though it should be said at once that I do not have any decisive refutation of it, and other approaches have their difficulties, too.

First, we may overlook the rather large number of forms of behavior in which motivation cannot be reduced to biological drive plus learning. Such behavior is most evident in higher species, and may be forgotten by those who work only with the rat or with restricted segments of the behavior of a dog or cat. (I do not suggest that we put human motivation on a different plane from that of animals (Brown, 1953); what I am saying is that certain peculiarities of motivation increase with phylogenesis, and though most evident in man can be clearly seen with other higher animals.) What is the drive that produces panic in the chimpanzee at the sight of a model of a human head; or fear in some animals, and vicious aggression in others, at the sight of the anesthetized body of a fellow chimpanzee? What about fear of snakes, or the young chimpanzee's terror at the sight of strangers? One can accept the idea that this is 'anxiety', but the anxiety, if so, is not based on a prior association of the stimulus object with pain. With the young chimpanzee reared in the nursery of the Yerkes Laboratories, after separation from the mother at birth, one can be certain that the infant has never seen a snake before, and certainly no one has told him about snakes; and one can be sure that a particular infant has never had the opportunity to associate a strange face with pain. Stimulus generalization does not explain fear of strangers, for other stimuli in the same class, namely, the regular attendants, are eagerly welcomed by the infant.

Again, what drive shall we postulate to account for the manifold forms of anger in the chimpanzee that do not derive from frustration objectively defined (Hebb and Thompson, 1954)? How account for the petting behavior of young adolescent chimpanzees, which Nissen (1953) has shown is independent of primary sex activity? How deal with the behavior of the female who, bearing her first infant, is terrified at the sight of the baby as it drops from the birth canal, runs away, never sees it again after it has

D. O. Hebb 121

been taken to the nursery for rearing; and who yet, on the birth of a *second* infant, promptly picks it up and violently resists any effort to take it from her?

There is a great deal of behavior, in the higher animal especially, that is at the very best difficult to reduce to hunger, pain, sex, and maternal drives, plus learning. Even for the lower animal it has been clear for some time that we must add an exploratory drive (if we are to think in these terms at all), and presumably the motivational phenomena recently studied by Harlow and his colleagues (Harlow, 1953; Harlow, Harlow and Meyer, 1950; Butler, 1953) could also be comprised under such a drive by giving it a little broader specification. The curiosity drive of Berlyne (1950) and Thompson and Solomon (1954), for example, might be considered to cover both investigatory and manipulatory activities on the one hand, and exploratory on the other. It would also comprehend the 'problem-seeking' behavior recently studied by Mahut and Havelka at McGill (unpublished studies). They have shown that the rat which is offered a short, direct path to food, and a longer, variable and indirect pathway involving a search for food, will very frequently prefer the more difficult, but more 'interesting' route.

But even with the addition of a curiosity-investigatory- manipulatory drive, and even apart from the primates, there is still behavior that presents difficulties. There are the reinforcing effects of incomplete copulation (Sheffield, Wulff and Backer, 1951) and of saccharin intake (Sheffield and Roby, 1950; Carper and Polliard, 1953), which do not reduce to secondary reward. We must not multiply drives beyond reason, and at this point one asks whether there is no alternative to the theory in this form. We come, then, to the conceptual nervous system of 1930 to 1950.

Motivation in the CNS of 1930–1950

About 1930 it began to be evident that the nerve cell is not physiologically inert, does not have to be excited from outside in order to discharge (Hebb, 1949, p. 8). The nervous system is alive, and living things by their nature are active. With the demonstration of spontaneous activity in c.n.s. it seemed to me that the conception of a drive system or systems was supererogation.

For reasons I shall come to later, this now appears to me to have been an oversimplification; but in 1945 the only problem of motivation, I thought, was to account for the *direction* taken by behavior. From this point of view, hunger or pain might be peculiarly effective in guiding or channeling activity but not needed for its arousal. It was not surprising, from this point of view, to see human beings liking intellectual work, nor to find evidence that an animal might learn something without pressure of pain or hunger.

The energy of response is not in the stimulus. It comes from the food, water, and oxygen ingested by the animal; and the violence of an epileptic convulsion, when brain cells for whatever reason decide to fire in synchrony, bears witness to what the nervous system can do when it likes. This is like a whole powder magazine exploding at once. Ordinary behavior can be thought of as produced by an organized series of much smaller explosions, and so a 'self-motivating' c.n.s. might still be a very powerfully motivated one. To me, then, it was astonishing that a critic could refer to mine as a 'motivationless' psychology. What I had said in short was that any organized process in the brain is a motivated process, inevitably, inescapably; that the human brain is built to be active, and that as long as it is supplied with adequate nutrition will continue to be active. Brain activity is what determines behavior, and so the only behavioral problem becomes that of accounting for *in*activity.

It was in this conceptual frame that the behavioral picture seemed to negate the notion of drive, as a separate energizer of behavior. A pedagogical experiment reported earlier (Hebb, 1930) had been very impressive in its indication that the human liking for work is not a rare phenomenon, but general. All of the six hundred-odd pupils in a city school, ranging from six to fifteen years of age, were suddenly informed that they need do no work whatever unless they wanted to, that the punishment for being noisy and interrupting others' work was to be sent to the playground to play, and that the reward for being good was to be allowed to do more work. In these circumstances, *all* of the pupils discovered within a day or two that, within limits, they preferred work to no work (and incidentally learned more arithmetic and so forth than in previous years).

The phenomenon of work for its own sake is familiar enough

to all of us, when the timing is controlled by the worker himself, when 'work' is not defined as referring alone to activity imposed from without. Intellectual work may take the form of trying to understand what Robert Browning was trying to say (if anything), to discover what it is in Dali's paintings that can interest others, or to predict the outcome of a paperback mystery. We systematically underestimate the human need of intellectual activity, in one form or another, when we overlook the intellectual component in art and in games. Similarly with riddles, puzzles, and the puzzle-like games of strategy such as bridge, chess, and *go*; the frequency with which man has devised such problems for his own solution is a most significant fact concerning human motivation.

It is, however, not necessarily a fact that supports my earlier view, outlined above. It is hard to get these broader aspects of human behavior under laboratory study, and when we do we may expect to have our ideas about them significantly modified. For my views on the problem, this is what has happened with the experiment of Bexton, Heron and Scott (1954). Their work is a long step toward dealing with the realities of motivation in the well-fed, physically comfortable, adult human being and its results raise a serious difficulty for my own theory. Their subjects were paid handsomely to do nothing, see nothing, hear or touch very little, for twenty-four hours a day. Primary needs were met, on the whole, very well. The subjects suffered no pain, and were fed on request. It is true that they could not copulate, but at the risk of impugning the virility of Canadian college students I point out that most of them would not have been copulating anyway and were quite used to such long stretches of three or four days without primary sexual satisfaction. The secondary reward, on the other hand, was high: $20 a day plus room and board is more than $7000 a year, far more than a student could earn by other means. The subjects then should be highly motivated to continue the experiment, cheerful and happy to be allowed to contribute to scientific knowledge so painlessly and profitably.

In fact, the subject was well motivated for perhaps four to eight hours, and then became increasingly unhappy. He developed a need for stimulation of almost any kind. In the first preliminary exploration, for example, he was allowed to listen to recorded material on request. Some subjects were given a talk for six-year-old children on the dangers of alcohol. This might be requested, by a grown-up male college student, fifteen to twenty times in a thirty-hour period. Others were offered, and asked for repeatedly, a recording of an old stock-market report. The subjects looked forward to being tested, but paradoxically tended to find the tests fatiguing when they did arrive. It is hardly necessary to say that the whole situation was rather hard to take, and one subject, in spite of not being in a special state of primary drive arousal in the experiment but in real need of money outside it, gave up the secondary reward of $20 a day to take up a job at hard labor paying $7 or $8 a day.

This experiment is not cited primarily as a difficulty for drive theory, although three months ago that is how I saw it. It *will* make difficulty for such theory if exploratory drive is not recognized; but we have already seen the necessity, on other grounds, of including a sort of exploratory-curiosity-manipulatory drive, which essentially comes down to a tendency to seek varied stimulation. This would on the whole handle very well the motivational phenomena observed by Heron's group.

Instead, I cite their experiment as making essential trouble for my own treatment of motivation (Hebb, 1949) as based on the conceptual nervous system of 1930 to 1945. If the thought process is internally organized and motivated, why should it break down in conditions of perceptual isolation, unless emotional disturbance intervenes? But it did break down when no serious emotional change was observed, with problem-solving and intelligence-test performance significantly impaired. Why should the subjects themselves report that after four or five hours in isolation they could not follow a connected train of thought, and their motivation for study or the like was seriously disturbed for twenty-four hours or more after coming out of isolation? The subjects were reasonably well adjusted, happy, and able to think coherently for the first four or five hours of the experiment; why, according to my theory, should this not continue, and why should the organization of behavior not be promptly restored with restoration of a normal environment?

You will forgive me perhaps if I do not dilate further on my own theoretical difficulties, paralleling those of others, but turn now to the conceptual nervous system of 1954 to ask what psychological values we may extract from it for the theory of motivation. I shall not attempt any clear answer for the difficulties we have considered – the data do not seem yet to justify clear answers – but certain conceptions can be formulated in sufficiently definite form to be a background for new research, and the physiological data contain suggestions that may allow me to retain what was of value in my earlier proposals while bringing them closer to ideas such as Harlow's (1953) on one hand and to reinforcement theory on the other.

Motivation and CNS in 1954

For psychological purposes there are two major changes in recent ideas of nervous function. One concerns the single cell, the other an 'arousal' system in the brain stem. The first I shall pass over briefly; it is very significant, but does not bear quite as directly upon our present problem. Its essence is that there are two kinds of activity in the nerve cell: the spike potential, or actual firing, and the dendritic potential, which has very different properties. There is now clear evidence (Clare and Bishop, 1955) that the dendrite has a 'slow-burning' activity which is not all-or-none, tends not to be transmitted, and lasts fifteen to thirty milliseconds instead of the spike's one millisecond. It facilitates spike activity (Li, Choh-Luh and Jasper, 1953), but often occurs independently and may make up the greater part of the EEG record. It is still true that the brain is always active, but the activity is not always the transmitted kind that conduces to behavior. Finally, there is decisive evidence of primary inhibition in nerve function (Lloyd, 1941; Eccles, 1943) and of a true fatigue that may last for a matter of minutes instead of milliseconds (Brink, 1951; Burns, 1955). These facts will have a great effect on the hypotheses of physiological psychology, and sooner or later on psychology in general.

Our more direct concern is with a development to which attention has already been drawn by Lindsley (1951): the nonspecific or diffuse projection system of the brain stem, which was shown by Moruzzi and Magoun (1949) to be an *arousal* system whose activity in effect makes organized cortical activity possible. Lindsley showed the relevance to the problem of emotion and motivation; what I shall attempt is to extend his treatment, giving more weight to cortical components in arousal. The point of view has also an evident relationship to Duffy's (1941).

The arousal system can be thought of as representing a second major pathway by which all sensory excitations reach the cortex, as shown in the upper part of Figure 1; but there is also feedback from the cortex and I shall urge that the *psychological* evidence further emphasizes the importance of this 'downstream' effect.

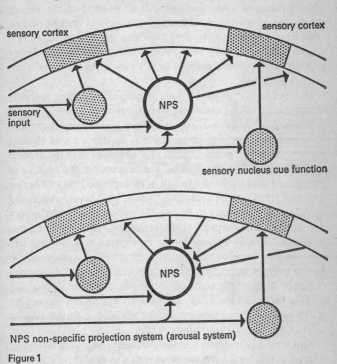

NPS non-specific projection system (arousal system)

Figure 1

In the classical conception of sensory function, input to the cortex was via the great projection systems only: from sensory nerve to sensory tract, thence to the corresponding sensory nucleus of the thalamus and thence directly to one of the sensory projection areas of the cortex. These are still the direct sensory routes, the quick efficient transmitters of information. The second pathway is slow and inefficient; the excitation, as it were, trickles through a tangled thicket of fibers and synapses, there is a mixing up of messages and the scrambled messages are delivered indiscriminately to wide cortical areas. In short, they are messages no longer. They serve, instead, to tone up the cortex, with a background supporting action that is completely necessary if the messages proper are to have their effect. Without the arousal system, the sensory impulses by the direct route reach the sensory cortex, but go no farther; the rest of the cortex is unaffected, and thus learned stimulus-response relations are lost. The waking center, which has long been known, is one part of this larger system; any extensive damage to it leaves a permanently inert, comatose animal.

Remember that in all this I am talking of the conceptual nervous system: making a working simplification, and abstracting for psychological purposes; and all these statements may need qualification, especially since research in this area is moving rapidly. There is reason to think, for example, that the arousal system may not be homogeneous, but may consist of a number of subsystems with distinctive functions (Olszewski, 1954). Olds and Milner's (1954) study, reporting 'reward' by direct intracranial stimulation, is not easy to fit into the notion of a single, homogeneous system. Sharpless' (1954) results also raise doubt on this point, and it may reasonably be anticipated that arousal will eventually be found to vary qualitatively as well as quantitatively. But in general terms, psychologically, we can now distinguish two quite different effects of a sensory event. One is the *cue function*, guiding behavior; the other, less obvious but no less important, is the *arousal* or *vigilance function*. Without a foundation of arousal, the cue function cannot exist.

And now I propose to you that, whatever you wish to call it, arousal in this sense is synonymous with a general drive state, and the conception of drive therefore assumes anatomical and physiological identity. Let me remind you of what we discussed earlier: the drive is an energizer, but not a guide; an engine but not a steering gear. These are precisely the specifications of activity in the arousal system. Also, learning is dependent on drive, according to drive theory, and this too is applicable in general terms – no arousal, no learning; and efficient learning is possible only in the waking, alert, responsive animal, in which the level of arousal is high.

Thus I find myself obliged to reverse my earlier views and accept the drive conception, not merely on physiological grounds but also on the grounds of some of our current psychological studies. The conception is somewhat modified, but the modifications may not be entirely unacceptable to others.

Consider the relation of the effectiveness of cue function, actual or potential, to the level of arousal (Figure 2). Physiologically, we may assume that cortical synaptic function is facilitated by the

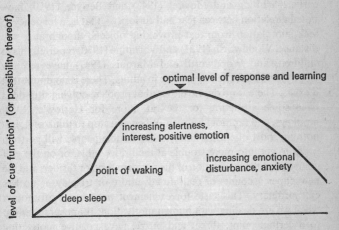

Figure 2

diffuse bombardment of the arousal system. When this bombardment is at a low level an increase will tend to strengthen or maintain the concurrent cortical activity; when arousal or drive is at a low level, that is, a response that produces increased stimulation and greater arousal will tend to be repeated. This is represented by the rising curve at the left. But when arousal is at a high level, as at the right, the greater bombardment may interfere with the delicate adjustments involved in cue function, perhaps by facilitating irrelevant responses (a high D arouses conflicting $_sH_R$s?). Thus there will be an optimal level of arousal for effective behavior, as Schlosberg (1954) has suggested. Set aside such physiologizing completely, and we have a significant behavioral conception left, namely, that the same stimulation in mild degree may attract (by prolonging the pattern of response that leads to this stimulation) and in strong degree repel (by disrupting the pattern and facilitating conflicting or alternative responses).

The significance of this relation is in a phenomenon of the greatest importance for understanding motivation in higher animals. This is the *positive attraction of risk taking*, or mild fear, *and of problem solving*, or mild frustration, which was referred to earlier. Whiting and Mowrer (1943) and Berlyne (1950) have noted a relation between fear and curiosity – that is, a tendency to seek stimulation from fear-provoking objects, though at a safe distance. Woodworth (1921) and Valentine (1930) reported this in children, and Woodworth and Marquis (1947) have recently emphasized again its importance in adults. There is no doubt that it exists. There is no doubt, either, that problem-solving situations have some attraction for the rat, more for Harlow's (1953) monkeys, and far more for man. When you stop to think of it, it is nothing short of extraordinary what trouble people will go to in order to get into more trouble at the bridge table, or on the golf course; and the fascination of the murder story, or thriller, and the newspaper accounts of real-life adventure or tragedy, is no less extraordinary. This taste for excitement *must* not be forgotten when we are dealing with human motivation. It appears that, up to a certain point, threat and puzzle have positive motivating value, beyond that point negative value.

I know this leaves problems. It is not *any* mild threat, *any* form of problem, that is rewarding; we still have to work out the rules for this formulation. Also, I do not mean that there are not secondary rewards of social prestige for risk taking and problem solving – or even primary reward when such behavior is part of lovemaking. But the animal data show that it is not always a matter of extrinsic reward; risk and puzzle can be attractive in themselves, especially for higher animals such as man. If we can accept this, it will no longer be necessary to work out tortuous and improbable ways to explain why human beings work for money, why school children should learn without pain, why a human being in isolation should dislike doing nothing.

One other point before leaving Figure 2: the low level of the curve to the right. You may be skeptical about such an extreme loss of adaptation, or disturbance of cue function and S–R relations, with high levels of arousal. Emotion is persistently regarded as energizing and organizing (which it certainly is at the lower end of the scale, up to the optimal level). But the 'paralysis of terror' and related states do occur. As Brown and Jacobs (1949, p. 753) have noted, 'the presence of fear may act as an energizer . . . and yet lead in certain instances to an increase in immobility'. Twice in the past eight months, while this address was being prepared, the Montreal newspapers reported the behavior of a human being who, suddenly finding himself in extreme danger but with time to escape, simply made no move whatever. One of the two was killed; the other was not, but only because a truck driver chose to wreck his truck and another car instead. Again, it is reported by Marshall (1947), in a book that every student of human motivation should read carefully, that in the emotional pressure of battle no more than 15 to 25 per cent of men under attack even fire their rifles, let alone use them efficiently.

Tyhurst's (1951) very significant study of behavior in emergency and disaster situations further documents the point. The adult who is told that his apartment house is on fire, or who is threatened by a flash flood, may or may not respond intelligently. In various situations 12 to 25 per cent did so; an equal number show 'states of confusion, paralyzing anxiety, inability to move out of bed, "hysterical" crying or screaming, and so on.' Three-quarters or more show a clear impairment of intelligent behavior, often with aimless and irrelevant movements, rather than (as one might expect) panic reactions. There seems no doubt: the curve at the right must come down to a low level.

Now back to our main problem: If we tentatively identify a general state of drive with degree of arousal, where does this leave hunger, pain, and sex drives? These may still be anatomically separable, as Stellar (1954) has argued, but we might consider instead the possibility that there is just one general drive state that can be aroused in different ways. Stellar's argument does not seem fully convincing. There are certainly regions in the hypothalamus that control eating, for example; but is this a *motivating* mechanism? The very essence of such a conception is that the mechanism in question should energize *other* mechanisms, and Miller, Bailey and Stevenson (1950) have shown that the opposite is true.

But this issue should not be pressed too far, with our present knowledge. I have tried to avoid dogmatism in this presentation in the hope that we might try, for once, to see what we have in common in our views on motivation. One virtue of identifying arousal with drive is that it relates differing views (as well as bringing into the focus of attention data that may otherwise be neglected). The important thing is a clear distinction between cue function and arousal function, and the fact that at low levels an increase of drive intensity may be rewarding, whereas at high levels it is a decrease that rewards. Given this point of view and our assumptions about arousal mechanisms, we see that what Harlow has emphasized is the exteroceptively aroused, but still low-level, drive, with cue function of course directly provided for. In the concept of anxiety, Spence and Brown emphasize the higher-level drive state, especially where there is no guiding cue function that would enable the animal to escape threat. The feedback from cortical functioning makes intelligible Mowrer's (1952) equating anxiety aroused by threat of pain, and anxiety aroused in some way by cognitive processes related to ideas of the self. Solomon and Wynne's (1950) results with sympathectomy are also relevant, since we must not neglect the arousal effects of interoceptor activity; and so is clinical anxiety due to metabolic and nutritional disorders, as well as that due to some conflict of cognitive processes.

Obviously these are not explanations that are being discussed, but possible lines of future research; and there is one problem in particular that I would urge should not be forgotten. This is the cortical feedback to the arousal system, in physiological terms: or in psychological terms, the *immediate drive value of cognitive processes*, without intermediary. This is psychologically demonstrable, and *has* been demonstrated repeatedly.

Anyone who is going to talk about acquired drives, or secondary motivation, should first read an old paper by Valentine (1930). He showed that with a young child you can easily condition fear of a caterpillar or a furry animal, but cannot condition fear of opera glasses, or a bottle; in other words, the fear of some objects, that seems to be learned, was there, latent, all the time. Miller (1951) has noted this possibility but he does not seem to have regarded it very seriously, though he cited a confirmatory experiment by Bergmann; for in the same passage he suggests that my own results with chimpanzee fears of certain objects, including strange people, may be dealt with by generalization. But this simply will not do, as Riesen and I noted (1943). If you try to work this out, for the infant who is terrified on *first* contact with a stranger, an infant who has never shown such terror before, and who has always responded with eager affection to the only human beings he has made contact with up to this moment, you will find that this is a purely verbal solution.

Furthermore, as Valentine observed, you cannot postulate that the cause of such fear is simply the strange event, the thing that has never occurred before. For the chimpanzee reared in darkness, the first sight of a human being is of course a strange event, by definition; but fear of strangers does not occur until later, until the chimpanzee has had an opportunity to learn to recognize a few persons. The fear is not 'innate' but depends on some sort of cognitive or cortical conflict of learned responses. This is clearest when the baby chimpanzee, who knows and welcomes attendant *A* and attendant *B*, is terrified when he sees *A* wearing *B*'s coat. The role of learning is inescapable in such a case.

The cognitive and learning element may be forgotten in other motivations, too. Even in the food drive, some sort of learning is fundamentally important: Ghent (1951) has shown this, Sheffield and Campbell (1954) seem in agreement, and so does the work of Miller and his associates (Berkun *et al.*, 1952; Miller, Kessen and Marion, 1952; Miller, 1953) on the greater reinforcement value of food by mouth, compared to food by stomach tube. Beach (1939) has shown the cortical-and-learning element in sex behavior. Melzack (1954) has demonstrated recently that even pain responses involve learning. In Harlow's (1953) results, of course, and Montgomery's (1953), the cognitive element is obvious.

These cortical or cognitive components in motivation are clearest when we compare the behavior of higher and lower species. Application of a *genuine* comparative method is essential, in the field of motivation as well as of intellectual functions (Hebb and Thompson, 1954). Most disagreements between us have related to so-called 'higher' motivations. But the evidence I have discussed today need not be handled in such a way as to maintain the illusion of a complete separation between our various approaches to the problem. It *is* an illusion, I am convinced; we still have many points of disagreement as to relative emphasis and as to which of several alternative lines to explore first, but this does not imply fundamental and final opposition. As theorists, we have been steadily coming together in respect of ideational (or representative, or mediating, or cognitive) processes; I believe that the same thing can happen, and is happening, in the field of motivation.

References

BEACH, F. A. (1939), 'The neural basis at innate behavior: III, Comparison of learning ability and instinctive behavior in the rat' *J. compar. Psychol.*, vol. 28, pp. 225–62.

BERGMANN, G. (1953), 'Theoretical psychology', *Ann. Rev. Psychol.*, vol. 4, pp. 435–58.

BERKUN, M. M., KESSEN, M. L., and MILLER, N. E. (1952), 'Hunger-reducing effects of food by stomach fistula versus food by mouth measured by a consummatory response', *J. compar. physiol. Psychol.*, vol. 45, pp. 550–54.

BERLYNE, D. E. (1950), 'Novelty and curiosity as determinants of exploratory behavior', *Brit. J. Psychol.*, vol. 41, pp. 68–80.

BEXTON, W. H., HERON, W., and SCOTT, T. H. (1954), 'Effects of decreased variation in the sensory environment', *Canad. J. Psychol.*, vol. 8, pp. 70–76.

BRINK, F. (1951), 'Excitation and conduction in the neuron', in S. S. Stevens (ed.), *Handbook of Experimental Psychology*, Wiley, pp. 50–93.

BROWN, J. S. (1953), 'Problems presented by the concept of acquired drives', in *Current Theory and Research in Motivation: A Symposium*, University of Nebraska Press, pp. 1–21.

BROWN, J. S., and JACOBS, A. (1949), 'The role of fear in the motivation and acquisition of responses', *J. exper. Psychol.*, vol. 39, pp. 747–59.

BURNS, B. D. (1955), 'The mechanism of afterbursts in the cerebral cortex', *J. Physiol.*, vol. 127 pp. 168–88.

BUTLER, R. A. (1953), 'Discrimination learning by rhesus monkeys to visual-exploration motivation', *J. compar. physiol. Psychol.*, vol. 46, pp. 95–8.

CARPER, J. W., and POLLIARD, F. A. (1953), 'Comparison of the intake of glucose and saccharin solutions under conditions of caloric need', *Amer. J. Psychol.*, vol. 66, pp. 479–82.

CLARE, M. H., and BISHOP, G. H. (1955), 'Properties of dendrites; apical dentrites of the cat cortex', *EEG clin. Neurophysiol.*, vol. 7, pp. 85–98.

DUFFY, E. (1941), 'An explanation of "emotional" phenomena without the use of the concept "emotion"', *J. gen. Psychol.*, vol. 25, pp. 283–93.

ECCLES, J. C. (1953), *The Neurophysiological Basis of Mind*, Oxford University Press.

GHENT, L. (1951), 'The relation of experience to the development of hunger', *Canad. J. Psychol.*, vol. 5, pp. 77–81.

HARLOW, H. F. (1953), 'Mice, monkeys, men and motives', *Psychol. Rev.*, vol. 60, pp. 23–32.

HARLOW, H. F., HARLOW, M. K., and MEYER, D. R. (1950), 'Learning motivated by a manipulation drive', *J. exper. Psychol.*, vol. 40 pp. 228–34.

HEBB, D. O. (1930), 'Elementary school methods', *Teach Mag.*, vol. 12, pp. 23–6.

HEBB, D. O. (1949), *Organization of Behavior*, Wiley.

HEBB, D. O. (1953), 'On human thought', *Canad. J. Psychol.*, vol. 7, pp. 99–110.

HEBB, D. O., and RIESEN, A. H. (1943), 'The genesis of irrational fears', *Bull. Canad. Psychol. Ass.*, vol. 3, pp. 49–50.

HEBB, D. O., and THOMPSON, W. R. (1954), 'The social significance of animal studies', in G. Lindzey (ed.), *Handbook of Social Psychology*, Addison-Wesley, pp. 532–61.

LI, CHOH-LUH, and JASPER, H. (1953), 'Microelectrode studies of the cerebral cortex in the cat', *J. Physiol.*, vol. 121, pp. 117–40.

LINDSLEY, D. B. (1951), 'Emotion', in S. S. Stevens (ed.), *Handbook of Experimental Psychology*, Wiley, pp. 473–516.

LLOYD, D. P. C. (1941), 'A direct central inhibitory action of dromically conducted impulses', *J. Neurophysiol.*, vol. 4, pp. 184–90.

MACCORQUODALE, K., and MEEHL, P. E. (1948), 'A distinction between hypothetical constructs and intervening variables', *Psychol. Rev.*, vol. 55, pp. 95–107.

MARSHALL, S. L. A. (1947), *Men Against Fire*, Morrow.

MELZACK, R. (1954), 'The effects of early experience on the emotional responses to pain', unpublished doctor's dissertation, McGill University.

MILLER, N. E. (1951), 'Learnable drives and rewards', in S. S. Stevens (ed.), *Handbook of Experimental Psychology*', Wiley, pp. 435–72.

MILLER, N. E. (1953), 'Some studies of drive and drive reduction', paper read at Amer. Psychol. Ass., Cleveland.

MILLER, N. E., BAILEY, C. J., and STEVENSON, J. A. F. (1950), 'Decreased "hunger" but increased food intake from hypothalamic lesions', *Science*, vol. 112, pp. 256–9.

MILLER, N. E., and KESSEN, M. L. (1952), 'Reward effects of food via stomach fistula compared with those of food via mouth', *J. compar. physiol. Psychol.*, vol. 45, pp. 555–64.

MONTGOMERY, K. C. (1953), 'The effect of activity deprivation upon exploratory behavior', *J. compar. physiol. Psychol.*, vol. 46, pp. 438–41.

MORUZZI, G., and MAGOUN, H. W. (1949), 'Brain stem reticular formation and activation of the EEG', *EEG clin. Neurophysiol.*, vol. 1, pp. 455–73.

MOWRER, O. H. (1952), 'Motivation', *Ann. Rev. Psychol.*, vol. 3, pp. 419–38.

NISSEN, H. W. (1953), 'Instinct as seen by a psychologist', *Psychol. Rev.*, vol. 60, pp. 291–4.

OLDS, J., and MILNER, P. (1954), 'Positive reinforcement produced by electrical stimulation of septal area and other regions of rat brain', *J. compar. physiol. Psychol.*, vol. 47, pp. 419–27.

OLSZEWSKI, J. (1954), 'The cytoarchitecture of the human reticular formation', in E. D. Adrian, F. Brenner, and H. H. Jasper (eds.), *Brain Mechanisms and Consciousness*, Blackwell.

SCHLOSBERG, H. (1954), 'Three dimensions of emotion', *Psychol. Rev.*, vol. 61, pp. 81–8.

SHARPLESS, S. K. (1954), 'Role of the reticular formation in habituation', unpublished doctor's dissertation, McGill University.

SHEFFIELD, F. D., and CAMPBELL, B. A. (1954), 'The role of experience in the "spontaneous" activity of hungry rats', *J. compar. physiol. Psychol.*, vol. 47, pp. 97–100.

SHEFFIELD, F. D., and ROBY, T. B. (1950), 'Reward value of a non-nutritive sweet taste', *J. compar. physiol. Psychol.*, vol. 43, pp. 471–81.

SHEFFIELD, F. D., WULFF, J. J., and BACKER, R. (1951), 'Reward value of copulation without sex drive reduction', *J. compar. physiol. Psychol.*, vol. 44, pp. 3–8.

SOLOMON, R. L., and WYNNE, L. C. (1950), 'Avoidance conditioning in normal dogs and in dogs deprived of normal autonomic functioning', *Amer. Psychologist*, vol. 5, (Abstract).

STELLAR, E. (1954), 'The physiology of motivation', *Psychol. Rev.*, vol. 61, pp. 5–22.

THOMPSON, W. R., and SOLOMON, L. M. (1954), 'Spontaneous pattern discrimination in the rat', *J. compar. physiol. Psychol.*, vol. 47, pp .104–7.

TYHURST, J. S. (1951), 'Individual reactions to community disaster: the natural history of psychiatric phenomena', *Amer. J. Psychiat.*, vol. 107, pp. 764–9.

VALENTINE, C. W. (1930), 'The innate bases of fear', *J. Genet. Psychol.*, vol. 37, pp. 394–419.

WHITING, J. W. M., and MOWRER, O. H. (1943), 'Habit progression and regression – a laboratory study of some factors relevant to human socialization', *J. comp. Psychol.*, vol. 36, pp. 229–53.

WOODWORTH, R. S. (1921), *Psychology*, Holt, Rinehart & Winston.

WOODWORTH, R. S., and MARQUIS, D. G. (1947), *Psychology*, Holt, Rinehart & Winston, 5th edn.

Part Three
Motivation as a Correlate of Reinforcement

Spencer formally introduced the idea that actions of animals and man are influenced and modified by pleasure and pain. Thorndike noted that the conditions that instigate animal actions are frequently the same as those required to train or strengthen particular actions. Hunger and food not only may instigate eating and general activity, but may also be used to strengthen a certain response by giving a hungry animal food when it makes that response. Thus, Thorndike's 'law of effect' may be considered as a statement on the parallel between motivating and reinforcing (rewarding or punishing) conditions. Hull introduced a particular hypothesis of reinforcement; he postulated that responses that reduce drive (Hull's motivational factor) are strengthened and that drive reduction constitutes positive reinforcement (reward). This view was criticized by many, including Skinner. But the concept of reinforcement became an important one in discussions of motivation. Spence showed how certain conditions of reinforcement can generate a learned motivational factor, called incentive motivation (K). Black has recently reviewed the various interpretations of reinforcement in trying to define the essential features that enable an object or event to serve as a reinforcing stimulus. And Bindra has suggested that no motivational instigation of a response can take place without the presence of reinforcing (or incentive) stimulus.

14 H. Spencer

On Pleasure and Pain

Excerpt from H. Spencer, *The Principles of Psychology*,
Appleton-Century-Crofts, 1872, volume 1, chapter 9.

Let us first glance at the fact, sufficiently obvious and sufficiently significant, that the extreme states, positive and negative, along with which pains occur, are states inconsistent with that due balance of the functions constituting health; whereas that medium state along with which pleasure occurs is consistent with, or rather is demanded by, this due balance. This we may see *a priori*. In a mutually dependent set of organs having a *consensus* of functions the very existence of a special organ having its special function implies that the absence of its function must cause disturbance of the *consensus* – implies, too, that its function may be raised to an excess which must cause disturbance of the *consensus* – implies, therefore, that maintenance of the *consensus* goes along with a medium degree of its function. The *a priori* inference involved, that these medium actions productive of pleasure must be beneficial and the extreme actions productive of pain detrimental, is abundantly confirmed *a posteriori* where the actions are of all essential kinds. Here are a few cases.

Intense cold and intense heat both cause acute suffering, and if the body is long exposed to them both cause death; while a moderate warmth is pleasurable and conduces to physical well-being. Extreme craving for food accompanies a hurtful inaction of the digestive organs, and if this craving and this inaction persist the result is fatal. Conversely, if solid food, or liquid, continues to be swallowed under compulsion, regardless of the painful sensations produced, the effect is also detrimental, and may even kill. But between these pains attending deficient and excessive action there are the pleasures of eating, which are keenest when the benefit to be derived is greatest. To a person in health duly rested, the feeling that accompanies absolute inaction of the muscles is unbearable; and this inaction is injurious. On the other hand, extreme exertion of the muscles in general is alike distressing and productive of prostration, while exertion of a particular muscle pushed to a painful excess leaves a temporary paralysis, and occasionally, by rupturing some of the muscular fibres, entails prolonged uselessness. Arrest of breathing by forcible closure of the air-passages causes an intolerable state of consciousness; and life soon ceases if there is no relief. The breathing of foul air is injurious as well as repugnant; while the breathing of air that is exceptionally fresh and pure is both pleasurable and physically advantageous. So, too, is it with the feelings caused by contacts with objects. Though, as above pointed out, we cannot be debarred from these, and therefore have no craving for them and little or no pleasure in them, yet we are liable to excesses of them and the accompanying pains; and these pains are the correlatives of detrimental results – crushings, and bruises, and lacerations. It is even so with extremely strong tastes and smells. The intense vegetal bitters are poisonous in any considerable quantities, and the intensest are poisonous in very small quantities. Powerful acids, too, are poisonous – being, indeed, immediately destructive of the membranes they touch. And gases that violently irritate when inhaled, as concentrated ammonia, or as pure chlorine, or as hydrochloric acid, work deleterious effects.

These facts should of themselves suffice to produce the conviction, in spite of apparent exceptions, that pains are the correlatives of actions injurious to the organism, while pleasures are the correlatives of actions conducive to its welfare. We need not, however, rest satisfied with an induction from these instances yielded by the essential vital functions; for it is an inevitable deduction from the hypothesis of evolution that races of sentient creatures could have come into existence under no other conditions.

If we substitute for the word Pleasure the equivalent phrase: a feeling which we seek to bring into consciousness and retain there; and if we substitute for the word Pain the equivalent phrase: a feeling which we seek to get out of consciousness and to keep out, we see at once that, if the states of consciousness which a creature endeavours to maintain are the correlatives of injurious actions, and if the states of consciousness which it endeavours to expel are the correlatives of beneficial actions, it must quickly disappear through persistence in the injurious and avoidance of the beneficial. In other words, those races of beings only can have survived in which, on the average, agreeable or desired feelings went along with activities conducive to the maintenance of life, while disagreeable and habitually-avoided feelings went along with activities directly or indirectly destructive of life; and there must ever have been, other things equal, the most numerous and long-continued survivals among races in which these adjustments of feelings to actions were the best, tending ever to bring about perfect adjustment.

If we except the human race and some of the highest allied races, in which foresight of distant consequences introduces a complicating element, it is undeniable that every animal habitually persists in each act which gives pleasure, so long as it does so, and desists from each act which gives pain. It is manifest that, for creatures of low intelligence, unable to trace involved sequences of effects, there can be no other guidance. It is manifest that in proportion as this guidance approaches completeness, the life will be long; and that the life will be short in proportion as it falls short of completeness. Whence it follows that as, other things equal, the longer-lived individuals of any species will more frequently produce and rear progeny than the shorter-lived, the descendants of the one must tend to replace those of the other – a process which, equally operative among the multiplying families of these surviving descendants, cannot but work towards maintenance and improvement of the guidance.

How then, it will be asked, does it happen that animals sometimes die from eating poisonous plants, or surfeit themselves fatally with kinds of food which, though wholesome in moderate quantities, are injurious in large quantities? The reply is that, by natural selection, the guidance of pleasures and pains can be adjusted only to the circumstances of the habitat within which the special type has been evolved. Survival of the fittest cannot bring the inclinations and aversions into harmony with unfelt conditions. And since each species under pressure of increasing numbers is ever thrusting itself into adjacent environments, its members must from time to time meet with plants, with prey, with enemies, with physical actions, of which neither they nor their ancestors have had experience, and to which their feelings are unadapted. Not only by migration into other habitats, but also by changes, inorganic and organic, within its own habitat, does each species suffer from failures of adjustment. But misadjustment inevitably sets up re-adjustment. Those individuals in whom the likes and dislikes happen to be most out of harmony with the new circumstances are the first to disappear. And if the race continues to exist there cannot but arise, by perpetual killing-off of the least adapted, a variety having feelings that serve as incentives and deterrents in the modified way required.

15 E. L. Thorndike

The Law of Effect

Excerpt from E. L. Thorndike, *Animal Intelligence*, Macmillan Co., 1911, chapter 6.

The Law of Effect is that:

Of several responses made to the same situation, those which are accompanied or closely followed by satisfaction to the animal will, other things being equal, be more firmly connected with the situation, so that, when it recurs, they will be more likely to recur; those which are accompanied or closely followed by discomfort to the animal will, other things being equal, have their connections with that situation weakened, so that, when it recurs, they will be less likely to occur. The greater the satisfaction or discomfort, the greater the strengthening or weakening of the bond.

For more detailed and perfect prophecy, the phrases 'result in satisfaction' and 'result in discomfort' need further definition, and the other things that are to be equal need comment.

By a satisfying state of affairs is meant one which the animal does nothing to avoid, often doing such things as attain and preserve it. By a discomforting or annoying state of affairs is meant one which the animal commonly avoids and abandons.

The satisfiers for any animal in any given condition cannot be determined with precision and surety save by observation. Food when hungry, society when lonesome, sleep when fatigued, relief from pain, are samples of the common occurrence that what favors the life of the species satisfies its individual members. But this does not furnish a completely valid rule.

The satisfying and annoying are not synonymous with favorable and unfavorable to the life of either the individual or the species. Many animals are satisfied by deleterious conditions. Excitement, overeating, and alcoholic intoxication are, for instance, three very common and very potent satisfiers of man.

Conditions useful to the life of the species in moderation are often satisfying far beyond their useful point: many conditions of great utility to the life of the species do not satisfy and may even annoy its members.

The annoyers for any animal follow the rough rule that alterations of the animal's 'natural' or 'normal' structure – as by cuts, bruises, blows, and the like – and deprivations of or interference with its 'natural' or 'normal' activities – as by capture, starvation, solitude, or indigestion – are intolerable. But interference with the structure and functions by which the species is perpetuated is not a sufficient criterion for discomfort. Nature's adaptations are too crude.

Upon examination it appears that the pernicious states of affairs which an animal welcomes are not pernicious *at the time*, *to the neurones*. We learn many bad habits, such as morphinism, because there is incomplete adaptation of all the interests of the body-state to the temporary interest of its ruling class, the neurones. So also the unsatisfying goods are not goods to the neurones at the time. We neglect many benefits because the neurones choose their immediate advantage. The neurones must be tricked into permitting the animal to take exercise when freezing or quinine when in a fever, or to free the stomach from certain poisons.

Satisfaction and discomfort, welcoming and avoiding, thus seem to be related to the maintenance and hindrance of the life processes of the neurones rather than of the animal as a whole, and to temporary rather than permanent maintenance and hindrance.

The chief life processes of a neurone concerned in learning are absorption of food, excretion of waste, reception and conduction of the nerve impulse, and modifiability or change of connections. Of these only the latter demands comment.

The connections formed between situation and response are represented by connections between neurones and neurones, whereby the disturbance or neural current arising in the former is conducted to the latter across their synapses. The strength or weakness of a connection means the greater or less likelihood that the same current will be conducted from the former to the latter rather than to some other place. The strength or weakness of the connection is a condition of the synapse. What condition of the synapse it is remains a matter for hypothesis. Close connection might mean protoplasmic union, or proximity of the neurones in space, or a greater permeability of a membrane, or a lowered electrical resistance, or a favorable chemical condition of some other sort. Let us call this undefined condition which parallels the strength of a connection between situation and response the intimacy of the synapse. Then the modifiability or connection-changing of a neurone equals its power to alter the intimacy of its synapses.

As a provisional hypothesis to account for what satisfies and what annoys an animal, I suggest the following:

A neurone modifies the intimacy of its synapses so as to keep intimate those by whose intimacy its other life processes are favored and to weaken the intimacy of those whereby its other life processes are hindered. The animal's action-system as a whole consequently does nothing to avoid that response whereby the life processes of the neurones other than connection-changing are maintained, but does cease those responses whereby such life processes of the neurones are hindered.

This hypothesis has two important consequences.

1. Learning by the law of effect is then more fully adaptive for the neurones in the changing intimacy of whose synapses learning consists, than for the animal as a whole. It is adaptive for the animal as a whole only in so far as his organization makes the neurones concerned in the learning welcome states of affairs that are favorable to his life and that of his species and reject those that are harmful.

2. A mechanism in the neurones gives results in the behavior of the animal as a whole that seem beyond mechanism. By their unmodifiable abandonment of certain specific conditions and retention of others, the animal as a whole can modify its behavior. Their one rule of conduct causes in him a countless complexity of habits. The learning of an animal is an instinct of its neurones.

I have limited the discussion to animals in whom the connection-system is a differentiated organ, the neurones. In so far as the law of effect operates in an animal whose connection-system is not anatomically distinguishable and is favored and hindered in its life by the same conditions that favor and hinder the life of the animal as a whole, the satisfying and annoying will be those states of affairs which the connection-system, whatever it be, maintains and abandons.

The other things that have to be equal in the case of the law of effect are: first, the frequency, energy and duration of the connection – that is, the action of the law of exercise; second, the closeness with which the satisfaction is associated with the response; and, third, the readiness of the response to be connected with the situation.

The first of these accessory conditions requires no comment. A slightly satisfying or indifferent response made often may win a closer connection than a more satisfying response made only rarely.

The second is most clearly seen in the effect of increasing the interval between the response and the satisfaction or discomfort. Such an increase diminishes the rate of learning. If, for example, four boxes were arranged so that turning a button caused a door to open (and permit a cat to get freedom and food) in one, five, fifty and five hundred seconds, respectively, a cat would form the habit of prompt escape from the first box most rapidly and would almost certainly never form that habit in the case of the fourth. The electric shock administered just as an animal starts on the wrong path or touches the wrong mechanism is potent, but the same punishment administered ten or twenty seconds after an act will have little or no effect upon that act.

Close temporal sequence is not the only means of insuring the connection of the satisfaction with the response producing it. What is called attention to the response counts also. If a cat pushes a button around with its nose, while its main occupation, the act to which its general 'set' impels it, to which, we say, it is chiefly attentive, is that of clawing at an opening, it will be less aided in the formation of the habit than if it had been chiefly concerned in what its nose was doing. The successful response is as a rule only a part of all that the animal is doing at the time. In proportion as it is an eminent, emphatic part of it, learning is aided. Similarly discomfort eliminates most the eminent, emphatic features of the total response which it accompanies or shortly follows.

The third factor, the susceptibility of the response and situation to connection, is harder to illustrate. But, apparently, of those responses which are equally strongly connected with a situation by nature and equally attended to, some are more susceptible than others to a more intimate connection.

16 C. L. Hull

Law of Primary Reinforcement

Excerpt from C. L. Hull, *Principles of Behavior*, Appleton-Century-Crofts, 1943, chapter 6.

The infinitely varied and unpredictable situations of need in which the higher organisms find themselves make any form of ready-made receptor–effector connections inadequate for optimal probability of survival. This natural defect of inherited reaction tendencies, however varied, is remedied by learning. Learning turns out upon analysis to be either a case of the differential strengthening of one from a number of more or less distinct reactions evoked by a situation of need, or the formation of receptor–effector connections *de novo*; the first occurs typically in simple selective learning and the second, in conditioned-reflex learning. A mixed case is found in which new receptor-effector connections are set up at the same time that selective learning is taking place.

An inductive comparison of these superficially rather divergent forms of learning shows one common principle running through them all. This we shall call the Law of Primary Reinforcement. It is as follows:

Whenever an effector activity occurs in temporal contiguity with the afferent impulse, or the perseverative trace of such an impulse, resulting from the impact of a stimulus energy upon a receptor, and this conjunction is closely associated in time with the diminution in the receptor discharge characteristic of a need, there will result an increment to the tendency for that stimulus on subsequent occasions to evoke that reaction.

From this principle it is possible to derive both the differential receptor–effector strengthening of simple selective learning and the acquisition of quite new receptor–effector connections, characteristic of conditioned-reflex learning as well as of certain forms of selective learning.

17 B. F. Skinner

Why is a Reinforcer Reinforcing?

Excerpt from B. F. Skinner, *Science and Human Behavior*, Macmillan Co., 1953, chapter 5.

The Law of Effect is not a theory. It is simply a rule for strengthening behavior. When we reinforce a response and observe a change in its frequency, we can easily report what has happened in objective terms. But in explaining *why* it has happened we are likely to resort to theory. Why does reinforcement reinforce? One theory is that an organism repeats a response because it finds the consequences 'pleasant' or 'satisfying'. But in what sense is this an explanation within the framework of a natural science? 'Pleasant' or 'satisfying' apparently do not refer to physical properties of reinforcing events, since the physical sciences use neither these terms nor any equivalents. The terms must refer to some effect upon the organism, but can we define this in such a way that it will be useful in accounting for reinforcement?

It is sometimes argued that a thing is pleasant if an organism approaches or maintains contact with it and unpleasant if the organism avoids it or cuts it short. There are many variations on this attempt to find an objective definition, but they are all subject to the same criticism – the behavior specified may be merely another product of the reinforcing effect. To say that a stimulus is pleasant in the sense that an organism tends to approach or prolong it may be only another way of saying that the stimulus has reinforced the behavior of approaching or prolonging. Instead of defining a reinforcing effect in terms of its effect upon behavior in general, we have simply specified familiar behavior which is almost inevitably reinforced and hence generally available as an indicator of reinforcing power. If we then go on to say that a stimulus is reinforcing *because* it is pleasant, what purports to be an explanation in terms of two effects is in reality a redundant description of one.

An alternative approach is to define 'pleasant' and 'unpleasant' (or 'satisfying' and 'annoying') by asking the subject how he 'feels' about certain events. This assumes that reinforcement has two effects – it strengthens behavior and generates 'feelings' – and that one is a function of the other. But the functional relation may be in the other direction. When a man reports that an event is pleasant, he may be merely reporting that it is the sort of event which reinforces him or toward which he finds himself tending to move because it has reinforced such movement. One could probably not acquire verbal responses with respect to pleasantness as a purely private fact unless something like this were so. In any case, the subject himself is not at an especially good point of vantage for making such observations. 'Subjective judgements' of the pleasantness or satisfaction provided by stimuli are usually unreliable and inconsistent. As the doctrine of the unconscious has emphasized, we may not be able to report at all upon events which can be shown to be reinforcing to us or we may make a report which is in direct conflict with objective observations; we may report as unpleasant a type of event which can be shown to be reinforcing. Examples of this anomaly range from masochism to martyrdom.

It is sometimes argued that reinforcement is effective because it reduces a state of deprivation. Here at least is a collateral effect which need not be confused with reinforcement itself. It is obvious that deprivation is important in operant conditioning. We used a *hungry* pigeon in our experiment, and we could not have demonstrated operant conditioning otherwise. The hungrier the bird, the oftener it responds as the result of reinforcement. But in spite of this connection it is not true that reinforcement always reduces deprivation. Conditioning may occur before any substantial change can take place in the deprivation measured in other ways. All we can say is that the *type* of event which reduces deprivation is also reinforcing.

The connection between reinforcement and satiation must be sought in the process of evolution. We can scarcely overlook the great biological significance of the primary reinforcers. Food, water, and sexual contact, as well as escape from injurious conditions, are obviously connected with the well-being of the organism. An individual who is readily reinforced by such events will acquire highly efficient behavior. It is also biologically advantageous if the behavior due to a given reinforcement is especially likely to occur in an appropriate state of deprivation. Thus it is important, not only that any behavior which leads to the receipt of food should become an important part of a repertoire, but that this behavior should be particularly strong when the organism is hungry. These two advantages are presumably responsible for the fact that an organism can be reinforced in specific ways and that the result will be observed in relevant conditions of deprivation.

Some forms of stimulation are positively reinforcing although they do not appear to elicit behavior having biological significance. A baby is reinforced, not only by food, but by the tinkle of a bell or the sparkle of a bright object. Behavior which is consistently followed by such stimuli shows an increased probability. It is difficult, if not impossible, to trace these reinforcing effects to a history of conditioning. Later we may find the same individual being reinforced by an orchestra or a colorful spectacle. Here it is more difficult to make sure that the reinforcing effect is not conditioned. However, we may plausibly argue that a capacity to be reinforced by any feed-back from the environment would be biologically advantageous, since it would prepare the organism to manipulate the environment successfully before a given state of deprivation developed. When the organism generates a tactual feed-back, as in feeling the texture of a piece of cloth or the surface of a piece of sculpture, the conditioning is commonly regarded as resulting from sexual reinforcement, even when the area stimulated is not primarily sexual in function. It is tempting to suppose that other forms of stimulation produced by behavior are similarly related to biologically important events.

When the environment changes, a capacity to be reinforced by a given event may have a biological *disadvantage*. Sugar is highly reinforcing to most members of the human species, as the ubiquitous candy counter shows. Its effect in this respect far exceeds current biological requirements. This was not true before sugar had been grown and refined on an extensive scale. Until a few hundred years ago, the strong reinforcing effect of sugar must have been a biological advantage. The environment has changed, but the genetic endowment of the organism has not followed suit. Sex provides another example. There is no longer a biological advantage in the great reinforcing effect of sexual contact, but we need not go back many hundreds of years to find conditions of famine and pestilence under which the power of sexual reinforcement offered a decisive advantage.

A biological explanation of reinforcing power is perhaps as far as we can go in saying why an event is reinforcing. Such an explanation is probably of little help in a functional analysis, for it does not provide us with any way of identifying a reinforcing stimulus as such before we have tested its reinforcing power upon a given organism. We must therefore be content with a survey in terms of the effects of stimuli upon behavior.

18 K. W. Spence

Incentive Motivation

Excerpt from K. W. Spence, *Behavior Theory and Conditioning*, Yale University Press, 1956, chapter 5.

The implication of Hull's theory with regard to reduction of incentive magnitude was never worked out in detail in the *Principles*. Hull merely stated that reduction of incentive size would be expected to lead on successive trials to a progressive lowering of performance level. Strictly speaking, Hull's hypothesis that the magnitude of H is a function of the magnitude of the reward, taken in conjunction with his assumption that habit (H) was a relatively permanent condition left by reinforcement within the nervous system, implied, as far as the value of H itself is concerned, that a shift to a smaller reward should not lead to a decrement in performance. However, the well-known fact that reduction to zero reward (experimental extinction) results in response decrement apparently led Hull to believe that any reduction in reward size less than to zero was related in some manner to experimental extinction and thus would result in some response decrement. Apparently he intended to return to this topic in the later chapter on experimental extinction, but he did not do so.

Incentive motivational interpretations of the effects of reward magnitude

In subsequent formulations of his theoretical system Hull (1950, 1951, 1952) abandoned this hypothesis that habit strength varied with the magnitude of the reward and instead conceived of variations in this experimental variable as affecting the strength of an incentive motivational factor which he designated by the symbol K. Like the motivational factor, D, this K factor was assumed to multiply habit strength to determine the excitatory potential (E). In this modification of his theory Hull was anticipated by Crespi (1944), who on the basis of his experimental findings rejected

Hull's differential habit interpretation and proposed in its stead an emotional drive or, as he anthropomorphically described it, an eagerness theory. According to this notion the basis of the differential drive strength was a variation in the amount of anticipatory tension or excitement that developed with different amounts of reward.

My own approach to these experimental phenomena has also always been a motivational one. Indeed, at the time that Hull was writing the chapter on magnitude of reinforcement for his *Principles of Behavior* our correspondence reveals a vigorous disagreement over his learning (habit) interpretation. The basis of my disagreement, in part, was the finding of Nissen and Elder (1935) and Cowles and Nissen (1937) with respect to variation of the magnitude of the goal object in delayed-response experiments with chimpanzees. After showing that the level of performance in this situation was a function of the magnitude of the incentive, these investigators further demonstrated that, after attaining a certain level of response with a given size of food, a drop in level of performance occurred if a smaller piece of food was used. Similarly, a shift to a larger piece of food was shown to lead to improvement in performance. These shifts up and down seemed to me to suggest changes in a motivational rather than a habit factor, and it is interesting to note that Cowles and Nissen interpreted their findings in terms of a mechanism which they described as reward expectancy.

My preference for a motivational interpretation was also greatly influenced, as I have already indicated, by our theorizing concerning the role of the fractional anticipatory goal response in our latent learning experiments with the simple T-maze (Spence, Bergmann and Lippitt, 1950). This theory assumed, it will be recalled, that stimulus cues in the goal box and from the alley just preceding the goal box become conditioned to the goal response, R_g. Through generalization the stimulus cues at earlier points in the runway are also assumed to acquire the capacity to elicit R_g, or at least noncompetitional components of R_g that can occur without the actual presence of the food (e.g. salivating and chewing movements). As a result this fractional conditioned response, which we shall designate as r_g, moves forward to the beginning of the instrumental sequence. Furthermore, the interoceptive stimulus cue (s_g) produced by this response also becomes a part of the stimulus complex in the alley and thus should become conditioned to the instrumental locomotor responses. But more important, in addition to this associative function we have assumed that this r_g–s_g mechanism also has motivational properties that vary with the magnitude or vigor with which it occurs.

A number of different conceptions of the manner in which the r_g–s_g mechanism may operate to affect motivational level have been suggested. One that was mentioned in my chapter on theories of learning in Stevens' *Handbook of Experimental Psychology* (Spence, 1951) was that the occurrence of these fractional goal responses results in a certain amount of conflict and hence in heightened tension or excitement. This heightened tension, it was assumed, might contribute to an increase in the existing state of general drive level, D. This conception, it will be seen, is very similar to that of Crespi. Another possibility is that variation of the intensity of s_g provides an internal stimulus dynamism akin to Hull's notion of stimulus dynamism (V) resulting from different intensities of external stimulation. However, my preference is merely to introduce an intervening variable, K, which is regarded as representing, quantitatively, the motivational property of the conditioned r_g–s_g mechanism and which is defined in terms of the experimental variables that determine the vigor of the latter.

From our assumption that the basic mechanism underlying this incentive motivational factor, K, is the classical conditioned r_g, we are necessarily committed to a number of assumptions as to the variables that determine its strength. Thus, being itself a conditioned response, r_g will vary with the number of conditioning trials given in the goal box. Secondly we must assume that its intensity or vigor will be a negatively accelerated, exponential function of the number of these conditioning trials. Furthermore, on the basis of experimental studies of generalization of conditioning we will need to assume that its strength at any point in the alley distant from the goal box will be a function of the similarity of the environmental cues at that point and those in the goal box. If internal proprioceptive cues from the running response play an important role, the differences in these cues at different distances from the goal box will have to be considered. Unfortunately we know very little, as yet, concerning either of these variables. Finally, any property of the goal object that produces unconditioned consummatory responses of different intensity or vigor will presumably determine the value of K, for there is some evidence to support the notion that the intensity or vigor of the response may be conditioned *as such* (Hull, 1943).

The diagram shown in Figure 1 attempts to summarize these various assumptions relating K on the one hand to the experimental variables of which it is a function and on the other to the intervening variables and behavior. Actually, as will become apparent, considerably more research needs to be done before we can specify in a systematic and precise manner the experimental variables that affect K. The listing in the diagram is in terms of the

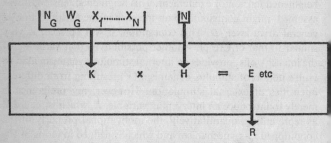

Figure 1 Diagram summarizing some of the assumptions of incentive motivation theory. Some of the experimental variables which are assumed to contribute to the level of incentive motivation (K) are shown above the rectangle on the left. The multiplicative assumption of K and H combination is shown inside the rectangle. For definition of symbols and further explanation see text

specific experimental operations that different investigators have so far employed. Thus N_G refers to the number of classical conditioning trials, which has typically been designated as the number of times the subject enters the goal box and responds to (consumes or sees) the goal object. W_G refers to the amount, e.g., the number, weight, or volume, of the goal objects consumed, while $X_1 \ldots X_n$ refers to a number of known and as yet unknown variables that presumably determine the vigor of the consummatory response, e.g., the sweetness of the object, the amount of sucking effort required to obtain the object in the case of liquids, possibly the hardness of the reward object, and so on. Again, as we shall see, these variables are not entirely independent of one another. The tentative hypothesis being proposed here is that these different experimental variations of reinforcing agents will determine K, either through the habit strength of r_g or through the particular r_g, i.e. the particular vigor of r_g being conditioned.

Having defined K in terms of these experimental variables, we must next relate it to our other intervening variables and thus eventually to the response variables. Being conceived of as a motivational factor, K is assumed to multiply the habit strength of the instrumental response to determine its excitatory strength. Thus, with D held constant E equals $K \times H$. This is not, of course, a complete picture of our current theorizing concerning K.

References

COWLES, J. T., and NISSEN, H. W. (1937), 'Reward-expectancy in delayed responses of chimpanzees', *J. compar. physiol. Psychol.*, vol. 24, pp. 345–58.

CRESPI, L. P. (1944), 'Amount of reinforcement and level of performance', *Psychol. Rev.*, vol. 51, pp. 341–57.

HULL, C. L. (1943), *Principles of Behavior*, Appleton-Century-Crofts.

HULL, C. L. (1950), 'Behavior postulates and corollaries – 1949' *Psychol. Rev.*, vol. 57, pp. 173–80.

HULL, C. L. (1951), *Essentials of Behavior*, Yale University Press.

HULL, C. L. (1952), *A Behavior System*, Yale University Press.

NISSEN, H. W., and ELDER, J. H. (1935), 'The influence of amount of incentive on delayed response performances of chimpanzees', *J. Genet. Psychol.*, vol. 47, pp. 49–72.

SPENCE, K. W., BERGMANN, G., and LIPPITT, R. (1950), 'A study of simple learning under irrelevant motivational-reward conditions', *J. exper. Psychol.*, vol. 40, pp. 539–51.

SPENCE, K. W. (1951), 'Theoretical interpretations of learning', in S. S. Stevens (ed.), *Handbook of Experimental Psychology*, Wiley.

19 R. W. Black

Theories of Reward

Excerpt from R. W. Black, 'Incentive motivation and the parameters of reward in instrumental conditioning', in W. J. Arnold and D. Levine (eds.), *Nebraska Symposium on Motivation*, University of Nebraska Press, 1969, pp. 90–137.

Sources of reward

I have already mentioned the problem of attempting to discover what it is about some stimuli which makes them rewarding. In the context of an empirical 'catalogue of rewards' this is the equivalent of identifying the characteristics which are common to 'rewarding stimuli' and which, therefore, might be considered the 'basis' or 'source' of their facilitory effect on performance. By a 'source of reward', then, is meant that aspect of the reinforcement situation which is primarily responsible for the behavioral effects of reinforcement.

For purposes of exposition, consider the simple and familiar runway conditioning situation. Here the apparatus often consists of a straight alley divided into a start box, runway, and goal box. A typical training trial might consist of placing S in the start box, opening the start box door and measuring the speed with which S runs through various segments of the alley. When S enters the goal box, a 'retrace door' is closed to confine the animal to the goal box for some specified period. If there is no food, water, or other appropriate reward in the goal box, very little improvement in performance can be expected over successive trials. On the other hand, if S has been deprived, say, of food and if food is present in the goal box, performance will probably show progressive improvement over successive trials. Thus, according to the current definition, the food in the goal box constitutes a 'reward' and E's operation of placing it there constitutes a 'reinforcement'. In this context, one may ask, What *specifically* is the 'source of reward' in this situation? Several solutions to this problem have been proposed.

1. *Stimulus Factors*. It may be that the sensory effects associated with, or produced by, the food used as reward constitute the crucial events or the 'source of reward' – that is, there may be certain stimuli which are 'palatable', or rewarding *per se*. Some evidence for this view is provided by the fact that performance in instrumental conditioning does seem to vary with the 'quality' (e.g. taste) of the rewarding stimulus as well as with its 'quantity'. For example, response strength has been shown to vary significantly with the 'sweetness' of the rewarding solution in the Skinner box (e.g. Guttman, 1953), in a straight runway (Homzie and Ross, 1962), and in a Y-maze (Black, 1965). Moreover, performance also varies with changes in sweetness even when the nutritional value of the solutions is equal (e.g. Sheffield, Roby and Campbell, 1954). Similarly, it has been demonstrated that incomplete copulation is rewarding to male rats in spite of the termination of the act prior to its completion – that is, before ejaculation (e.g. Sheffield, Wulff and Backer, 1951). Further, an apparently powerful reward effect resulting from certain types of intracranial stimulation has apparently been demonstrated (e.g. Olds and Milner, 1954). Finally, it appears that, under the appropriate circumstances, a stimulus need have no other property to be a reward other than that of being 'novel' (Berlyne, 1950). Thus, the hypothesis that the stimulus itself (or, more correctly, the sensory consequences of the stimulus) may be the source of reward does have a certain plausibility.

2. *Response Factors*. When a hungry animal enters the goal box of a straight alley and there encounters familiar and palatable food, it is very likely that the animal will eat that food – that is, a vigorous 'consummatory response' is likely to be elicited. It has been suggested (e.g. Sheffield, Roby and Campbell, 1954) that it is such consummatory activity itself which is rewarding rather than the stimulus or sensory properties of the food or its nutritional effect on the organism. A detailed statement of this position requires, of course, the specification of the parameters of consummatory activity which are considered important (e.g. the duration, frequency, consistency, and vigor of the consummatory response, etc.). Thus, one implication of this position is that the strength of the instrumental response should show a strong posi-

tive correlation with the amount or vigor of consummatory activity, and with exceptions noted later, this relationship has typically been obtained (e.g. Sheffield, Roby and Campbell, 1954). A further implication of this position is that if a vigorous consummatory response can be elicited, immediately preceding responses should be strengthened, even though the consummatory response fails to result in drive reduction. This implication seems to be confirmed, for example, by the observations that incomplete copulation is apparently rewarding (Sheffield, Wulff and Backer, 1951) and that animals with esophageal fistulas (which prevent swallowed food from reaching the stomach) learn new responses which allow them to engage in such 'sham feeding'.

3. *Difficulties with the Stimulus and Consummatory Response Views.* There seems to be little question that both stimulus and consummatory-response factors may contribute to the behavioral consequences of reinforcement. Unfortunately, in the case of much of this research the effects of the stimulus and those of consummatory activity tend to be almost completely confounded. Thus, when *E* varies the 'amount of consummatory activity' by manipulating the amount of food presented, he often simultaneously varies the 'amount of stimulation' as well. On the other hand, if he seeks to vary the 'quality' or 'palatability' of the rewarding stimulus, he may at the same time be increasing the vigor or consistency of consummatory activity. Thus, the apparently rewarding effect of incomplete copulation could be equally well attributed to the vigorous consummatory response (copulation) or to the stimulation associated with that response. In short, the relative contributions to reward of these two potential sources is difficult to assess, since a consummatory response is usually accompanied by considerable resulting stimulation, while the presentation of a palatable stimulus is likely to elicit consummatory activity.

Beyond the problem of distinguishing between stimulus and consummatory-response factors as sources of reward in instrumental conditioning, there is the question of whether either of these factors is a *necessary* condition for reward. Thus, for example, Miller and Kessen (1952) reported that rats with esophageal fistulas learned a spatial discrimination in which the reinforcement consisted of the direct injection of milk into the animal's stomach following a correct choice. If one assumes that this procedure involved neither consummatory activity nor gustatory and olfactory stimulation, then it might be concluded that 'reward' had been demonstrated in the absence of both of these factors. One might wonder, however, to what extent the direct injection of milk into the stomach might be considered to simulate a portion of the normal 'consummatory response' of the intact organism. In this connection, Glickman and Schiff (1967) have commented:

Miller (1963) described several problems for Sheffield's theory which the formulation of a consummatory response theory might handle. He pointed out that the main difficulties with the earlier theory derive from the emphasis on the peripheral consummatory response. The present authors, however, have considered the neural activity in the motor paths to be the sufficient condition for the reinforcement of new responses. Accordingly, the data of Miller and Kessen (1952) and of Clark, Schuster and Brady (1961), which are demonstrations of learning in the absence of overt consummatory activity, present no necessary problem. We would conclude that the injection of foodstuffs directly into the stomach or bloodstream would differ from ordinary ingestion only in providing less facilitation of the motor pathways, and the demonstrated, and relatively weaker, reinforcing effects would be expected (Glickman and Schiff, 1967, p. 101).

4. *Premack's Response Theory.* Premack (1961, 1962, 1965) has proposed an interpretation of reinforcement which might be described as a 'response theory of reinforcement', although it is certainly not a 'consummatory response theory'. Premack, in fact, insists that no fundamental distinction should be made between consummatory responses and other responses so far as their potential reward value is concerned. Specifically, he states:

For any pair of responses, the more probable one will reinforce the less probable one. . . . Reinforcement is a relative property. The most probable response of a set of responses will reinforce all members of the set; the least probable will reinforce no member of the set. However, responses of intermediate probability will reinforce those less probable than themselves but not those more probable than themselves (Premack, 1965, p. 132).

Premack's theory has led to a variety of intriguing experimental results, some of which have apparently indicated that consummatory activity can actually be made to act as an instrumental response which is reinforced by other, nonconsummatory behaviors. From the point of view of the present paper, Premack's position is an attempt to specify the crucial characteristics which make a stimulus a reward. He is, as noted above, quite explicit on this point: a reinforcer is a response rather than a stimulus; it is a response the probability or operant level of which is greater than that of the response which it strengthens. Thus, Premack has clearly stated the criterion for identifying the 'source of reward', but the mechanism by which such rewards affect performance remains uncertain.

5. *Drive-Reduction Factors.* It frequently has been argued that in appetitive conditioning it is neither the stimulus qualities of the rewarding stimulus nor the consummatory responses which that stimulus may elicit which is the primary source of reward, but rather the metabolic or motivational effects of that stimulus which constitute 'reward'. In its most familiar form, this view asserts that a reward is a stimulus which reduces the intensity of drive or of drive stimuli. The intuitive appeal of this hypothesis is obvious when one considers the fact that the great majority of investigations of appetitive conditioning with animals involve the establishment of a metabolic drive (e.g. hunger or thirst) and the selection of rewarding stimuli (food or water) which at least partially satiate that drive. In such investigations, performance is typically found to vary directly with both the level of drive and the degree of drive reduction presumably produced by the reward. Unfortunately, these experiments typically confound the 'amount of drive reduction' with both the 'amount of stimulation' and the 'amount of consummatory activity'. Thus, if the rewarding stimulus is a 'large quantity of food', a 'large amount of drive reduction' will normally result from its ingestion. A 'large amount of consummatory activity' will, however, also be required to ingest that reward, which will result in a 'large amount of stimulation'. Thus, if a 'large increment in performance' follows such a reinforcement, its source remains ambiguous. Nevertheless, there seem to be some situations, mentioned later, in which these factors become at least partially disentangled.

Mechanisms of reinforcement

I wish to turn now from the discussion of hypotheses regarding the characteristics essential to stimuli which have the property of strengthening responses which they closely follow (i.e. 'sources of reward') to a consideration of the mechanisms by which the operations called 'reinforcement' result in such strengthening of instrumental performance. Theories regarding the manner in which reinforcement affects performance may be divided into two general categories: 'associative interpretations' which assume that reinforcement, in some manner, directly or indirectly, affects learning or conditioning *per se*; and 'incentive interpretations' which assume that reinforcement affects only performance by contributing to S's level of motivation, excitement, or arousal. Some representative instances of each of these points of view are presented below, although this discussion is not intended to be exhaustive.

Associative interpretations of reinforcement

Probably the earliest explicit associative interpretation of reinforcement was that proposed by Thorndike (1913, 1932), who assumed that the effect of a reward (or 'satisfying state of affairs') was to directly strengthen the connection between a response and the stimulus which immediately preceded or was coincidental with it. Thus, Thorndike considered rewards to make a direct and positive contribution to learning by 'cementing' the association between specific stimuli and responses.

Guthrie also interpreted the empirical effect of rewards in associative terms. Thus, he assumed that 'a combination of stimuli which has accompanied a movement will on its occurrence tend to be followed by the same movement'. Moreover, 'a stimulus pattern gains its full associative strength on the occasion of its first pairing with a response' (Guthrie, 1942, p. 30). This is, of course, a so-called strict contiguity interpretation of learning. Nevertheless, Guthrie, like all other learning theorists, had to account for the empirical facts of reinforcement. To do so, he relied on the stimulus properties of the reward. Consider again the case of the rat traversing a straight runway: 'What encountering the food does is not to intensify a previous item of behavior but to protect that item from being unlearned. The whole situation and action of the animal is so changed by the food that the pre-food situation is shielded from new associations' (Guthrie, 1940, p. 144). Thus, rewards do not contribute directly to 'S-R connections' for Guthrie as they did for Thorndike. Instead, they affect performance indirectly by 'protecting' an S-R association which has been previously learned solely on the basis of contiguity. Nevertheless, like Thorndike's, Guthrie's interpretation of reward was associative – that is, rewards affect S-R connections.

Guthrie (1935) also advanced an associative interpretation of the effect of reinforcement in instrumental appetitive conditioning. In its most general form, this position asserts that the behavior of *S* in the goal box may be dichotomized into 'consummatory activity' and 'nonconsummatory activity'. Consummatory activity, of course, consists of such responses as eating or drinking the reward, etc. while nonconsummatory behaviors may involve grooming, exploration, remaining inactive, retracing toward the runway, etc. In any event, it is often assumed that both consummatory and nonconsummatory activities tend to become conditioned to the cues present in the goal box and to generalize to the runway and start box. Further, it might be assumed that conditioned or generalized consummatory responses, since they cannot genuinely occur in the absence of the rewarding stimulus, do not interfere with the instrumental (e.g. locomotor) response. On the other hand, nonconsummatory responses, such as grooming or exploring, can occur in the runway before entrance to the goal box and may, therefore, interfere with and depress the speed or vigor of the instrumental response. Thus, an important function of reinforcement may be the degree to which it 'encourages' *S* to engage in consummatory activity and 'discourages' it from engaging in nonconsummatory responses which have the potential of interfering with the instrumental response.

A final instance of an associative interpretation of the effect of reinforcement is found in Hull's 1943 version of his behavior theory. Hull assumed that reinforcement contributed to his primary associative variable, 'habit strength $(_{S}H_{r})$', in two ways. First, he assumed that habit strength theoretically increased only on those occasions when an S-R sequence was closely followed by reinforcement. Second, he assumed that the magnitude of reinforcement set the maximum or limit to which habit strength could grow. As a matter of fact, in his 1943 formulation, Hull proposed no construct other than habit strength to which reward was considered ·a direct contributor. Thus, at this point his interpretation of reinforcement, like that of Thorndike and Guthrie, was purely associative.

Incentive interpretations of reinforcement

While a variety of 'incentive theories' of reinforcement have been proposed, they have in common the assumption that rewards, in one way or another, add to the S's level of motivation or arousal. Hull (1952), for example, was led to modify his views in the direction of an incentive interpretation of reward as a result, at least in part, of experiments which involved shifts in the magnitude of reward. Thus, Crespi (1942) and Zeaman (1949) reported that shifts in the quantity of food reward administered to rats in a straight alley resulted in very rapid and 'appropriate' changes in the speed with which Ss ran in that alley. Of particular importance was the fact that decremental shifts in reward magnitude produced an almost immediate decline in performance. Since Hull (1943) had assumed that reward primarily affects habit strength, and since habit strength was considered to be a relatively permanent variable, this result was unexpected. To account for these rapid changes in performance following shifts in reward magnitude, Hull introduced a new construct, 'incentive motivation (K)', the value of which was determined by the magnitude of reward and the function of which was, like D, to multiply $_sH_r$. On the other hand, Hull continued to insist that reinforcement influenced habit strength to the extent that at least some minimal amount of reinforcement must follow the occurrence of the instrumental response before any increment in $_sH_r$ for that response can occur. Thus, Hull's final (1952) position with respect to reward might be described as being both associative and motivational (i.e. incentive) in character.

In his modifications and extensions of Hull's position, Spence (1956) placed still more emphasis on the incentive-motivational aspects of reward. Thus, Spence discarded the assumption that reinforcement was a necessary determinant of the associative variable, H, in instrumental reward conditioning. Rather, according to Spence (1956) K is the molar theoretical variable that summarizes the motivational consequences of the r_g-s_g mechanism which is assumed to consist of implicit components of the overt consummatory response (R_g) that become conditioned to the stimulus situation in which the instrumental response is appetitively reinforced. The strength of the r_g-s_g mechanism depends, in turn, upon at least two variables. First, since it results from classical conditioning to goal box cues, the strength of r_g-s_g will be an increasing function of the frequency and duration with which R_g has been elicited in the presence of those cues. Thus, K is assumed to be an increasing function of the number of rewarded trials and approaches an asymptote determined, in part, by the magnitude of reward. Second, since the strength of r_g-s_g is assumed to reflect the vigor of the overt consummatory response (R_g) of which it is a component, any variable which contributes to the vigor of R_g will also affect the theoretical value of K (Black, 1965, p. 310).

Although he emphasized the motivational (incentive) effects of reward, Spence's analysis of this variable also had associative components. Thus, the basis or source of K (i.e. r_g) was itself conceived of as a conditioned response subject to all the rules or laws governing other conditioned responses. Moreover, r_g was assumed to result in distinctive internal cues, s_g, which presumably serve as part of the stimulus complex which evokes the instrumental response. In fact, at least in personal conversations, Spence repeatedly expressed the view that the motivational or facilitative effects of K would benefit only those responses which had previously become conditioned to s_g. Thus, Spence considered K, unlike D, not to be a general or non-specific energizer of all response tendencies.

A similar interpretation of the mechanism of reward was also proposed by Sheffield and his associates. According to this view components of the consummatory response become conditioned to cues in the goal box and subsequently come to be evoked by similar cues before the goal box is reached. This anticipatory and incomplete arousal of the consummatory response is further assumed to create a state of 'excitement' which is 'channeled into whatever response is being performed at the moment' (Sheffield, Roby and Campbell, 1954, p. 354). To emphasize the incentive-motivational nature of their position, Sheffield and his associates describe it as a 'drive-induction' theory of reinforcement. Seward (1950, 1951, 1956) has also proposed a 'drive induction' interpretation of the effects of reward based on the notion of the conditioning and generalization of consummatory activity (R_g). Thus, he states:

When a response (R) is followed by a reward, R_g is conditioned to concurrent stimuli. By generalization of this conditioning, stimuli accompanying R now serve to intensify r_g. ... This intensification called tertiary motivation is endowed with the property of facilitating R, the activity in progress (Seward, 1951, p. 130).

Miller (1963) has more recently suggested an interpretation of reinforcement which is essentially incentive-motivational in character, although he relates it more explicitly than prior theorists to hypothesized events in the CNS. Specifically, Miller assumes 'that there are one or more "go" or "activating" mechanisms in the brain which act to intensify ongoing responses to cues and traces of immediately preceding activities, producing a stronger intensification the more strongly the "go mechanism" is activated' (Miller, 1963, p. 95). He further assumes that this 'go mechanism' can be activated in a variety of different ways, including 'by the taste of food to a hungry animal, possibly by feedback from still more central effects of eating'. He also states that the 'go mechanism' will depend in large part on the strength of the UCR (presumably consummatory activity). Finally, he assumes that the 'go mechanism' will be weakened or extinguished if it is repeatedly elicited without reinforcement from the UCS (e.g. food). With the exception of its emphasis on a central as opposed to a peripheral locus, Miller's 'go mechanism' has, quite obviously, most of the properties of the conditionable components of consummatory behavior (r_g) as discussed by Spence, Sheffield, Seward, etc.

Theories of reinforcement: a common parameter

I have attempted to classify and briefly describe some of the major hypotheses regarding two fundamental problems in the analysis of the effects of reinforcement on performance in instrumental, appetitive conditioning. With respect to the source of reward, these hypotheses have emphasized the potential importance of the sensory consequences of the stimulus characteristics of the reward, the properties of the consummatory response which the rewarding stimulus typically evokes, and the motivational or metabolic effects on the organism of the ingestion of the reward. While these factors are admittedly difficult to separate experimentally, they are, nevertheless, quite different in principle.

The problem of specifying the mechanism by which the operation termed reinforcement strengthens or otherwise affects performance has also resulted in a variety of alternative hypotheses. Perhaps arbitrarily, I have categorized these hypotheses as being *primarily* 'associative' or *primarily* 'motivational (incentive)' in character. Within these categories, however, important differences exist. Thus, an associative interpretation of reinforcement may assume that rewards directly strengthen S-R connections, that they 'protect' already established connections against unlearning, or that they reduce the likelihood of the learning of responses which subsequently interfere with the instrumental response. Similarly, while incentive interpretations of reward generally emphasize the importance of the conditioned or anticipated consummatory response, the details of the analysis vary considerably from one theorist to another.

In spite of these several and significant differences, there is at least one parameter of the general 'reinforcement situation' which is critically important to any interpretation of the effect of reinforcement on the *normal, intact organism*: the behavior of S in relation to the reward. Thus, food, water, and other primary rewards will not be expected to strengthen performance unless S consumes them. This expectation would appear to follow from a 'stimulus theory', a 'consummatory response theory' or a 'drive-reduction theory' of the source of reward. With respect to the mechanism of reinforcement, an available but nonconsumed reward would not be expected to fulfill any of the associative criteria of a 'reward' – for example, 'strengthening connections', 'protecting S-R bonds', or 'preventing the establishment of competing responses'. Even more obviously, an incentive interpretation of reward would not predict an enhancement of performance as the result of a 'reward' which failed to produce a consummatory response. In short, regardless of one's theoretical views regarding the sources and mechanisms of reward, it must be recognized that no set of operations on the part of the experimenter nor any physical characteristic of the rewarding stimulus can ensure an enhancement in the performance of *S* unless the behavior of *S* with respect to that reward is 'appropriate'.

References

BERLYNE, D. E. (1950), 'Novelty and curiosity as determinants of exploratory behavior', *Brit. J. Psychol.*, vol. 41, pp. 68–80.

BLACK, R. W. (1965), 'Discrimination learning as a function of varying pairs of sucrose reward', *J. exper. Psychol.*, vol. 70, pp. 452–5.

CLARK, R., SCHUSTER, C. R., and BRADY, J. V. (1961), 'Instrumental conditioning of jugular self-infusion in the rhesus monkey', *Sci.*, vol. 133, pp. 1829–30.

CRESPI, L. P. (1942), 'Quantitative variation of incentive and performance in the white rat', *Amer. J. Psychol.*, vol. 55, pp. 467–517.

GLICKMAN, S. E., and SCHIFF, B. B. (1967), 'A biological theory of reinforcement', *Psychol. Rev.*, vol. 74, pp. 81–109.

GUTHRIE, E. R. (1935), *The Psychology of Learning*, Harper & Row.

GUTHRIE, E. R. (1940), 'Association and the law of effect', *Psychol. Rev.*, vol. 47, pp. 127–48.

GUTHRIE, E. R. (1942), 'Conditioning: a theory of learning in terms of stimulus response and association', in Nat. Soc. Stud. Educ., *The Psychology of Learning*, vol. 41, pt 2, pp. 17–60.

GUTTMAN, N. (1953), 'Operant conditioning extinction, and periodic reinforcement in relation to concentration of sucrose used as reinforcing agent', *J. exper. Psychol.*, vol. 46, pp. 213–24.

HOMZIE, M. J., and ROSS, L. E. (1962), 'Runway performance following a reduction in the concentration of a liquid reward', *J. compar. physiol. Psychol.*, vol. 55, pp. 1029–33.

HULL, C. L. (1943), *Principles of Behavior*, Appleton-Century-Crofts.

HULL, C. L. (1952), *A Behavior System*, Yale University Press.

MILLER, N. E. (1963), 'Some reflections on the law of effect produce a new alternative to drive reduction', in M. R. Jones (ed.), *Nebraska Symposium on Motivation*, University of Nebraska Press.

MILLER, N. E., and KESSEN, M. L. (1952), 'Reward effects of food via stomach fistula compared with those of food via mouth', *J. compar. physiol. Psychol.*, vol. 45, pp. 555–64.

OLDS, J., and MILNER, P. (1954), 'Positive reinforcement produced by electrical stimulation of septal area and other regions of the rat brain', *J. compar. physiol. Psychol.*, vol. 47, pp. 419–27.

PREMACK, D. (1961), 'Predicting instrumental performance from the independent rate of the contingent response', *J. exper. Psychol.*, vol. 61, pp. 163–71.

PREMACK, D. (1962), 'Reversibility of the reinforcement relation', *Sci.*, vol. 136, pp. 255–7.

PREMACK, O. (1965), 'Reinforcement theory', in D. Levine (ed.), *Nebraska Symposium on Motivation*, University of Nebraska Press.

SEWARD, J. P. (1950), 'Secondary reinforcement as tertiary motivation: a revision of Hull's revision', *Psychol. Rev.*, vol. 57, pp. 362–74.

SEWARD, J. P. (1951), 'Experimental evidence for the motivating function of reward', *Psychol. Bull.*, vol. 48, pp. 130–49.

SEWARD, J. P. (1956), 'Drive, incentive and reinforcement', *Psychol. Rev.*, vol. 63, pp. 195–203.

SHEFFIELD, F. D., ROBY, T. B., and CAMPBELL, B. A. (1954), 'Drive reduction versus consummatory behavior as determinants of reinforcement', *J. compar. physiol. Psychol.*, vol. 47, pp. 349–54.

SHEFFIELD, F. D., WULFF, J. J., and BACKER, R. (1951), 'Reward value of copulation without sex drive reduction', *J. compar. physiol. Psychol.*, vol. 44, pp. 3–8.

SPENCE, K. W. (1956), *Behavior Theory and Conditioning*, Yale University Press.

THORNDIKE, E. L. (1913), *Educational Psychology*, Teachers College, Columbia University.

THORNDIKE, E. L. (1932), *The Fundamentals of Learning*, Teachers College, Columbia University.

ZEAMAN, D. (1949), 'Response latency as a function of the amount of reinforcement', *J. exper. Psychol.*, vol. 39, pp. 466–83.

20 D. Bindra

Drive and Incentive-Motivation

Excerpts from D. Bindra, 'Neuropsychological interpretation of the effects of drive and incentive-motivation on general activity and instrumental behavior', *Psychological Review*, volume 75, 1968, pp. 1–22.

Drive and incentive-motivation as sources of motivational effects

The concept of drive was introduced into psychology (Richter, 1922, 1927; Woodworth, 1918) to account for the fact that animals 'worked' (e.g. ran through a maze or exhibited conditioned responses) only in certain biological states, such as those of hunger and thirst. These biological states or drives were thought directly to instigate increased level of general activity, as well as to facilitate the occurrence of particular consummatory acts and instrumental responses. This drive view of motivation has in recent years been increasingly subordinated to what might be described as the incentive-motivation view (Bolles, 1967; Cofer and Appley, 1964). Though the exact proportion of explanatory burden placed on incentive-motivation varies from theorist to theorist, ranging from little (e.g. Brown, 1961) to moderate (e.g. Seward, 1956; Spence, 1956), to great (e.g. Mowrer, 1960), their theories are addressed to a common central issue. It is this: are drive and incentive-motivation individually necessary for explaining motivational effects? Are they, individually, sufficient? Two types of evidence bear upon this issue: evidence from studies of general activity, and evidence from studies of particular-response facilitation.

Studies of general activity

Richter's (1922, 1927) work, showing how a variety of drive manipulations (e.g. food deprivation, lowering of environmental temperature, estrus) increase the level of general activity, led to the view that drives, the physiological consequences of experimental manipulations, directly release an energizing factor that induces activity. Increased activity came to be regarded as a *sine qua non* of the presence of a drive state.

A series of investigations, starting around 1950, has demonstrated that animals also show an increase in activity when placed in a stimulus situation that has been repeatedly associated with a positive reinforcer. Such incentive-motivational increases are commonly seen around the normal time of feeding in animals maintained on fixed schedules of food or water deprivation. It has been established experimentally that these activity increases are a function of conditioning, with the situational cues serving as CS and the reinforcement (e.g. food) as UCS (Baumeister, Hawkins and Cromwell, 1964; Bolles, 1963; Finger, Reid and Weasner, 1957, 1960; Sheffield and Campbell, 1954). Clearly, positive incentive-motivational stimuli (i.e. those linked to appetitive reinforcers) can enhance the level of activity. However, in a recent experiment Bindra and Palfai (1967) found that while incentive-motivational stimuli were effective in raising activity level of animals in the medium and high drive-level groups, the introduction of incentive-motivational stimuli had little effect on activity level in the low-drive group. Thus incentive-motivational stimuli are sufficient to increase general activity, provided a certain minimum level of drive is present. This could mean that drive is one of the determiners of the level of incentive-motivation (see p. 176).

The efficacy of incentive-motivational stimuli in producing increases in general activity raises the question whether they are necessary for obtaining motivational increases in activity level or whether drive alone may be sufficient. Though there is little in print that would constitute an explicit answer to this question, there are indications of a sentiment favoring the position that all motivational increases in activity must involve an obvious or hidden incentive-motivational factor (e.g. Baumeister, Hawkins and Cromwell, 1964; Bolles, 1967). But such a position would not be tenable. It is true that in earlier experiments the possibility existed that the activity increases observed following, say, food deprivation arose not from drive *per se* but from some confounding reinforcement effects associated with periodic feeding. But recent experiments, which have eliminated this possibility by placing animals on continuous (terminal) deprivation without any scheduled feeding periods, have shown that hunger *per se* is a sufficient condition for obtaining an increase in the level of general activity (Bolles, 1965; Campbell, Teghtsoonian and Williams, 1961; Duda and Bolles, 1963). Further, Bindra and Palfai (1967) varied drive and incentive-motivation in the same experiment and found that higher drive levels produced higher activity levels even before the incentive-motivational stimuli were introduced. Since the incentive-motivational training was identical for all animals, the differences in activity level must be attributed to drive *per se*. Again, estrus, a drive condition that may have never been accompanied by reinforcement (as in the adult virgin female rat), produces marked activity increase (Wang, 1923). Thus, the presence of incentive-motivational stimuli is not a necessary condition for obtaining activity increases; in certain cases drive alone is sufficient. Clearly, we must recognize two separate types of motivational effects so far as general activity is concerned: those induced by drive *per se* and incentive-motivational.

If some drive manipulations can by themselves, in the absence of the incentive-motivational factor, raise activity level, three further questions arise. The first is whether *all* different types of drive manipulations are, individually, sufficient to raise the increase of general activity. As noted above, food deprivation and estrus are sufficient. However, water deprivation has not been found consistently to produce an increase; for example, in the absence of an incentive-motivational factor, no increment in activity was found by Campbell and Cicala (1962) or Bolles (1965). The discrepancy in the results obtained with water deprivation and food deprivation may not result from differences in methods of activity measurement; Bolles (1965), observing the effects of both hunger and thirst on rat activity in the home cage, found that only hunger increased the level of general activity. These findings raise doubt about the view that a common energizing factor is made operative by all drive manipulations. Rather they suggest that the relation between each drive manipulation and activity level is a specific one, the exact changes in the level and form of activity being dependent upon the particular neurophysiological mechanisms involved.

The second question is whether a drive manipulation that is effective in raising activity level under one set of conditions will do so under all sets of conditions; in other words, whether activity level can be considered as a reliable indicator of drive state. It has been clear for a long time that the answer to this question is No. Whether or not activity changes are observed depends upon the activity-measuring technique, the species and strain of animals, the age and physical condition of the subjects, and on a variety of other experimental details (for a review, see Baumeister, Hawkins and Cromwell, 1964; Bolles, 1967). Besides, the specific acts that make up 'general activity' may differ from situation to situation, so that different techniques may sample different acts (Bindra, 1961; Bindra and Spinner, 1958; Bolles, 1965). Clearly, an increase in activity level cannot serve as a *sine qua non* of drive state. But note that this fact does not detract from my earlier conclusion that under certain conditions certain drive states are in themselves sufficient to increase the level of general activity, and that, therefore, incentive-motivational stimuli are not necessary for obtaining a motivational increase in activity.

The third question is this: are the *forms* of drive-induced and incentive-motivational activity the same or different? While the above considerations allow us to formulate this question, it cannot yet be answered unequivocally on the basis of existing evidence. Bindra and Palfai (1967) have noted that incentive-motivational activity has all the marks of anticipatory excitement, such as that frequently seen during classical appetitive conditioning (Zener, 1937) and that described by ethologists as 'appetitive behavior' (e.g. Lorenz, 1950; Tinbergen, 1951, ch. 5). Further, the activity elicited by incentive-motivational stimuli is best described as exploration of the environment – the rat systematically sniffs around the experimental chamber as if looking for something. Such systematic investigation does not appear to be a feature of rat behavior when drive is the only independent variable; as Bolles (1963, p. 460) has noted, it is only activity that is contingent upon particular stimuli that makes deprived animals 'look motivated'. Though differences in the form of activity require further study, it may be tentatively concluded that the activity elicited by incentive-motivational stimuli is more investigatory or goal directed than is activity induced by drive alone.

Particular-response facilitation

The traditional view (Warden, 1931; Woodworth, 1918) regarded drive to be necessary and sufficient for facilitating the occurrence of all particular reactions. But evidence shows this to be correct only so far as consummatory acts[1] are concerned. That the occurrence of consummatory acts can be facilitated by appropriate drive manipulations, in the absence of specific reinforcement of those acts, is supported by the following facts. Several investigators have shown that, when food is present, electrical stimulation of the midlateral hypothalamic area produces feeding responses in sated rats (see Anand, 1961). The probability of elicitation of lordosis in prepuberal virgin female rats is increased by injections of appropriate gonodal hormones (Beach, 1942). Vaughan and Fisher (1962) have noted that electrical stimulation of the anterior dorsolateral hypothalamus in the sexually naïve male rat facilitates the onset of mounting on a receptive female. Various components of maternal behavior of several species are known to be affected by changing hormonal levels (e.g. Kinder, 1927; Lehrman, 1956; Wiesner and Sheard, 1933).

Obviously, consummatory acts can occur only if appropriate stimulus objects (e.g. food, a sexual partner) are present – this is true whether drive manipulations or incentive-motivational stimuli are employed to elicit the acts. But in the experiments cited above the presence of the appropriate objects by itself did not elicit the consummatory acts; they occurred only when the proper drive state was experimentally introduced. Notwithstanding the possibility that the occurrence of such consummatory acts may, as a result of reinforcing experiences, come under the control

---

1. For our purpose, a consummatory response may be defined as an organized series of acts, involved in a basic biological function (e.g. eating, drinking, or copulating), that can be reliably elicited under a defined set of conditions in all normal members of the species. A test of such organization is that the acts may be made to occur in a more or less normal manner by electrical or chemical stimulation of particular brain sites in the presence of appropriate stimulus objects (e.g. food, water, a sexually ready partner). For example, such stimulation has been shown to induce consummatory acts of eating (Mendelson and Chorover, 1965; Miller, 1957), drinking (Andersson and McCann, 1955), mating (Vaughan and Fisher, 1962), attack (Roberts and Kiess, 1964), and exploration (Gastaut, Vigouroux and Naquet, 1952; Roberts and Kiess, 1964).

of incentive-motivational stimuli, we can safely conclude that, when the objects required for the response are present, the physiological consequences of certain drive manipulations can in themselves be sufficient to alter the probability of consummatory-act occurrence. The mechanism of interaction of the appropriate objects and drive state will be discussed in a later section of this paper.

Turn now to the facilitation of instrumental responses. Though there is considerable evidence that drive manipulations facilitate instrumental performance (see Cofer and Appley, 1964, ch. 11; Kimble, 1961, ch. 13), it is not clear that the observed facilitation is attributable to drive *per se*. In the early theoretical formulations of learning it was assumed that the facilitation of performance was the direct result of increased drive; thus Hull (1943) regarded reaction potential ($S^E R$) to be a function of habit (H) multiplied by drive (D). But this did not take into account the possibility that the facilitating effects attending drive manipulations may result from some confounding reinforcement-linked factors. As the response facilitating role of incentive-motivational stimuli became known, the emphasis gradually shifted toward considering instrumental-response facilitation as an incentive-motivational rather than a drive-induced phenomenon (Hull, 1950; Seward, 1951; Sheffield, 1966; Spence, 1956). Though an incentive-motivational factor (K) was thus added to the performance equation, theorists still regarded drive (D) as a direct and sufficient, though now only a partial, determiner of instrumental performance.

The above interpretation is open to question, for drive may not facilitate instrumental responses directly, but only indirectly through its influence on the strength of reinforcing effects and hence of incentive-motivation (R. W. Black, 1965; Mendelson, 1965). If, as we have noted, drive manipulations (e.g. food deprivation, hormonal injections) increase the likelihood and strength of consummatory acts, and, as appears to be the case, the extent of the elicitation of consummatory acts is at least a rough correlate of the degree of reinforcing effects (see Bindra, 1959; Glickman and Schiff, 1967; Sheffield, Roby and Campbell, 1954), then an increase in drive should increase the strength of incentive motivation. But in order to be able to prove that the facilitation of instrumental responses following an increase in drive results not from drive *per se* but from its effect on the degree of reinforcement (i.c. the extent of elicitation of consummatory acts), it is necessary to separate the effects of drive from those of drive-plus-reinforcement. If drive affects performance through its influence on re-inforcement, then drive would be required only at the time of reinforcement, not during the performance of the instrumental responses that lead to the reinforcement. Mendelson (1966) has isolated the role of drive by employing a technique that permitted him to turn hunger drive on and off instantaneously.

The drive manipulation employed by Mendelson was intra-cranial electrical stimulation (ICS) of the lateral hypothalamic feeding areas. This stimulation induces the consummatory re-sponse of eating in sated rats, and it has been shown that such electrically induced predispositions to display various consum-matory acts have all the properties of natural drives (e.g. Coons, Levak and Miller, 1965; Roberts and Kiess, 1964; Tenen and Miller, 1964). Mendelson first demonstrated that sated animals so stimulated in a T-maze would learn to go to the goal box which contained food in preference to the one that did not. Since ICS was given in both maze arms and end boxes, it was the consump-tion of food (while being stimulated) that provided the differential reinforcement in the rewarded end (goal) box. Mendelson then showed that the animals continued to perform correctly and promptly even when the stimulation was eliminated from the start box and the arms of the maze; as long as ICS was given in the correct goal box (which resulted in eating), the performance did not deteriorate. But the elimination of stimulation from the rewarded end box, even when stimulation was present in the start box and the rest of the maze, quickly reduced the choice-point behavior to a random level and greatly increased running time. Thus, the facilitation of instrumental responding occurred only when hunger drive (produced by ICS) was accompanied by reinforcement (eating) in the goal box, the presence or absence of the drive in nongoal-box parts of the maze made no difference. These results are not consistent with the view that drive *per se* is sufficient for instrumental-response facilitation; they are consistent with the view that drive merely creates the conditions under which the animals would be likely to display the consummatory acts and be reinforced. Reinforcement in the goal box is essential for both response instigation and response choice. Reinforcement in the goal box could affect start-box and choice-point behavior only if the cues there had become associated with the reinforcement and had acquired incentive-motivational properties. Pending further investigations of the type that Mendelson has conducted, it may be tentatively concluded that incentive-motivational stimuli are necessary for the facilitation of instrumental responses.

Current views of the mechanisms of motivational effects

In this section, the current views of the mechanisms by which drive and incentive-motivational stimuli affect behavior shall be examined. These views are discussed here with reference to interpretations of motivational effects on general activity, and instrumental responses. [. . .]

Motivational effects on general activity

The most commonly encountered explanation of the observed incentive-motivational increase in general activity is that the increase is the outcome of strengthening by reinforcement of locomotory and other acts that spontaneously occur in the experimental situation (Amsel and Work, 1961; Baumeister, Hawkins and Cromwell, 1964; Bolles, 1963; Finger, Reid and Weasner, 1957, 1960). Specific situational cues are thought to become instrumentally conditioned to certain specific 'activity responses' by virtue of the reinforcement provided by, say, food in the case of a hungry animal. The other, less common, view regards the conditioning as consisting, not in the association of specific responses with the stimulus situation, but in the association of some sort of a central state with the situational cues (Campbell, 1960). The central state, originally created only by the UCS (reinforcer), through a process of classical conditioning, comes to be evoked in advance of the UCS by the stimulus situation (CS); this central incentive-motivational state then facilitates the responses that make up 'general activity'.

Bindra and Palfai (1967) have experimentally examined the above explanations. They exposed thirsty rats to paired presentations (classical conditioning) of a CS (metronome) and UCS (water), while the animals were immobilized in restraining cages.

Then they measured their activity in another situation both in the presence and absence of the CS. This arrangement insured that the stimulus characteristics of the conditioning situation were different from those of the situation in which activity was to be measured. Also, as the animals were tightly restrained during conditioning, they were prevented from displaying the type of acts (e.g. rearing, walking) that could contribute to the activity scores in the test situation. Nevertheless, the level of rat activity during CS presentation in the test situation was higher than the level in the absence of CS. Further, the acts displayed in the test situation were quite different from those that occurred in the conditioning situation; thus the former could not have become associated with the CS during conditioning. Bindra and Palfai interpret these data by assuming that, during conditioning, a central state that facilitates the organization of environmentally oriented acts became associated with the CS.

Concerning the mechanism of drive-induced increase in activity, perhaps the most frequently cited explanation is that of Campbell and Sheffield (1953). They state that an increase in drive increases the animal's 'sensitivity to minimal stimulus changes in the environment' (p. 321), and that this enhanced excitability is responsible for the observed increase in activity. Two types of evidence tend to argue against this view. First, sensory loss (e.g. deafening or blinding) does not always reduce the level of general activity (Hall and Hanford, 1954; Zucker and Bindra, 1961). Second, if activity level is crucially determined by environmental stimulation, then the form of activity should be the same regardless of the type of drive so long as the test environment remains constant, but this is not so. For example, Bolles (1965) has noted that the diurnal cycles of hungry rats are considerably shallower than those of thirsty rats, and that thirsty rats sleep more and groom less than hungry ones. Though none of this evidence is crucial for the Campbell and Sheffield hypothesis, it does suggest that drive, apart from any increase in excitability it might produce, may also determine activity in some other way. Bindra and Palfai (1967) have suggested that changes in drive alter the 'motor readiness' of the animal. This concept of motor readiness is similar to that of excitability of the response system proposed by Campbell and Sheffield (1953), but is more explicitly linked to motor or response-occurrence mechanisms; in contrast, Campbell and Sheffield's concept appears to be linked to the sensory system. According to the Bindra and Palfai hypothesis, drive states that enhance motor readiness would facilitate the motor outflow of whatever response tendencies are evoked by the prevailing central state and environmental stimuli.

Motivational effects on instrumental responses

Typically, the instigation of an instrumental response is separated spatially (and, therefore, temporally as well) from the location where the response is terminated and rewarded. In order to explain response instigation at the starting location, any postulated motivational factor must be made to bridge the gap between the reward and starting locations. Watson (1919, p. 295 ff.) placed the burden of explanation on the concept of response chaining. Hull (1943) suggested that a response chain emerges in the course of learning and extends gradually backwards from reward location to the starting location. Individual elements of the response chain were thought by him to become conditioned to the cues of the various specific areas of the apparatus. Response instigation was thus simply the elicitation by start-area cues of the early components of the response chain. More recently, the emphasis has shifted from the elicitation of instrumental-response components to the elicitation of components of the consummatory response (Spence, 1956). It is supposed that, during acquisition, the cues of the starting location come to elicit certain components of the unconditioned response to the reward, and that this fractional anticipatory goal response (r_g) is responsible for the observed incentive-motivational effects. This is the currently favored view and should be examined in detail.

According to this view, r_g's (e.g. components of the consummatory acts of eating) become classically conditioned to the reward-area cues; later the start-area cues, inasmuch as they resemble the reward-area cues, begin to evoke r_g's as well. The r_g's of special significance are thought to be the components of visceral and other responses controlled by the autonomic nervous system. In general, those who offer this explanation of response instigation (e.g. Amsel, 1962; Mowrer, 1960; Seward, 1950; Sheffield, 1965; Spence, 1956) consider sensory feedback from the anticipatory response ($r_g \rightarrow s_g$) to be the crucial factor. The promptness of response instigation is thought to vary with the strength of the feedback, which in turn reflects the vigor of the r_g elicited by the cues at the starting location.

There are two versions of this view. One of these, linked to the Hullian view of $H \times D$ interaction, regards sensory feedback as a (secondary) drive, contributing to the total drive (D) and hence to response instigation. The other version regards the sensory feedback as a contribution to the stimulus complex that becomes conditioned to the instrumental response; that is, motivational effects are thought to result from variations in effective habit. Some seem to favor the first version (e.g. Seward, 1956; Sheffield, 1965), others the second version (e.g. Estes, 1958), and still others seem to regard both versions to be tenable (Amsel, 1962; Brown and Farber, 1951; Spence, 1956). Both versions imply that the occurrence of some fractional components of the unconditioned goal response should be correlated with the instrumental responses they support. But the evidence tends to be against this.

In the case of positive reinforcers, the experimental search has been directed at licking and salivation reactions as the r_g's facilitating instrumental responses leading to food or water. Williams (1965) recorded salivation as dogs pressed a panel for food on various reinforcement schedules. His results show that, though a high output of salivation generally occurred in the neighborhood of panel pressing, frequently, in situations involving response chaining, the two responses became 'dissociated'. Williams concludes that his results 'cast doubt upon the possibility that incentive motivation is directly linked to the actual occurrence of classically conditioned responses' (p. 345). This conclusion is supported by Ellison and Konorski (1964, 1966) who have demonstrated relative independence of salivary and motor responses in instrumental learning. Studies of licking in relation to instrumental feeding responses have also failed to prove a dependence of instrumental responses on licking (Miller and DeBold, 1965).

Roberts and his collaborators have come to a similar conclusion in their studies of aggression and gnawing induced by hypothalamic stimulation (Roberts and Carey, 1965; Roberts and Kiess, 1964). They showed that cats receiving hypothalamic stimulation would learn a discriminative habit in a Y-maze provided an object appropriate to the hypothalamic stimulation (i.e. an attackable or gnawable object) was present in the goal box. But they noted that the occurrence of the instrumental response did not depend on the elicitation of the consummatory acts of aggression or gnawing by alley cues. In fact, no evidence of conditioning of the electrically induced consummatory responses could be found, but the animals persisted in choosing the correct arm of the Y-maze so long as the appropriate object was present in the goal box.

In the case of avoidance training, the instigational stimuli are presumed to arise from a set of classically conditioned anticipatory visceral reactions, collectively called 'fear' or 'anxiety'. However, surgical and pharmacological blocking of the peripheral autonomic nervous system seems not to disrupt avoidance performance (Wynne and Solomon, 1955). Similarly, though changes in heart rate often occur during avoidance training, these changes do not show any systematic relation with instrumental performance when the response is well-established (Bersh, Notterman and Schoenfeld, 1956; A. H. Black, 1959, 1965). Nor does there seem to be any close relation between heart rate and behavioral suppression as seen in a conditioned emotional response situation (DeToledo and Black, 1966). And Solomon and Turner (1962) have shown that incentive-motivational effects can be generated under curare, which eliminates the possibility of occurrence of skeletal responses, such as muscular tension.

Of course, it is possible that the sensory feedback from some other, hitherto unsuspected, classically conditioned reactions may be the crucial factor in the performance of instrumental responses, but the available evidence does not encourage belief in such a proposition. There is certainly no justification for restricting speculation concerning the mechanism of incentive-motivation within a framework that assumes that the occurrence of classically conditioned anticipatory reactions is essential for the instigation of instrumental responses.

If the anticipatory reactions are not necessary for instrumental response instigation, the incentive-motivational stimuli must be capable of influencing instrumental behavior in other ways. As in the case of general activity, a hypothesis worth considering is that the facilitation of specific instrumental responses is attributable to some central states created by incentive-motivational stimuli. If it could be shown that one and the same incentive-motivational stimulus can exert influences on several different aspects of behavior, then the postulate of a central incentive-motivational state would become a reasonable one. The question to be asked is whether the influence of an incentive-motivational stimulus is limited to the type of behavior in connection with which the incentive-motivational properties were acquired or extends to a wider variety of behavior. Weinrich, Cahoon, Ambrose and Laplace (1966) have shown that incentive-motivational properties generated in connection with the training of one instrumental response (lever pressing) are general enough to influence the performance of another response (chain pulling).

Following a demonstration by Bower and Kaufman (1963), Bacon and Bindra (1967) posed this question of generality in another way. Do incentive-motivational properties acquired by a CS under one set of drive-reinforcement conditions affect responses developed or maintained under a different set of drive-reinforcement conditions? For example, will a CS, whose incentive-motivational properties have been developed in relation to thirst drive and water reward, affect the acquisition or performance of responses acquired in relation to hunger drive and food reward or electric shock and escape reward? They studied the effects of a CS (metronome), previously paired (classical procedure) with a reinforcer (water), on the acquisition of an instrumental running response in the rat. In one experiment the instrumental response was trained on the same drive-reinforcement combination (thirst-water) as was used during classical conditioning, in another the drive-reinforcement combination was changed to hunger-food during instrumental training, and in a third experiment to shock-avoidance. In all cases the presence of the incentive-motivational CS facilitated the acquisition of the instrumental response.

If the incentive-motivational properties of a stimulus can be independent of the response (if any) in connection with which the properties were acquired, as well as of drive-reinforcement conditions under which the conditioning occurred, then it seems reasonable to assume that an incentive-motivational stimulus creates a central state with widespread influences. But how many different types of such central states can be created? The answer probably lies in the different types of drive-reinforcement conditions used to create incentive motivation. Certain concepts already widely used in psychology, such as fear or anxiety (Miller, 1951; Mowrer, 1939), frustration (Amsel, 1958; Spence, 1960), and excitement or activation (Hebb, 1955; Miller, 1963), may be thought of as central states capable of affecting a variety of responses. The question of the number of separable incentive-motivational states is an empirical one, to be answered by studying the effects on behavior of incentive-motivation generated in different ways. [. . .]

References

AMSEL, A. (1958), 'The role of frustrative non-reward in non-continuous reward situations', *Psychol. Bull.*, vol. 55, pp. 102–19.

AMSEL, A. (1962), 'Frustrative non-reward in partial reinforcement and discrimination learning: Some recent history and a theoretical extension', *Psychol. Rev.*, vol. 69, pp. 306–28.

AMSEL, A., and WORK, M. S. (1961), 'The role of learned factors in "spontaneous" activity', *J. compar. physiol. Psychol.*, vol. 54, pp. 527–32.

ANAND, B. K. (1961), 'Nervous regulation of food intake', *Physiol. Rev.*, vol. 41, pp. 677–708.

ANDERSSON, B., and McCANN, S. M. (1955), 'A further study of polydipsia evoked by hypothalamic stimulation in the goat', *Acta Physiologica Scandinavia*, vol. 33, pp. 333–46.

BACON, W. E., and BINDRA, D. (1967), 'The generality of the incentive-motivational effects of classically conditioned stimuli in instrumental learning', *Acta Biologiae Experimentalis*, Warsaw, vol. 27, p p. 185-97.

BAUMEISTER, A., HAWKINS, W. F., and CROMWELL, R. L. (1964), 'Need states and activity level', *Psychol. Bull.*, vol. 61, pp. 438–53.

BEACH, F. A. (1942), 'Sexual behavior of prepuberal male and female rats treated with gonodal hormones', *J. compar. Psychol.*, vol. 34, pp. 285–92.

BERSH, P J., NOTTERMAN, J. M., and SCHOENFELD, W. N. (1956), 'Extinction of human cardiac-response during avoidance conditioning', *Amer. J. Psychol.*, vol. 69, pp. 244–51.

BINDRA, D. (1959), 'Stimulus change, reactions to novelty, and response decrement', *Psychol. Rev.*, vol. 66, pp. 96–103.

BINDRA, D. (1961), 'Components of general activity and the analysis of behavior', *Psychol. Rev.*, vol. 68, pp. 205–15.

BINDRA, D., and PALFAI, T. (1967), 'The nature of positive and negative incentive-motivational effects on general activity', *J. compar. physiol. Psychol.*, vol. 63, pp. 288–97.

BINDRA, D., and SPINNER, N. (1958), 'Response to different degrees of novelty: The incidence of various activities', *J. exper. Psychol.*, vol. 1, pp. 341–50.

BLACK, A. H. (1959), 'Heart rate changes during avoidance learning in dogs', *Canad. J. Psychol.*, vol. 13, pp. 229–42.

BLACK, A. H. (1965), 'Cardiac conditioning in curarized dogs: The relationship between heart rate and skeletal behavior', in W. F. Prokasy (ed.), *Classical Conditioning: A Symposium*, Appleton-Century-Crofts, pp. 20–47.

BLACK, R. W. (1965), 'On the combination of drive and incentive motivation', *Psychol. Rev.*, vol. 72, pp. 310–17.

BOLLES, R. C. (1963), 'Effect of food deprivation upon the rat's behavior in its home cage', *J. compar. physiol. Psychol.*, vol. 56, pp. 456–60.

BOLLES, R. C. (1965), 'Effects of deprivation conditions upon the rat's home cage behavior', *J. compar. physiol. Psychol.*, vol. 60, pp. 244–8.

BOLLES, R. C. (1967), *Theory of Motivation*, Harper & Row.

BOWER, G., and KAUFMAN, R. (1963), 'Transfer across drives of the discriminative effect of a Pavlovian conditioned stimulus', *J. exper. Anal. Behav.*, vol. 6, pp. 445–8.

BROWN, J. S. (1961), *The Motivation of Behavior*, McGraw-Hill.

BROWN, J. S., and FARBER, I. E. (1951), 'Emotions conceptualized as intervening variables – with suggestions toward a theory of frustration', *Psychol. Bull.*, vol. 48, pp. 465–95.

CAMPBELL, B. A. (1960), 'Effects of water deprivation on random activity', *J. compar. physiol. Psychol.*, vol. 53, pp. 240–41.

CAMPBELL, B. A., and CICALA, G. A. (1962), 'Studies of water deprivation in rats as a function of age', *J. compar. physiol. Psychol.*, vol. 55, pp. 763–8.

CAMPBELL, B. A., and SHEFFIELD, F. D. (1953), 'Relation of random activity to food deprivation', *J. compar. physiol. Psychol.*, vol. 46, pp. 320–22.

CAMPBELL, B. A., TEGHTSOONIAN, R., and WILLIAMS, R. A. (1961), 'Activity, weight loss, and survival time of food-deprived rats as a function of age', *J. compar. physiol. Psychol.*, vol. 54, pp. 216–19.

COFER, C. N., and APPLEY, M. H. (1964), *Motivation: Theory and Research*, Wiley.

COONS, E. E., LEVAK, M., and MILLER, N. E. (1965), 'Lateral hypothalamus: Learning of food-seeking response motivated by electrical stimulation', *Sci.*, vol. 152, pp. 1320–21.

DETOLEDO, L., and BLACK, A. H. (1966), 'Heart rate: Changes during conditioned suppression in rats', *Sci.*, vol. 152, pp. 1404–6.

DUDA, J. J., and BOLLES, R. C. (1963), 'Effects of prior deprivation, current deprivation, and weight loss on the activity of the hungry rat', *J. compar. physiol. Psychol.*, vol. 56, pp. 569–71.

ELLISON, G. D., and KONORSKI, J. (1964), 'Separation of the salivary and motor responses in instrumental conditioning', *Sci.*, vol. 146, pp. 1071–2.

ELLISON, G. D., and KONORSKI, J. (1966), 'Salivation and instrumental responding to an instrumental CS pretrained using the classical conditioning paradigm', *Acta Biologiae Experimentalis*, vol. 26, pp. 159–65.

ESTES, W. K. (1958), 'Stimulus-response theory of drive', in M. R. Jones (ed.), *Nebraska Symposium on Motivation: 1958*, University of Nebraska Press, pp. 35–69.

FINGER, F. W., REID, L. S., and WEASNER, M. H. (1957), 'The effect of reinforcement upon activity during cyclic food deprivation', *J. compar. physiol. Psychol.*, vol. 50, pp. 495–8.

FINGER, F. W., REID, L. S., and WEASNER, M. H. (1960), 'Activity changes as a function of reinforcement under low drive', *J. compar. physiol. Psychol.*, vol. 53, pp. 385–7.

GASTAUT, H., VIGOUROUX, R., and NAQUET, R. (1952), 'Comportements posturaux et cinétiques provoqués par stimulation sous-corticale chez le chat non anesthésié. Leur relation avec le "réflexe d'orientation"', *J. Psychol. normale pathol.*, vol. 45, pp. 257–71.

GLICKMAN, S. E., and SCHIFF, B. B. (1967), 'A biological theory of reinforcement', *Psychol., Rev.*, vol. 74, pp. 81–109.

HALL, J. F., and HANFORD, P. V. (1954), 'Activity as a function of a restricted feeding schedule', *J. compar. physiol. Psychol.*, vol. 47, pp. 362–3.

HEBB, D. O. (1955), 'Drives and the CNS (Conceptual Nervous System)' *Psychol. Rev.*, vol. 62, pp. 243–54.

HULL, C. L. (1943), *Principles of Behavior*, Appleton-Century-Crofts.

HULL, C. L. (1950), 'Behavior postulates and corollaries – 1949', *Psychol. Rev.*, vol. 57, pp. 173–80.

KIMBLE, G. A. (1961), *Hilgard and Marquis' Conditioning and Learning*, Appleton-Century-Crofts.

KINDER, E. F. (1927), 'A study of nest-building activity of the albino rat', *J. exper. Zool.*, vol. 47, pp. 117–61.

LEHRMAN, D. S. (1956), 'The organization of maternal behavior and the problem of instinct', in *L'Instinct dans les Comportements des Animaux et de L'Homme*, Masson.

LORENZ, K. (1950), 'The comparative method in studying innate behavior patterns', *Symposia Soc. exper. Biol.*, vol. 4, pp. 221–68.

MENDELSON, J. (1965), 'Electrical stimulation in the hypothalamic feeding area of the rat: Motivational, reinforcing, and cue properties', unpublished doctoral dissertation, Massachusetts Institute of Technology.

MENDELSON, J. (1966), 'The role of hunger in T-maze learning for food by rats', *J. compar. physiol. Psychol.*, vol. 62, pp. 341–53.

MENDELSON, J., and CHOROVER, S. L. (1965), 'Lateral hypothalamic stimulation in satiated rats: T-maze learning for food', *Sci.*, vol. 149, pp. 559–61.

MILLER, N. E. (1951), 'Learnable drives and rewards', in S. S. Stevens (ed.), *Handbook of Experimental Psychology*, Wiley, pp. 435–72.

MILLER, N. E. (1957), 'Experiments on motivation', *Sci.*, vol. 126, pp. 1271–8.

MILLER, N. E. (1963), 'Some reflections on the law of effect produce a new alternative to drive reduction', in M. R. Jones (ed.), *Nebraska Symposium on Motivation: 1963*, University of Nebraska Press, pp. 65–112.

MILLER, N. E., and DeBOLD, R. C. (1965), 'Classically conditioned tongue-licking and operant bar pressing recorded simultaneously in the rat', *J. compar. physiol. Psychol.*, vol. 59, pp. 100–111.

MOWRER, O. H. (1939), 'A stimulus-response analysis of anxiety and its role as a reinforcing agent', *Psychol. Rev.*, vol. 46, pp. 553–65.

MOWRER, O. H. (1960), *Learning Theory and Behavior*, Wiley.

RICHTER, C. P. (1922), 'A behavioristic study of the activity of the rat', *Compar. Psychol. Monogr.*, vol. 1, no. 2.

RICHTER, C. P. (1927), 'Animal behavior and internal drives', *Q. Rev. Biol.*, vol. 2, pp. 307–43.

ROBERTS, W. W., and CAREY, R. J. (1965), 'Rewarding effect of performance of gnawing aroused by hypothalamic stimulation in the rat', *J. compar. physiol. Psychol.*, vol. 59, pp. 317–24.

ROBERTS, W. W., and KIESS, H. O. (1964), 'Motivational properties of hypothalamic aggression in cats', *J. compar. physiol. Psychol.*, vol. 58, pp. 187–93.

SEWARD, J. P. (1950), 'Secondary reinforcement as tertiary motivation: A revision of Hull's revision', *Psychol. Rev.*, vol. 57, pp. 362–74.

SEWARD, J. P. (1951), 'Experimental evidence for the motivating function of reward', *Psychol. Bull.*, vol. 48, pp. 130–49.

SEWARD, J. P. (1956), 'Drive, incentive, and reinforcement', *Psychol. Rev.*, vol. 63, pp. 195–203.

SHEFFIELD, F. D. (1966), 'New evidence on the drive-induction theory of reinforcement', in R. N. Haber (ed.), *Current Research in Motivation*, Holt, Rinehart & Winston, pp. 111–22.

SHEFFIELD, F. D. (1965), 'Relation between classical conditioning and instrumental learning', in W. F. Prokasy (ed.) *Classical Conditioning: A Symposium*, Appleton-Century-Crofts, pp. 302–22.

SHEFFIELD, F. D., and CAMPBELL, B. A. (1954), 'The role of experience in the "spontaneous" activity of hungry rats', *J. compar. physiol. Psychol.*, vol. 47, pp. 97–100.

SHEFFIELD, F. D., ROBY, T. B., and CAMPBELL, B. A. (1954), 'Drive reduction versus consummatory behavior as determinants of reinforcement', *J. compar. physiol. Psychol.*, vol. 47, pp. 349–54.

SOLOMON, R. L., and TURNER, L. H. (1962), 'Discriminative classical conditioning in dogs paralyzed by curare can later control discriminative avoidance responses in the normal state', *Psychol. Rev.*, vol. 69, pp. 202–19.

SPENCE, K. W. (1956), *Behavior Theory and Conditioning*, Yale University Press.

SPENCE, K. W. (1960), *Behavior Theory and Learning*, Prentice-Hall.

TENEN, S. S., and MILLER, N. E. (1964), 'Strength of electrical stimulation of lateral hypothalamus, food deprivation, and tolerance for quinine in food', *J. compar. physiol. Psychol.*, vol. 58, pp. 55–62.

TINBERGEN, N. (1951), *The Study of Instinct*, Oxford University Press.

VAUGHAN, E., and Fisher, A. E. (1962), 'Male sexual behavior induced by intercranial electrical stimulation', *Sci.*, vol. 137, pp. 758–60.

WANG, G. H. (1923), 'Relation between "spontaneous" activity and oestrus cycle in the white rat', *Compar. Psychol. Monogr.*, vol. 2, no. 6.

WARDEN, C. J. (1931), *Animal Motivation*, Columbia University Press.

WATSON, J. B. (1919), *Psychology from the Standpoint of a Behaviorist*, Lippincott.

WIENRICH, W. W., CAHOON, D. D., AMBROSE, G., and LAPLACE, R. (1966), 'Secondary stimulus control of a "new" operant incompatible with "running to the food magazine"', *Psychonomic Sci.*, vol. 5, pp. 189–90.

WIESNER, B. P., and SHEARD, N. M. (1933), *Maternal Behaviour in the Rat*, Oliver & Boyd.

WILLIAMS, D. R. (1965), 'Classical conditioning and incentive motivation', in W. F. Prokasy (ed.), *Classical Conditioning: A Symposium*, Appleton-Century-Crofts, pp. 340–57.

WOODWORTH, R. S. (1918), *Dynamic Psychology*, Columbia University Press.

WYNNE, L. C., and SOLOMON, R. L. (1955), 'Traumatic avoidance learning: Acquisition and extinction in dogs deprived of normal peripheral autonomic function', *Genet. Psychol. Monogr.*, vol. 52, pp. 241–84.

ZENER, K. (1937), 'The significance of behavior accompanying conditioned salivary secretion for theories of the conditioned response' *Amer. J. Psychol.*, vol. 50, pp. 384–403.

ZUCKER, I., and BINDRA, D. (1961), 'Peripheral sensory loss and exploratory behaviour', *Canad. J. Psychol.*, vol. 15, pp. 237–43.

Part Four Motivation as Incentive Stimulation

The concern with the nature of objects and events that have the property of reinforcing responses led gradually to the idea that reinforcing stimuli themselves might be the basis of motivation. The essential point of this view is that certain stimuli and stimulus configurations are intrinsically pleasurable or painful to individuals of certain species, and that such 'incentive stimuli' generate motivation in the animal and instigate approach or withdrawal actions in relation to themselves (incentive stimuli). In other words, it is the sensory processes arising from incentive (or reinforcing) stimuli themselves, rather than their response-reinforcement properties that are the basis of motivation. This idea had been discussed by Troland and has recently been elaborated by Young and Pfaffmann. Some of the work of ethologists and comparative psychologists, concerned with analysing what specific stimulus configurations are essential in making certain objects and events incentive stimuli, contributed further to the acceptance of the view that incentive stimulation plays a role in motivation. This analytical work on incentive stimuli is represented here by the papers of Levison and Flynn, and Harlow and Suomi.

21 L. T. Troland

Pleasure–Pain and Facilitation Inhibition

Excerpts from L. T. Troland, *The Principles of Psychophysiology*, Van Nostrand, 1932, volume 3, chapter 23, sections 87 and 88.

Sherrington (1911) has signalized a class of receptive systems which he calls *nociceptive*, because they are particularly attuned to noxious or injurious agencies. His interest, however, seems to have been restricted mainly to the observation that the arousal of such sense channels gives rise to particularly energetic reactions on the motor side. The outstanding examples of this class of afferent mechanisms are, of course, the pain nerves, but many other special sensory systems can be added, as we shall see below. Nociceptive afferent paths can be contrasted with those which have no special sensitivity to injurious forces, by designating the latter as *neutroceptive*. However, in order to make the classification complete, we must define a third group to include those afferent channels which are specially attuned to beneficial stimuli. I have suggested the term, *beneceptive*, to designate systems of this sort. The sweet sensibility of the tongue may be cited as an example.

The definition and identification of nociceptive or beneceptive sensory systems can be carried out quite independently of any reference to consciousness. We have only to note whether or not the agencies which characteristically arouse the given receptors are typically injurious or beneficial. The concepts of injury and of benefit must, of course be established from a general biological standpoint; injury means reduction of the chances of species survival and multiplication, while benefit has the opposite significance. However, in applying criteria of this sort, we must recognize that we are dealing only with average tendencies, and not with rules which allow of no exception. In the state of nature, tissue lesions are typically injurious, even if, at the hands of a surgeon, they may be highly beneficial. Similarly, sexual relations are favorable to the maintenance of a species, although in human civilization they frequently lead to venereal infection and death.

Using such criteria, we may classify the various departments of sensation somewhat as follows. The principal neutroceptive systems are those of vision, audition, cutaneous touch, and attitudinal kinaesthesis. Among the nociceptive systems, we may include the various forms of pain sensibility, bitter taste, salt and sour at high intensity, the olfactory responses which correspond to the alliaceous, caprillic, repugnant, and nauseating items of the Zwaardemaker classification, cold, excessive heat, the senses of hunger, thirst, and numerous other visceral afferent processes. The latter include the desires to micturate, to defecate, afferent processes underlying the feeling of suffocation, etc. Each of these sense mechanisms is to be conceived in purely physiological terms, although the nomenclature may be suggested by the psychical accompaniments in many instances. The class of beneceptors has a somewhat smaller number of representatives. The erotic sensibility heads the list, followed by gustatory sweet response, the olfactory reactions corresponding to ethereal, aromatic and balsamic items of Zwaardemaker's classification, salt and sour at low intensities, warmth at low intensity, and certain viscerally aroused afferent currents, such as those underlying coenaesthesia and the satisfaction of organic needs.

We must note, furthermore, that whether or not a given afferent excitation should be regarded as nociceptive, beneceptive, or neutroceptive may not be determined exclusively by the anatomical identity of the sensory channel. It may also depend upon the intensity of the process, and upon the given temporary condition of the organism. Thus, in the gustatory cases of salt and sour, low intensity excitation is beneceptive, while stimulation at a higher intensity must be classed as nociceptive. This distinction is not made primarily upon the basis of any physiological criterion, but wholly from a general biological standpoint. We know that small amounts of salt and acid are beneficial, but that large quantities of either of these substances will upset the metabolic equilibrium. Similarly, in the case of thermal sensibility, a low degree of warmth is beneceptive, whereas a higher degree' must be regarded as nociceptive. Cold, on the other hand, is always nociceptive except when it follows excessive exposure to heat, but in this latter case it may be regarded as a beneceptive response. With the passage of time, as the body cools off, it must go over into the nociceptive category again.

Considerations of this sort lead us to define more or less abstract functions of *nociception* and *beneception*, which are not rigidly attached to any special afferent channels. However, a study of the general biological situation should enable us to state the conditions under which any given sensory department will be operating in either of these two ways. Intensity, adaptation, organic condition, anatomical identity, and even spatial extent and temporal rhythm may be features in determining the answer.

We are now in a position to note a rather reliable psychophysiological relationship. This is to the effect that beneception tends to be accompanied by pleasantness in consciousness, while nociception ordinarily brings unpleasantness. Neutroceptive processes, on the other hand, are uniformly inclined to yield an indifferently affective experience. This correlation applies not only to the rough classification of sensory departments on an anatomical basis, but to the quantitative dependency of nociception and beneception upon such factors as intensity and adaptation. Pains of all kinds, bitterness, hunger, nausea, etc., are practically always unpleasant; sexual excitation, sweet taste, etc., quite reliably yield pleasure. But also: low intensity saltiness is pleasant, while high intensities of the same process give unpleasantness. Cold is normally unpleasant, but is accompanied by pleasure when it follows excessive exposure to heat. We do not need to claim that this psychophysical correlation between affectivity and nociception–beneception is perfect, and exceptions can easily be found. Nevertheless, the magnitude of the correlation is such as to make it strikingly significant.

Relation of affection to facilitation and inhibition

In seeking out an appropriate determinant for affectivity, we may find our first clue in the logical nature of the affective variable. We have noted that the latter presents two algebraically opposed modes of variation, with a zero point of indifference between them. Although it is by no means a logical necessity that the cortical determinant of affection should have a similarly algebraic constitution, nevertheless, we shall naturally make this assumption unless reasons appear to the contrary. Now, a very superficial glance at the general physiology of the nervous system immediately reveals a set of functions having the required properties, namely *facilitation* and *inhibition*. These processes are very wide-spread and of extreme importance. They are definitely opposed to each other in an algebraic manner, and are bound up with the dynamics of nervous activity in a very intimate way. Indeed, we can readily note a correlation between these processes and affective experience, on the basis of everyday observations. Everyone will recognize that pain and other forms of discomfort are inhibitory whereas pleasures facilitate concurrent modes of action.

It is very reasonable to suppose that the operations of the essential thalamic nuclei upon the cortex have general facilitative or inhibitory effects, as the case may be.

When we come to consider the more intimate nature of these processes, we note, first, that facilitation is closely allied to excitation. In fact, it seems, superficially, to involve a mere summation of concomitant excitatory values. Inhibition, on the other hand, apparently stands for a decrease in excitation, as if the combination were of negative with positive amounts. It is thus evident that, although facilitation may possibly involve no elementary features in addition to excitation, inhibition must incorporate an additional feature, to account for the interference. This suggests that facilitation, also, may have a basis which is distinct from that of mere nerve activity. Such a conception is provided in the notion of *Bahnung*, or an opening up of conduction pathways, the reduction of resistance or the raising of *conductance*. Inhibition can be defined in the same fundamental terms, as the opposed process of augmenting resistances or of depressing conductances. It is by no means necessary to insist that all cases of facilitation and inhibition must be explained in this manner, but there is plenty of evidence that such changes in conducting power actually do occur and play a part in the phenomena which we have been considering above. At any rate, they provide the most fruitful basis for developing a psycho-physiological theory of affectivity.

Reference

SHERRINGTON, C. S. (1911), *The Integrative Action of the Nervous System*, Yale University Press, pp. 227–31.

22 P. T. Young

Affective Processes and Motivation

Excerpts from P. T. Young, 'The role of affective processes in learning and motivation', *Psychological Review*, volume 66, 1959, pp. 104–25.

The common sense hedonistic explanation of learning implies that subjective feelings of pleasantness and unpleasantness influence behavior. This view involves the mind–body tangle. Thorndike tried to give a better formulation with his law of effect and concepts of satisfiers and annoyers; he later revised the theory, attempting to make it more objective. Troland introduced the concepts of beneception and nociception, but his views have never been widely accepted.

The aim of the present paper is to show that affective processes can be studied within a strictly objective frame of reference. I will argue that the affective processes are intervening variables, in Tolman's sense. For the present they may be viewed as logical constructs which bring together in an orderly way a large body of facts. Eventually affective processes will be described in physiological terms; current research indicates that their bodily nature and locus will some day be known. In the meantime the affective processes can be anchored firmly to events within the physical world.

The construct of affective processes

Let us begin by postulating that affective processes have an objective existence within the organism and that their nature and functions can be discovered.

Definition of the affective processes by their attributes

Affective processes can be defined objectively in terms of their attributes: sign, intensity, duration:

1. *Sign.* What one observes in laboratory situations is that naïve animals develop approach-maintaining or avoidance-terminating

patterns of behavior. If they develop the approach-maintaining pattern, I would assume that the underlying affective process is positive in sign. If they develop the avoidance-terminating pattern, I would assume that the affective process is negative in sign. If neither positive nor negative behavior develops, I would make no assumption concerning the sign of affective arousal.

It is important to note that the bare existence of adient or abient behavior is not a sufficient ground for inferring affective processes. Approach-maintaining and avoidance-terminating behavior may be habitual, automatic and affectively indifferent; but the *development* of approach-maintaining or avoidance-terminating patterns by *naïve animals* is the criterion for the sign of affective processes.

2. *Intensity.* In addition to sign, affective processes differ in intensity, or degree. Affective processes vary along a bipolar continuum between the extremes of maximal negative and maximal positive intensity.

One way to demonstrate the relative intensity of affective processes is to give animals a brief-exposure preference test with foods. A brief-exposure test is recommended because with prolonged exposures the level of acceptability of test-foods declines as the terminal state of satiation is approached.

In the brief-exposure test the animal is offered a series of choices between two test-foods (A and B). The series of choices reveals whether a preference for one food (A) or the other (B) develops. There is no way to force an animal to show a preference. Either a preference develops, with repeated choices, or it does not develop. Weak preferences, strong preferences, alternating preferences, and no preferences at all, have been found. In some tests the preference is obvious but, in others, statistical methods are needed to determine whether or not a particular body of data indicates a significant preference or a mutation of preference.

If both test-foods are accepted, I would assume that the preferred food arouses a higher intensity of positive affectivity than the nonpreferred. This is what is meant, objectively, by the statement that the preferred food is the more palatable. Again, it must be emphasized that the *development* of a preference *in naïve animals* indicates relative hedonic intensity and not the bare existence of a preference, since a preferential discrimination can be purely habitual and automatic.

3. *Duration.* In addition to sign and intensity, affective processes differ in duration and temporal course. Insofar as affective processes are induced by taste solutions, the duration of stimulation can be used to control the duration of affective arousal. The number of seconds that an animal is in contact with a food can be controlled or the number of individual licks of a fluid can be counted by an electronic device. The frequency and schedule of affective processes can also be controlled

With painful stimulations it would seem that the intensity frequency, and schedule are all subject to precise experimental control. In addition to direct stimulation, negative affectivity can be produced by frustration and conflict; but these conditions can be controlled less precisely than the conditions of sensory stimulation.

The hedonic continuum

The sign, intensity, and temporal changes of affective processes can be represented upon the hedonic continuum. Figure 1 shows this continuum extending from the extreme of negative affectivity (distress) to the extreme of positive affectivity (delight). Different intensities of affective arousal are represented by arbitrary units marked off upon the continuum. Midway between negative and positive affectivity is the range of indifferent, neutral processes and others that are weakly affective.

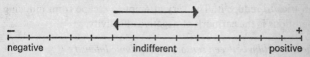

Figure 1 The hedonic continuum

The arrows represent two opposed directions of hedonic change. The upper arrow, pointing away from the negative end and towards the positive end of the continuum, represents a kind of hedonic change that is of great importance in the organization of behavior. According to the hedonic hypothesis, neuro-behav-

P. T. Young 197

ioral patterns are organized that minimize negative affectivity (distress) and maximize positive affectivity (delight). That is to say, organization is dependent upon hedonic change in the positive direction. Changes in the negative direction necessarily and frequently occur, and the lower arrow represents such changes. The total figure implies a principle of affective opposition or antagonism: there can be a change towards either pole but not a change in opposite directions at the same moment of time.

Although there are two opposed directions of change, there are, logically and psychologically, four main kinds of affective change that need to be considered: (*a*) increasing positive affectivity, (*b*) decreasing positive affectivity, (*c*) increasing negative affectivity, (*d*) decreasing negative affectivity. The first kind of hedonic change (increasing positive affectivity) is present when an animal tastes a sugar solution and organizes an approach-maintaining pattern of behavior. The fourth kind of change (decreasing negative affectivity) is present when an animal succeeds in relieving the 'distress' associated with an electric shock or reducing a need produced by dietary depletion. 'Distress reduction' is the hedonic equivalent of 'drive reduction' in the organization of instrumental behavior.

Changes in the negative direction occur under various circumstances. When an organism continues eating an acceptable food, the level of acceptability gradually declines as the final state of satiation is approached. Hedonic changes in the negative direction are also produced by shocks, burns, cuts, shrill sounds, and similar conditions. When negative affectivity is present the organism tries to reduce it. The very attempt to escape from inducing conditions is the earmark of negative affectivity.

The distinction between sensory and hedonic intensity

To a psychology that is limited by stimulus-response concepts the postulate of central affective processes may appear superfluous. I believe, however, that any theory of behavior which ignores the concept of affectivity will be found inadequate as an explanation of the total facts. To prove the point let us consider the following facts which are difficult, if not impossible, to explain in strictly S–R terms:

If pairs of sucrose solutions are presented to rats briefly for choice, the animals select the higher of two concentrations in preference to the lower. Scale values based upon preference tests 'show that the level of acceptability is directly proportional to the logarithm of the concentration. The relation holds all the way up the intensive scale from the preferential threshold to a saturated solution (Young and Greene, 1953).

From the facts about sucrose solutions one might argue that *sensory* intensity or physical concentration of solution is the critical determinant of behavior. But difficulty with the sensory interpretation appears when one considers the relative palatability of solutions of sodium chloride.

Young and Falk (1956) ran a series of preference tests between distilled water and sodium chloride solutions of different concentrations, and between pairs of sodium chloride solutions. They found that need-free rats revealed an optimal concentration for sodium chloride within the range of 0·75 to 1·5 per cent. When concentrations were below this range, need-free rats preferred the higher concentration; when above this optimal range, they preferred the lower concentration. Within the optimal range there were marked individual differences in preference and there was much indiscriminate behavior. The experimenters concluded that there is a *range of acceptance* within which acceptability increases with rising concentration of NaCl and a *range of rejection* within which the level of acceptability falls as concentration rises. The optimum of acceptability appears to be determined by the intersection of two gradients – one of acceptance and one of rejection. Incidentally, this finding agrees well with the work of Bare (1949), and others, who relied upon an intake method of studying acceptability of NaCl solutions.

It is clear, therefore, that with solutions of sodium chloride hedonic intensity does not have a one-to-one relation with sensory intensity. *Sensory* intensity is an increasing monotonic function of concentration of solution; *hedonic* intensity is a discontinuous function of concentration.

In another experiment, Young and Asdourian (1957) selected a 1 per cent sodium chloride solution as representative of the optimal range of NaCl concentrations. This near-optimal concentration was tested for preference against distilled water and four concentrations of sucrose solutions (54, 18, 6 and 2 per cent). The 1 per cent NaCl solution was preferred to distilled water by need-free rats; but *all* sucrose solutions were preferred to the standard 1 per cent NaCl solution. In the study it was estimated that a 1 per cent NaCl solution is isohedonic to a sucrose concentration of 0·38 per cent, which is very near to the preferential taste threshold for sucrose (about 0·50 per cent). In other words, practically all sucrose solutions are more palatable to need-free rats than all NaCl solutions. The hedonic intensity of all NaCl solutions is so low, in fact, that it is impossible to discover isohedonic pairs of sucrose and NaCl solutions.

It is difficult at best to equate sensory intensities across modalities but it is impossible to equate hedonic intensities if we employ solutions of sucrose and NaCl. High concentrations of sucrose are hedonically positive and high concentrations of NaCl are hedonically negative. This finding underscores the principle that *sensory* intensity is very different from *hedonic* intensity.

The scaling of hedonic intensities through preference tests yields an order of fact quite different from the facts of sensory intensity. This comes to light clearly in tests (unpublished) by Kent Christensen, who worked with compound solutions containing both sucrose and NaCl. When the sucrose concentration was 1 per cent and the NaCl 0·75 per cent (near optimal), the rats preferred the compound solution to both the 1 per cent sucrose solution and the 0·75 per cent NaCl solution. In other words, the two solutes – sucrose and NaCl – made independent additive contributions to palatability. The experiment demonstrated summation of two positive hedonic intensities. But, to take an extreme example, when the sucrose concentration was 4 per cent and the NaCl concentration was also 4 per cent, the rats showed a marked and consistent preference for the sucrose solution to the compound (very salty) solution. In this instance, positive and negative hedonic values summated algebraically. Christensen demonstrated, therefore, that the palatability of some sucrose solutions can be raised by adding small quantities of NaCl and lowered by adding larger quantities. Although he did not succeed in mapping out isohedonic contours for compound solutions, in an area determined by the concentration of sucrose and the concentration of sodium chloride, he demonstrated their existence and the possibility of charting them.

I believe that these facts demonstrate convincingly the necessity of distinguishing between *sensory* intensity and *hedonic* intensity and hence between the sensory and affective aspects of neural excitation. Stimulation of the taste receptors has both sensory and affective consequences.

Objective principles of experimental hedonism

Some of the objective principles of experimental hedonism are stated briefly below. These statements should be regarded as tentative formulations and as a basis for further experimental studies:

1. *Stimulation has affective as well as sensory consequences.* Along with gustatory stimulation by sugar solutions, for example, there is a positive affective arousal which, by its very nature, is something to be prolonged and intensified. Along with painful stimulation, there is a negative affective arousal which, by its very nature, is something to be avoided.

2. *An affective arousal orients the animal toward or against the stimulus-object.* This orientation can be readily observed. For example, when a rat, in the course of exploratory activity, makes contact with a sugar solution he may pause for a moment, then continue to explore. Sooner or later, however, he returns to the solution and takes more. After repeated sips he becomes oriented toward the solution. If an experienced animal is delayed in his approach to the cup, he shows a postural orientation toward the cup and approaches it quickly when released. If, however, the animal is offered a quinine solution, he fails to develop a positive orientation or an existing positive orientation is inhibited.

3. *Affective processes lead to the development of motives.* An orientation toward the goal-object is a motive that instigates and regulates behavior. The sign of an affective arousal determines whether an approach-maintaining motive or an avoidance-terminating motive will develop. This principle can be illustrated by numerous runway experiments in which animals acquire,

through affective arousals, motives that lead to approach or to avoidance.

4. *The strength of a recently acquired motive is correlated with the intensity, duration, frequency, and recency of previous affective arousals.* On the positive side, at least, the speed with which need-free rats approach a sucrose solution is related to the concentration and to the duration, frequency, and recovery of contact. With practice, however, animals speed up their running as they approach a physiological limit. This speeding up with practice may obscure initial differences due to affective arousals.

5. *The growth of motives is dependent upon learning as well as upon affective arousals.* Learning of a simple pattern such as running down a straight alley or running back and forth upon the preference tester is dependent directly on exercise (practice, drill, training); but affective arousals play an essential motivating role in the organizing, activating, regulating, and sustaining of neurobehavioral patterns.

It is necessary, therefore, to distinguish between learning through exercise (practice, drill, training) and the hedonic regulation of behavior. Affective processes regulate and organize neurobehavioral patterns in the sense that they determine what will be learned and what not; but such hedonic regulation and organization are not to be confused with learning through practice. Learning is here defined as a change in neurobehavioral pattern that depends upon exercise. Affective processes do not *cause* learning. They are motivational in nature and they influence performance.

6. *The laws of conditioning apply to affective processes.* Psychologists ordinarily describe conditioning in terms of S–R bonds, but this view is inadequate unless it can be made to include central affective processes.

An environmental situation, through conditioning, comes to arouse affective processes directly. To illustrate: if a rat is placed upon a piece of apparatus, he learns to respond to the stimulus-pattern of his surroundings; but, in addition to the usual S–R patterns, the stimulus-situation produces an affective arousal. If there is a positive affective arousal, the whole situation becomes hedonically positive so that the animal comes to react positively to environmental stimulus-cues. If the situation is hedonically negative, the environmental stimulus-cues come to arouse negative affectivity – call it distress, anxiety, fear, or whatever you will.

There is definitely an internal conditioning of affective processes along with the usual conditioning described in S–R terms. By human analogy it can be said that the animal learns how to *feel* in the situation as well as what cognitive discriminations to make and what acts to perform.

7. *Affective processes regulate behavior by influencing choice.* Numerous experiments upon the development of food preferences show that the sign and intensity of affective processes influence choice. The development of a food preference between two acceptable foods indicates which food-stimulus arouses the more intense affective process.

The acquisition of a preferential discrimination is not an instance of pure learning because affective processes determine whether one preference or its opposite will develop and, further, the relative hedonic intensities associated with two stimuli determine the rate of growth of a preferential pattern.

8. *Neurobehavioral patterns are organized according to the hedonic principle of maximizing the positive and minimizing the negative affective arousal.* This principle has a very wide range of application. It is seen most clearly in situations that involve choice. The stimulus associated with the more intense affective arousal dominates the preferential discrimination.

Conclusion

Although feelings of pleasantness and unpleasantness are known directly only in human experience, the facts of animal behavior make it necessary to postulate that affective processes have an objective existence. Since affective processes are not directly observed in behavior, they must be postulated as intervening variables. The postulate brings together in an orderly way a large and complex body of interrelated facts. Moreover, there are indications that the hypothetical construct of affective processes can some day be replaced by a physiological account of the intervening events.

Affective processes are motivational in the sense that they arouse, sustain, regulate, direct, and organize neurobehavioral patterns. Reinforcement and extinction are viewed as changes in performance dependent upon affective processes. Reinforcement must be distinguished from a change in habit strength due to exercise (practice, drill, training).

The postulate that affective processes have an objective existence is demanded by the facts of food acceptance but the postulate has a wider range of possible application – to sexual behavior, play, manipulation, and exploration, as well as to human action. Some principles of experimental hedonism have been tentatively formulated and it is suggested that they be tested in the laboratory.

References

BARE, J. K. (1949), 'The specific hunger for sodium chloride in normal and adrenalectomized white rats', *J. compar. physiol. Psychol.*, vol. 42, pp. 242–53.

YOUNG, P. T., and ASDOURIAN, D. (1957), 'Relative acceptability of sodium chloride and sucrose solutions', *J. compar. physiol. Psychol.*, vol. 50, pp. 499–503.

YOUNG, P. T., and FALK, J. L. (1956), 'The acceptability of tap water and distilled water to nonthirsty rats', *J. compar. physiol. Psychol.*, vol. 49, pp. 336–8.

YOUNG, P. T., and GREENE, J. T. (1953), 'Quantity of food ingested as a measure of relative acceptability', *J. compar. physiol. Psychol.*, vol. 46, pp. 288–94.

23 C. Pfaffmann

The Pleasures of Sensation[1]

C. Pfaffmann, 'The pleasures of sensation', *Psychological Review*, volume 67, 1960, pp. 253–68.

That the senses are the channels of communication between the external environment and the nervous system is so much a truism that, except for those who espouse ESP, the senses are held to be the sole mediators of transactions between the organism and its environment. But students of the senses tend to emphasize primarily the nature of their information handling function, their discriminative capacities and limits as well as the physiological processes upon which they are based. Behavior theorists have given heed to such function in another context when they speak of the cue function of stimuli. According to these conceptions discriminative stimuli serve to steer behavior, to guide it or set the stage for the response. But in this paper I do not plan to elaborate upon such processes. Rather I wish to call attention to certain other aspects of sensory function.

In recent years, neurophysiologists have emphasized that sensory systems may mediate important functions other than discrimination. Attention has been focused on such generalized effects as arousal or alerting of the nervous system as a whole. Bremer (1935) first showed that a state of cerebral somnolence could be produced in experimental animals in which the cerebrum had been surgically isolated from the brainstem and its incoming afferent pathways. He attributed this to the interruption of sensory influx itself. Later analysis (Magoun, 1958) showed that the somnolence resulted largely from interference with the centripetal influence exerted by the reticular system, the ascending reticular activating or arousal system. Much subsequent research

1. Slightly revised version of Presidential Address presented at the Annual Meeting of the Eastern Psychological Association, Atlantic City, 13 April 1959.

has shown that this system controls not only the state of arousal of the 'higher centers' of the nervous system, but that it can also modulate and influence activity within the classical sensory pathways themselves (Galambos, 1956; Hagbarth and Kerr, 1954; Hernandez-Peon, 1955). The reticular system may also be significant for a variety of other psychological processes (Lindsley, 1951; Schlosberg, 1954).

Most sense organs were found to have at least two central neural pathways. One, the well-known primary projection pathway via the thalamic sensory relays to the cerebral cortex, and the second, a nonspecific pathway by way of the reticular activating system with diffuse projections to the cortex and other neural structures. The reticular system is multimodal and intramodal, for it receives inputs from many modalities. The classical projection systems are specific to one modality and may be said to mediate primarily the cognitive or discriminatory sensory functions, the nonspecific system to mediate physiological and behavioral arousal (Magoun, 1958).

Psychologists especially have emphasized that stimuli may have still other functions, especially that of reinforcement (Hebb, 1958a; Keller and Schoenfeld, 1950; Skinner, 1953; Spence, 1956). This concept has most often been discussed in purely behavioral terms until the more recent studies of direct reinforcement by intracranial stimulation (Brady, 1958; Miller, 1957; Olds, 1958; Olds and Milner, 1954). In the ensuing discussion I shall limit myself to the so-called *primary reinforcement* for there is almost no limit to the range of previously neutral stimuli that, by one method or another, can be made to acquire reinforcing properties. That *primary aversive reinforcement* has been a function of stimuli has long been known, particularly for those stimuli of high intensity which elicit defense reactions or 'reflexes'. Certain of these seem qualitatively more prepotent as, for example, the pain of electric shock; 'rat runners' have frequently used shock as a primary negative reinforcer in their mazes or lever boxes. Some theorists hold that the pain reduction by shock termination provides the prototype of all reinforcement in the form of drive or tension reduction (Miller, 1959). The study of stimuli as *positive primary reinforcers* has, until recently, been restricted to those stimuli which are naturally related to such biologically functional activities as eating, drinking, or sexual activity. These stimuli could often be assigned a role in processes that mediated the satisfaction of a need or 'homeostatic drive'. Thus they were said to be related in some way to the primary biological drives. But there has been increasing evidence of late that sensory stimulation, divorced from its need or drive reducing concomitants, may function as a reinforcer in its own right. 'Exteroceptive motivation' sometimes called by such names as curiosity or stimulus change (Harlow, 1953; Hebb, 1958a; Kling, Horowitz, and Delhagen, 1956; Montgomery, 1952) has been demonstrated in a number of situations. And one theorist (Hebb, 1958, pp. 451–67, 1958b) has attempted to link such reinforcement to the reticular activating system on the grounds that changes in level of activation are reinforcing, *per se*, depending upon the prevailing level at the time of stimulation. Thus, in sensory isolation experiments, 'the subject experienced great swings of motivation, which alternated between periods of apathy and intense desire to get back to a normal environment'. Hebb concludes, 'clearly man's motivation is a function of his exteroceptive stimulation'. Thus, although the reinforcing function of stimuli has long been recognized and is the stock in trade of many experimentalists, there is still considerable debate as to the basis for this effect. Does it depend upon some secondary effect as need reduction, drive reduction, or change in arousal patterns in the reticular activating system? Or can we attribute these effects to sensory stimulation directly?

In this paper I shall discuss the proposition that sensory stimulation *per se* together with its ensuing central neural events be considered as a prime determinant of reinforcement. In this context I shall discuss our experiments on the sense of taste with emphasis on the sensory physiology of taste-mediated motivation as revealed in the correlation between gustatory nerve discharges and food preferences in animals. This will lead into a consideration of the relation between hedonic processes and afferent nerve discharges, preference behavior, and taste reinforcement. Finally the relation between affective sensory processes and discriminative functions will be discussed in the light of some speculations on the physiological bases for these two aspects of sensory function and their significance in behavior.

Taste as a model system

Although I began my studies of the sense of taste with a traditional sensory emphasis, it became increasingly apparent that the gustatory sense has certain unique features for the further understanding of behavior in general. Not only does the sense of taste possess selective receptor sensitivity that permits the discrimination of different taste stimuli, but these stimuli will elicit a number of specific consummatory responses: drinking and eating or, on the other hand, rejection. It is a relatively simple matter to demonstrate the control of behavior that taste stimuli can manifest by giving the animal a choice of water and taste solutions as Richter (1942) showed in his classic studies of self-selection. In

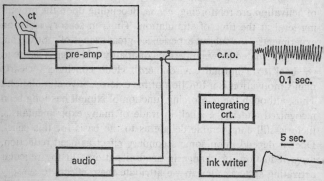

Figure 1 A block diagram of the recording apparatus showing two types of record. The upper trace shows a typical asynchronous, multi-fiber discharge from a large number of nerve fibers; the lower trace shows how such activity appears when processed through the integrator. (After a diagram in the *American Journal of Clinical Nutrition*)

addition, these stimuli can act as powerful reinforcers of instrumental responses leading to ingestion. Thus one and the same sense modality possesses easily demonstrable discriminative and reinforcing functions. In this respect it is an ideal model sensory-behavioral system in which to examine the relation between sensory stimulation and the reinforcing mechanisms in behavior as well as to permit the manipulation of the state of the organism by certain deprivation operations. I should, therefore, like to review briefly some of the methods we have employed and some of our experiments on taste,[2] to show how we look at the sensory continuum and its afferent neural input to the CNS which both motivates and directs behavior. In so doing I shall make use of the behavioral data of other workers, as well as the results of our own physiological and behavioral experiments. Our behavioral studies to date have utilized primarily the preferential ingestion method.

The gustatory afferent discharge and preference

Afferent nerves, like all nerves of the body, carry a series of electrical pulses which are the signs of impulse traffic up the sensory nerve. These can be recorded by appropriate electronic devices as shown in Figure 1 (cf. Pfaffmann, 1959). I shall present only data for the over-all activity in the taste nerve as afforded by the integrating circuit illustrated in the lower trace in Figure 1. The gustatory response curves for the cat are shown in Figure 2 in terms of the magnitude of the electrical signal generated in the nerve when each of the basic taste stimuli is applied to the tongue receptor surface. By such curves we can map out the taste sensitivity of different animals (Pfaffmann, 1955). These curves do not tell us about 'qualitative' differences in the nerve response. For that, analysis of the activity of single nerve fibers in the nerve is required (Pfaffmann, 1959).

From the point of view of behavior, the basic response to taste solutions is either one of acceptance or rejection so that the classical manifold of four tastes, salt, sour, bitter and sweet, may be reduced to two behavioral classes: acceptance and rejection. We have used a typical two-bottle Richter-type preference situation to study such behavior in different species (Bare, 1949; Carpenter, 1956; Pfaffmann, 1957). Certain substances may be accepted at low, but rejected at the higher concentrations. This is so for NaCl in the rat where the well-known preference-aversion response can be demonstrated to be a function of concentration as shown in Figure 3. The solid line shows relative preference behavior.

$$\frac{\text{cc. intake taste sol.}}{\text{cc. intake taste} + \text{cc. intake } H_2O}$$

2. These experiments have been supported in part by projects and grants from the Office of Naval Research, National Science Foundation, and the General Foods Corporation.

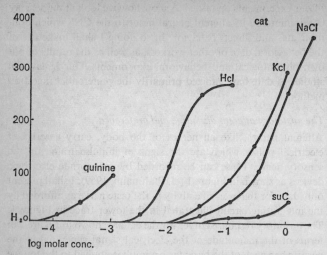

Figure 2 Curves of taste responses in the cat to four different taste stimuli as indicated by the integrated response method. (After a graph in the *Journal of Neurophysiology*)

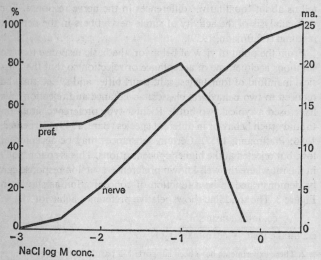

Figure 3 Preference response to different salt concentrations and magnitude of the chorda tympani nerve discharge in the rat. Ordinate to the left corresponds to preference response, ordinate to the right shows magnitude of integrator deflection. (After Pfaffmann, 1958)

Most acceptable solutions including sugar will follow this pattern when ingestion measures are used. Figure 3 also shows the neural response in the rat chorda tympani nerve to the same salt solutions. The broken line shows the integrated neural responses as a percentage of the maximum response observed. Clearly the preference behavior (i.e. response greater than 50 per cent) is not apparent until some substantial neural input has been achieved (20–30 per cent of maximal discharge). The peak preference occurs at about 60 per cent of maximal input, and the aversion rapidly sets in while the afferent discharge is still climbing. There is no change in the afferent input signal that corresponds to the behavioral inversion point – at least we have not been able to detect any such change. Up to the inversion point, the behavior parallels the afferent discharge curve as if the positive approach to the stimulus were due directly to the afferent input. The inversion and the subsequent aversion suggest the intrusion of a secondary 'stop' system. The fact that the inversion point is close to the isotonic point for sodium chloride solutions (0·9 per cent NaCl (0·15M) is isosmotic with the body fluids) suggests that some post-ingestion or metabolic factor related to water balance has become operative.

Indeed Stellar, Hyman and Samet (1954) have shown that the salinity of the gastric contents does affect the salt preference. Strong salt solutions intubated directly into the stomach depress the drinking of the more concentrated salt solutions. On the other hand, this is not the only stop factor for, in the same study, animals with an esophageal fistula showed the preference for hypotonic solutions and aversions for hypertonic ones even though the solutions never reached the stomach. Taste factors alone appear capable of eliciting the typical salt preference-aversion function. Thus the stop may indicate a change in 'sign' of the afferent input merely as a consequence of its increasing intensity. Perhaps there is a central-neural switching when the intensity of the afferent salt discharge reaches a critical value. Most intense sensory stimuli have aversive effects.

The relation of behavior to sensory afferent discharge for some of the other basic taste stimuli is shown in Figure 4. The upper figure shows the preference response curves for sugar, acid, and quinine as well as salt. We show here only the intakes above 50 per cent for salt and sugar, remembering that at higher concentrations, the curves fall below the 50 per cent value. The responses for acid and quinine are both aversions; no preference is shown. Note in are lower curves that the absolute magnitudes of neural response the quite different for the electrolytes as compared with the non-electrolytes. The behavioral response to quinine is quite definite and appears before there is a clear signal 'greater than the noise' for the nerve response. Here the behavioral indicator is the more sensitive. In an analogous way, the response to sucrose behaviorally is clear and definite, yet the neural response is disappointingly small. Intrinsic differences in the magnitude of the neural response, due in part to fiber size, etc., mean that sheer size of electrical signal itself cannot be correlated with behavioral effect. On the other hand, the range of effective stimulus concentration values in the two sets of determinations for each stimulus shows good agreement. The exact form or position of the preference aversion curves along the abscissa may be shifted depending upon such factors as order of presentation of stimuli, degree of hunger or physiological need, and amount of experience with the taste stimuli. It is the general nature of the relations between sensory input and preference that is shown in Figure 4.

The behavioral response to sugar solutions has been studied rather extensively, and it now seems possible to give an account of the start and stop factors in relation to sensory input. The preference curve just shown is based on ingestion of sugar over a twenty-four-hour or longer period. Ingestion is a rising function of concentration to a peak preference when the typical inflection occurs and intake declines. This relation is found also in the single stimulus method. McCleary (1953) was one of the first to show that the intake of sugar solution is limited by an osmotic post-ingestion factor. Others have shown similar effects of gastric factors by studying the effects of intubation upon intake (Le Magnen, 1955; Miller, 1957; Smith and Duffy, 1957; Stellar, Hyman and Samet, 1954). The relative frequency of choice in the brief exposure preference method, however, does not show the inflection (Young and Greene, 1953). Here there appears to be a linear relation between the level of acceptability and logarithm of concentration. Guttman's (1953) study of the rate of bar pressing as a function of concentration of sucrose solution used as the

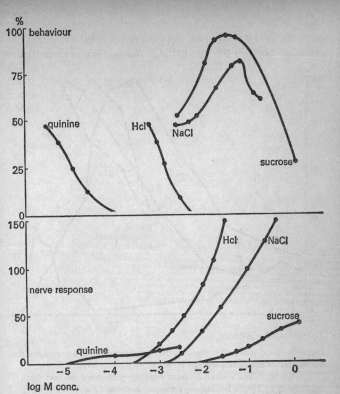

Figure 4 Composite graph of behavioral and electrophysiological responses in the rat. Upper graphs show the percentage preference (or aversion) as a function of stimulus concentration. The integrator responses in the chorda tympani nerve to the same stimuli are shown in arbitrary units in the lower graph

reinforcement showed that, on a continuous schedule, rate increased for the weaker concentrations but showed an inversion at the higher value. On a periodic schedule, however, the rate of bar press was found to be linear with the log of the concentration. The latter schedule provides relatively little drinking per response. But bar press rate also can be depressed by intragastric injections (Smith and Duffy, 1955).

The relations between bar pressing on the two schedules and the preference ingestion data of Richter and Campbell (1940) are shown in Figure 5 together with the electrophysiological response curve for the rat (Hagstrom and Pfaffmann, 1959). Note that the inversion point in the two-bottle preference test is close to the

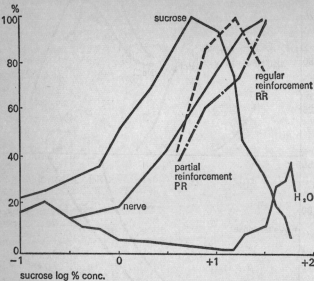

Figure 5 Composite graph showing the neural response to sucrose and the behavioral measures obtained by three different procedures in the rat. Pref. is the typical two bottle 24-hour ingestion preference method. Both the sucrose and water intakes are shown as smoothed curves, based on data by Richter and Campbell. RR is the rate of bar pressing during a test period for a small drop of sucrose on a regular reinforcement schedule, and PR is the same on a periodic reinforcement schedule, both based on Guttman (1953). Ordinates have been adjusted to make the maximum values in the original curves equal to 100

inversion point of the continuous reinforcement schedule. Both points lie close to the top of the electrophysiological sensory function. On the periodic schedule, rate rises as the sensory function increases. The fact that there is no inversion where the amount ingested is small appears to implicate the post-ingestion factor as a primary stop mechanism (Collier and Siskel, 1959; Shuford, 1959). Such a formulation would agree with Young's (1959) statement 'that sugar solutions are basically hedonically positive for the rat as compared with salt which is first positive but then negative'.

Studies which compared the effect of two different sugars, glucose and sucrose, on consummatory behavior, choice response, and rate of bar press likewise point to the importance of post-ingestive factors. Isohedonic concentrations, equally accepted in short comparative tests, were not consumed in equal amount when presented singly for longer periods. The glucose solutions were consumed in less volume than their isohedonically matched sucrose solutions, and the cumulative mean intake of both sugars was linearly related to osmotic pressure for the longer periods (Shuford, 1959). In the Skinner box the concentration of these two sugars which give equal rate of response on an aperiodic schedule (i.e. have equal reinforcing value) corresponds to the isohedonic concentrations (Shuford, 1959; Young, 1957). Guttman (1954) previously showed that the equal reinforcing solutions correspond to the equally sweet concentrations found in psycho-physical experiments (Cameron, 1947; MacLeod, 1952).

Hagstrom and Pfaffmann (1959) have also compared the relative efficacy of sucrose and glucose as gustatory stimuli for the rat, using the electrophysiological recording method. This could be done even though the magnitude of response to sugar is relatively small. Figure 6 shows the relative responses to the two sugars, and Figure 7 shows the comparison of the equi-effective concentrations of the two sugars as determined in the bar pressing experiment, in the preference choice test, and by the electrophysiological measure. All measures agree that sucrose is more effective than glucose of equimolar concentration, although the quantitative relation is not precise, for the electrophysiological data is curvilinear, the behavioral data, linear. However, it should be remembered that the physiological data reflect only the chorda tympani response and not the taste receptors at the back of the mouth. Perhaps the curvilinear relation between the behavioral and physiological measures arises from this.

Where ingestion is minimal, behavior and sensory effectiveness seem to go together. Actually the post-ingestion factor seems to be especially significant in preferences based on ingestion. The glucose preference threshold is lower than that for sucrose and the intake of glucose greater than that predicted by the sensory

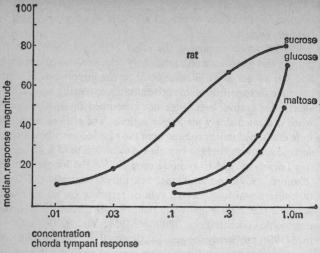

Figure 6 Integrator response magnitudes to three sugars for the rat chorda tympani nerve. Ordinate is relative magnitude, 100 equals the response to 0·01 M NaCl. (After graph in *Journal of Comparative and Physiological Psychology*)

measures. Soulairac (1947) has shown that the relative preference for sugars in a typical two-bottle preference test is correlated with their relative rates of absorption from the gastrointestinal tract.

Experiments utilizing other learning situations have been concerned with the action of sugar or saccharin as reinforcers (Collier and Siskel, 1959; Hughes, 1957; Sheffield and Roby, 1950; Sheffield, Roby and Campbell, 1954; Smith and Duffy, 1957; Young and Shuford, 1954, 1955). There is ample evidence that the sweet taste is rewarding whether it is nutritive or non-nutritive. Performance here too is an increasing function of stimulus concentration where conditions appear to maximize the sensory effects and minimize the post-ingestion factor. When amount or temporal factor is such that the absolute amount or volume of stimulus or nutrient ingested per unit time is low, then purely stimulus factors seem best to account for the results. When the amount consumed per unit is large, either because of a large amount of reinforcing agent or short time between presentations, then the secondary post-ingestive factors intrude. As Collier and Siskel (1959) point out, it should be possible with the proper

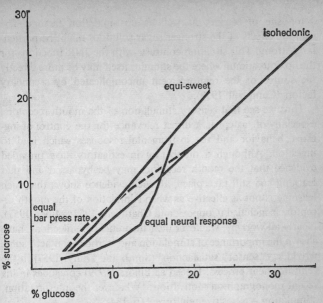

Figure 7 Equal response concentrations of glucose and sucrose for electro-physiological measures, equal bar press rates, equi-sweet solutions and isohedonic solutions. (After graph in *Journal of Comparative and Physiological Psychology*)

combination of concentration, volume, interval between reinforcement, and number of reinforcements to obtain a monotonic stimulus function, a non-monotonic function with inversion points at different volumes or concentrations, or even no relation at all between amount of reinforcement and performance.

These considerations presumably apply to Campbell's (1958) measurements of the JNR, the just noticeable reinforcing difference for sucrose solutions. He determined the minimal concentration increment necessary to produce a 75 per cent preference for the stronger of a pair of sucrose solutions in a two-bottle preference situation. Stronger solutions required a larger concentration increment than did the weak ones, and the plot of JNR against stimulus concentration showed a U-shaped function reminiscent of the more familiar Weber intensity discrimination functions. The resemblance may be due only in part to the properties of the sensory input because, as we have just shown, preference is the composite of sensory as well as post-ingestion factors. The osmotic effects of the stronger sugar solutions might be particularly strong. This situation contrasts with the JNR functions for the noxious stimuli where the stimulus itself may be more directly the source of the reinforcement uncomplicated by secondary factors (Campbell, 1958).

Thus we see that sensory stimulation of the mouth receptors, especially of taste, has a direct relevance for the control of ingestive behavior and the instrumental responses which lead to ingestion. Although a number of investigators have provided evidence that the mouth receptors may be bypassed and that learning can still take place, all such evidence shows that such learning is not as effective as when stimulation of the mouth receptors is included (Coppock and Chambers, 1954; Miller, 1957). Nearly all workers, whatever their theoretical predilections, have shown the importance of stimulation and 'sensory contact', some would say 'sensory satisfaction' (Smith and Duffy, 1957) in the reinforcement process. Indeed as Bindra (1959) concludes in his recent monograph on motivation: 'Whatever the interpretation, stimulation is a positive reinforcer' (p. 134).

The fact that certain taste stimuli control ingestion directly appears to be biologically determined. Frings (1946) has pointed out that nearly all organisms accept sugar solutions. There are exceptions perhaps related to certain aspects of metabolic or other biochemical divergences among the species. Cats cannot taste or discriminate sugar solutions (Carpenter, 1956; Pfaffmann, 1955), and birds (Pick and Kare, 1959) do not appear to show strong sucrose preferences; but these examples are remarkable largely for their divergence from what otherwise appears to be a general rule. Further there is no convincing evidence that the 'sweet tooth', where it does exist, depends upon the concomitant nourishment. The drinking of nonnutritive saccharin solutions under prolonged exposure to them shows no sign of extinction such as might be expected if the preference for saccharin or 'sweet' were acquired by past association with nourishment (Sheffield and Roby, 1950). Here we have 'sweet for sweet's sake'.

On the other side of the coin, we have been able to show that a 'bitter' aversive stimulus can be made more acceptable *only temporarily* when it is paired with the alleviation of thirst in early infancy (Warren and Pfaffmann, 1958). Newborn guinea pigs were raised on a normally avoided solution of sucrose octaacetate (SOA) as the only source of water for a three-week period. At an older age these organisms showed the usual rejection of SOA. Gustatory stimuli, therefore, appear to be biologically determined as the instigator of consummatory or avoidance responses and as primary positive or negative reinforcing stimuli.

So far I have discussed the mechanisms of a variety of behavior which appear to be under the control of sensory stimulation *qua* 'sensory stimulation'. I have not discussed the question of the affective or hedonic aspects of sensory stimulation, the pleasure of sensation, so to speak. To do so, I should now like to turn to other kinds of data derived from studies of man.

Hedonic aspects of sensory stimulation

Of all the applied psychophysical fields, none has made greater use of the affective or hedonic rating scale methods, along with purely sensory testing procedures, than has the field of flavor technology. In a series of carefully controlled tests the Army Quartermaster Food Acceptance Laboratory (Pilgrim, 1957), using a ninepoint hedonic rating scale, has been able to predict, with good reliability, the actual choices of food and the acceptance of menus on the part of soldiers in the field. These ratings frankly ask such questions as the following: like extremely, like very much, indifferent, dislike very much, etc. In this case the hedonic ratings are not determined solely by stimulus properties of food, for other studies by the Quartermaster group have documented the important role played by familiarity and past experience. None the less, the frankly hedonic rating initiated by the sensory stimulation is a good predictor of actual acceptance and ingestion.

I have been impressed by the apparent similarity of our rat preference curves with those of hedonic value obtained many years ago by Engel (1928). In those experiments, subjects were asked to rate different intensities of taste stimuli as either pleasant, unpleasant, or indifferent. The data can be treated in a number of ways, but in Figure 8 we see the ratings of four different taste modalities expressed as percentage of pleasant ratings minus the percentage of unpleasant ratings for a group of seven observers using summed ratings of all observers. The abscissa is propor-

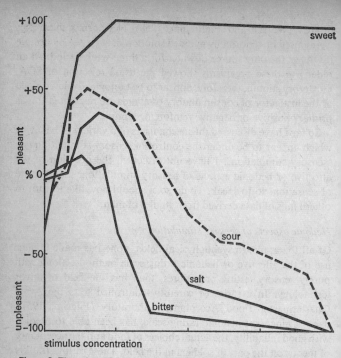

Figure 8 The preponderance of 'pleasant' or 'unpleasant' judgements in relation to the concentration of taste solution. Ordinate gives percentage of 'pleasant' minus percentage 'unpleasant'. The abscissa is proportional to concentration, the full length of the base line standing for 40% cane sugar, 1·12% tartaric acid, 10% NaCl, and 0·004% quinine sulphate (by weight). (After Pfaffmann, 1958)

tional to the concentrations adjusted for each of the different stimulus solutions. Note that sugar begins at a slightly unpleasant value and rises with concentration to reach a plateau. Sour, bitter, and salt all start from indifference, rise to a peak, and then fall off to unpleasantness. Sweet is predominantly pleasant, bitter predominantly unpleasant, with salt and sour intermediate. In Figure 9 I have plotted the animal preference curve and the hedonic rating by Engel's *S*s for sodium chloride solutions by concentration. The hedonic ratings here were computed simply as the percentage of the total ratings that are pleasant. Except for position along the abscissa, the two curves show a striking

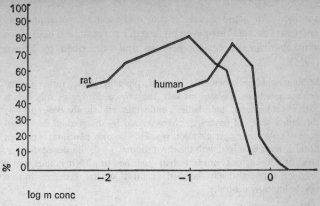

Figure 9 Comparison of animal preference and hedonic ratings of man in response to sodium chloride solutions. (After Pfaffmann 1958)

similarity. Beebe-Center (1951) earlier called attention to these same relations and compared the animal preference responses with hedonic ratings. Actually the more recent analysis of the post-ingestive factors that control the intake of sucrose solutions has done much to clarify the discrepancy between Engel's hedonic curve for sugar and the rat's preference for sugar. The sucrose hedonic curve does not turn down at the higher concentrations (see Figure 8). As noted earlier, rate of bar pressing on a periodic schedule and frequency of choice in the brief exposure test are likewise monotonically related to concentration. Thus hedonic rating and reinforcement bear the same relation to stimulus concentration.

In the preference-aversion curves for other substances, the stop mechanism may be sensory (gustatory) in origin or might arise from other than post-ingestive effects. If the taste of strong salt solutions is aversive *per se*, then we might expect that, regardless of reinforcement schedule, response will fall off above the optimal salt concentration in a manner resembling the 'fall-off' in Engel's curves. The same might hold for saccharin which has a 'bitter' sensory component at the higher concentrations. Further study of these effects is needed.

I have been emphasizing stimulus properties as prime determinants of the hedonic effect, but let me hastily point out that

C. Pfaffmann 221

specific training and experience may make some unpleasant odors and tastes acceptable or even preferred. I am reminded here of the whiskey drinker's development so aptly described by Brown (1955).

Straight whiskey, when first ingested, typically effects rather violent defense reactions. Because of this, the novice drinker usually begins with sweet liqueurs, 'pink ladies', and wines, and slowly works his way through a series of beverages characterized by the gradual disappearance of cola and ginger ale additives. Finally, only plain water or even nothing need be mixed with the raw product. To the hardened drinker, straight whiskey does not taste bad – *not bad at all!* (It is thus that a product euphemistically labelled 'neutral spirits' becomes indeed psychologically neutral.)

Although this description appeared in defense of a drive reduction formulation of behavior and learning, the mere fact that drive reduction was supported and buttressed by the use of sweet and 'pleasant' stimuli seems to have been overlooked. There is no convincing evidence that the primary relation between hedonic tone and sensory stimulation is entirely acquired. Indeed, quite the converse seems to be true.

The relation of sensory stimulation to hedonic process has been noted by earlier workers. Sherrington (1906) noted that the stimulation of contact receptors, as contrasted with distance receptors, is characterized by strong affective tone and that the contact receptors stand in very close relation to consummatory responses. Stimulation of the touch receptors of the lips and touch and taste in the mouth initiates reflex movements that precede the act of swallowing. Troland (1928) spoke of three classes of stimulus reception: nociception, beneception, and neutroception. The principal nociceptor system was pain, but other examples were hunger, thirst, the taste of bitter, strong salts and acids, and certain foul or repugnant odors, etc. In the beneceptor class were the sense organs mediating erotic behavior, the taste of sugar, and certain other odors. Vision, hearing, touch, and proprioception were relegated to neutroception. Although Troland's criterion was that of biological utility, Young (1936) pointed to the high correlation between pleasantness and beneception, unpleasantness and nociception. He also notes that there is a frequent correlation between pleasantness and approach, and unpleasantness and avoidance; and further that the affective responses to simple colors and tones are much weaker than those evoked by odors, tastes, cutaneous or organic stimuli.

In his work on palatability, Young espouses a clearly hedonistic theory of reinforcement in which he treats the affective process as a postulate, an intervening variable (Young, 1959). The reactions of animals to taste solutions then can only be described when reference is made to their positive or negative hedonic effects. Thus, sugar solutions are hedonically positive, and the level of acceptability is directly proportional to the logarithm of the concentration. Salt on the other hand does not show this one-to-one correspondence with sensory intensity. Low concentrations of salt are said to be hedonically positive for the rat, but at high concentrations are hedonically negative. Such terminology often appears simply to rename approach or avoidance behavior with hedonistic synonyms for we all know what we mean when we say in laboratory jargon that the rat likes sugar. We know he will take it in preference to water, he may press a bar for it, he may take it even when it is adulterated with something 'doesn't like' such as quinine. But such usage does not necessarily indicate the primacy of the hedonic process; we must have further experimental study of acceptance and rejection and of their relation to hedonic or affective processes.

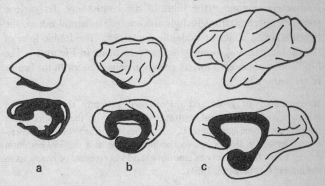

Figure 10 Lateral and medial surfaces of brains of rabbit (a), cat (b), and monkey (c) drawn roughly to scale. The drawings illustrate that the limbic lobe, represented in black, forms a common denominator in the brains of all mammals. (After a drawing in *Journal of Neurosurgery*)

Thus it is abundantly clear that, instigation of consummatory response (or of rejection), reinforcement of instrumental responses and elicitation of hedonic effect are all closely related and that reproducible stimulus functions can be demonstrated for each. A definitive choice as to which of these is primary cannot yet be made. I would like to propose that sensory stimulation *per se* together with its ensuring central neural events be considered as a prime determinant in the chain of events culminating in acceptance behavior, reinforcement and hedonic effect. The further study of such stimulus functions and their analysis particularly at the physiological level is a problem that should merit the highest priority.

I should like to turn to the possible physiological mechanisms in the reinforcing and hedonic functions of stimuli.

The physiology of reinforcement and sensory affect

The studies of cranial self-stimulation (Brady, 1958; Olds, 1958; Olds and Milner, 1954) show that the reward and punishment systems within the brain itself, but particularly the reward systems, have been found to depend in large measure upon the limbic system. In classical neuroanatomy this was known as the rhinencephalon or smell brain, but its relation to olfaction seems less and less particular. The limbic lobe including the hippocampus completely surrounds the hilus of the hemisphere. Its various subcortical cell stations include the amygdala, septal nuclei, the hypothalamus, anterior thalamic nuclei, etc. The limbic lobe of the rabbit, cat, and monkey is shown in black in Figure 10. The limbic lobe appears to form a common denominator in the brains of all mammals.

Its constancy of gross and microscopic structure throughout the phylogeny of the mammal contrasts strikingly with the mushrooming neopallium which surrounds it. . . . Papez theorized that the experimental evidence also points to the limbic lobe as a cortical common denominator for a variety of emotional and viscerosomatic reactions in the mammal (MacLean, 1954).

There is increasing evidence of a sensory viscerosomatic influx into the limbic system. In pathological involvements, particularly of the temporal lobe, discharges in this part of the brain may be associated with a wide variety of auras involving all the body senses as well as a great number of feeling and emotional states. Among the more purely sensory auras are crude olfactory sensations; alimentary symptoms including taste, thirst, hunger, nausea; and somatic sensations ranging from pains to paresthesia. Prolonged rhythmic responses can be elicited in the pyriform area by olfactory, gustatory, and painful stimulation (MacLean, 1954). MacLean notes that all three of these senses accent the quality and intensity of a stimulus rather than its spatial relationships.

I do not wish to give the impression that this system is essentially one for viscerosomatic sensation, for it is also implicated in a variety of complex effects such as the Klüver–Bucy syndrome (1958), memory losses (Penfield, 1958), the lowering of rage thresholds in some cases or increased docility after ablation in others (Bard and Mountcastle, 1947; Green, 1958; Schreiner and Kling, 1953; Spiegel, Miller and Oppenheimer, 1940), and a variety of cranial self-stimulation effects (Brady, 1958; Olds, 1958; Olds and Milner, 1954). The details of these relations are beyond the scope of the present discourse. What I wish to emphasize is that there are significant sensory inputs into this system which may relate to the hedonic and reinforcing features of stimulation as compared with either the cognitive or arousal functions.

Stellar and his colleagues (Sprague, Chambers, Stellar, Liu and Robson, 1958; Stellar, Chambers, Liu, Levitt and Sprague, 1958) at the University of Pennsylvania have made some interesting studies of chronic animals with extensive lesions in the lateral lemniscal, primary sensory pathways. I was struck with their description of the lemniscal animals, i.e the sensorially restricted animals displayed little affect in any situation, except, perhaps the most extreme. They flex and tend to pull away from a pinch, but do not attack or show any autonomic response. They showed little or no aversive reaction to an ether cone, although they lacrimated and sneezed. Prior to the operation, they solicited petting and responded to it well; afterwards they gave no reaction to petting.

These observations suggest that the affective response to sensory stimuli might be mediated by the lemniscal and not the diffuse arousal system, which, it might be noted, already seems to have been theoretically overworked by psychologists. I would like to remind you of the 'thalamic syndrome', described by Head and Holmes (1911). Lesions in the region of the thalamus are characterized by 'overreaction', by excessive affectivity, for both pleasurable as well as painful sensations. This is pathology characterized by the affective modification of sensation. Although the 'syndrome thalamique' is well known to clinical neurologists, its exact mechanism is still not clear. For our purposes, it is sufficient to note that in this condition, the basic hedonic responses to sensory stimulation, some of the 'pleasures of sensation' as well as the displeasures, can be unmasked. In short, I am suggesting that the affective consequences of sensory stimulation are mediated by processes that depend upon the primary projection systems and their ramifications in thalamic and old brain neural connections. Obviously much work is required to place these speculations upon a more solid foundation.

Summary

And now let me briefly summarize. I alluded briefly to the different roles of stimuli and sensory processes in the behavioral economy of the organism. I pointed out that traditionally sensory processes were studied largely in relation to discrimination or so-called cognitive functions. But stimuli have been shown to have other neural and behavioral functions as arousal and reinforcement. I then went on to discuss in further detail certain of our own experiments on taste as a model system to show the relation of gustatory stimulation to the control of consummatory responses and the reinforcement of instrumental behavior. It was shown that there is increasing support for the idea that gustatory stimulation *per se* is capable of eliciting and reinforcing behavior in its own right. We might say 'sweet for sweet's sake'. I then led into the problem of hedonic or affective responses to such stimuli; and, although a good correlation between affective response and reinforcement could be demonstrated, a statement as to their exact relation must await further study, particularly at the physiological level. Finally, I speculated as to the psychophysiological mechanisms that might underlie reinforcement and the affective responses to sensory stimuli. My basic theme has been that sensory stimulation '*qua* stimulation' plays a significant role in the motivation as well as guidance of behavior – euphemistically we might say, in controlling behavior for the 'pleasures of sensation'.

References

BARD, P., and MOUNTCASTLE, V. B. (1947), 'Some forebrain mechanisms involved in expression of rage with special reference to suppression of angry behavior', *A.R.N.M.D.*, vol. 27, pp. 362–404.

BARE, J. K. (1949), 'The specific hunger for sodium chloride in normal and adrenalectomized white rats', *J. compar. physiol. Psychol.*, vol. 42, pp. 242–53.

BEEBE-CENTER, J. G. (1951), 'Feeling and emotion', in H. Helson (ed.), *Theoretical Foundations of Psychology*, Van Nostrand, pp. 254–317.

BINDRA, D. (1959), *Motivation, a Systematic Reinterpretation*, Ronald.

BRADY, J. V. (1958), 'Temporal and emotiona lfactors related to electrical self-stimulation of the limbic system', in H. H. Jasper, L. D. Proctor, R. S. Knighton, W. C. Noshay and R. T. Costello (eds.), *Reticular Formation of the Brain*, Little, Brown, pp. 689–704.

BREMER, F. (1935), 'Cerveau "isole" et physiologie du sommeil', *CR Soc. Biol.*, vol. 118, pp. 1235–41.

BROWN, J. S. (1955), 'Pleasure-seeking behavior and the drive-reduction hypothesis', *Psychol. Rev.*, vol. 62, pp. 169–79.

CAMERON, A. T. (1947), 'The taste sense and the relative sweetness of sugars and other substances', *Sci. Rep. Ser.*, no. 9, Sugar Research Foundation.

CAMPBELL, B. A. (1957), 'Auditory and aversion thresholds of rats for bands of noise', *Sci.*, vol. 125, pp. 596–7.

CAMPBELL, B. A. (1958), 'Absolute and relative sucrose preference thresholds for hungry and satiated rats', *J. compar. physiol. Psychol.*, vol. 51, pp. 795–800.

CARPENTER, J. A. (1956), 'Species differences in taste preference', *J. compar. physiol. Psychol.*, vol. 49, pp. 139–44.

COLLIER, G., and SISKEL, M. Jr (1959), 'Performance as a joint function of amount of reinforcement and interreinforcement interval', *J. exper. Psychol.*, vol. 57, pp. 115–20.

COPPOCK, H. W., and CHAMBERS, R. M. (1954), 'Reinforcement of position preference by automatic intravenous injection of glucose', *J. compar. physiol. Psychol.*, vol. 47, pp. 355–7.

ENGEL, R. (1928), 'Experimentelle Untersuchungen über die Abhängigkeit der Lust und Unlust von der Reizstärke beim Geschmackssinn', *Arch. ges. Psychol.*, vol. 64, pp. 1–36.

FRINGS, H. (1946), 'Biological backgrounds of the "sweet tooth"' *Turtox News*, vol. 24, no. 8.

GALAMBOS, R. (1956), 'Suppression of auditory nerve activity by stimulation of efferent fibers to cochlea', *J. Neurophysiol.*, vol. 19 pp. 424–37.

GREEN, J. D. (1958), 'The rhinencephalon and behavior', in *Neurological Basis of Behavior*, Ciba Foundation Symposium, Little, Brown, pp. 222–35.

GUTTMAN, N. (1953), 'Operant conditioning, extinction and periodic reinforcement in relation to concentration of sucrose used as reinforcing agent', *J. exper. Psychol.*, vol. 46, pp. 213–24.

GUTTMAN, N. (1954), 'Equal reinforcement values for sucrose and glucose solutions compared with equal sweetness values', *J. compar. physiol. Psychol.*, vol. 47, pp. 358–61.

HAGBARTH, K. E., and KERR, D. I. B. (1954), 'Central influences on spinal afferent conduction', *J. Neurophysiol.*, vol. 17, pp. 295–307.

HAGSTROM, E. C., and PFAFFMANN, C. (1959), 'The relative taste effectiveness of different sugars for the rat', *J. compar. physiol. Psychol.*, vol. 52, pp. 259–62.

HARLOW, H. F. (1953), 'Motivation as a factor in the acquisition of new responses', in *Current Theory and Research in Motivation*, University of Nebraska Press, pp. 24–49.

HEAD, H., and HOLMES, G. (1911), 'Sensory disturbances from cerebral lesion', *Brain*, vol. 34, pp. 102–254.

HEBB, D. O. (1958), 'Alice in wonderland or psychology among the biological sciences', in H. F. Harlow and C. N. Woolsey (eds.), *Biological and Biochemical Bases of Behavior*, University of Wisconsin Press, pp. 451–67.

HEBB, D. O. (1958a), *A Textbook of Psychology*, Saunders.

HERNANDEZ-PEON, R. (1955), 'Central mechanisms controlling conduction along central sensory pathways', *Acta. neurol. latino. Amer.*, vol. 1, pp. 256–64.

HUGHES, L. H. (1957), 'Saccharine reinforcement in a T maze', *J. compar. physiol. Psychol.*, vol. 50, pp. 431–35.

KELLER, F. S., and SCHOENFELD, W. N. (1950), *Principles of Psychology*, Appleton-Century-Crofts.

KLING, J. W., HOROWITZ, L., and DELHAGEN, J. E. (1956), 'Light as a positive reinforcer for rat responding', *Psychol. Rep.*, vol. 2, pp. 337–40.

KLÜVER, H. (1958), 'The temporal lobe syndrome produced by bilateral ablations', in *Neurological Foundations of Behavior*, Ciba Foundation Symposium, Little, Brown, pp. 175–86.

LEMAGNEN, J. (1955), 'Le rôle de la receptivité gustative au chlorure de sodium dans le mécanisme de régulation de la pris d'eau chez le rat blanc', *J. Physiol. Path. gen.*, vol. 47, pp. 405–18.

LINDSLEY, D. B. (1951), 'Emotion', in S. S. Stevens (ed.), *Handbook of Experimental Psychology*, Wiley, ch. 14.

MCCLEARY, R. A. (1953), 'Taste and postingestion factors in specific hunger behavior', *J. compar. physiol. Psychol.*, vol. 46, pp. 411–21.

MACLEAN, P. D. (1954), 'The limbic system and its hippocampal formation in animals and their possible application to man', *J. Neurosurg.*, vol. 11, pp. 29–44.

MacLean, P. D., Horwitz, N. H., and Robinson, F. (1952), 'Olfactory-like responses in pyriform area to non-olfactory stimulation', *Yale J. Biol. Med.*, vol. 25, pp. 159–72.

MacLeod, S. (1952), 'A construction and attempted validation of sensory sweetness scales', *J. exper. Psychol.*, vol. 44, pp. 316–23.

Magoun, H. W. (1958), *The Waking Brain*, Charles C. Thomas.

Miller, N. E. (1957), 'Experiments on motivation', *Sci.*, vol. 126, pp. 1271–8.

Miller, N. E. (1959), 'Liberalization of basic S–R concepts: extensions to conflict behavior, motivation, and social learning', in S. Koch, (ed.), *Psychology: A Study of a Science*, McGraw-Hill, vol. 2.

Montgomery, K. C. (1952), 'Exploratory behavior and its relation to spontaneous alterations in a series of maze exposures', *J. compar. physiol. Psychol.*, vol. 45, pp. 50–57.

Olds, J. (1958), 'Self-stimulation of the brain', *Sci.*, vol. 127, pp. 315–24.

Olds, J. S., and Milner, P. (1954), 'Positive reinforcement produced by electrical stimulation of septal area and other regions of the rat brain', *J. compar. physiol. Psychol.*, vol. 47, pp. 419–27.

Penfield, W. (1958), 'The role of the temporal cortex in recall of past experience and interpretation of the present', in *Neurological Foundations of Behavior*, Ciba Foundation Symposium, Little, Brown, pp. 149–74.

Pfaffmann, C. (1955), 'Gustatory nerve impulses in rat, cat and rabbit' *J. Neurophysiol.*, vol. 18, pp. 429–40.

Pfaffmann, C. (1957), 'Taste mechanisms in preference behavior', *Amer. J. clin. Nutr.*, vol. 5, pp. 142- 7.

Pfaffmann, C. (1958), *Flavor Research and Food Acceptance*, Reinhold.

Pfaffmann, C. (1959), 'The afferent code for sensory quality', *Amer. Psychologist*, vol. 14, pp. 226–232.

Pilgrim, F. J. (1957), 'The components of food acceptance and their measurement', *Amer. J. clin. Nutr.*, vol. 5, pp. 142–7.

Richter, C. P. (1942), 'Self-regulatory functions', *Harvey Lectures*, vol. 38, pp. 63–103.

Richter, C. P., and Campbell, K. H. (1940), 'Taste thresholds and taste preferences of rats for five common sugars', *J. Nutr.*, vol. 20, pp. 31–46.

Schlosberg, H. (1954), 'Three dimensions of emotion', *Psychol. Rev.*, vol. 61, pp. 81–8.

Schreiner, L., and Kling, A. (1953), 'Behavioral change following rhinencephalic injury in the cat', *J. Neurophysiol.*, vol. 16, pp. 643–59.

Sheffield, F. D., and Roby, T. B. (1950), 'Reward value of a nonnutritive sweet taste', *J. compar. physiol. Psychol.*, vol. 43, pp. 471–81.

Sheffield, F. D., Roby, T. B., and Campbell, B. A. (1954), 'Drive reduction versus consummatory behavior as determinants of reinforcement', *J. compar. physiol. Psychol.*, vol. 47, pp. 349–54.

Sherrington, C. (1906), *The Integrative Action of the Nervous System*, Constable.

SHUFORD, E. H. Jnr (1959), 'Palatability and osmotic pressure of glucose and sucrose solutions as determinants of intake', *J. compar. physiol. Psychol.*, vol. 52, pp. 150–53.

SKINNER, B. F. (1953), *Science and Human Behavior*, Macmillan Co.

SMITH, M., and DUFFY, M. (1955), 'The effects of intragastric injection of various substances on subsequent bar pressing', *J. compar. physiol. Psychol.*, vol. 48, pp. 387–91.

SMITH, M., and DUFFY, M. (1957), 'Evidence for a dual reinforcing effect of sugar', *J. compar. physiol. Psychol.*, vol. 50, pp. 242–7.

SOULAIRAC, A. (1947), 'La physiologie d'un comportement: l'Appetit glucidique et sa régulation neuro-endocrinienne chez les rongeurs', *Bull. biol.*, vol. 81, pp. 273–432.

SPENCE, K. W. (1956), *Behavior Theory and Conditioning*, Yale University Press.

SPIEGEL, E., MILLER, H., and OPPENHEIMER, J. (1940), 'Forebrain and rage reactions' *J. Neurophysiol.*, vol. 3, pp. 538–48.

SPRAGUE, J. M., CHAMBERS, W. W., STELLAR, E., LIU, C. N., and ROBSON, K. (1958), 'Chronic reticular and lemniscal lesions in cats', *Fed. Proc.*, vol. 17, p. 154.

STELLAR, E., CHAMBERS, W. W., LIU, C. N., LEVITT, M., and SPRAGUE, J. M. (1958), 'Behavior of cats with chronic reticular and lemniscal lesions', *Fed. Proc.*, vol. 17, p. 156.

STELLAR, E., HYMAN, R., and SAMET, S. (1954), 'Gastric factors controlling water and salt solution drinking', *J. compar. physiol., Psychol.*, vol. 47, pp. 220–26.

TROLAND, L. T. (1928), *The Fundamentals of Human Motivation*, Van Nostrand.

WARREN, R. P., and PFAFFMANN, C. (1958), 'Early experience and taste aversion', *J. compar. physiol. Psychol.*, vol. 52, pp. 263–6.

YOUNG, P. T. (1936), *Motivation of behavior*, Wiley.

YOUNG, P. T. (1957), 'Psychologic factors regulating the feeding process' *Amer. J. clin. Nutr.*, vol. 5, pp. 154–61.

YOUNG, P. T. (1959), 'The role of affective processes in learning and motivation', *Psychol. Rev.*, vol. 66, pp. 104–25.

YOUNG, P. T., and GREENE, J. T. (1953), 'Quantity of food ingested as a measure of relative acceptability', *J. compar. physiol. Psychol.*, vol. 46, pp. 288–94.

YOUNG, P. T., and SHUFORD, E. H. Jr (1954), 'Intensity, duration and repetition of hedonic processes as related to acquisition of motives', *J. compar. physiol. Psychol.*, vol. 47, pp. 298–305.

YOUNG, P. T., and SHUFORD, E. H. Jr (1955), 'Quantitative control of motivation through sucrose solution of different concentrations' *J. compar. physiol. Psychol.*, vol. 48, pp. 114–18.

24 P. K. Levison and J. P. Flynn

The Objects Attacked by Cats during Stimulation of
the Hypothalamus[1]

P. K. Levison and J. P. Flynn, 'The objects attacked by cats during
stimulation of the hypothalamus', *Animal Behaviour*, volume 13, 1965
pp. 217–20.

Introduction

Many laboratory cats never attack a rat spontaneously. If electrodes are properly implanted in the hypothalamus of one of these
cats, the animal will, when stimulated electrically, regularly
launch a directed attack upon a rat in its cage (Wasman and
Flynn, 1962). The initiation of attack, its latency, duration, and
termination can be controlled by the experimenter. The question
the present study sought to answer is whether or not such a cat
would attack other objects similar to a rat as readily as it attacks a
rat. Is the cat indiscriminate in its attack or is the range of objects
attacked limited? Furthermore, is the persistence of the attack
related to the particular object of attack?

Method

Electrodes were aseptically implanted in the hypothalamus of
each of 9 cats which had been tested previously and found not to
attack rats spontaneously. These electrodes had their tips bared
for 0·5 mm. An additional electrode whose tip was in the table of
the skull served as an indifferent electrode.

The electrical stimulus to the hypothalamus consisted of a
train of biphasic square waves whose frequency was 62·5 p.p.s.
The duration of the pulse train was limited to a maximum of 32
seconds. Ordinarily it was terminated less than 2 seconds after the
cat attacked the object. Given this procedure, the attack might
appear to be a response that has been reinforced by withdrawal of
an aversive stimulus. However, unpublished data indicate the
attack can be independent of the termination of the stimulus.

1. Our thanks go to Mildred Groves for her work in preparing the
histological material for this study.

Furthermore, Roberts and Kiess (1964) have demonstrated that there is positive reinforcement in the cat's attacking a rat, a finding that contradicts the idea that the stimulation is aversive. The peak-to-peak current of the pulses were kept stable for each cat during the experiment. The current used for different cats ranged from 0·2 mA. to 0·65 mA. Two durations of the individual pulses were used. One was 1 ms. for each half of the biphasic wave (producing an attack latency of 6 to 8 seconds at the selected intensity); the other was increased to produce an attack latency of 2 to 4 seconds, being of the order of 2·5 ms. These stimulus parameters were selected prior to the formal experiment. The stimulation was monopolar for 7 cats, bipolar in the case of 2 animals. The initial testing of the electrodes was carried out with the 3 test objects in the cage to avoid associating a particular object with attack. The apparatus has been described in greater detail by Wasman and Flynn (1962).

The placements of the electrodes were determined histologically, except for the electrodes in cat 1313P whose brain could not be suitably prepared. At the completion of the experiment, the cats were perfused with a normal saline solution, and then with 10 per cent formalin. The brains were removed and sectioned, and the sections were stained for cell bodies.

In the choice situation 3 objects were placed at the front of a cage and the cat was positioned in the centre of the cage, facing front. The trials were carried out in a glass fronted cage 25·5 inches wide, 21·5 inches deep, 24 inches high. There were 2 experimental sessions, with typically at least 1 day intervening between sessions. Thirty-three trials were given in a session, and a 5 minute interval occurred between trials. In addition to the object attacked, the cat's persistence in attacking was noted. Initially the criterion for persistence was at least 3 bites after first contact. It was observed that these took place within 2 seconds, and thereafter persistence was defined as continuing to attack for 2 seconds. The stimulation was terminated 2 seconds after attack or after thirty seconds if the cat failed to attack. Some cats did not attack on every trial (5 per cent of the trials). Attack is defined as biting the object or striking it with a paw.

An anaesthetized white rat and a stuffed white rat were present on each trial, the third object in the cage being varied from trial to trial. The stuffed rat was prepared by skinning a rat, stuffing the skin with cotton batting, and drying the preparation in a moderate heat, so that the skin retained some flexibility. A new stuffed rat was prepared for each animal because they became stiff as they aged and were torn apart in the course of the experiment. To a human being the odour of the stuffed rat was detectable and different from that of the anaesthetized or recently killed rat. Preliminary experiments indicated that preference between anaesthetized and unanaesthetized rats as attack objects was small.

The third object was either a hairy toy dog, or a rectangular block of styrofoam, or a block of foam rubber all similar in size to a live rat. Each cat had its own set of objects.

There is a tendency for cats stimulated in the hypothalamus to turn in the direction contralateral to the side stimulated. This increases the likelihood that an object located on that side will be attacked first. In order to control for this effect, the positions of the objects were varied in blocks of trials.

Results
Object selection

Eight of the nine cats attacked the third object in the cage less frequently than the anaesthetized rat or the stuffed rat (Figure 1). Separate X^2 analyses of the results of the first eight cats yielded a $p < 0.01$ in each instance. The ninth cat attacked indiscriminately. The two levels of stimulation did not lead to differing results, so the data from them were combined.

The object in the third group that was most frequently attacked was the hairy toy dog ($p < 0.01$ by X^2 analyses). Seven of the nine cats never attacked the hard styrofoam block or the soft rubber block.

Six of the cats attacked the stuffed rat and the anaesthetized rat equally often, within the limits of random variation. Three of the cats, those on the top row of Figure 1, attacked the anaesthetized rat significantly more often than they attacked the stuffed rat.

Persistent attacks

The cats made persistent attacks on the anaesthetized rat more often than on the stuffed rat. For the group, 89 per cent of the attacks made on the anaesthetized rat were persistent ones, while

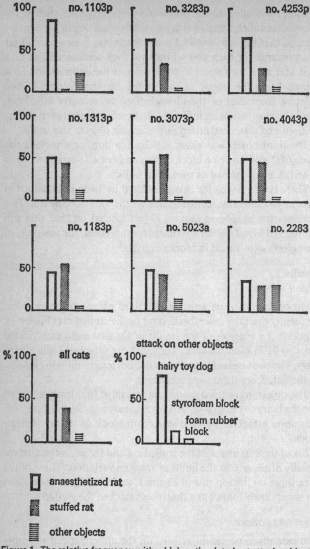

Figure 1 The relative frequency with which a stimulated cat attacks objects other than a stuffed or anaesthetized rat is significantly lower than when it attacks rats. Only in the case of the last animal, No. 2283, is the cat indiscriminate. Most of the attacks in the third category were made upon a hairy toy dog

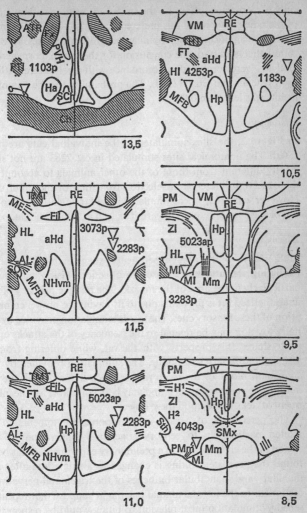

Figure 2 The sites within the hypothalamus from which attack was elicited are indicated by triangles, and the sites are accompanied by the number of the animal. The numbers at the right bottom corner of each section indicate frontal sections of the Horsley-Clarke coordinates as given by Ajmone-Marsan and Jasper. The stimulation was bipolar in the case of cat 2283 P. Cat 5023 P was stimulated monopolarly at two different sites, each site being used for one complete session

only 67 per cent of those on the stuffed rat were persistent. Eight of the nine cats showed this preference. In the individual animals, statistical significance was obtained in only three cases. In order to test the validity of the conclusion for the group, corrected X^2 analyses were combined in accordance with a procedure outlined by Mosteller and Bush (1954). The probability for the combined results was less than 0·001.

Histology

In Figure 2, the sites stimulated in the individual cats are indicated. The anatomical sites stimulated in cat 2283 are not sufficiently different from those of the other animals to account for the observed difference in selection from that of the other cats. However, cat 2283, when stimulated would frequently look to the top of the cage and jump toward it as well as attack the rat.

Discussion

Preliminary extirpation experiments suggest that the senses mediating the attack response are olfaction, vision and touch, particularly in the area of the muzzle. The relative primacy of the anaesthetized rat is probably due to its having the proper combination of these sensory cues. The tactile stimulation provided by the hairy toy dog may be related to the frequency of the attacks upon it. It shares this property with the rat, while differing from it visually and in terms of odour. The stimulation provided by the styrofoam block or the foam rubber block differed from the rat in all three sensory aspects, and may be accountable for the infrequent attacks made upon these objects.

The persistence of a cat's attack upon a rat appears to be related particularly to sensory trigeminal innervation in the region of the cat's mouth. In a preliminary experiment, it has been found that persistent biting is changed to a single bite after the maxillary and mandibular branches of the trigeminal nerve were sectioned. In the normal animal one might suppose that repeated sensory stimulation most relevant to biting would be responsible for the persistence of the attack.

One can regard the stimulation of the hypothalamus as not only inducing certain initial forms of activity, such as movement around the cage, and sniffing, but as also setting limits to the sensory objects which are capable of modifying this initial behaviour and bringing it to the level of a full blown attack.

The data indicate that the range of objects attacked by cats electrically stimulated is limited and that persistence of attack is also related to the attack objects.

Summary

Cats that attack as a result of electrical stimulation of the hypothalamus are not indiscriminate in their attack. They attack rats more frequently than other objects. Seven of the nine cats never attacked blocks of styrofoam or foam rubber comparable in size to a rat. Even though the majority of the cats attacked stuffed rats as often as they attacked anaesthetized rats, they persisted more frequently in their attack upon an anaesthetized rat than upon a stuffed rat.

References

JASPER, H. H., and AJMONE-MARSAN, C. A., 'Stereotaxic atlas of the diencephalon of the cat', National Research Council of Canada, n.d.

MACDONNELL, M., and FLYNN, J. P., 'The senses mediating attack by a cat upon a rat', in preparation.

MOSTELLER, F., and BUSH, R. R. (1954), 'Selected quantitative techniques', in G. Lindzey (ed.), *Handbook of Social Psychology*, Addison-Wesley.

ROBERTS, W. W., and KIESS, H. O. (1964), 'Motivational properties of hypothalamic aggression in cats', *J. compar. physiol. Psychol.*, vol. 58, pp. 187–93.

WASMAN, M., and FLYNN, J. P. (1962), 'Directed attack elicited from the hypothalamus', *Arch. Neurol.*, vol. 6, pp. 220–27.

25 H. F. Harlow and S. J. Suomi

Nature of Love – Simplified

H. F. Harlow and S. J. Suomi, 'Nature of love – simplified'
American Psychologist, volume 25, 1970, pp. 161–8.

The cloth surrogate and its wire surrogate sibling (see Plate 1) entered into scientific history as of 1958 (Harlow, 1958). The cloth surrogate was originally designed to test the relative importance of body contact in contrast to activities associated with the breast, and the results were clear beyond all expectation. Body contact was of overpowering importance by any measure taken, even contact time, as shown in Figure 1.

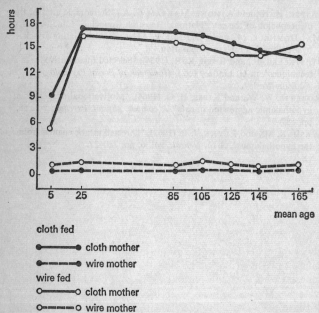

Figure 1 Contact time to cloth and wire surrogate

However, the cloth surrogate, beyond its power to measure the relative importance of a host of variables determining infant affection for the mother, exhibited another surprising trait, one of great independent usefulness. Even though the cloth mother was inanimate, it was able to impart to its infant such emotional security that the infant would, in the surrogate's presence, explore a strange situation and manipulate available physical objects (see Plate 2), or animate objects (see Plate 3). Manipulation of animate objects leads to play if these animate objects are age-mates, and play is the variable of primary importance in the development of normal social, sexual, and maternal functions, as described by Harlow and Harlow (1965). It is obvious that surrogate mothers, which are more docile and manipulative than real monkey mothers, have a wide range of experimental uses.

Simplified surrogate

Although the original surrogates turned out to be incredibly efficient dummy mothers, they presented certain practical problems. The worst of the problems was that of cleanliness. Infant monkeys seldom soil their real mothers' bodies, though we do not know how this is achieved. However, infant monkeys soiled the bodies of the original cloth surrogates with such efficiency and enthusiasm as to present a health problem and, even worse, a financial problem resulting from laundering. Furthermore, we believed that the original cloth surrogate was too steeply angled and thereby relatively inaccessible for cuddly clinging by the neonatal monkey.

In the hope of alleviating practical problems inherent in the original cloth surrogate, we constructed a family of simplified surrogates. The simplified surrogate is mounted on a rod attached to a lead base 4 inches in diameter, angled upward at 25°, and projected through the surrogate's body for 4 inches, so that heads may be attached if desired. The body of the simplified surrogate is only 6 inches long, $2\frac{1}{2}$ inches in diameter, and stands approximately 3 inches off the ground. Plate 4 shows an original cloth surrogate and simplified surrogate placed side by side.

As can be seen in Plate 5, infants readily cling to these simplified surrogates of smaller body and decreased angle of inclination. Infant monkeys do soil the simplified surrogate, but the art and act of soiling is very greatly reduced. Terry cloth slip-covers can be made easily and relatively cheaply, alleviating, if not eliminating, laundry problems. Thus, the simplified surrogate is a far more practical dummy mother than the original cloth surrogate.

Surrogate variables
Lactation

Although the original surrogate papers (Harlow, 1958; Harlow and Zimmermann, 1959) were written as if activities associated with the breast, particularly nursing, were of no importance, this is doubtlessly incorrect. There were no statistically significant differences in time spent by the babies on the lactating versus nonlactating cloth surrogates and on the lactating versus non-lactating wire surrogates, but the fact is that there were consistent preferences for both the cloth and the wire lactating surrogates and that these tendencies held for both the situations of time on surrogate and frequency of surrogate preference when the infant was exposed to a fear stimulus. Thus, if one can accept a statistically insignificant level of confidence, consistently obtained from four situations, one will properly conclude that nursing is a minor variable but one of more than measurable importance operating to bind the infant to the mother.

To demonstrate experimentally that activities associated with the breasts were variables of significant importance, we built two sets of differentially colored surrogates, tan and light blue; and using a two by two Latin square design, we arranged a situation such that the surrogate of one color lactated and the other did not. As can be seen in Figure 2, the infants showed a consistent preference for the lactating surrogate when contact comfort was held constant. The importance of the lactational variable probably decreases with time. But at least we had established the hard fact that hope springs eternal in the human breast and even longer in the breast, undressed.

Facial variables

In the original surrogates we created an ornamental face for the cloth surrogate and a simple dog face for the wire surrogate. I

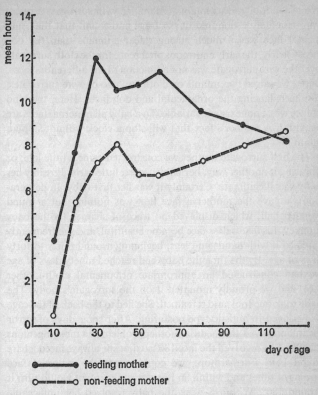

Figure 2 Infant preference for lactating cloth surrogate

was working with few available infants and against time to prepare a presidential address for the 1958 American Psychological Association Convention. On the basis of sheer intuition, I was convinced that the ornamental cloth-surrogate face would become a stronger fear stimulus than the dog face when fear of the unfamiliar matured in the monkeys from about seventy to a hundred and ten days (Harlow and Zimmermann, 1959; Sackett, 1966). But since we wanted each surrogate to have an identifiable face and had few infants, we made no effort to balance faces by resorting to a feebleminded two by two Latin square design.

Subsequently, we have run two brief unpublished experiments.

We tested four rhesus infants unfamiliar with surrogate faces at approximately a hundred days of age and found that the ornamental face was a much stronger fear stimulus than the dog face. Clearly, the early enormous preference for the cloth surrogate over the wire surrogate was not a function of the differential faces. Later, we raised two infants on cloth and two on wire surrogates, counterbalancing the ornamental and dog faces. Here, the kind of face was a nonexistent variable. To a baby all maternal faces are beautiful. A mother's face that will stop a clock will not stop an infant.

The first surrogate mother we constructed came a little late, or phrasing it another way, her baby came a little early. Possibly her baby was illegitimate. Certainly it was her first baby. In desperation we gave the mother a face that was nothing but a round wooden ball, which displayed no trace of shame. To the baby monkey this featureless face became beautiful, and she frequently caressed it with hands and legs, beginning around thirty to forty days of age. By the time the baby had reached ninety days of age we had constructed an appropriate ornamental cloth-mother face, and we proudly mounted it on the surrogate's body. The baby took one look and screamed. She fled to the back of the cage and cringed in autistic-type posturing. After some days of terror the infant solved the medusa-mother problem in a most ingenious manner. She revolved the face 180° so that she always faced a bare round ball! Furthermore, we could rotate the maternal face dozens of times and within an hour or so the infant would turn it around 180°. Within a week the baby resolved her unfaceable problem once and for all. She lifted the maternal head from the body, rolled it into the corner, and abandoned it. No one can blame the baby. She had lived with and loved a faceless mother but she could not love a two-faced mother.

These data imply that an infant visually responds to the earliest version of mother he encounters, that the mother he grows accustomed to is the mother he relies upon. Subsequent changes, especially changes introduced after maturation of the fear response, elicit this response with no holds barred. Comparisons of effects of baby-sitters on human infants might be made.

Body-surface variables

We have received many questions and complaints concerning the surrogate surfaces, wire and terry cloth, used in the original studies. This mountain of mail breaks down into two general categories: that wire is aversive, and that other substances would be equally effective if not better than terry cloth in eliciting a clinging response.

The answer to the first matter in question is provided by observation: wire is not an aversive stimulus to neonatal monkeys, for they spend much time climbing on the sides of their hardware-

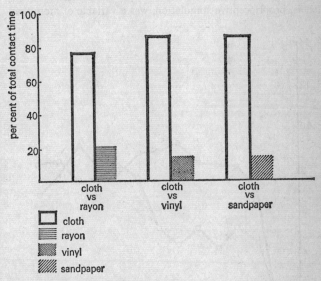

Figure 3 Effect of surface on surrogate contact

cloth cages and exploring this substance orally and tactually. A few infants have required medical treatment from protractedly pressing their faces too hard and too long against the cage sides. Obviously, however, wire does not provide contact comfort.

In an attempt to quantify preference of various materials, an exploratory study[1] was performed in which each of four infants

1. We wish to thank Carol Furchner, who conducted this experiment and the described experiment in progress

was presented with a choice between surrogates covered with terry cloth versus rayon, vinyl, or rough-grade sandpaper. As shown in Figure 3, the infants demonstrated a clear preference for the cloth surrogates, and no significant preference difference between the other body surfaces. An extension of this study is in progress in which an attempt is being made to further quantify and rank order the preference for these materials by giving infants equal exposure time to all four materials.

Motion variables

In the original two papers, we pointed out that rocking motion, that is, proprioceptive stimulation, was a variable of more than

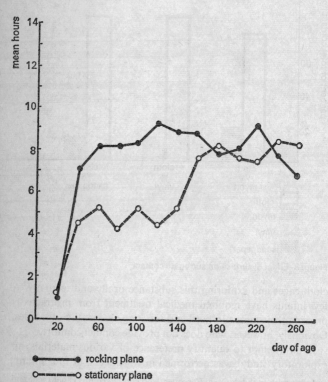

Figure 4 Infant contact to stationary and rocking planes

statistical significance, particularly early in the infant's life, in binding the infant to the mother figure. We measured this by comparing the time the infants spent on two identical planes, one rocking and one stationary (see Figure 4) and two identical cloth surrogates, one rocking and one stationary (see Figure 5).

Temperature variables

To study another variable, temperature, we created some 'hot mamma' surrogates. We did this by inserting heating coils in the maternal bodies that raised the external surrogate body surface about 10° F. In one experiment, we heated the surface of a wire surrogate and let four infant macaques choose between this

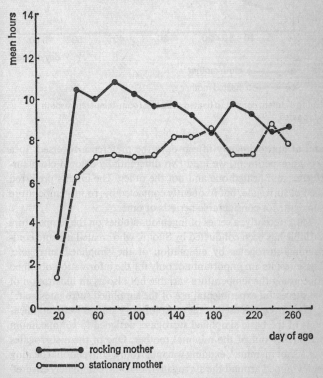

Figure 5 Infant contact to stationary and rocking surrogates

heated mother and a room-temperature cloth mother. The data are presented in Figure 6. The neonatal monkeys clearly preferred the former. With increasing age this difference decreased,

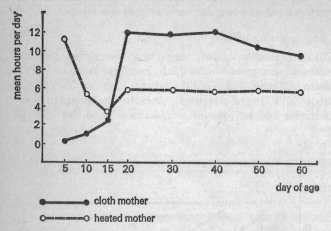

Figure 6 Infant contact to heated-wire and room-temperature cloth surrogate

and at approximately fifteen days the preference reversed. In a second experiment, we used two differentially colored cloth surrogates and heated one and not the other. The infants preferred the hot surrogate, but frequently contacted the room-temperature surrogate for considerable periods of time.

More recently, a series of ingenious studies on the temperature variable has been conducted by Suomi, who created hot and cold-running surrogates by adaptation of the simplified surrogate. These results are important not only for the information obtained concerning the temperature variable but also as an illustration of the successful experimental use of the simplified surrogate itself.

The surrogates used in these exploratory studies were modifications of the basic simplified surrogate, designed to get maximum personality out of the minimal mother. One of these surrogates was a 'hot mamma', exuding warmth from a conventional heating pad wrapped around the surrogate frame and completely covered by a terry cloth sheath. The other surrogate was a cold female;

beneath the terry cloth sheath was a hollow shell within which her life fluid – cold water – was continuously circulated. The two surrogates are illustrated in Plate 6, and to the untrained observer they look remarkably similar. But looks can be deceiving, especially with females, and we felt that in these similar-looking surrogates we had really simulated the two extremes of womanhood – one with a hot body and no head, and one with a cold shoulder and no heart. Actually, this is an exaggeration, for the surface temperature of the hot surrogate was only 7° F. above room temperature, while the surface temperature of the cold surrogate was only 5° F. below room temperature.

In a preliminary study, we raised one female infant from the fifteenth day on the warm surrogate for a period of four weeks. Like all good babies she quickly and completely became attached to her source of warmth, and during this time she exhibited not only a steadily increasing amount of surrogate contact but also began to use the surrogate as a base for exploration (see Plate 7). At the end of this four-week period, we decided that our subject had become spoiled enough and so we replaced the warm surrogate with the cold version for one week. The infant noticed the switch within two minutes, responding by huddling in a corner and vocalizing piteously. Throughout the week of bitter maternal cold, the amount of surrogate contact fell drastically; in general, the infant avoided the surrogate in her feeding, exploratory, and sleeping behaviors. Feeling somewhat guilty, we switched surrogates once more for a week and were rewarded for our efforts by an almost immediate return to previously high levels of surrogate contact. Apparently, with heart-warming heat, our infant was capable of forgiveness, even at this tender age. At this point, we switched the two surrogates daily for a total two weeks, but by this time the infant had accepted the inherent fickle nature of her mothers. On the days that her surrogate was warm, she clung tightly to its body, but on the days when the body was cold, she generally ignored it, thus providing an excellent example of naïve behaviorism.

With a second infant we maintained this procedure but switched the surrogates, so that he spent four weeks with the cold surrogate, followed by one week with the warm, an additional week with the cold, and finally a two-week period in which the surrogates were switched daily. This infant became anything but attached to the cold surrogate during the initial four-week period, spending most of his time huddling in the corner of his cage and generally avoiding the surrogate in his exploratory behavior (see Plate 8). In succeeding weeks, even with the warm surrogate, he failed to approach the levels of contact exhibited by the other infant to the cold surrogate. Apparently, being raised with a cold mother had chilled him to mothers in general, even those beaming warmth and comfort.

Two months later both infants were exposed to a severe fear stimulus in the presence of a room-temperature simplified surrogate. The warm-mother infant responded to this stimulus by running to the surrogate and clinging for dear life. The cold-mother infant responded by running the other way and seeking security in a corner of the cage. We seriously doubt that this behavioral difference can be attributed to the sex difference of our subjects. Rather, this demonstration warmed our hopes and chilled our doubts that temperature may be a variable of importance. More specifically, it suggested that a simple linear model may not be adequate to describe the effects of temperature differences of surrogates on infant attachment. It is clear that warmth is a variable of major importance, particularly in the neonate, and we hazard the guess that elevated temperature is a variable of importance in the operation of all the affectional systems: maternal, mother-infant, possibly age-mate, heterosexual, and even paternal.

Prospectives

Recently we have simplified the surrogate mother further for studies in which its only function is that of providing early social support and security to infants. This supersimplified surrogate is merely a board $1\frac{1}{2}$ inches in diameter and 10 inches long with a scooped-out, concave trough having a maximal depth of $\frac{3}{4}$ inch. As shown in Plate 10, the supersimplified surrogate has an angular deviation from the base of less than 15°, though this angle can be increased by the experimenter at will. The standard cover for this supremely simple surrogate mother is a size 11, cotton athletic sock, though covers of various qualities, rayon, vinyl (which we call the 'linoleum lover'), and sandpaper, have been used for experimental purposes.

Linoleum lover, with you I am through,
The cause of smooth love never runs true.

This supersimplified mother is designed to attract and elicit clinging responses from the infant during the first fifteen days of the
infant's life.

We have designed, but not yet tested, a swinging mother that
will dangle from a frame about two inches off the floor and have
a convex terry cloth or cotton body surface. Observations of real
macaque neonates and mothers indicate that the infant, not the
mother, is the primary attachment object even when the mother
locomotes, and that this swinging mother may also elicit infantile
clasp and impart infant security very early in life. There is nothing
original in this day and age about a swinger becoming a mother,
and the only new angle, if any, is a mother becoming a swinger.

Additional findings, such as the discovery that six-month social
isolates will learn to cling to a heated simplified surrogate, and
that the presence of a surrogate reduces clinging among infant-
infant pairs, have substantiated use of the surrogate beyond
experiments for its own sake. At present, the heated simplified
surrogate is being utilized as a standard apparatus in studies as
varied as reaction to fear, rehabilitation of social isolates, and
development of play. To date, additional research utilizing the cold
version of the simplified surrogate has been far more limited,
possibly because unused water faucets are harder to obtain than
empty electrical outlets. But this represents a methodological, not
a theoretical problem, and doubtlessly solutions will soon be
forthcoming.

It is obvious that the surrogate mother at this point is not
merely a historical showpiece. Unlike the proverbial old soldier,
it is far from fading away. Instead, as in the past, it continues to
foster not only new infants but new ideas.

References

HARLOW, H. F. (1958), 'The nature of love', *Amer. Psychologist*, vol.
13, pp. 673–85.
HARLOW, H. F., and HARLOW, M. K. (1965), 'The affectional systems',
in A. M. Schrier, H. F. Harlow and F. Stollnitz (eds.), *Behavior of
Nonhuman Primates*, vol. 2, Academic Press.

HARLOW, H. F., and ZIMMERMANN, R. R. (1959), 'Affectional responses in the infant monkey', *Sci.*, vol. 130, pp. 421–32.
SACKETT, G. P. (1966), 'Monkeys reared in visual isolation with pictures as visual input: Evidence for an innate releasing mechanism', *Sci.*, vol. 154, pp. 1468–72.

Part Five
Unified Interpretation of Motivation and Reinforcement

The intermingling of discussions of motivation and reinforcement suggested that the phenomena of motivation and response reinforcement may be explained in terms of certain common processes. This suggestion was supported by the discovery that electrical stimulation of certain sites in the brain not only produce rewarding or response-reinforcing effects but also motivate the animal to engage in actions that lead to the stimulation. The early findings on such motivating-reinforcing effects of intracranial electrical stimulation are reviewed here by Olds. Prompted by these and other findings, Miller proposed a combined motivating-reinforcing 'go mechanism' as the basis of response facilitation. Glickman and Schiff, reviewing the mass of experiments in which the occurrence of species-typical consummatory actions (eating, drinking, copulating, etc.) is facilitated by electrical stimulation of hypothalamic sites, also suggested a unified treatment of motivation and reinforcement phenomena. An incentive–motivational interpretation of the findings on rewarding electrical stimulation of the brain has been recently suggested by Trowill *et al.* This section ends with a paper by Bindra, who argues that the principle of response reinforcement is a special case of the more fundamental principle of motivation.

26 J. Olds

Self-Stimulation Experiments and Differentiated Reward Systems

J. Olds, 'Self-stimulation experiments and differentiated reward systems', in H. H. Jasper, L. D. Proctor, R. S. Knighton, W. C. Noshay and R. T. Costello (eds), *Reticular Formation of the Brain*, Little, Brown, 1958, pp. 671–87.

In self-stimulation experiments (Olds and Milner, 1954; Olds, 1956a, 1956b; Olds, Killam and Bach-y-Rita, 1956) electrodes are chronically implanted in the brain, and a circuit is arranged so that the experimental animal can deliver the shock to himself.

For rats, we use the electrode arrangement shown in the upper left of Figure 1. The plastic block is screwed to the skull, and a pair of insulated silver wires penetrates the brain to stimulate only at the tips. Electrodes in place in an intact animal are shown in the X-ray photograph of Figure 1. The circuit is shown in the lower left. Here the rat steps on a pedal to deliver to his brain a shock of 60-cycle current which lasts for about half a second. The shock level ranges from 10 to 150 microamperes, as will be shown. The electrode track following a completed experiment appears as the darkened area of the photomicrograph in Figure 1.

When electrodes are in certain places, animals stimulate their brains more than 5000 times an hour. With electrodes in other places, a negative effect can be achieved. Once the animal learns how to get the shock, he avoids it from then on.

The positive effect can be achieved in extreme or mild form through electrodes placed anywhere within a broad system of structures centered in the hypothalamus and including most of the rhinencephalon plus parts of the thalamus, tegmentum, and caudate nucleus (see lined areas in Figure 2). The negative or punishing effect is much less extensive, according to our studies. Animals avoid the electric shock when electrodes are in certain lateral and posterior parts of the diencephalon and in certain lateral parts of the tegmentum (see stippled area in Figure 2). Our studies of over 200 electrodes placed in all parts of the brain have indicated that about 60 per cent of all electrodes placed are motivationally neutral – the animal neither approaches nor

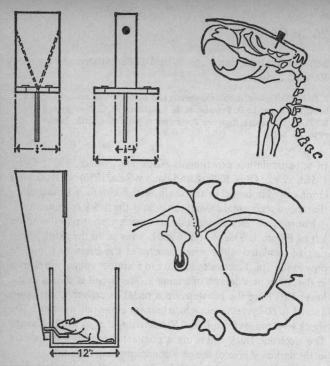

Figure 1 Electrode implants for self-stimulation experiments. Upper left electrode placement used for rats. Upper right, electrodes in place. Lower left, circuit for self-stimulation. Lower right, electrode track as darkened area, after stimulation

avoids the shock. Only about 5 per cent are motivationally negative – the animal avoids the shock; the other 35 per cent are motivationally positive – the animal approaches the shock.

In the case of positive effects, we wished to establish categorically that we were dealing with a rewarding process rather than with automatism or compulsion. For this purpose we trained rats in a complicated maze and an obstruction box with electrical brain shock as the only reward. We compared results so obtained with results obtained when food was the reward for hungry rats (Figure 3).

The time to run the maze declined rapidly in the first three days whether the reward was food or electric stimulation. On the

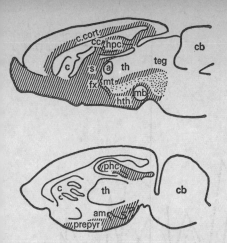

c.cort: cingulum cortex
cc: corpus callosum
s: septum
hpc: hippocampus
a: anterior commissure
th: thalamus
fx: fornix

mt: mammillo-thalamic fasciculus
hth: hypothalamus
cb: cerebellar
mb: mammillary body
am: amygdala
prepyr: prepyriformis cortex

Figure 2 Lined areas indicate brain areas where positive effects can be achieved with electrodes. Stippled area represents regions of avoidance effects

fourth day, when the reward was withdrawn, both groups showed extinction of the running response. The first runs of the day showed a steady decline during the four days (see Figure 3). This indicates that no 'priming' with an hors d'oeuvre is necessary to start a rat self-stimulating.

In the obstruction box experiment done with Mr J. Sinclaire (Figure 4) the rat got three self-stimulations at one end, then had to cross the grid for three more, and so forth. Here we also ran hungry rats with food for reward. They were pretrained for a month to eat three bites at one end, then three at the other, and back and forth. Then shock was introduced by electrifying the grid, and was increased day by day until the rats would no longer cross the grid for food. It is clear from the data on the left in Figure 5 that most of the rats were stopped in their quest for food

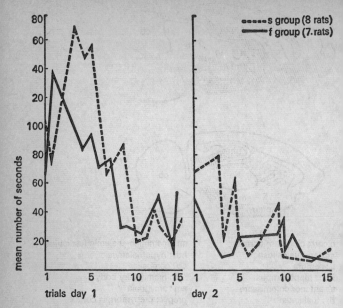

Figure 3 Maze results when rat is offered food (f group, solid line) or electric stimulation (s group, dotted line)

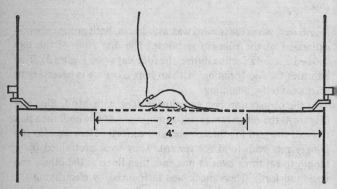

Figure 4 Obstruction box experiment

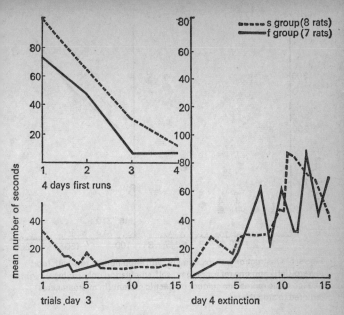

mean number of seconds

4 days first runs

trials day 3

day 4 extinction

s group (8 rats)
f group (7 rats)

by about 50 to 60 microamperes, but a few rats kept going until given almost 300 microamperes.

The chart on the right in Figure 5 (one rat running for self-stimulation) shows microamperes along both the ordinate and the abscissa. From left to right are increasing microamperes of head shock (reward). From bottom to top are increasing microamperes of foot shock (obstruction). At 100 microamperes of shock to the head, this rat crossed an area through which he received about 200 microamperes of shock to the feet. At 150 to the head he crossed about 280 to the feet, and at 200 to the head, he crossed more than 420 to the feet. A shock of 420 microamperes is very high and painful for rat or human.

Our conclusion from these preliminary experiments is that we are stimulating genuine reward systems in the brain. We believe that the effect derives from no mere compulsion or automatism, but from stimulation of cells actually involved in food, sexual, or other reward processes. We have therefore hoped that a study of the variables affecting self-stimulation may lead us toward a knowledge of the differentiations within these reward systems and

J. Olds 257

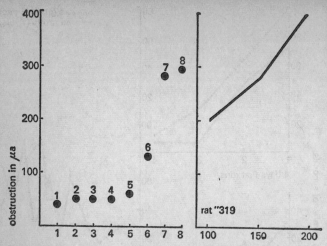

Figure 5 Obstruction box experiment with eight hungry rats with food reward (left) and one rat running for self-stimulation only (right). Height of each circle represents amount of electric current (in microamperes) required to stop the rat

the mechanisms involved in the control of behavior by rewards.

A brief glance suggests that the primary variables are (1) the location of the stimulating electrode, (2) the amount and kind of electric shock, and (3) the state of the neural units and pathways that mediate the effect.

Relationship of location of stimulating electrode to animal's response

In the posterior hypothalamus (except for the mammillary bodies) self-stimulation rates are very high. Figure 6 shows cumulative response curves for a rat with a posterior electrode. Each sawtooth represents 500 responses, and each block represents an hour. Here we see a very stable rate of 4500 responses per hour maintained for 15 days of testing. Such rates are maintained for many months.

Figure 7 shows much slower rates when the electrodes are in the anterior hypothalamus. Within the tegmental hypothalamic system the decline in rates appears to be steady as we progress forward along the ventromedial surface.

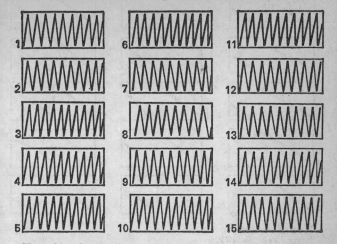

fifteen days of responding
posterior hypothalamic electrode #315

Figure 6

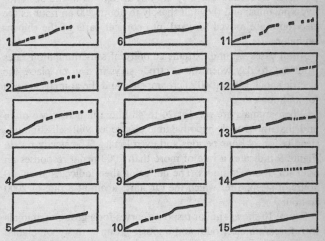

fifteen days of responding
middle hypothalamic electrode #124

Figure 7

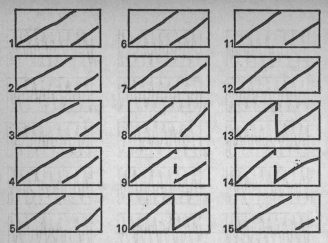

fifteen days of responding
forebrain electrode #215

Figure 8

Rates rise again slightly (Figure 8) in the preoptic region and posterior forebrain, but they are not as high as in the posterior hypothalamus, and they fall sharply to about 200 an hour as the electrodes are moved forward into cortical parts of the rhinencephalon.

In all cases we find extreme stability of self-stimulation rates from day to day when the electrode stays in a given place, the electric shock is set at 60 microamperes, and the animals are run for an hour a day.

When animals are run for 24 to 48 hours in a row, we often find that those with hypothalamic electrodes will self-stimulate steadily for 24-hour periods and even longer. The steady rise in Figure 9 indicates a rate of more than 2000 pedal responses an hour for about 24 hours. The flattening then indicates about 20 hours of sleep, after which the rat starts again at a rate of 2000 an hour.

Figure 10 shows similar response curves for a group of animals with forebrain electrodes and another group with hypothalamic ones. It is quite apparent that slowing in the second group is moderate and could be attributed to general fatigue. Slowing in

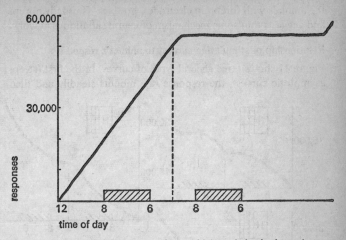

Figure 9 Self-stimulation response of a rat with hypothalamic electrodes, run continually for over 24 hours

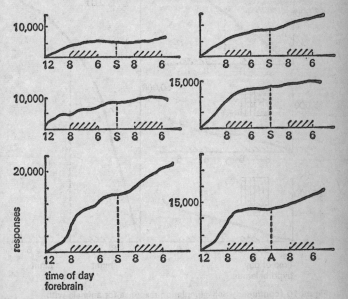

Figure 10 Self-stimulation response for animals with forebrain electrodes and with hypothalamic electrodes

the animals with forebrain electrodes, however, is usually abrupt and suggests that some mechanism of neural satiation is at work.

Relationship of stimulating current to animal's response

Figure 11 shows three general types of curves. In the first (steep, asymptotic curves), the response rate mounts steadily and then

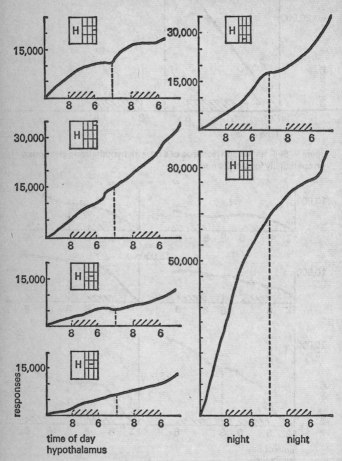

Figure 10 (continued) Self-stimulation response for animals with forebrain electrodes and with hypothalamic electrodes

levels off at a very high point. These results appear to be achieved with electrodes in the anterior or posterior portions of the medial forebrain bundle, and the rates appear to rise steadily with increases in electric shock to the head. The point of leveling off may be due to some limit of skill, and declines at the tops of the curves are usually accounted for by seizures. We assume that in these cases our electrode sits in a region of positive motivational units, and that all the cells in a millimeter sphere surrounding the electrode tip are homogeneous in this positive effect. We have some evidence from obstruction experiments that these rats will continue to increase their willingness to take pain for higher brain shocks after response rate has leveled off.

The second type of curve (undulating) suggests that the electrode is placed in a set of cells or fibers giving positive results, but that increases in electric current bring in a lamina of negative motivational units, after which there are more positives. This

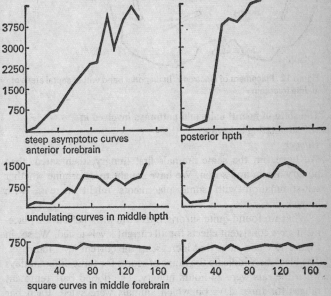

Figure 11 Self-stimulation responses with varying amounts of electric current. The current increases in 10-microampere steps along the abscissa, and response rate increases along the ordinate

result is achieved from electrodes placed in parts of the middle hypothalamus where we have previously found rewarding and punishing effects from neighboring electrodes.

The third type of curve (square) suggests that the electrodes are placed directly in a tract of fibers with positive motivational effects, but that all other cells in the region are neutral. So far, this result has been obtained only with electrodes placed in the diagonal band within the septal areas (Figure 12). This suggests that in this septal area proper, the diagonal band is the only active structure.

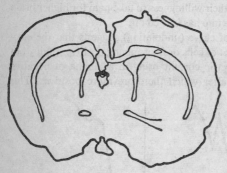

Figure 12 Placement of electrodes in diagonal band within septal areas of middle forebrain

The state of neural units and pathways involved in self-stimulating behavior

Hunger

We have run the same animals first hungry, then sated, then hungry again, and so on. We have sought to determine whether self-stimulation with some placements might increase with hunger.

What we found quite surprised us at first. No electrode placement gave consistent effects for all current levels tested. We see in Figure 13 again rates that increase as the current level increases. The black bars indicate the range of scores for three different days when the rats were 24-hours hungry. The dotted bars represent ranges for three days on which animals were sated. Each bar represents the range for just one voltage level. The rat whose scores are on the left shows a marked difference between hunger and sated conditions only at 10 microamperes. At all other levels the scores overlap. The rat whose data are on the right shows clearcut differences only at the top of the microampere scale.

We have surmised here, as before, that increases in electric current widen the circle of cells stimulated. Cells far outside the circle will not be affected even when their thresholds are low; those deep within the sphere are stimulated by a supra-threshold current. Cells close to the boundary, however, are questionable, and drive variations may change the threshold of these cells to move them into or out of the ring. We must surmise, then, that only when this boundary includes hunger-sensitive cells can we expect a hunger difference to appear.

To look for a pattern, we plotted on a brain map the current levels at which hunger differences occur. We have, of course, found areas, particularly in the anterior hypothalamus, where there were apparently no hunger differences at all. Hunger differences are, however, particularly frequent in the posterior hypothalamus (Figure 14). It is apparent from the arrows that

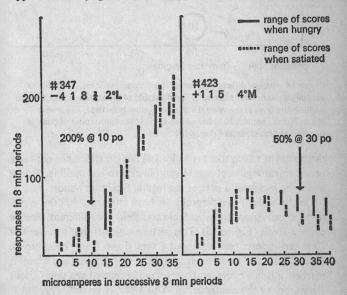

Figure 13

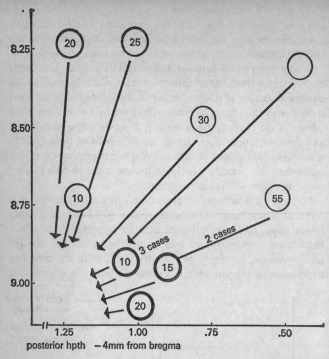

Figure 14 Hunger differences shown on diagrammatic cross-section of ventral posterior hypothalamus. The right side of the square is about at the midline, the base at the ventral surface ($9\frac{1}{2}$ mm. from top). The area is about $1\frac{1}{2}$ mm. square. Number within circle indicates amount of current required to give clearcut hunger difference

the points at which there is a clearcut hunger difference converge on a ventral region about $1\frac{1}{4}$ mm. lateral to the midline. This is again the region of a part of the medial forebrain bundle.

On the basis of this diagram, we have attempted to draw a picture of our supra-threshold electric field for different electric current levels (Figure 15). This picture suggests that a current of 20 microamperes reaches about $\frac{3}{4}$ mm. down from the electrode tip but less than $\frac{1}{2}$ mm. to either side. A 60-microampere stimulus reaches cells in a circle of about 1·5 mm. centered at a point about $\frac{1}{2}$ mm. below the electrode tip. This work is preliminary, but it gives us a useful tool for further analysis and suggests that in

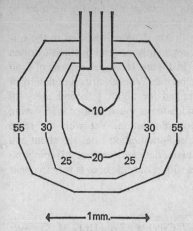

Figure 15 Supra-threshold electric field for different electric current levels

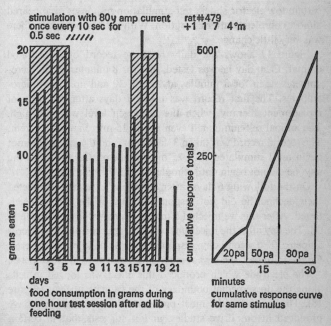

stimulation with 80μ amp current once every 10 sec for 0.5 sec //////

rat#479
+1 1 7 4°m

grams eaten

days
food consumption in grams during one hour test session after ad lib feeding

cumulative response totals

minutes
cumulative response curve for same stimulus

Figure 16

order to study the effects of electrode placement, we must be careful in specifying the level of electric current.

Other work on hunger with Mr R. Wendt has led to the surprising conclusion that an apparently rewarding stimulus often increases the hunger drive. In Figure 16 we see records of food intake during an hour test period. With electric stimulation of about 80 microamperes applied for about $\frac{1}{2}$ second every 10 seconds, the amount of food eaten is much greater than during comparable periods without stimulation. Yet with the same stimulus at the same point, self-stimulation rates are about 800 responses per hour. Wendt's later data indicate that this combination of drive increase effects with rewarding ones is very frequent in the hunger system.

Androgens

In studies done with Mr C. V. Critchlaw from Dr C. H. Sawyer's laboratory, we found that with some electrode placements and certain low electric shock, self-stimulation responses disappeared almost completely after castration. With other placements, there was very little change.

Figure 17 shows the daily response record of a castrated animal. Each day he was tested, first for 8 minutes at 15 microamperes, then for 8 minutes at 20, 25, 30 and up to 55 microamperes. The first record was taken 7 days after cessation of replacement therapy, when the androgen level was still high. The animal self-stimulated even at the 15-microampere current. The second record was taken 3 days later, and the animal did not begin until stimulated with 25 microamperes. On the following day, he did not begin until stimulated with 55 microamperes.

On the following 6 days, after androgen levels had completed their decline, he did not respond for any of the current levels tested. After this we injected 5 mg. of testosterone propionate in oil. The day after the injection, responding occurred at 55 microamperes. The second day, responding began at 45 microamperes. On the third day, there was responding again at 15 microamperes.

The electrode which produced this effect was lodged in cells along the dorsomedial boundary of the caudate nucleus (Figure 18). This is by far the most pronounced effect which we have produced in our drive studies, and it suggests that in certain

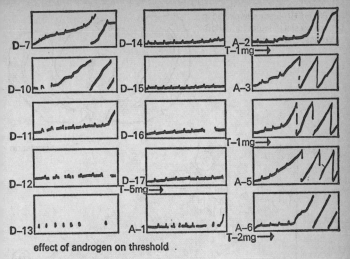

D-7 D-14 A-2 T-1mg→

D-10 D-15 A-3

D-11 D-16 T-1mg→

D-12 D-17 A-5 T-5mg→

D-13 A-1 A-6 T-2mg→

effect of androgen on threshold .

Figure 17

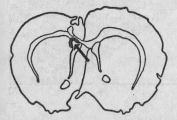

Figure 18 Arrow indicates electrode placement along the dorsomedial boundary of the caudate nucleus for testing the effect of androgens on self-stimulation

parts of the caudate nucleus, drive effects may be more clearly separated anatomically than in the hypothalamus.

Another androgen effect shown by a different technique was found with an electrode in the mesial reticular formation (Figure 19). Here we obtained a rapid but unstable response rate prior to castration, using a stimulus of 65 microamperes. After castration, we often obtained practically no response with the same stimulus. About a week after the commencement of replacement therapy, the animal was responding regularly again at about 1500 an hour.

Figure 19 Electrode placed in the mesial reticular formation, to test androgen effect

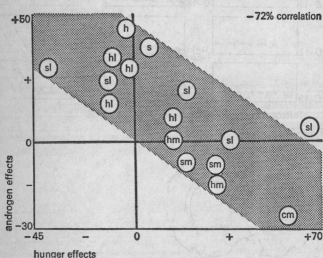

Figure 20 Negative correlation of androgen and hunger effects. Each circle stands for one animal. The letters inside the circles indicate electrode placement: s, septal; h, hypothalamic; c, caudate; l, lateral; m, medial. Animals are assumed to differ from one another only in electrode placement. The y axis indicates per cent improvement of self-stimulation rates by giving androgens to the castrated animals; the x axis indicates per cent improvement of self-stimulation rates by starving the animal for about 23 hours

Figure 21 see right Sections through the ventral portion of the diencephalon and telencephalon of the rat, showing places of extreme and mild inhibition of self-stimulation rates by chlorpromazine (2mg./kg.). The numbers inside the circles indicate the number of 8-minute intervals of testing during which self-stimulation was abolished by the drug. (Thus, a 1·5 would mean that half of the normal output was inhibited for one 8-minute interval and the whole normal output for another interval after drug injection.) Triangles indicate mild effects (depression of 1·5 or less): circles indicate moderate effects (depression of 1·5 to 3 intervals): squares indicate extreme effects (depressions of more than 3 intervals)

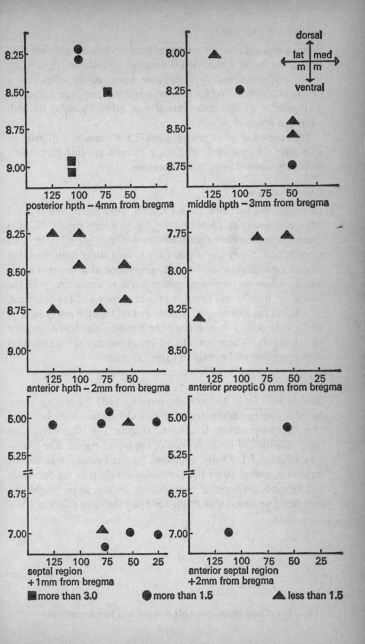

posterior hpth – 4mm from bregma

middle hpth – 3mm from bregma

dorsal
lat | med
m | m
ventral

anterior hpth – 2mm from bregma

anterior preoptic 0 mm from bregma

septal region +1mm from bregma

anterior septal region +2mm from bregma

■ more than 3.0   ● more than 1.5   ▲ less than 1.5

Hunger and androgens

When a series of animals was tested for both hunger and androgen effects, we found a remarkable negative correlation (Figure 20). When androgens improved response rates, hunger often had a detrimental effect. When hunger increased response rates, the performance of the same animal was often impaired by high androgen levels.

This certainly gives strong ground for expecting to find an anatomic differentiation of hunger reward systems from those positively affected by male sex hormone.

Chlorpromazine

In studies started with Dr K. Killam, chlorpromazine injected intraperitoneally at a rate of 2 mg./kg. had very greatly differing effects depending on the point of stimulation (Figure 21). In some cases it had a very slight effect for a very short time. In other cases it completely abolished self-stimulation at all current levels tested. When we map these effects on a schematic map of the posterior, middle and anterior hypothalamus and the posterior, middle, and anterior septal region, we find that the heavy inhibitory effects collect in the posterior hypothalamus and anterior septal region. There are almost no effects on self-stimulation with electrodes in the anterior hypothalamus.

LSD

Studies with Dr S. Eiduson showed that LSD 0·2 mg./kg. never has the massive inhibitory effects of chlorpromazine, but does give very dependable inhibitions (Figure 22). The effects are most pronounced in some parts of the septal region. The inhibitory effects of LSD are abolished by preliminary injection of serotonin, except when the electrodes are deep in the forebrain just beyond the anterior commissure. In this same place, and only here, we found that Brom-LSD had the same effect as LSD.

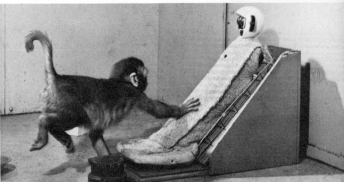

Above: Plate 1 Cloth and wire surrogate mothers

Middle: Plate 2 Infant monkey security in the presence of the cloth surrogate

Plate 3 Infant play in the presence of the surrogate

Above left: Plate 4 Original surrogate and simplified surrogate

Above right: Plate 5 Infant clinging to simplified surrogate

Left: Plate 6 Warm (left) and cold simplified surrogates

Below left: Plate 7 Infant clinging to and exploring from warm simplified surrogate

Below right: Plate 8 Typical infant reactions to cold simplified surrogate

Plate 9 The supersimplified surrogate

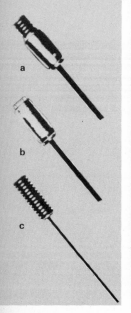

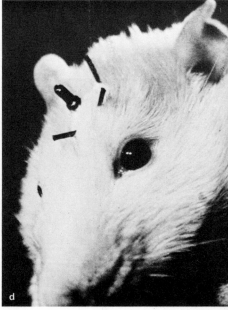

Plate 10 Double cannula
system for chemo-stimulation:
(a) the complete implant;
(b) the outer cannula;
(c) the inner cannula;
(d) rat with double cannula implant
and three additional pins for
electrical stimulation and recording

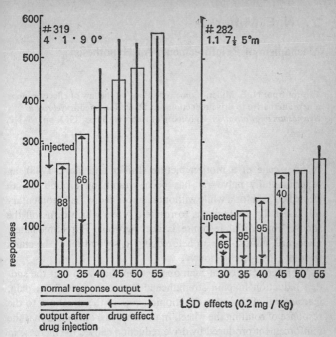

Figure 22 LSD effects on self-stimulation. Response output during successive 8-minute intervals is plotted as the electric current is raised from 30 to 55 microamperes. The open rectangles denote normal output; the black bars represent output under the effects of the drug

References

OLDS, J., and MILNER, P. (1954), 'Positive reinforcement produced by electrical stimulation of septal area and other regions of the rat brain', *J. compar. physiol. Psychol.*, vol. 47, p. 419.

OLDS, J. (1956a), 'A preliminary mapping of electrical reinforcing effects in the rat brain', *J. compar. physiol. Psychol.*, vol. 49, p. 281.

OLDS, J. (1956b), 'Runway and maze behavior controlled by baso-medial forebrain stimulation in the rat', *J. compar. physiol. Psychol.*, vol. 49, p. 507.

OLDS, J., KILLAM, K. F., and BACH-Y-RITA, P. (1956), 'Self-stimulation of the brain used as a screening method for tranquilizing drugs', *Sci.*, vol, 124, p. 265.

27 N. E. Miller

Mechanism of Reinforcement: An Hypothesis

Excerpt from N. E. Miller, 'Some reflections on the law of effect produce a new alternative to drive reduction', in M. R. Jones (ed.), *Nebraska Symposium on Motivation*, University of Nebraska Press, 1963, pp. 65–112.

In one scene of a motion picture (Miller and Hart, 1948), an experimentally naïve rat has been scrambling around on an electrified grid for a while without securing more than momentary relief. Finally, he happens to rotate a wheel which turns off the shock. This initial response is not vigorous. But immediately afterward, almost like an actor doing a 'second take', he starts to rotate the wheel furiously.

My interpretation of such observations has been that the sudden reduction in pain strengthened the connection from pain, fear and all of the other functioning cues in the situation, to the response of rotating the wheel. In other words, I assumed that the reinforcement produced by drive reduction caused the increase in vigor of this response. This may be true. But what happens if one assumes that the causal relationship runs in the opposite direction?

Let us explore the assumption that the sudden relief from pain produces an automatic increase in the activity of any neural circuits that have just been firing. Let us further assume that it is this energization that is responsible for the strong performance (in this case appearing as vigorous overt rehearsal) which in turn is responsible for learning by contiguity. Such energization could involve the reticular activating system or it could involve something as different as a DC potential. Let us see where such speculations can lead us.

There are a number of ways of proceeding from this point. At one extreme, one can assume that each of the stimulus situations in the long list known to be empirically rewarding is individually wired up so that it will have its own separate network (DC potential or other means) for facilitating any ongoing activity, including the trace of an immediately preceding activity. At the other extreme, one can assume that there is a single 'go network' or 'go mechanism'. It is obvious that the latter would be much more parsimonious to construct, but natural selection does not always result in maximum parsimony.

Let us make the following tentative assumptions:

1. That there are one or more 'go' or 'activating' mechanisms (or 'mechanisms', as will be understood but not repeated here-after) in the brain which act to intensify ongoing responses to cues and the traces of immediately preceding activities, producing a stronger intensification the more strongly the 'go mechanism' is activated.

2. That this 'go mechanism' can be activated in a variety of ways, such as by reduction in noxious stimulation, by the taste of food to a hungry animal, possibly by feedback from still more central effects of eating, by the release of a stimulated but inhibited response from blocking, by the removal of a discrepancy between an intention and an achievement, etc. (The similarity between the 'go' mechanism and the 'confirming response' will be recognized, but it is assumed that the primary effect of the 'go' mechanism is to intensify current activities, including dynamic or other traces, rather than *directly* to strengthen connections. As will be seen from 3 and 4 below, however, a secondary effect of such intensification is to strengthen connections, or in other words, habits.)

3. That all responses, including the activation of this 'go mechanism' are subject to conditioning with contiguity being sufficient. (Note that this is a crucial difference from Mowrer (1960a and 1960b) which avoids the fatal weakness that has already been pointed out.)

4. That the strength of the CR is determined to a great degree by the strength of the UCR (including the intensified trace which automatically serves as a UCR since the activities are similar), but also by the number of pairings. (This is a key assumption, which together with the preceding ones, means that more strongly rewarded responses will be prepotent over competing less strongly rewarded ones. The number of pairings could act to build up

more functional units in an all-or-none way as Guthrie (1952) assumes; we do not need to decide that point now.)

5. That when a chain of cues leads to a UCS for the 'go mechanism', it is most strongly conditioned to those nearer to the UCS, but can be conditioned (perhaps via lingering traces and/or by successive higher-order conditioning) to those farther away with a progressive decline in strength.

6. That every time a CR (including a conditioned 'go response') is repeated without reinforcement from the UCS (or perhaps it should be – a CS is presented without a UCS, or the CR is stronger than the UCR), it is subject to a certain amount of weakening, or in other words, experimental extinction. (With instrumental responses it will be remembered that the intensified trace serves as the UCS, so that non-intensification of the trace will, according to the present assumption, produce experimental extinction.)

It can be seen that, after various conditioning trials in its environment, an organism or other device, constructed along these principles, would tend to be guided cybernetically toward the UCS for the 'go system', and that it would tend to drop out sequences that doubled back on themselves (blind alleys). It also would learn specific S–R connections[1] which could be the basis for immediate choice, without the necessity for sampling various cues, or in other words, showing VTE's before every choice. Thus the theory avoids the fatal weakness of Mowrer's (1960a and 1960b) formulation. Such an organism would learn fear by classical conditioning, but would not learn to approach pain, because it is only the offset of pain that is the UCS for the 'go' mechanism.

1. Please note carefully that the word 'connection' is used in the sense defined by Miller and Dollard (1941 p. 21): 'The word "connection" is used to refer to a causal sequence, the details of which are practically unknown, rather than to specific neural strands.' There is nothing to prevent a 'connection' from being a modulation of an ongoing activity, a complex processing of information, or a complex pattern of permanent traces in different parts of different networks, provided that the end result is that under specified conditions a cue has a tendency to be followed by a response, as we have broadly defined both of these terms.

In developing this line of speculation I use the extended definitions of stimulus and response, including central activities and attention, which were advanced before such notions were fashionable (Miller and Dollard, 1941), and have been repeated and extended recently (Miller, 1959, pp. 238–52; 1963b), including the extension to different 'programs' suggested in this paper. The key assumption is that all of these apparently diverse processes follow the same basic laws of learning (Miller, 1959, p. 243).

Some similarities and differences with other theories

The present hypothesis has obvious resemblances to Mowrer (1960a, 1960b) except for the crucial fact that, like the original analysis of copying (Miller and Dollard, 1941), it does *not* rule out connections between cues and motor responses, and therefore does have a way of eliciting immediate responses. Thus, it overcomes a fatal weakness of Mowrer's theory.

The present formulation also resembles Sheffield's (1954) drive-induction hypothesis, and some of the recent emphasis by Spence (1956) on the incentive value of the anticipatory goal response, except that it does *not* limit itself to incentives based on the conditioning of peripheral consummatory responses, and does specifically include an incentive based on the termination of noxious stimulation.[2] While Spence, who has primarily used the empirical law of effect, prudently has not clearly made up his mind, the present formulation differs from what seems to be Spence's present position in that it clearly and definitely does not assume different processes for appetitive and aversive learning, or for the acquisition of habit strength and incentive strength.

While the present formulation does use association by contiguity, it differs from Guthrie (1952) in using the booster or 'go

2. In his latest version of his drive-induction hypothesis, Sheffield (1960) is moving toward a 'central response' position, more similar to the one advanced in the present paper, but he still seems to emphasize the consummatory response. In discussing the problem of what aspect of the consummatory response is conditionable and what aspect moves forward to produce consummatory excitement, he says: '. . . we will all have to give up the idea that what moves forward is some overt or peripheral portion of the consummatory response. I am already thinking instead of a central-nervous-system phenomenon which may show up in various ways at the behavioral level.'

mechanism' to explain the obvious selectivity of learning, instead of relying on stimulus change to protect certain elements of completely indiscriminate learning from being unlearned. It also differs from Guthrie in having a specific assumption about experimental extinction. Conceivably, this assumption can later be derived from the more basic phenomenon of habituation, or from the learning of interfering activities, but this is a tricky problem.

The present formulation is similar to Tolman (1932) in that reward serves to elicit performance and that there is a possibility of learning by contiguity. It differs, however, in (a) that activated performance clearly is essential for the learning of responses, including central ones, that must compete with other strong responses at the time of such learning or that are strong enough to do so during performance, and (b) that it is assumed that direct responses can be learned without always having an expectancy as a mediating link. It is similar to Tolman's and different from most other CR formulations in that it does not place all of its emphasis on peripheral mediating responses, but allows for the possibility of central perceptual, imaged or other processes utilizing the myriad potential interconnections in the brain. It is different from Tolman in that it conceives of these central processes as obeying the same fundamental laws as overt responses, and hence refers to them as cue-producing 'responses'.

The central responses, which have been a part of my thinking for a long time, obviously resemble Hebb's (1949) cell assemblies and phase sequences, but in the 'go mechanism' and experimental extinction, the present formulation has selective factors which are essential to prevent Hebb's cell assemblies and phase sequences from continuing to grow from association by contiguity until they elicit one grand convulsion.

In short, while certain assumptions of the present tentative formulation necessarily resemble previous theories, I believe that this particular combination of assumptions is unique and that it is precisely this particular combination that actually will work. Certainly, difficulties will be encountered and revisions or extensions will be needed. Only a few lines of further development may be briefly suggested here.

Look for direct evidence of 'go' mechanism

One of the first things that should be done is to try to secure some direct evidence that something like the 'go mechanism' outlined in the first assumption actually exists and, if it does, to investigate the degree to which it can be demonstrated to intensify or prolong the activity of neural traces or overt motor activity. What are the effects in different parts of the brain when a given response first gives sudden relief from prolonged pain or causes food to be delivered to a hungry animal which has been thoroughly trained to promptly seize and eat it in the experimental situation? What are the effects during the first trial on which a CS, to which the investigatory response has been habituated, is paired with the UCS of food? We know that after several trials, the CS shows no habituation and that effects of it are more intense and widespread than they otherwise would be. The occurrence of such effects during the very first trial would be evidence for the type of 'go' or 'booster' mechanism we have postulated. If, however, such effects occurred only on the second trial, this would be evidence for the more conventional conception of a retroactive effect of reward on the strengthening of a connection.

Experimental tests of cybernetic guidance

We also need to know the extent to which drive induction and reduction can cybernetically guide responses as emphasized by Mowrer (1960a). Is such guidance very effective on the very first trial, or only after S–R connections have been strengthened either by the new process we have just proposed or by some other means? Let us place a rat in an open-field apparatus, wearing a little headlight casting the brightest beam directly ahead. Place a photocell at a given point in the field and have the illumination of this photocell reduce the intensity of electric shock delivered via body electrodes (or electrodes on an aversive area of the brain) placed so that the shock elicits a minimum of interfering motor responses. Will the rat be guided efficiently to that point on the very first trial? Will it be more effective to turn the shock off completely whenever the rat starts to move in the desired direction? If this is done, will the beneficial effects appear only as the strength of the shock is gradually built up again? We need to know more facts about the possibilities, and difficulties, of such guidance as contrasted with learning specific directional responses to specific directional cues.

It seems reasonable to assume that the areas in which Olds (1958) secured self-reward are either a part of the 'go mechanism' or are directly connected with it. On the behavioral side, it would be interesting to see whether or not one can guide a rat cybernetically toward a goal by playing 'you're getting hotter or colder' with an area in which the animal will hold a bar down continuously in order to get continuous brain stimulation.

The fact that there are so many areas in which the rats do not give themselves continuous stimulation by holding down such a bar continuously, and where they will even perform a second response to turn the stimulation off (Roberts, 1958; Bower and Miller, 1958), poses certain problems for such an experiment, and perhaps also for the hypothesis. Perhaps responses are facilitated, not by the absolute level of activity of the 'go system', but only by increases in its level of activity. Perhaps a succession of brief episodes or rises and falls in motivating stimulation will be found to be more effective in cybernetic shaping than continuous feedback.

Relationships between 'go' and 'stop' mechanisms

While we are clumsily groping along, it is tempting to endow our organism with one or more 'stop' mechanisms which have effects directly opposite to those of the 'go' one. But this might cause trouble. Desirable as it may be to have pain and fear stop behavior under certain circumstances, as indeed it seems to do in the CER, there are other circumstances, namely escape and avoidance learning, in which it is desirable to have them elicit vigorous activity. The same seems to be true of frustration. Perhaps we might want to have a generalized freezing mechanism with connections from pain and fear that could be strengthened if it was active when their termination activated the 'go' mechanism by sudden reductions in pain, fear, and frustration.

Although it does not seem desirable to assume a 'stop' mechanism with effects on all responses that are directly opposite to those assumed for the 'go' mechanism, it does seem worthwhile to make the following additional assumption which is more tentative than the preceding ones:

7. That there is a certain amount of reciprocal inhibition between the central mechanisms involved in pain, fear, and frustration and the 'go' mechanism.

Such inhibition would explain the counterconditioning of fear, which it will be remembered is badly in need of additional detailed experimental study. The activation of the 'go' mechanism would tend to inhibit fear, rather than to boost it. The converse aspect of such inhibition would cause pain at the goal to tend to subtract from the effectiveness of reward there. Furthermore, the activation of the 'go' mechanism by the termination of pain would be prevented by the inhibiting effects of the pain from being strongly conditioned to cues occurring during the pain. This would account for the apparent difficulty of establishing strong secondary reinforcement based on the termination of pain. (If such secondary reinforcement were strong enough, it could even lead to the performance of responses leading to pain.) The particular responses energized by the termination of pain would not, however, be subject to such inhibition and hence could become anticipatory. Before being too explicit about the inevitability, symmetry, and strength of such reciprocal inhibition, however, it will be wise to have more exact experimental evidence concerning the phenomena to be accounted for. We have already suggested some experiments which might contribute to this goal.

Speed versus prepotency

As one tries to apply the hypothesis to a greater variety of situations, problems arise. For example, how can one account for the experiment in which Egger and Miller (1962) found that, if a first and second cue always are immediately associated with food, the redundant second one has relatively little secondary reinforcing value, and at the same time have the subject take the shortcut of choosing the second cue when subsequently confronted with both simultaneously? A careful analysis of the stimulus changes involved may provide the answer.

Another difficulty arises from the fact that, if rats are specifically rewarded for running slowly down one alley, and allowed to run rapidly down another, they will learn to run at different speeds in the two alleys, but if they are given better rewards for running slowly, they will choose the slow alley (Logan, 1962). In short, the most vigorous response in terms of speed (and presumably amplitude also) is not necessarily the one that is strongest in terms of prepotency. Therefore, we probably shall have to be careful to define strength in terms of prepotency, rather than speed and amplitude.

The lesson is that it is dangerous to regard one hypothesis as more promising than another when it has not been worked out in as much detail. Nevertheless, each hypothesis has to start out in a tentative manner and there is an advantage in trying to work from the general to the specific by a strategy analogous to that employed in the game of 'twenty questions'.

Changes in rewards

We know that performance declines when one shifts from a larger reward to a smaller one. Such a decline would be expected if we assume that extinction occurs whenever the CR is stronger than the UCR, or than some given fraction of the UCR.

There is also some disturbance when an animal is shifted from one reward to another, although the laws of such disturbance need to be experimentally determined in more detail, especially since many experiments have confounded shifts in the type of reward with shifts to a less preferred one. We need to find out the extent to which the disturbance is a function of the goal responses elicited by the reward, biting dry food versus lapping sweet water, and the extent to which it can also be produced by distinctive changes in the flavor of food without apparently introducing any change into the motor responses of eating. To what extent do such disturbances become greater as one advances from the rat to the dog to the monkey? Perhaps we shall have to assume a number of 'go' mechanisms, or that different strengths of the 'go' mechanism function as incompatible responses, or that a conflict between an image and a perceptual response produces a disturbance. In the absence of better data, there is not much point in making overly specific theoretical assumptions.

Furthermore, the problems of sensory preconditioning and

latent learning seem to me to be closely related to the foregoing ones.

You will note that in a previous context I said 'functioning cues'. Having been one of the few stimulus-response psychologists who used the concept of 'attention' before our entry into World War II (Miller and Dollard, 1941), I use functioning cues to mean ones that are receiving at least some attention, a concept that has been given a physiological basis by recent work on the reticular formation (Magoun, 1958) and has been extended and clarified by detailed experimental work such as that which Broadbent (1948, 1962) has summarized in support of his filter theory.

References

BOWER, G. H., and MILLER, N. E. (1960), 'Effect of amount of reward on strength of approach in an approach-avoidance conflict', *J. compar. physiol. Psychol.*, vol. 53, pp. 59–62.

BROADBENT, D. E. (1958), *Perception and Communication*, Basic Books.

EGGER, M. D., and MILLER, N. E. (1962), 'Secondary reinforcement in rats as a function of information value and reliability of the stimulus', *J. exper. Psychol.*, vol. 64, pp. 97–104.

GUTHRIE, E. R. (1952), *The Psychology of Learning*, Harper & Row, rev. edn.

HEBB, D. O. (1949), *The Organization of Behavior*, Wiley.

LOGAN, F. A. (1962), 'Conditional-outcome choice behavior in rats' *Psychol. Rev.*, vol. 69, pp. 467–76.

MAGOUN, H. W. (1958), *The Waking Brain*, Charles C. Thomas.

MILLER, N. E. (1959), 'Liberalization of basic S–R concepts: extensions to conflict behavior, motivation and social learning', in S. Koch (ed.), *Psychology: A Study of a Science*, McGraw-Hill, study 1, vol. 2.

MILLER, N. E. (1963), 'Some implications of modern behavior theory for personality change and psychotherapy', in P. Worchel and D. Byrne (eds.), *Personality Change*, Wiley.

MILLER, N. E., and DOLLARD, J. (1941), *Social Learning and Imitation*, Yale University Press.

MILLER, N. E., and HART, G. (1948), 'Motivation and reward in learning', Psychological Cinema Register, Pennsylvania State University.

MOWRER, O. H. (1960a), *Learning Theory and Behavior*, Wiley.

MOWRER, O. H. (1960b), *Learning Theory and Symbolic Processes*, Wiley.

OLDS, J. A. (1958), 'Self-stimulation of the brain used to study local effects of hunger, sex, and drugs', *Sci.*, vol. 127, p. 315.

ROBERTS, W. W. (1958), 'Both rewarding and punishing effects from stimulation of posterior hypothalamus with same electrode at same intensity', *J. compar. physiol. Psychol.*, vol. 51, pp. 400–7.

SHEFFIELD, F. D. (1954), 'A drive-induction theory of reinforcement', paper read at Psychology Colloquium, Brown University.

SHEFFIELD, F. D. (1960), 'New evidence on the drive-induction theory of reinforcement', paper read at Psychology Colloquium, Stanford University.

SPENCE, K. W. (1956), *Behavior Theory and Conditioning*, Yale University Press.

TOLMAN, E. C. (1932), *Purposive Behavior in Animals and Men*, Appleton-Century-Crofts.

28 S. E. Glickman and B. B. Schiff

A Theory of Reinforcement

Excerpts from S. E. Glickman and B. B. Schiff, 'A biological theory of reinforcement', *Psychological Review*, volume 74, 1967, pp. 81–109.

Outline of a theory
The classification of behavior

Behavior sequences will be classified, using Schneirla's (1959) terms, into those involving approach and those involving withdrawal. Approach sequences include investigatory activity, feeding, drinking, sexual activity, maternal activity, care of the body, aggressive responses of a carnivore and probably the defensive activities of any species in protection of home territory. Withdrawal includes escape from painful stimulation, flight from a predator, and the less dramatic withdrawal from an aversive taste, smell, or other simple sensory stimulus. Most of these sequences are directly related to the patterns characterized by ethologists (Lorenz, 1950; Tinbergen, 1951) as Fixed Action Patterns. It is clear that environmental stimulation may be essential for the proper integration of these behaviors (Moltz, 1965; Schneirla, 1959), however, it may do so by acting upon and maintaining innate patterns of neural organization (Wiesel and Hubel, 1963).

Valenstein (1964) has found that sites in the brain which yield positive reinforcing effects in self-stimulation situations tend to produce forward approach movements when electrically stimulated under other test conditions. Conversely, stimulation in negative reinforcement areas frequently produces freezing or backward movements. Brain stimulation in complex test situations has been shown to produce more complicated sequences of behavior (see p. 289). It is likely that serious confusions have arisen in the brain stimulation literature from investigators failing to properly discriminate whether these sequences of behavior constitute approach or withdrawal. Judgements of this sort must take into account the normal response repertoires of the species in question and the conditions under which these repertoires developed. For example, there has been a tendency for scientists observing a domestic cat growling and attacking objects with claws unsheathed to assume that the cat is experiencing something unpleasant and striking out at the world in its helpless rage. It does not look like behavior that the average human would enjoy. On the other hand, it is critical for the survival of a carnivore in its natural habitat that it engage in such activities, either in territorial defense or before eating its prey. It would be a cruel and unadaptive trick of nature to render such behavior 'negatively reinforcing' or 'unpleasant' to the animal, and there is every reason to believe that the evocation of an attack pattern is a substantial positive reinforcement for a cat (Roberts and Kiess, 1964). There are also purely defensive patterns which might be activated in the cat. Such patterns normally include elements of both attack and flight, as well as characteristic postural adjustments and growling or hissing, the growling constituting a more aggressive sign than the hissing (Leyhausen, 1956). We shall soon consider in detail the identification of elicited approach or withdrawal behaviors, with positive or negative reinforcing effects coincident with brain stimulation. Proper classification of elicited behavior and the extent to which a sequence approximates approach, withdrawal, or a mixture of the two, may clarify the complex and sometimes paradoxical self-stimulation effects noted in the literature (Bower and Miller, 1958; Brown and Cohen, 1959; Roberts, 1958).

The organization of motor patterns

It has become increasingly plausible that complex motor patterns, involving the sequential performance of a variety of movements, are organized in some 'preformed' state within the brainstem (Bullock, 1961). Such patterns range from relatively simple head (Hyde, 1965) or circling movements (Skulkety, 1962), through complex standing-walking-climbing sequences (Delgado, 1965), to the extraordinarily complex patterns which fit the approach-withdrawal classification (Brown and Hunsperger, 1963; Delgado, 1964; Strumwasser and Cade, 1957; von Holst and von Saint Paul, 1963). Some selected studies involving the elicitation of feeding, drinking, aggression, defense and many related patterns, through electrical or chemical stimulation of brainstem and basal forebrain regions, will be reviewed. We shall try to localize the structures crucial to the integration of these sequences by reference to some brain lesion experiments. In regard to such lesion studies the role of the neocortex in the execution of motor sequences must be considered. The classic view of voluntary behavior in corticalized species implies the organization of each muscle twitch in appropriate sequence through sequential firing from the precentral gyrus, which produces axonal discharge in the corticospinal tracts. There are many reasons to doubt this view (Ruch, 1960), but few alternative hypotheses have been available. We shall review some evidence which at least makes it conceivable that, in the intact animal, motor control involves the sequential facilitation of motor sequences already preformed in the brainstem and conducted caudally through the extrapyramidal, rather than the corticospinal, pathways. If this latter argument should prove feasible, it would provide an anatomical basis for the operation of reinforcement mechanisms in learned behaviors at the brainstem level.

This would be a conservative method of control from an evolutionary standpoint. Assuming these preformed patterns exist in the brainstem, it seems unlikely that they would be completely bypassed for a technique of activation that relied solely upon the fantastically delicate sequential firing demanded by a pure corticospinal tract theory of voluntary behavior.

Reinforcement: approach or withdrawal motor sequences

Olds and Olds (1965, p. 381) have observed that there is apparently a neural system which functions: '. . . to facilitate *ongoing* motor mechanisms and, possibly, to reinforce the firing pattern of *antecedently active* motor systems. This interstitial system might be thought of as the final common path of a reinforcement mechanism which controls all the voluntary or operant behavior of the organism.' The facilitation of ongoing motor mechanisms would be a simpler mechanism and could be used to account for the manner in which a novel environment supports the locomotor exploration of a mammal, or the consummatory activity which might ensue if a hungry animal were to stumble upon some food.

The latter role of reinforcement is invoked to explain its apparently retroactive effects in operant learning situations. The thesis presented here is similar in that the facilitation of motor patterns is considered the sufficient condition for reinforcement. However, our formulation differs from that of Olds and Olds (1965) in the absence of a generalized reinforcement mechanism. Rather, we visualize sets of parallel neural pathways regulating species-typical response patterns. It is the activation of these independent paths by whatever means which constitutes what is conventionally described as reinforcement. Those stimuli which are uniquely capable of reliably activating particular primitive approach or withdrawal sequences would be especially potent reinforcing agents. The learning of new responses would take place by contiguity.

This physiological theory has much in common with the consummatory response theory which Sheffield and his colleagues used to explain the reinforcing properties of nonnutritive sweet substances (Sheffield and Roby, 1950; Sheffield, Roby and Campbell, 1954), or of incomplete copulatory activities (Sheffield, Wulff and Backer, 1951). It is also compatible with Premack's (1959) theoretical framework, which places emphasis on the frequency of occurrence of response sequences as indexes of their reinforcing properties. However, it is more closely related to the ethological theories of reinforcement which have been proposed to account for the performance of species characteristic behaviors.

Lorenz has pointed out that . . . the end of purposive behavior is . . . the performance of consummatory action, which is attained as a consequence of the animal's arrival at an external situation which provides the special sign stimuli releasing the consummatory act (Tinbergen, 1951, p. 106).

In our theory the activation of the underlying neural systems is considered the sufficient condition for reinforcement. The experiments of Thompson (1963, 1964) illustrate this position. He found that Siamese fighting fish and roosters would learn a response which was rewarded by the sight of their respective rivals (sign stimuli which elicit attack responses).

Sensory filtering and the activation of reinforcement pathways

In the intact animal, activation of an approach or withdrawal motor sequence will depend upon information arriving through the primary sensory channels and its interacting with ongoing activity in the brainstem or limbic system. As Pfaffmann (1960) has suggested, it seems reasonable that sensory stimuli exert their reinforcing effects via limbic-system structures. It is tempting to interpret the effects of amygdaloid lesions including docility (Schreiner and Kling, 1956; Woods, 1956), impaired attack behavior (Karli, 1956), or the insensitivity of monkeys to shifts in reward magnitude (Schwartzbaum, 1960), as due to interruption of the sensory mechanism normally involved in the activation of approach or withdrawal sequences. However, the amygdala, which seems ideally suited for this role, possesses a disappointingly small number of units which are responsive to other than olfactory stimulation (Creutzfeldt, Bell and Adey, 1963).

Gross electrode recordings have demonstrated that the different sensory modalities do converge on the amygdala (Gloor, 1960). The paucity of units responsive to these other modalities is accordingly somewhat surprising. It is possible that the difficulty in finding responsive units derives from the use of inappropriate stimuli. Hubel and Wiesel (1962) and Lettvin, Maturana, Pitts and McCulloch (1959) have found units in the visual systems of the cat and frog, respectively, which respond selectively and exclusively to particular patterns of stimulation. The proposed role for the amygdala is that of a sensory filter which mediates the effects of biologically salient stimuli. Accordingly, its afferent pathways may be so organized as to render its units selectively responsive to these complex stimuli. The observation by Sawa and Delgado (1963) that the sight of a rat and the meowing of a cat were particularly effective in driving amygdaloid units in cats is indicative of such a conclusion. Nevertheless, the specification of limbic pathways which may mediate sensory influence over the approach and withdrawal sequences remains unclear.

We may still proceed with certain assumptions regarding the ultimate nature of reinforcing activity. For example, it seems reasonable that, in the normal animal, summation of facilitation from many channels can serve in reinforcing a motor sequence. Thus, activation of the chewing-swallowing sequence might involve facilitation from the lateral hypothalamus, as well as from the primary systems involved with taste and smell, and the corticofugal pathways mediating the learned visual recognition of food stimuli. The magnitude of the reinforcing effects, that is, the strength of activation of the feeding pathway, would be the summated effect of converging facilitatory discharge upon a final common pathway.

Some recent data of MacDonnell and Flynn (1966) showed how the reinforcement of a motor sequence may depend on the summation of environmental and central events. They found that jaw opening, one of the final events in the sequence of attack behavior in cats, depended upon facilitation from tactile stimulation and hypothalamic stimulation. Cats with section of the trigeminal nerve showed no jaw opening during hypothalamically elicited attack without there being any evidence of motor impairment. Furthermore, in the intact animal, tactile stimulation of the perioral and lipline regions elicited jaw opening, but only in cats who were receiving electrical stimulation of the hypothalamus.

Within the above scheme, the conventional operations used to manipulate primary drives (deprivation or modification of circulating hormone levels) serve a variety of functions. They directly influence transmission in the facilitatory pathway, as ventromedial hypothalamic activity apparently regulates facilitation from the lateral hypothalamic feeding pathway (Hoebel and Teitelbaum, 1962). They regulate arousal level (Bélanger and Feldman, 1962; Hebb, 1955). And they provide the stimulus cues associated with deprivation or hormonal states. Such cues might serve as conditioned stimuli eliciting a particular sequence, or as potential conditioned stimuli in a new learning situation.

This formulation places drive reduction in a new light. The stimuli which reduce drives are now seen as but one of a class of stimuli which potentially facilitate a motor sequence. However, these stimuli may possess a unique self-governing mechanism. For example, in hunger, food simultaneously facilitates a particular motor sequence and produces changes in blood chemistry which ultimately inhibit facilitation in the system. Presumably with non-drive-reducing reinforcing stimuli there are other factors which could either enhance or decrease the ability of a stimulus to facilitate a given motor sequence. Enhanced neural reactivity might be associated with sheer deprivation of stimulation within the sensory pathway (Sharpless, 1964). Decrements would be attributed to receptor adaptation or some central habituatory process resulting from sheer stimulus repetition, as in the gradual diminution of the orienting response to a repetitively presented tone (Sharpless and Jasper, 1956; Thompson and Welker, 1963). There is some evidence that one of the key characteristics distinguishing a reinforcing from a non-reinforcing central stimulus is the relatively slow habituation of orienting responses elicited by the former as opposed to the latter (Glickman and Feldman, 1961).

Among the non-drive-reducing stimuli capable of facilitating motor patterns would be those capable of evoking investigatory behaviors. However, habituation to simple stimuli proceeds fairly rapidly in most mammalian species (Glickman and Sroges, 1966; Welker, 1956) and we would infer that there is a correspondingly rapid decrement in facilitation, that is, reinforcement.

The selective preferences for mild salt or sweet solutions exhibited by rats (Young and Schulte, 1963; Young and Shuford, 1965) presumably result from some unique stimulus properties of the agents in question which give them direct access to reinforcing pathways (Pfaffmann, 1960). In the terminology of our theory, they are viewed as having direct access to the pathways involved in the facilitation of the feeding or drinking sequence, and are resistant to the habituatory process which quickly destroys the facilitating properties of most sensory stimuli. The fact that degrees of hunger or thirst affect the intake of saccharine (Smith and Duffy, 1957) or weak salt (Deutsch and Jones, 1960) solutions, suggests that the facilitatory effects upon the consummatory response are mediated by the same pathways which mediate normal feeding and drinking.

Some relevant data

The identity of approach or withdrawal and reinforcement pathways

A major feature of this theory is the identity of regions yielding approach sequences upon electrical stimulation with positive reinforcement and those yielding withdrawal with negative reinforcement. It should be kept in mind that: (1) each approach or withdrawal sequence is postulated to operate through a pathway which is anatomically separable at the level of the upper brainstem; and (2) it is possible to summate total stimulus effects within a pathway through interaction of central and environmentally applied stimuli.

One problem that frequently arises in the studies to be reviewed concerns the 'purity' of intracranial stimulation. All of the approach sequences to be described can be elicited from the lateral hypothalamic-medial forebrain bundle regions. It seems likely that stimulation in this area invades more than one approach pathway. A given experimenter might be unaware of this unless he provided the subject with an adequate range of environmental stimuli to support the appearance of the overt behavior sequence in question. There is now ample evidence for the dependence of elicited sequences upon stimuli present in the test situation (Delgado, 1964; von Holst and von Saint Paul, 1963). Many experimenters stimulating in the lateral hypothalamus of the rat to study feeding have probably been simultaneously facilitating separate nest-building or gnawing sequences (Roberts and Carey, 1965), but were unaware of this because of the lack of suitable materials in the test situation.

Feeding. The identification of elicited behavior and reinforcing qualities of stimulation is best established in feeding. Stimulation through the same electrode in the lateral hypothalamus of the rat can yield either self-stimulation or feeding dependent upon the conditions of testing (Hoebel and Teitelbaum, 1962; Margules and Olds, 1962). Hoebel and Teitelbaum further demonstrated that simultaneous stimulation of the ventromedial hypothalamus, or extensive feeding, will suppress both stimulation-induced feeding and self-stimulation, while ablation or depression of ventromedial hypothalamic activity leads to increments in feeding and self-stimulation. As Olds (1962, p. 567) has observed: '. . . such findings appear to indicate a very near identity of the lateral mechanisms responsible for lowering the threshold for eating reflexes and that responsible for hunger-related positive reinforcement.' Covariation of self-stimulation rate with food deprivation has also been observed in the medial septal area of the rat (Brady, Boren, Conrad and Sidman, 1957; Hodos and Valenstein, 1960). Robinson and Mishkin (1962) have recently mapped a great many loci in the basal forebrain and diencephalon of the monkey where stimulation may elicit feeding, or sometimes ejection of food from the mouth. There is a crude correlation between the structures from which these latter experimenters were able to evoke feeding responses and those which have been found to yield positive reinforcement in other species, although there were some points of discrepancy (Olds, 1962). They also observed positive reinforcement from seven of twelve points yielding 'ejection', however, this evidence is not a critical refutation of the point of view presented here. It is quite likely that, within the regions explored by Robinson and Mishkin, there was overlap with reinforcement systems other than feeding and drinking (e.g. see MacLean and Ploog, 1962). As Robinson and Mishkin (1962, p. 261) note: '. . . little was seen to suggest the nature of the point if food and water were removed.' It is highly likely that without proper environmental support these other motivational pathways could also pass unnoticed. In a more recent study directly concerned with the 'overlap' issue, Plutchick, McFarland and Robinson (1966) have observed feeding, drinking, biting, defecating and urinating as elicited behaviors coincident with self-stimulation in the monkey.

An experiment by Mendelson (1965) is also relevant to our formulation. He has found that rats in a T-maze will choose the side offering lateral hypothalamic stimulation plus food over the side offering lateral hypothalamic stimulation alone. This is what would be expected if reinforcement were a function of total facilitation in the feeding pathway, with corresponding summation of exteroceptive-proprioceptive and intracranial stimulation.

Gnawing and nesting. Roberts and Carey (1965) have made the important discovery that stimulation of separable pathways in the lateral hypothalamus of the rat can elicit nest building, paper gathering, or gnawing. The latter responses can be differentiated from feeding, as the rat will terminate feeding when appropriately stimulated and start gnawing a block of wood. They have further shown that a rat will learn a Y-maze if the reinforcement is simultaneous stimulation in a 'gnawing' region and presentation of a

S. E. Glickman and B. B. Schiff 293

wooden block upon which to gnaw. Olds and Olds' (1962) results indicate that the lateral hypothalamic region contains pathways mediating potent positive reinforcement effects. We suggest that such effects do not simply correlate with feeding but also with activation of any of these approach systems, including gnawing, nest building and paper gathering. The latter types of behavior have also been elicited in rats through chemical stimulation (Fisher, 1956) of the preoptic regions. We accordingly predict that all of these regions would support self-stimulation behavior, and that selective covariation of such self-stimulation behavior would occur with these variables regulating the intensity of nest building (temperature or hormonal state), or gnawing (possibly deprivation of opportunity to gnaw).

The significance and magnitude of non-feeding chewing responses is not often appreciated by psychologists working with rats maintained in the usual barren wire environment (unless the rats happen to chew down the edges of their metal food dishes). The paper-shredding response of the Mongolian gerbil (*Meriones unquiculatus*) has recently been examined.[1] A quantitative study of such behavior revealed that an average gerbil would completely shred more than two sheets of $8\frac{1}{2} \times 11$-inch bond paper per day, even when fed ad lib with hard pellets and maintained in an environment offering adequate warmth, burrowing material and a place of retreat. Males chewed equally as much as females, and chewing continued at a high rate even after their cages were virtually filled to the brim with the shredded remnants of previous days. Preliminary observation also suggested that deprivation of opportunity to chew facilitated subsequent chewing. The results bear a mixed relationship to 'conventional' drives, for example, hunger, but they fit neatly within a consummatory response formulation which emphasizes the biological utility of such species-typical response patterns.

Drinking. The relation between drinking and self-stimulation has not been as clearly defined as in the case of feeding.[2] However,

1. S. E. Glickman, B. Morrison, and P. Bourke, unpublished observations, 1965.
2. Mogenson and Stevenson (1966) have recently been able to elicit self-stimulation and drinking behavior from the same electrode placement in the lateral hypothalamus of rats.

following Grossman's (1962) demonstration of cholinergic sites in the hypothalamus mediating drinking, Fisher and Coury (1962) have elicited the response from a wide range of areas between the forebrain and the mammillary-interpeduncular region. Fisher and Coury (1962) comment on the overlap between the drinking system and Papez circuit, and further observe that all of the areas yielding drinking also support positive intracranial reinforcement as defined in Olds' maps.

Sexual activity. Caggiula and Hoebel (1966) have found that constant stimulation of 'reward' loci in the posterior hypothalamus of male rats elicited copulation with estrous females. They also showed that during stimulation the rats would press a bar to open a door for access to females. Herberg (1963a, 1963b) has found that stimulation of loci within the medial forebrain bundle of the rat can both elicit ejaculation and reinforce self-stimulation behavior. In both studies it was also shown that self-stimulation rates covaried with androgen levels, which is compatible with a prior report of such covariation by Olds (1958). Vaughan and Fisher (1962) have successfully induced unusually vigorous male sexual behavior in the rat through intracranial electrical stimulation in the anterior dorsolateral hypothalamus. The behavior sequence appeared only if there was an estrous female present in the test situation. There were no tests of self-stimulation reported; however, the sites are again located within a diencephalic region designated as highly reinforcing by Olds and Olds (1963). Finally, a gross overlap may also be observed between the regions yielding penile erection upon electrical stimulation in the squirrel monkey (MacLean and Ploog, 1962) and those areas found to yield positive reinforcement in various species (Olds, 1962).

Attack. Wasman and Flynn (1962) have observed directed attack sequences following electrical stimulation of the lateral hypothalamus in the cat. Such sequences fall into two general categories: affective attack and stalking attack. The former included hissing, piloerection, growling, arching of the back, head low to the ground, circling the cage, striking with the forepaws and biting. This is the kind of pattern one might expect if the cat were defending its territory against a fairly equal opponent, where the growling and piloerection might serve an intimidating function. Stalking attack also involved the animal placing its nose to the ground and arching its back. But this was followed by movement directly to the rat and by biting, with less prominent use of the paws and only minimal growling, hissing, or piloerection. These stalking attacks, which Wasman and Flynn note were more deadly, seem more characteristic of the predatory response to a clearly weaker opponent and were elicited from more lateral points in the hypothalamus than the affective attacks. In accordance with our discussion of the classification of behavior, the stalking pattern would be classified as a pure approach sequence. Not so the affective attack which contains defensive elements (hissing, piloerection) that have been shown to presage possible conversion into a flight sequence (Fernandez de Molina and Hunsperger, 1959). We thus expect high positive reinforcing effects from the placements eliciting stalking attack, and mixed, but dominantly positive, effects from regions yielding affective attack. Wasman and Flynn present no direct information about this point. However, the data are compatible with the shift from pure positive to negative effects of intracranial stimulation as one moves from the lateral to the more medial hypothalamic areas (Olds, 1962). In addition, Roberts and Kiess (1964) have successfully motivated Y-maze learning in the cat by providing hypothalamic stimulation culminating in attack upon a rat placed in one of the goal boxes. Once again, we anticipate that stimulation in this region is positively reinforcing without the presence of the external stimulus (rat), although the latter may add considerably to the magnitude of reinforcement as in the previously cited study of Mendelson (1965).

Levison and Flynn (1965) found that the probability of eliciting aggressive attack with hypothalamic stimulation was very low when the environmental stimulus objects were blocks of styrofoam or foam rubber. The probability of persistent attack increased systematically as they substituted a stuffed rat, an anesthetized rat, and finally an unanesthetized rat. Presumably the reinforcement magnitude of the consummatory attack increased accordingly. It may be noted that the external stimulus, in addition to providing direct facilitation of the motor sequence, results in the introduction of new response-dependent stimulus cues in the situation – with emphasis on those regulating the directed attack. Such cues may be crucial in sustaining responding during extinction of self-stimulation behavior (Gibson, Reid, Sakai and Porter, 1965), and it is possible that we might obtain lever-pressing, but not efficient maze learning, without the environmental support that provokes an overt motor sequence.

Defensive or escape behaviors. We now come upon a group of experiments involving the elicitation of defensive or flight reactions. These studies are especially difficult to classify because effects shift with changes in current level and duration; the barren environments in which many of the tests were carried out and differences in descriptive terminology may create discrepancies that do not actually exist.

It has been known for some years that stimulation of various diencephalic regions can produce fearful, defensive motor sequences (Hess and Brügger, 1943). It was originally averred that such sequences were purely motor, since their elicitation apparently could not be used as an adequate UCS–UCR sequence in a conditioning situation (Massermann, 1941). However, both thalamic (Delgado, Roberts and Miller, 1954) and hypothalamic (Brown and Cohen, 1959) stimulation were subsequently shown to be capable of 'motivating' escape or avoidance learning.

Stimulation as far caudally as the mesencephalic gray matter has also been shown capable of mediating a conditioned response (Ross, Pineyrua, Prieto, Areas, Stirner and Galeano, 1965). However, our initial concern here is with the differentiation among varieties of defensive responses and the structures from which they can be elicited. To achieve some workable unit, we shall restrict ourselves to the effects of electrical stimulation within the central mesencephalon, hypothalamus and amygdala.

Hunsperger (1956) has described two systems coursing through the mid-brain and hypothalamus of the cat, stimulation of which can elicit either a pure flight response or a hissing–defensive pattern. The latter may terminate in directed attack toward a dog in the test room. Hissing was elicited from the perifornical regions of the hypothalamus and central gray and the pure flight response was induced from a 'common outer zone'. Fernandez de Molina and Hunsperger (1959) subsequently followed this system into the amygdala, where they obtained complex effects which shifted with the duration and strength of stimulation. Growling was elicited with low intensities of stimulation. With increasing frequency or voltage, growling might shift to hissing, or growling–hissing might terminate in flight. Similar effects were obtainable by simply maintaining stimulation for periods up to one minute. Unfortunately, there are discrepancies in the anatomical maps of amygdaloid sites which yield different defensive responses as reported by various investigators (MacLean and Delgado, 1953; Magnus and Lammers, 1956; Ursin and Kaada, 1960; Zbrozeyna, 1963). However, the basic responses – growling, hissing, crouching and gross locomotor running – can be found within most of the reports. It appears to the present authors that a central step in untangling this literature would be more precise delineation of the individual motor patterns elicited by stimulation in a complete range of biologically meaningful situations of the sort employed by von Holst and von Saint Paul (1963). Zbrozeyna's (1963) criticism of Ursin and Kaada (1960) for attempting to break down the total defensive pattern described by Hess seems unwarranted. Finer, not cruder, analytic methods are needed.

Assume that there are discrete pathways in the brainstem and basal forebrain mediating pure attack (Roberts and Kiess, 1964; Wasman and Flynn, 1962), pure flight (Hunsperger, 1956; Ursin and Kaada, 1960), or the mixed elements of attack, intimidation, and flight inherent in the defensive pattern (Fernandez de Molina and Hunsperger, 1959; Hunsperger, 1956; Ursin and Kaada, 1960; Wasman and Flynn, 1962). Given the information just cited regarding shifts in stimulus effects with changes in duration and intensity, many of the 'paradoxical' reinforcement effects in the literature can be resolved within the theoretical framework outlined previously. As long as stimulation is confined to a pure 'attack' (approach) pathway, it should prove positively reinforcing. Conversely, stimulation in a pure escape or flight (withdrawal) pathway should produce clear negative reinforcing effects. However, stimulation in a defensive pathway might well produce mixed effects, dependent on duration and intensity, since increasing either of these has been shown capable of converting a defensive response into a flight sequence. Studies reporting both approach and avoidance behavior from the same locus (Bower and Miller,

1958; Brown and Cohen, 1959; Roberts, 1958) have generally involved stimulation in medial and posterior hypothalamic regions where defense reactions have been elicited by electrical stimulation. Alternatively, primarily positive effects characterize stimulation in the immediately lateral areas merging with the medial forebrain bundle (Olds, 1962), as would be expected in terms of the concentration of approach behavior (including attack) pathways in that region. Poschel (1966) has recently documented the shift from positive to negative self-stimulation effects as one shifts from the lateral to the medial hypothalamus of the rat.

Wurtz and Olds (1963) in their study mapping self-stimulation effects from the amygdala, introduce their experiment with a review of the behavior patterns elicited by amygdaloid stimulation. They note that, '. . . these studies emphasized the aversive and aggressive effects observed, and positive reinforcement was not anticipated' (Wurtz and Olds, 1963, p. 941). It is further observed that it may be difficult to identify those elicited behaviors which characterize positive reinforcement. There are several points to be considered here. Stimulation in the amygdala of the rat may activate other approach pathways (Grossman, 1964). Then, we again propose the view that pure aggressive behavior is basically an approach pattern which should be maintained by a positive reinforcement mechanism. On the other hand, the defensive behavior frequently evoked by amygdaloid stimulation contains elements of both approach and withdrawal, and we would expect mixed effects, critically sensitive to intensity and duration of stimulation from these loci. A test of this position is difficult since 'elicited' behavior has been mapped in the cat with conflicting results, while self-stimulation regions within the amygdala have been studied in detail only in the rat. However, there is at least a crude agreement between Ursin and Kaada's location of a 'fear' area and Wurtz and Olds delineation of a self-stimulation escape area in the basolateral amygdaloid nuclei.

References

BÉLANGER, D., and FELDMAN, S. M. (1962), 'Effects of water deprivation upon heart rate and instrumental activity in the rat', J. compar. physiol. Psychol., vol. 55, pp. 220–25.

BOWER, G. H., and MILLER, N. E. (1958), 'Rewarding and punishing effects from stimulating the same place in the rat's brain', *J. compar. physiol. Psychol.,* vol. 51, pp. 669–74.

BRADY, J. V., BOREN, J. J., CONRAD, D., and SIDMAN, M. (1957), 'The effect of food and water deprivation upon intracranial self-stimulation', *J. compar. physiol. Psychol.,* vol. 50, pp. 134–7.

BROWN, G. W., and COHEN, B. D. (1959), 'Avoidance and approach learning motivated by stimulation of identical hypothalamic loci', *Amer. J. Physiol.,* vol. 197, pp. 153–7.

BROWN, J. L., and HUNSPERGER, R. W. (1963), 'Neurothology and the motivation of agonistic behaviour', *Animal Behav.,* vol. 11, pp. 439–48.

BULLOCK, H. T. (1961), 'Origins of patterned nervous discharge', *Behav.,* vol. 17, pp. 48–60.

CAGGIULA, A. R., and HOEBEL, B. G. (1966), '"Copulation-reward site" in the posterior hypothalamus', *Sci.,* vol. 153, pp. 1284–5.

CREUTZFELDT, O. D., BELL, F. R., and ADEY, W. R. (1963), 'The activity of neurons in the amygdala of the cat following afferent stimulation', in W. Bargmann and J. P. Schade (eds.), *The Rhinencephalon and Related Structures,* Elsevier, pp. 31–49.

DELGADO, J. M. R. (1964), 'Free behavior and brain stimulation' *Int. Rev. Neurobiol.,* vol. 6, pp. 349–449.

DELGADO, J. M. R. (1965), 'Sequential behavior induced repeatedly by stimulation of the red nucleus in free monkeys', *Sci.,* vol. 148, pp. 1361–3.

DELGADO, J. M. R., ROBERTS, W. W., and MILLER, N. E. (1954), 'Learning motivated by electrical stimulation of the brain', *Amer. J. Physiol.,* vol. 179, pp. 587–93.

DEUTSCH, J. A., and JONES, A. D. (1960), 'Diluted water: An explanation of the rat's preference for saline', *J. compar. physiol. Psychol.,* vol. 53, pp. 122–7.

FERNANDEZ DE MOLINA, A., and HUNSPERGER, R. W. (1959), 'Central representation of effective reactions in forebrain and brain stem: electrical stimulation of amygdala, stria terminalis and adjacent structures', *J. Physiol.,* vol. 145, pp. 251–265.

FISHER, A. E. (1956), 'Maternal and sexual behavior induced by intracranial chemical stimulation', *Sci.,* vol. 124, pp. 228–9.

FISHER, A. E., and COURY, J. N. (1962), 'Cholinergic tracing of a central neural circuit underlying the thirst drive', *Sci.,* vol. 138, pp. 691–3.

GIBSON, W. E., REID, L. D., SAKAI, M., and PORTER, P. B. (1965), 'Intracranial reinforcement compared with sugar water reinforcement' *Sci.,* vol. 148, pp. 1357–9.

GLICKMAN, S. E., and FELDMAN, S. M. (1961), 'Habituation of the arousal response to direct stimulation of the brainstem', *Electroencephalography clin. Neurophysiol.,* vol. 13, pp. 703–9.

GLICKMAN, S. E., and SROGES, R. W. (1966), 'Curiosity in zoo animals', *Behav.,* vol. 26, pp. 151–88.

GLOOR, P. (1960), 'Amygdala', in J. Field (ed.), *Handbook of Physiology*, Amer. Physiol. Soc., vol. 2, pp. 1395–420.

GROSSMAN, S. P. (1962), 'Direct adrenergic and cholinergic stimulation of hypothalamic mechanisms', *Amer. J. Physiol.*, vol. 202, pp. 872–82.

GROSSMAN, S. P. (1964), 'Behavioral effects of chemical stimulation of the ventral amygdala', *J. compar. physiol. Psychol.*, vol. 57, pp. 29–36.

HEBB, D. O. (1955), 'Drives and the CNS (conceptual nervous system)' *Psychol. Rev.*, vol. 62, pp. 243–54.

HERBERG, L. J. (1963a), 'Determinants of extinction in electrical self-stimulation', *J. compar. physiol. Psychol.*, vol. 56, pp. 686–90.

HERBERG, L. J. (1963b), 'Seminal ejaculation following positively reinforcing electrical stimulation of the rat hypothalamus', *J. compar. physiol. Psychol.*, vol. 56, pp. 679–85.

HESS, W. R., and BRÜGGER, M. (1943), 'Das subkorticale Zentrum der affectiven Abwehrreaktion', *Helvetia Physiologica Acta*, vol. 1, pp. 33–52.

HODOS, W., and VALENSTEIN, E. (1960), 'Motivational variables affecting the rate of behavior maintained by intracranial stimulation', *J. compar. physiol. Psychol.*, vol. 53, pp. 502–7.

HOEBEL, B. G., and TEITELBAUM, P. (1962), 'Hypothalamic control of feeding and self-stimulation', *Sci.*, vol. 135, pp. 375–6.

HUBEL, D. H., and WIESEL, T. N. (1962), 'Receptive fields, binocular interaction and functional architecture in the cat's visual cortex', *J. Physiol.*, vol. 160, pp. 106–54.

HUNSPERGER, R. W. (1956), 'Affektreaktionen auf elektrische Reizung im Hirnstamm der Katze', *Helvetia Physiologica Acta*, vol. 14, pp. 70–92.

HYDE, J. E. (1965), 'Effects of simultaneous application of opposing stimuli for head turning in cats', *Exper. Neurol.*, vol. 11, pp. 230–44.

KARLI, P. (1956), 'The Norway rat's killing response to the white mouse: An experimental analysis', *Behav.*, vol. 10, pp. 81–103.

LETTVIN, J. Y., MATURANA, H. R., PITTS, W. H., and McCULLOCH, W. S. (1959), 'What the frog's eye tells the frog's brain', *Proc. Inst. Radio Eng.*, vol. 47, pp. 1940–41.

LEVISON, P. K., and FLYNN, J. P. (1965), 'The objects attacked by cats during stimulation of the hypothalamus', *Animal Behav.*, vol. 13, pp. 217–20.

LEYHAUSEN, P. (1956), 'Verhaltensstudien an Katzen', *Zeitschrift für Tierpsychologie*, (Monogr. Suppl. no. 2), pp. 1–120.

LORENZ, K. (1950), 'The comparative method in studying innate behavior patterns', *Symposium of the Soc. of exper. Biol.*, vol. 4, pp. 221–68.

MACDONNELL, M. F., and FLYNN, J. P. (1966), 'Control of sensory fields by stimulation of hypothalamus', *Sci.*, vol. 152, pp. 1406–8.

MACLEAN, P. D., and DELGADO, J. M. R. (1953), 'Electrical and chemical stimulation of fronto-temporal portion of the limbic system in the waking animal', *Electroencephalography clin. Neurophysiol.*, vol. 5, pp. 91–100.

MacLean, P. D., and Ploog, D. W. (1962), 'Cerebral representation of penile erection', *J. Neurophysiol.*, vol. 25, pp. 29–55.

Magnus, O., and Lammers, H. J. (1956), 'The amygdaloid nuclear complex', *Folia Psychiatrica, Neurologica, et Neurochirurgica Neerlandica*, vol. 59, pp. 555–82.

Margules, D. L., and Olds, J. (1962), 'Identical "feeding" and "rewarding" systems in the lateral hypothalamus of rats', *Sci.*, vol. 135, pp. 374–5.

Massermann, J. H. (1941), 'Is the hypothalamus a center of emotion?', *Psychosomatic Medicine*, vol. 3, pp. 3–25.

Mendelson, J. (1965), 'Electrical stimulation in hypothalamic "feeding area" of rats: Motivational, reinforcing, and cue properties', unpublished doctoral dissertation. Massachusetts Institute of Technology.

Moltz, H. (1965), 'Contemporary instinct theory and the fixed action pattern', *Psychol. Rev.*, vol. 72, pp. 27–47.

Olds, J. (1958), 'Self-stimulation of the brain: Used to study local effects of hunger, sex and drugs', *Sci.*, vol. 126, pp. 315–24.

Olds, J. (1962), 'Hypothalamic substrates of reward', *Physiol. Rev.*, vol. 42, pp. 554–604.

Olds, M. E., and Olds, J. (1963), 'Approach-avoidance analysis of rat diencephalon', *J. compar. Neurol.*, vol. 120, pp. 259–95.

Olds, M. E., and Olds, J. (1965), 'Drives, rewards and the brain', in T. M. Newcomb (ed.), *New Directions in Psychology*, Holt, Rinehart & Winston, pp. 329–410.

Pfaffmann, C. (1960), 'The pleasures of sensation', *Psychol. Rev.*, vol. 67, pp. 253–68.

Plutchik, R., McFarland, W. L., and Robinson, B. W. (1966), 'Relationships between current intensity, self-stimulation rates, escape latencies, and evoked behavior in rhesus monkeys', *J. compar. physiol. Psychol.*, vol. 61, pp. 181–8.

Poschel, B. P. H. (1966), 'Comparison of reinforcing effects yielded by lateral versus medial hypothalamic stimulation', *J. compar. physiol. Psychol.*, vol. 61, pp. 346–52.

Premack, D. (1959), 'Toward empirical behavior laws. I: Positive reinforcement', *Psychol. Rev.*, vol. 66, pp. 219–33.

Roberts, W. W. (1958), 'Both rewarding and punishing effects from stimulation of posterior hypothalamus of cat with same electrode at same intensity', *J. compar. physiol. Psychol.*, vol. 51, pp. 400–7.

Roberts, W. W., and Carey, R. J. (1965), 'Rewarding effect of performance of gnawing aroused by hypothalamic stimulation in the rat', *J. compar. physiol. Psychol.*, vol. 59, pp. 317–24.

Roberts, W. W., and Kiess, H. O. (1964), Motivational properties of hypothalamic aggression in cats', *J. compar. physiol. Psychol.*, vol. 58 pp. 187–93.

Robinson, B. W., and Mishkin, M. (1962), 'Alimentary responses evoked from forebrain structures in Mucacca mulatta', *Sci.*, vol. 136, pp. 260–61.

Ross, N., Pineyrua, M., Prieto, S., Areas, L. P., Stirner, A., and Galeano, C. (1965), 'Conditioning of midbrain behavioral responses' *Exper. Neurol.*, vol. 11, pp. 263–76.

Ruch, T. C. (1960), 'The cerebral cortex: Its structure and motor functions', in T. C. Ruch and J. F. Fulton (eds.), *Med. Physiol. Biophysics*, Saunders, pp. 249–77.

Sawa, M., and Delgado, J. M. R. (1963), 'Amygdala unitary activity in the unrestrained cat', *Electroencephalography clin. Neurophysiol.*, vol. 15, pp. 637–50.

Schneirla, T. C. (1959), 'An evolutionary theory of biphasic processes underlying approach and withdrawal', in M. R. Jones (ed.), *Nebraska Symposium on Motivation*, University of Nebraska Press, pp. 1–42.

Schreiner, L., and Kling, A. (1956), 'Rhinencephalon and behavior', *Amer. J. Physiol.*, vol. 184, pp. 486–90.

Schwartzbaum, J. S. (1960), 'Changes in reinforcing properties of stimuli following ablation of the amygdaloid complex in monkeys', *J. compar. physiol. Psychol.*, vol. 53, pp. 388–95.

Sharpless, S. K. (1964), 'Reorganization of function in the nervous system – use and disuse', *Ann. Rev. Physiol.*, vol. 26, pp. 357–88.

Sharpless, S. K., and Jasper, M. H. (1956), 'Habituation of the arousal reaction', *Brain*, vol. 79, pp. 655–80.

Sheffield, F. D., and Roby, T. B. (1950), 'Reward value of a non-nutritive sweet taste', *J. compar. physiol. Psychol.*, vol. 43, pp. 471–81.

Sheffield, F. D., Roby, T. B., and Campbell, B. A. (1954), 'Drive reduction versus consummatory behavior as determinants of reinforcement', *J. compar. physiol. Psychol.*, vol. 47, pp. 349–54.

Sheffield, F. D., Wulff, J. J., and Backer, R. (1951), 'Reward value of copulation without sex drive reduction', *J. compar. physiol. Psychol.*, vol. 44, pp. 3–8.

Skulkety, F. M. (1962), 'Circus movements in cats following midbrain stimulation through chronically implanted electrodes', *J. Neurophysiol.*, vol. 25, pp. 152–64.

Smith, M., and Duffy, M. (1957), 'Consumption of sucrose and saccharine by hungry and satiated rats', *J. compar. physiol. Psychol.*, vol. 50, pp. 65–9.

Strumwasser, F., and Cade, T. (1957), 'Behavior elicited by brain stimulation in freely moving vertebrates', *Anat. Rec.*, vol. 128, pp. 630–31.

Thompson, R. F., and Welker, W. I. (1963), 'Role of the auditory cortex in reflex head orientation by cats to auditory stimuli', *J. compar. physiol. Psychol.*, vol. 56, pp. 996–1002.

Thompson, T. I. (1963), 'Visual reinforcement in Siamese fighting fish', *Sci.*, vol. 141, pp. 55–7.

Thompson, T. I. (1964), 'Visual reinforcement in fighting cocks', *J. exper. Anal. Behav.*, vol. 7, pp. 45–9.

Tinbergen, N. (1951), *The Study of Instinct*, Oxford University Press.

Ursin, H., and Kaada, B. R. (1960), 'Functional localization within the amygdaloid complex of the cat', *Electroencephalography clin. Neurophysiol.*, vol. 12, pp. 1–20.

Valenstein, E. S. (1964), 'Problems of measurement and interpretation with reinforcing brain stimulation', *Psychol. Rev.*, vol. 71, pp. 415–38.

Vaughan, E., and Fisher, A. E. (1962), 'Male sexual behavior induced by intracranial electrical stimulation', *Sci.*, vol. 137, pp. 758–60.

von Holst, E., and von Saint Paul, U. (1963), 'On the functional organization of drives', *Animal Behav.*, vol. 11, pp. 1–20.

Wasman, M., and Flynn, J. P. (1962), 'Directed attack elicited from the hypothalamus', *Arch. Neurol.*, vol. 6, pp. 220–27.

Welker, W. I. (1956), 'Some determinants of play and exploration in chimpanzees', *J. compar. physiol. Psychol.*, vol. 49, pp. 84–9.

Wiesel, T. N., and Hubel, D. H. (1963), 'Single cell responses in striate cortex of kittens deprived of vision in one eye', *J. Neurophysiol.*, vol. 26, pp. 1003–17.

Woods, J. W. (1956), '"Taming" of the wild Norway rat by rhinencephalic lesions', *Nature*, vol. 178, pp. 106–10.

Wurtz, R. H., and Olds, J. (1963), 'Amygdaloid stimulation and operant reinforcement in the rat', *J. compar. physiol. Psychol.*, vol. 56, pp. 941–9.

Young, P. T., and Schulte, R. H. (1963), 'Isohedonic contours and tongue activity in three gustatory areas of the rat', *J. compar. physiol. Psychol.*, vol. 56, pp. 465–75.

Young, P. T., and Shuford, E. H. (1955), 'Quantitative control of motivation through sucrose solutions of different concentrations', *J. compar. physiol. Psychol.*, vol. 48, pp. 114–18.

Zbrozeyna, A. W. (1963), 'The anatomical basis of the patterns and behavioural response effected via the amygdala', in W. Bargmann and J. P. Schadé (eds.), *The Rhinencephalon and Related Structures*, Elsevier, pp. 50–68.

29 J. A. Trowill, J. Panksepp and R. Gandelman

An Incentive Model of Rewarding Brain Stimulation

J. A. Trowill, J. Panksepp and R. Gandelman, 'An incentive model of rewarding brain stimulation', *Psychological Review*, volume 76, 1969, pp. 264–81.

Since its discovery by Olds and Milner (1954), rewarding electrical stimulation of the brain (ESB) has been shown from a range of areas covering the diencephalon and limbic system (see Olds and Olds, 1963; Olds, Travis and Schwing, 1960), and from a variety of species, including goldfish (Boyd and Gardner, 1962), pigeons (Goodman and Brown, 1966), rabbits (Bruner, 1966), cats (Roberts, 1958), dogs (Stark and Boyd, 1961), dolphins (Lilly and Miller, 1962), monkeys (Brady, 1961), and humans (Heath and Mickle, 1960). The evidence that organisms acquire new responses to obtain ESB establishes the effect as a reinforcement according to the empirical law of effect (see Spence, 1959, p. 33). However, performance aspects of responding for ESB have established the phenomenon as one which cannot be fully understood in terms of traditional variables of learning theory. For example, Deutsch (1963) has stated:

The discovery of this phenomenon was very important. One of the reasons for this is that it can be used to test the adequacy of existing theories, as Olds and Milner (1954) themselves rightly emphasized. So far such theories have found the phenomenon with its striking characteristics a complete enigma (p. 202).

The purpose of this paper is to review the behavioral evidence surrounding ESB, to assess the major theoretical treatments which have been proposed to account for it, and to analyse the effect in terms of an incentive model which is directly based on the incentive variable of learning theory (see Bolles, 1967; Hull, 1943; Spence, 1956). Furthermore, factors which are thought to contribute to the characteristics of the ESB effect will be analysed in light of their contribution for an understanding of incentive in a general sense.

ESB viewed as a unique reinforcement

Early evidence suggested that rewarding brain stimulation has properties differing from those exhibited by conventional rewards such as food and water. As a result, theories were proposed to account for ESB in terms of new variables or in terms of new combinations of traditional behavioral variables.

The data

Perhaps the most peculiar property of ESB is the extremely rapid extinction of a response previously rewarded with it. In their initial report, Olds and Milner (1954) included cumulative records of pedal pressing which showed a sharp decrease in responding when brain stimulation was discontinued. Furthermore, it was reported that once the animal stopped responding during extinction it seldom returned to the bar. Deutsch (1963) remarked that his subjects (Ss) have seldom bar-pressed more than thirty times during extinction. This observation agrees with the results reported by Seward, Uyeda and Olds (1959).

Rapid falling off of responding is also seen in situations where intermittent reward schedules are employed. Sidman, Brady, Conrad and Schulman (1955) showed an inverse relationship between the rate of responding and the interval between reinforcements. Rats did not maintain responding when the schedule extended beyond a variable interval 16 seconds (VI-16 seconds) or a fixed ratio 7 (FR-7). Furthermore, Brodie, Moreno, Malis and Boren (1960) demonstrated that in most cases monkeys would not respond when the schedule exceeded an FR-20 although one animal did reach a schedule of FR-150. In contrast, the responding of deprived animals for deprivation-specific rewards persists well beyond the scheduling limits typically found with ESB (Ferster and Skinner, 1957).

Performance in the runway situation is also maximized when the interreinforcement interval is short. Seward, Uyeda and Olds (1960) showed that running speed is faster when the animal is put directly back into the start box after receiving brain shock in the

goal than when a fifteen minute intertrial interval (ITI) is imp
between runs. The spaced group had a mean latency of
seconds while the massed *S*s had a mean latency of 15·6 secon
Also, massed practice, for example, immediate replacement
start box, has been shown to improve performance from trial to
trial more than spaced practice, for example, fourteen to sixteen
minutes ITI (Spear, 1962). Olds (1956) also reported a decrement
in running performance between the last trial on one day and the
first trial on the next day. Olds observed that this decrement is not
seen with rats running for conventional rewards.

From the above it appears that responses rewarded with ESB
extinguish or fall off rapidly when reinforcement is withheld.
Furthermore, in order to maintain ESB-directed responding and
in order to increase performance under partial reinforcement
schedules and in runways and mazes the delay between rewards
must not be too great.

Another peculiarity of ESB is the observation that non-contingent brain stimulation can rapidly reinstate an extinguished
response which was previously rewarded with ESB. This phenomenon, sometimes referred to as 'priming' (Gallistel, 1964), has
been reported by Lilly (1958) and Olds (1958d).

Unlike responding for conventional rewards, ESB-rewarded
responding also persists for very long periods of time in the
absence of deprivation or drive conditions, that is, responding
without satiation. Olds (1958b) reported that with the exception of
telencephalic placements where decrements in responding occur
after about eight hours, responding for ESB continues until the
animal quits from exhaustion (up to twenty-four hours). In addition to this seeming lack of satiation, animals also typically prefer
ESB to conventional rewards even when the latter are essential
for self-preservation. Falk (1961) trained rats to press one bar for
ESB and to press another bar for water. Up to extreme deprivation
conditions (ninety-four hours) *S*s consistently chose the bar which
delivered ESB. Also, rats with electrodes in the hypothalamus
will self-starve when given the opportunity to bar-press for ESB
during the daily one-hour feeding session (Routtenberg and Lindy,
1965).

From this it seems that ESB is of a greater reward value than
are conventional rewards. It is perhaps for this reason that Brady

it difficult to show a disruption of bar pressing for
... ditioned emotional response situation.

... ference between ESB and conventional rewards in-
... ficulty of imparting secondary reinforcing properties
... stimulus when brain stimulation is used as primary
... ment. Seward, Uyeda and Olds (1959), using rats main-
... on ad-lib food and water, failed to establish a light as a
... dary reinforcer when it was presented concomitantly with
...B, the reward for bar pressing. Stein (1958), employing a classical conditioning paradigm, did establish a tone as a weak secondary reward. The acquisition procedure consisted of four hundred
pairings of a tone with ESB. Two bars were present during
testing, one produced the tone, the other did not. The average
rate of tone bar presses, although significantly greater than the
operant rate and the rate on the non-tone bar, was only thirty-five
responses per hour. Unfortunately, since Stein did not give details
of the feeding regimen imposed on his animals during training
and testing, one cannot ascertain whether deprivation was a
necessary condition for the effect. Knott and Clayton (1966)
clearly demonstrated secondary reinforcement but again did not
state the feeding schedule. Using rats maintained on ad lib food
and water, Mogenson (1965) replicated both the Seward *et al.*
(1959) paradigm and that of Stein (1958). Secondary reinforcement was not demonstrated in either situation.

Theories

Olds (1958c) proposed that in positively stimulating subcortical
structures one is 'stimulating genuine reward systems in the
brain ... that the effect derives from no mere compulsion or
automatism, but from stimulation of the cells actually involved in
food, sexual, or other reward processes' (p. 675). However, others
proposed theories that were designed to account for the apparent
disparities between behavior maintained by ESB and behavior
maintained by conventional rewards. Due to these peculiar characteristics, all of the theories themselves are characterized by the
introduction of new explanatory concepts and variables. The
following will briefly summarize the major interpretations.

Noting that EEG seizure activity accompanies self-stimulation
(Nielson, Doty and Rutledge, 1958; Porter, Conrad and Brady,

1958), and that self-induced petit mal seizures are rewarding (Robertson, 1954), it has been surmised that seizures might be a necessary component of the reinforcement derived from ESB. However, Reid, Gibson, Gledhill and Porter (1964) showed that self-stimulation rates increase after the administration of anticonvulsant drugs such as phenobarbital and tridione. If seizures are involved in the reward component of ESB the above study would have had to show a decrease in rates of responding.

Another interpretation has considered possible aversive after-effects of rewarding brain stimulation. Ball and Adams (1965) showed that when brain shocks are widely spaced (one every thirty minutes), rats learn to go to an end box of a T-maze where no further shocks are obtained. However, if the intershock interval is reduced (one every twenty seconds) the animals learn to go to the end box where stimulation is given. This result was viewed as indicating that ESB reduces noxious after effects of the previous application of ESB. Thus, the animal is entrapped in a 'vicious circle' in which it *must* receive further electrical stimulation. If this is impossible, as when the intershock interval is long, animals avoid further stimulation.[1] In a subsequent study, Ball (1967) stimulated the infraorbital branch of the trigeminal nerve before, during and after bursts of ESB and recorded evoked potentials from the main sensory nucleus of the trigeminal nerve. The results showed that when infraorbital stimulation was preceded by ESB the postsynaptic potential recorded from the trigeminal nerve was inhibited. These data suggest that ESB could be part of a general inhibitory system which could reduce and/or delay abnormal sensory input perhaps resulting from a previous application of ESB. Other studies (Heath, 1954; Lilly, 1960) have reported that ESB at some locations inhibits pain. Numerous studies,

1. Although histological comparisons are difficult to make, the Ball and Adams (1965) data may be further interpreted in light of the report by Wasden, Reid and Porter (1965) that overnight decrements in responding are found only from electrode sites which are anatomically removed from the medial forebrain bundle, in areas that have been reported to contain aversive components during stimulation. More recently Wasden and Reid (1968) presented evidence that the approach–avoidance conflict confronting animals with such electrode placement is the cause of the overnight decrement in responding, and that sodium amytal, a fear-reducing drug, eliminates this decrement.

however, have damaged the aversive after effects proposal. For example, Scott (1967) demonstrated that rats can be trained to traverse a runway for ESB with the trials spaced at fifteen minutes. Furthermore, reports of human *S*s describe ESB as joyful, relaxing, or satisfying without mention of any aversive components (Heath and Mickle, 1960).

The most explicitly stated and rigorously tested theory of ESB is that of Deutsch and Howarth.[2] They posit that an application of electrical stimulation to a 'rewarding' area of the brain directly and simultaneously stimulates both drive and reinforcement systems of the brain.[3] This explanation accounts for both the rapid acquisition and reacquisition of responding seen with ESB. Since the two systems are stimulated directly while no consummatory response is required, the delay of reinforcement is eliminated as well as any concomitants of natural rewards such as stomach distention and sensory adaptation which might reduce the effectiveness of ordinary reinforcement. Because the drive pathway is stimulated with *every* reinforcement no satiation effects will be produced. Finally, since the drive is assumed to decay rapidly following the removal of ESB, extinction is rapid and there is no drive to maintain responding on partial reinforcement schedules with long intervals between stimulations. This 'dual process' interpretation of ESB can account, in theory, for the differences between the properties of ESB and conventional rewards. Furthermore, it has led to some interesting new predictions.

Direct support for the dual process position was obtained by Howarth and Deutsch (1962), who showed that extinction is a function of time since the last reinforcement rather than of the number of non-reinforced responses. Their procedure consisted of withdrawing the manipulandum, a lever, from the test box for periods of 2·5, 5·0, 7·5, and 10·0 seconds at the onset of extinction. It was found that the same number of extinction responses were

2. For a thorough review of the Deutsch and Howarth dual process position see Deutsch (1963), Gallistel (1964), and Deutsch and Deutsch (1966).

3. The terms 'drive' and 'motivation' have often been interchanged by the dual process theorists. While 'motivation' can involve either drive or incentive properties, it is clear that 'motivation' within the dual process context refers to drive, for example, the heading 'extinction or drive decay' (Deutsch, 1963, p. 203).

given whether or not the lever was present at the beginning of extinction. Thus, after 7 seconds of extinction *S*s bar-pressed an average of 1·92 times before reaching an extinction criterion while rats subjected to 7 seconds of lever withdrawal at the onset of extinction responded an average of 1·82 times. This supports the contention of rapidly decaying drive accrued from the electrical stimulus. The drive decay notion has been further supported in the runway situation (Gallistel, 1966, 1967). It was shown that an increase in the ITI from 5 to 60 seconds leads to an *immediate decrease* in running speed while a decrease in the ITI from 60 to 5 seconds leads to an *immediate increase* in running speed. These results were interpreted as indicating that an animal subjected to a shift in ITI from 5 to 60 seconds had a concomitant decrease in postshift drive since the drive accrued from the previous electrical stimulus had longer to decay. Conversely, those *S*s shifted from 60 to 5 seconds were, during the postshift period, under increased drive since the drive had less time to decay.

Other evidence lends support to the notion that brain stimulation simultaneously activates drive and reward systems in the brain. Assuming that nerve fibers exhibit a refractory period after being fired, and that the duration of the refractory period is a function of fiber diameter, Deutsch (1964) attempted to show that fibers of the reward and drive systems have different refractory periods; namely, different characteristic fiber diameters. Tests of preference and bar pressing presumably indicated that a short refractory period (range 0·5–0·6 milliseconds) is concerned with reinforcement while longer ones (range 0·8–1·0 milliseconds) involve drive. Deutsch, Howarth, Ball and Deutsch (1962) showed that if a low intensity electrical stimulus, previously shown to be ineffective in maintaining bar pressing when contingent upon responding, is intermittently and non-contingently given to the rat during extinction of a bar-pressing response previously rewarded with ESB, increased resistance to extinction results. This was thought to indicate that the drive effect of ESB has a lower threshold than does the reinforcing effect.

ESB viewed as a conventional reinforcement

In contrast to the evidence reviewed in the preceding section, other evidence suggests that behavior controlled by ESB is not as different from behavior maintained by conventional rewards as was assumed by these theories. Since most of this recent evidence suggests a similarity between ESB and more conventional rewards, it questions all of the reviewed interpretations.

The rapid extinction so often found when the current is disconnected from a self-stimulating animal has recently been shown to depend on the specific training conditions used with ESB rather than on any special characteristics of ESB itself. Conversely, and in opposition to the hypothesis of stimulation induced, rapidly decaying drive, manipulation of training conditions used with ESB can lead to changes in resistance to extinction. For example, Herberg (1963) demonstrated that an FR schedule leads to greater resistance to extinction than does a continuous reinforcement (CRF) schedule. This partial reinforcement effect (PRE) with self-stimulation has been strikingly demonstrated by Culbertson, Kling and Berkley (1966). Herberg (1963) also demonstrated that resistance to extinction is increased after a short bout of self-stimulation if the animal is accustomed to longer sessions. Clearly the self-stimulating animal is capable of demonstrating a discrimination of subtle manipulations in the experimental situation.

The contention that decaying performance depends on an invariably decaying drive has been further weakened by the Pliskoff and Hawkins (1963) demonstration that experience with retraction of the response lever abolishes the extinction without responding effect. Similarly, Gandelman, Panksepp and Trowill (1968) have shown that experience with lever retraction in a CRF situation leads to increased resistance to extinction. With a different approach, Stutz, Lewin and Rocklin (1965) corroborated the finding that self-stimulation behavior is more flexible than first thought by showing that a rat will wait up to twenty minutes between successive bouts of self-stimulation.

Furthermore, recent evidence suggests that in the absence of special training extinction of ESB-maintained behavior is not as rapid as was originally proposed. The variance of extinction scores obtained under similar training conditions is, in fact, quite large. Figure 1 shows cumulative records obtained in our laboratory during ESB extinction. All animals were permitted a thousand responses a day for three days on a CRF schedule. The fourth day consisted of two hundred and fifty reinforced responses followed by forty-five minutes of extinction. The mode of responding ranged from animals that give only a short burst of responding at the start of the extinction session to those that repeatedly return

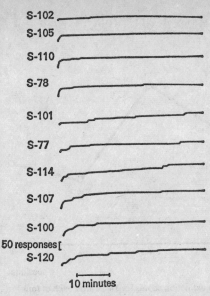

Figure 1 Cumulative extinction records of 10 Ss after continuously reinforced self-stimulation

to the bar for short bouts of responding throughout the session. At present it is not clear whether this large variance is due to differences in electrode location or is analogous to the large variance in extinction in the free-operant food-reward situation.

Another feature of ESB extinction is that with repeated extinctions and reacquisitions the first extinction session does not give the highest extinction score, as is the case with food reward (Bullock and Smith, 1953; Clark and Taylor, 1960). Figure 2 shows scores for four successive extinction sessions obtained in the authors' laboratory. Fourteen *S*s were allowed five hundred reinforcements on Day One and two hundred and fifty reinforcements followed by a fifteen-minute extinction period on Day Two. This two-day sequence was run four times. In general, the greatest resistance to extinction occurred on the second session, although several animals gave the highest score on the third or fourth sessions. Only one of the fourteen animals gave the highest score on the first session.

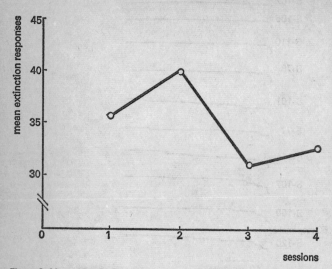

Figure 2 Mean 15-minute extinction scores for 14 Ss after each of four successive continuously reinforced acquisition sessions

The observation that long intermittent schedules of reinforcements are incapable of being maintained has also been disproved. Pliskoff, Wright and Hawkins (1965) were able to establish schedules of reinforcement with ESB as a reward that were comparable to those used with conventional rewards. This was accomplished by using a situation where pressing a permanent lever under various intermittent schedules produced a retractable lever where ESB was available on a CRF schedule. In this manner the following schedules of reinforcement on the permanent lever were maintained: FI-30 minutes, FR-200, VI-4 minutes, and differential reinforcement of low rates (DRL) three minutes. The authors have been able to get long intermittent schedules in the one-bar situation (Figure 3). The figure suggests close similarity between response patterns for ESB on these schedules and response patterns typically reported for natural rewards (Ferster and Skinner, 1957). The post-reinforcement pause typical of long FR schedules, the 'scalloping' of FI schedules, and the steady responding under VI schedules are similar for all rewards.

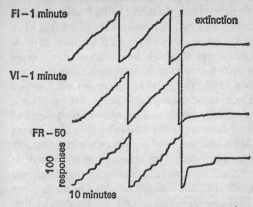

Figure 3 Circulative records from three Ss demonstrating typical schedule dependent response gradients. (The F1-1 minutes and V1-1 minute Ss received five consecutive brain stimulations as a reward. The FR-50 S was allowed only one brain stimulation after the completion of each FR segment)

Direct comparisons between performance for ESB and performance for natural rewards are hampered by the difficulty of equating the reward value of ESB and natural rewards. Pliskoff, Wright and Hawkins (1965) have suggested that ten intracranial reinforcements are more similar to a standard food unit (forty-five milligram pellet) than a single brain stimulation. Such considerations make it difficult to judge the validity of direct comparisons between ESB and conventional rewards since only a single burst of ESB has been used in most studies. In such comparisons Culbertson, Kling and Berkley (1966) and McIntyre and Wright (1965) have reported a significant reinforcer effect – ESB exhibiting lower resistance to extinction than either food or water. However, Kling and Matsumiya (1962) reported that performance maintained by ESB is more stable than performance maintained by food pellets in a discrimination reversal situation.

It has also been recognized that performance measures from instrumental learning situations using conventional reinforcers cannot be adequately compared with situations using ESB as reward unless the temporospatial relation between response and reinforcement is equated (Gibson, Reid, Sakai and Porter, 1965; McIntyre and Wright, 1965; Pliskoff, Wright and Hawkins, 1965; Terman and Kling, 1968). All these studies found that when the response-reinforcement delay in the ESB situation is made similar to the delay typical of the conventional free-operant situation, extinction of the self-stimulation response is significantly prolonged. Gibson *et al.* (1965) also ran a conventional reward group that tried to simulate the negligible delay of reward that is found in the typical ESB situation. They allowed food-deprived rats to receive either sugar water or ESB immediately upon licking a liquid dipper. Since both groups of animals extinguished equally rapidly, they concluded that when delay of reinforcement is equated between the ESB and food situations, the reinforcer effect is non-significant. The validity of this conclusion was questioned by Panksepp and Trowill (1967), who showed that rapid extinction of bar pressing is not obtained in deprived animals who are rewarded by injections of chocolate milk directly into the mouth.

Despite the inadequacy of explaining the rapid extinction with the simple variable of delay of reinforcement, other common motivational variables have been neglected in the search for a behavioral analogue of self-stimulation. A striking aspect of the majority of brain stimulation studies is that they employ animals maintained on free feeding schedules. It has been pointed out that the laws derived from animals maintained on high drive levels may not necessarily hold for animals at low drive levels (Bolles, 1967, p. 349). In spite of this, the behavior of animals working for conventional rewards at low levels of drive has been ignored. A recognition of this problem can help clarify an inconsistency between food and ESB-maintained behavior, namely, the apparent inability of ESB to impart secondary reinforcing characteristics to a neutral stimulus. The fact that stimuli paired with conventional primary rewards are ineffective in satiated animals (Miles, 1956; Schlosberg and Pratt, 1956) suggests why secondary reinforcement is so elusive with ESB as reward. Recently, DiCara (1966) concluded that secondary reinforcement can be demonstrated with ESB but that an appropriate drive has to be present during training.

Other data also lead to the conclusion that drive level is a potent variable that has to be controlled in comparisons between food and ESB-maintained behavior. It has been demonstrated that the rate of responding for ESB at certain hypothalamic sites is directly related to the level of food deprivation (Hodos and Valenstein, 1960; Hoebel and Teitelbaum, 1962; Olds, 1958a) and insulin-induced hunger (Balagura and Hoebel, 1967). Resistance to extinction (Deutsch and DiCara, 1967; Hodos and Valenstein, 1960) and the size of the terminal fixed ratio for which Ss maintain responding (Elder, Montgomery and Rye, 1965) are also increased by hunger. Conversely, however, it has not been adequately recognized that the rapid extinction of responses for ESB may be due exclusively to the use of free feeding schedules. A cogent comparison between ESB and conventional rewards should therefore be made using satiated animals. Panksepp and Trowill (1967a) demonstrated that animals on ad lib feeding maintain bar pressing for intra-oral injections of a highly appetitive chocolate milk solution. Using this preparation, evidence was presented for fast extinction, priming, agitation and excitement in responding, and extinction without responding.[4] The similarity of data collected from these animals and that from ESB situations supports the notion that deprivation level is a crucial factor in comparing ESB with other rewards. Furthermore, to the extent that a highly palatable reward delivered with minimal delay for responding best duplicates ESB-type performance, the authors suggested that a strong incentive or expectancy component elicited in the two situations, ESB and intra-oral feeding, is the crucial similarity between them.

ESB as an incentive condition

The preceding analysis suggests that while there are peculiarities apparently surrounding the nature of performing for ESB the

---

4. Agitation and excitement during responding is a commonly observed but rarely reported event associated with self-stimulation. Grover (1966) has systematically investigated behavioral activity accompanying self-stimulation.

crucial factor which contributes to these peculiarities is that of performing under low levels of drive. Specifically, while there is some evidence that the situational characteristics typically used in ESB free-operant procedures apparently contribute to the nature of the performance (Gibson *et al.*, 1965), the Panksepp and Trowill study (1967) suggests that a duplication of these characteristics in food-deprived rats working for immediate delivery of a highly palatable solution does not lead to a duplication of ESB performance. Rather, it seems that these characteristics of the reward and its delivery *and* the condition of a low drive level best duplicate responding for ESB.

Operationally, incentive has been defined in terms of the characteristics of reinforcement, such as its amount, quality, and delay of delivery (Bolles, 1967; Spence, 1956). It is impressive that the antecedents which contribute to incentive motivation are maximized in the behavioral situations where the peculiarities of ESB performance seem most prominent, namely, in free-operant, CRF situations where ESB is delivered with little or no delay. The consequents of incentive manipulation can be characterized in terms of a relatively rapid change in the strength of performance, such as the demonstration of contrast effects in running speed by Crespi (1942) and Zeaman (1949). It is compelling that the one major dependent variable which contributes to the enigma of ESB, a rapid change in strength of performance, seems dependent on an abrupt variation of reward variables. For example, the abrupt removal of ESB as in extinction or in non-reward portions of partial reinforcement situations leads to a relatively abrupt decrement in responding. Such decrements can easily be overcome in situations where the organism is specifically trained to continue to respond after periods of nonreinforcement, as in the Pliskoff, Wright and Hawkins (1965) and Gandelman, Panksepp and Trowill (1968) situations, showing that whatever the nature of the motivation for ESB, it is not totally dependent on the time since the last stimulation.

While the dependency of incentive variation on changes in need or drive states cannot be ignored, it is also apparent, according to several sources (Panksepp and Trowill, 1967b; Young and Shuford, 1954), that incentive motivation can maintain behavior even in the absence of regulated deprivation states. Although the complete absence of drive can never be conclusively demonstrated, the data demonstrating sustained performance for reinforcements with strong incentive characteristics in non-deprived organisms suggest that a similar process may account for the sustained responding of organisms working for ESB in the absence of known drive.

While incentive has long and increasingly been recognized as an important performance variable (Bolles, 1967; Hull, 1943; Spence, 1956), there has been no clear statement of its role in the ESB situation. However, the possibility of its importance has been recognized (Olds, 1956; Seward, Uyeda and Olds, 1959). For example, Seward, Uyeda and Olds (1959, p. 294) stated: 'Special interest attaches to the Olds-Milner phenomenon because it seems to be a pure case of "incentive motivation", i.e. a response energized by anticipation of a stimulus and reinforced by its realization.'

In spite of these suggestions, there has been a conspicuous absence of specific tests of the role of incentive in controlling ESB-related performance. Since properties of incentive variation have been investigated for conventional reward situations (see Bolles, 1967, for a review of the incentive literature) the possibility exists that similar properties may hold in the ESB situation. Furthermore, to the extent that performance for ESB is easily maintained under non-deprivation conditions, performance in the ESB situation may elucidate non-deprivation incentive properties.

Some tests of the ESB-incentive model

The explanation of the ESB effect in terms of incentive is appealing because it can account not only for a vast amount of the literature already in existence but also because of the diversity of predictions which can be generated. Essentially, the position taken here is that the behavior of organisms working for ESB should be comparable, in quality at least, to that of organisms working for any reward (and vice versa) as long as there is some similarity in terms of the conditions under which the organisms are run, for example, deprivation state, delivery of reward, etc. When these conditions are duplicated the behavior displayed should be basically the same regardless of the specific nature of the rewarding event. The predictions made with respect to ESB when taking an incentive position should, therefore, be similar to predictions made for other rewards.

Resistance to extinction and partial reinforcement responding

According to an incentive model, the rapid extinction typically displayed by organisms working for ESB should be a function of the characteristics of reward training. Where incentive magnitude is maximal during reward training, responding during extinction should be minimal due to the abrupt change occurring with the elimination of reward (Wagner, 1961; Zaretsky, 1965). A prominent explanation of this effect is based on a hypothetical 'frustration' response induced by shifting from high to low or no reward (Amsel, 1958, 1962; Wagner, 1963).

The removal of reward represents an extreme of shifting reward magnitude. Under such conditions two predictions result: (1) the vigor of behavior immediately following removal of reward should be enhanced (frustration effect); (2) total resistance to extinction should be inversely related to the amount of frustration present.

Merrill, Bromley and Porter (1967) tested for the frustration effect using ESB as reward. They trained rats on a multiple schedule consisting of FR-8 and FI-2 minute segments which were repeated over and over with 11-second time-outs between each successive segment. The results showed that withholding reinforcement at the end of an arbitrarily selected FR segment significantly increased responding in the subsequent FI segment. In a further test the time-out after an FR segment was increased from 11 seconds to 2·5 minutes. The frustrative delay produced the greatest increase in responding in the FI segment. Analogously, incidental observations from our laboratory indicate that when animals are placed on extinction after CRF training there is an initial burst of responding at a rate greater than when reinforcement is present.

According to the second prediction, extinction takes place due to the development of competing responses induced by the frustration of not receiving a reward when one is expected. Thus, responding during extinction should increase as a function of lowering frustration during non-reward, or as a function of reducing incentive during training such as by training Ss in the presence of periods of non-reward, for example, in partial reinforcement situations. The first possibility has been tested by introducing depressants, such as sodium amytal or alcohol, during extinction (Barry, Wagner and Miller, 1962). The observation that rats which received the drug ran faster during extinction than did placebo controls led Barry and his associates to suggest that the drugs reduce anticipatory frustration generated by non-reward.

A similar approach was taken by Gandelman and Trowill (1968) in attempting to explain the rapid extinction in the ESB situation. It was reasoned that if extinction is some function of frustration engendered by non-reward, then the typical ESB training conditions of continuous, immediate, and strong reinforcement should produce extremely rapid extinction due to a severe frustration response. Furthermore, any drug having properties of reducing reactions to aversive stimuli, such as a tranquilizer, should function in a manner similar to sodium amytal or alcohol. Chlordiazepoxide, a tranquilizer, has been shown to have these properties (Lewis and Feldman, 1964). The Ss were run under the four possible conditions of being trained and/or extinguished with or without the drug. The results indicated that while there was no difference in rate of reinforced responding between groups, the resistance to extinction scores of groups who received the drug during extinction were significantly higher than those of groups who did not receive the drug during extinction. It was further noted that the presence or absence of the drug did not differentially decrease the rapid and temporary burst of responding during the initial stage of extinction. Rather, Ss extinguished with the drug showed a tendency to respond, leave the bar and return, while those extinguished without the drug rarely returned to the bar after an initial two or three minutes of responding.

Incentive motivation is supposed to depend upon the most recent conditions of reinforcement (Bolles, 1967). A study done in our laboratory (Panksepp and Trowill, 1968) demonstrates the proactive effects of ESB training on resistance to extinction and thus further supports this position. Six Ss were allowed five hundred reinforcements on Day One and two hundred and fifty reinforcements followed by a fifteen-minute extinction period on Day Two. This two-day sequence was run five times. During a sixth sequence, the fifteen-minute extinction period followed the two hundred and fifty reinforcements by twenty-four hours. Figure 4 shows the mean extinction scores for Sessions One to Five, the mean of the highest score per animal during Sessions One to Five, and the mean score for the sixth session. Of interest is the fact that resistance to extinction during the sixth session, when no reward training immediately prior to extinction was given, was higher than that of any of the preceding sessions where extinction was always immediately preceded by a reinforcement period. These results agree with Herberg's demonstration (1963) of increased resistance to extinction after a short session of self-stimulation by animals accustomed to longer sessions.

It should be noted that none of these six Ss required priming or reshaping stimulation during the final session or the one immediately preceding. While the necessity for priming stimulation has been questioned elsewhere (Grossman, 1967), this is an impressive demonstration of the amount of responding which can occur without it.

Resistance to extinction can also be increased by maintaining responding in the presence of non-reward, such as in partial reinforcement (PR) situations. Presumably, the maintenance of responding during periods of non-reward establishes an association between the response and the cues of non-reward (Weinstock, 1958). Hence, to the extent that non-reward initially produces a frustration reaction, the organism is receiving training in the presence of cues associated with frustration. A shift to extinction conditions following PR training is not so readily discriminated from reward conditions and S continues to respond to the cues of non-reward.

This PRE effect has been found to hold true for ESB (Brodie *et al.*, 1960; Culbertson, Kling and Berkley, 1966; Herberg, 1963), as well as for natural rewards (Jenkins and Stanley, 1950). Work done in our laboratory has also shown that rats trained to respond for ESB on an FI-1 minute schedule show less resistance to extinction than do rats trained on a VI-1 minute schedule. This can be understood on the basis that the FI schedule is a condition on which reward can reliably be expected for the first response after a minute, a condition which produces scalloping of responding. On the other hand, the VI schedule is one on which there can be relatively little development of an expectancy of reward delivery due to the variability of the schedule, a condition which produces a steady rate of responding. Both groups, of course, showed greater resistance to extinction than a CRF group.

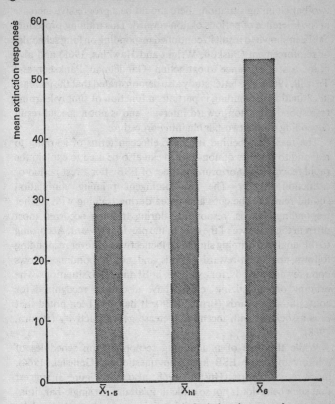

Figure 4 Mean extinction response for six Ss during six repeated acquisition and extinction periods. ($\bar{X}_{1\cdot5}$ represents the mean extinction response for the first five sessions. Each of these sessions was immediately preceded by a period of self-stimulation. $\bar{X}_{hi}$ represents the mean of the highest extinction scores of all animals during the first five sessions. $\bar{X}_6$ designates the mean extinction score during the sixth session when extinction was not immediately preceded by self-stimulation.)

The maintenance of responding on long schedules of reinforcement using a response chaining procedure can also be understood in terms of training in the presence of non-reward. To the extent that there is a persistence in responding on the non-reward manipulandum, as in the Pliskoff, Wright and Hawkins (1965) two-bar chaining situation, there should be a progressive increase in the tolerance of periods of non-reward. This training procedure has been shown to result in continued responding on long schedules of reinforcement (Pliskoff, Wright and Hawkins, 1965) and also in increased resistance to extinction (Gandelman, Panksepp and Trowill, 1968). The latter study also demonstrated that the increase in extinction responding is partially a function of simply learning to respond after non-reward intervals and is not a special result depending on the two-bar chaining procedure.

The reasoning behind the PRE effect in terms of learning to respond to the cues of non-reward can also be used to explain the rapid reacquisition or priming effect of ESB after a rest period or extinction session. The non-contingent priming stimulation should reinstate the cues associated during training with further responding, that is, responding during training occurred most often in the presence of the cues of the previous reward. According to this analysis, priming should be ineffective wherever responding follows upon non-reward periods and non-responding follows upon reward periods, for example, in FI and DRL situations. The priming or 'appetizing' effects have also been recognized for conventional rewards (Bruce, 1938). It has also been noted that cues associated with incentive increase general activity (Bindra, 1968).

While the ease of maintaining responding on schedules of reinforcement for ESB has been questioned (Gallistel, 1964), more recent reports (Huston, 1968; also, see Figure 3) suggest that such behavior is not so difficult to attain in a single-bar situation. In contrast to the special training procedure reported by Huston (1968), the crucial techniques used in developing scheduling behavior in our laboratory are: (1) a gradual exposure to the PR conditions after a limited amount of CRF training; and (2) the use of several, rather than one, ESB bursts for rewards. The latter was originally suggested and used by Pliskoff, Wright and Hawkins (1965) to maintain responding in the two-bar chaining situation. The need for a limited, rather than an extended, amount of CRF training follows from the observation that resistance to extinction is increased after a small amount of training trials as compared to a larger amount of training trials (Ison, 1962; Siegel and Wagner, 1963). This follows from the notion that the greater the amount of training, the stronger is the learned expectancy of reward (incentive) and so the greater is the frustration contributing to response fall-off when non-reward is experienced. In support of this in the ESB situation, Herberg and Watkins (1966) have shown that extinction scores asymptote after approximately 3,000 rewards and then decrease.

Since the rapid fall-off of responding can be understood in terms of the development of frustration as a function of non-confirmed expectancy of reward, drugs which have characteristics which might act to combat the effects of frustration should modulate the rapid response fall-off in PR situations as they do in extinction (Gandelman and Trowill, 1968). Elder, Montgomery and Rye (1965) have shown that methamphetamine (a sympathomimetic which decreases hunger) increases the terminal FR for which rats will respond from sites that exhibit lower terminal FRs under satiation than deprivation conditions. This effect is reasonable when consideration is given to the energizing effects of the drug which would be expected to combat effects of frustration. This result has also been confirmed with both d-amphetamine and the tranquilizer, chlordiazepoxide, in our laboratory. One S under d-amphetamine showed consistent responding on an FR-200 schedule.

Positive and negative contrast effects with ESB

The interpretation of ESB in terms of incentive suggests the possibility of demonstrating positive and negative contrast effects with shifts in the variables contributing to incentive, such as amount, quality, and delay of reward. Although there has been some variability in terms of the literature relating to the effects of such shifts when natural rewards are used (see Bolles, 1967), all of these variables have been consistently interpreted as contributing to incentive level.

With respect to ESB, it can be said that while several authors have alluded to apparent incentive shifts in their data (Brady, 1961; Lilly, 1958; Pliskoff and Hawkins, 1963; Valenstein, 1964), there have been no studies specifically addressed to this problem.

For example, Lilly (1958) reported that monkeys respond for less rewarding ESB at significantly reduced rates after being exposed to stimulation in highly rewarding areas than after no stimulation. Valenstein (1964) has reported a similar finding and has pointed out the potentially distorting effect such intensity shifts may have on reinforcement threshold determinations. These 'negative contrast' effects with ESB are analogous to the effect on bar pressing described by Pieper and Marx (1963) and Marx, Tombaugh, Cole and Dougherty (1963) when rewarding sucrose concentrations are shifted downward.

An attempt has been made in our laboratory at directly investigating contrast effects with ESB. In this study, shifts in intensity of ESB were correlated with shifts in rate of bar pressing. Threshold determinations of current intensity-response rate correlations were initially taken. During the contrast test sessions, Ss were given fifteen minutes of responding at either a high or a low-intensity level followed immediately by fifteen minutes at the other intensity level. Care was taken in choosing intensity levels so as to avoid ceiling and floor response levels. The range of intensity shifts was from approximately ten microamperes to fifteen microamperes. Every animal underwent two counterbalanced shifts, from low to high and from high to low. Figure 5 shows the minute-by-minute response rates for ten Ss, each of whom underwent each direction of shift once. The positive and negative contrast effects occurred relatively rapidly (within two to three minutes) and were quite large. In contrast to the positive effect, however, the duration of the negative contrast effect extended for the full fifteen-minute duration. In a follow-up study, preliminary results indicate a replication of these results with both bar pressing and running speed measures.

The observation of abrupt and direct shifts in running time with shifts in ITI (Gallistel, 1967) may also be viewed in terms of shifting incentive. Panksepp, Gandelman and Trowill (1968) showed that postshift running times, though initially showing appropriate changes, eventually converge. This convergence is untenable with respect to a drive decay explanation.

Gallistel (1966) has also reported that running speed is dependent upon the characteristics of the preceding reinforcement rather

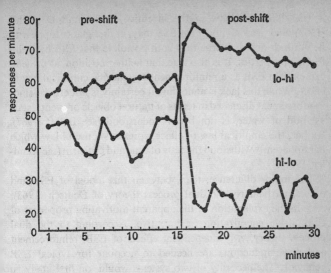

Figure 5 Minute-by-minute response rates during shifts in intensity of brain stimulation. (Ten Ss were run under each of the intensity shifts.)

than on those of the anticipated reinforcement. It is assumed that these results should be replicable using conventional rewards as long as there is no deprivation.

Implications of ESB for the areas of drive and incentive

It has been said about scientific theories that 'a theory is only overthrown by a better theory, never merely by contradictory facts' (Conant, 1947, p. 36). The present effort has been to assimilate performance properties of ESB events in terms of incentive as defined by antecedents and consequents derived from performance for natural rewards. Furthermore, recent data testing a variety of specific predictions derived from the incentive model have been reviewed. It will be the purpose of this section to compare the incentive position with the prevalent theoretical model of ESB, namely, the dual process theory, and to point out the relevance of ESB to understanding drive, as well as incentive, in a general sense.

The difference between the incentive model and Deutsch's (1963) dual process model[5] of ESB may, at first glance, appear to be a minor one. It is true that both postulate that ESB has reinforcing properties. It is also true that neither position, at present, can explain ESB as a reinforcement beyond the empirical law of effect. While this lack is annoying, it certainly is not crucial since reinforcement discussed in terms of natural objects or events, such as food or water, is not better understood (see Bolles, 1967). Rather, the empirical law of effect represents a useful law which has apparently withstood the tests of time and criticism (see Kendler, 1951).[6]

The major difference, then, between this model of ESB and others, particularly the dual process theory of Deutsch (1963), rests in the explanation of the apparent motivating properties of ESB, drive energization or incentive. According to the dual process theory, two independent effects of ESB, reinforcement and drive induction, are needed to account for typical ESB behavior. The necessity of two systems would, on first analysis, seem to be supported by the common observation that various drive-specific behaviors may be elicited from stimulation of areas that support self-stimulation. Stimulation of well-defined hypothalamic sites in the rat may elicit behaviors such as eating (Miller, 1960), drinking (Greer, 1955; Mogenson and Morgan,

5. A recent theoretical paper by Routtenberg (1968) formulating a 'two-arousal hypothesis' for maintaining behavior essentially explains ESB from certain locations, for example, posterior hypothalamus, in the same way as the dual process theory. For example, hypothalamic stimulation is rewarding because of both Arousal System I (drive) and Arousal System II (reinforcement-incentive) activation. On the other hand, telencephalic stimulation, for example, septal area, only activates Arousal System II. We have sampled a wide range of electrode placements in the anterior, middle and lateral hypothalamus and have found no evidence necessitating the inclusion of Arousal System I activation in explaining self-stimulation. It is our contention that behavioral differences from stimulation of different sites is due to quantitative and/or qualitative differences in reinforcement and/or incentive. This is not to suggest that there is no evidence for Arousal System I; rather, the role of Arousal System I in relation to ESB may be extraneous to the explanation of ESB properties.

6. The circularity of the empirical law of effect has been criticized in a recent article by Glickman and Schiff (1967). The authors' suggestion that positive and negative reinforcement be defined in terms of approach and withdrawal sequences seems equally circular.

1967), copulation (Caggiula and Hoebel, 1966), gnawing (Roberts and Carey, 1965), and hoarding (Herberg and Blundel, 1967). Furthermore, it has been shown that at certain current intensities, self-stimulation is only obtained when food (Coons and Cruce, 1968) or water (Mendelson, 1967) is also available. In fact, it has been suggested (Mendelson, 1967) that when an appropriate incentive object, for example, water, is available animals will respond for stimulation, which supposedly only induces an appropriate drive, for example, thirst. It thus seems that at these levels of stimulation the addition of the incentive consequences of the external reward makes the drive-inducing stimulation rewarding. Since self-stimulation is maintained at higher intensities without such peripheral rewards (Coons and Cruce, 1968), it is to be assumed that some aspects of the more intense stimulation are capable of replacing the incentive consequences of the peripheral reward. The present authors contend that the aspect of this stimulation is the incentive component that is part of natural rewards. A recent study by Poschel (1968) suggests that biological reinforcers do act via the substrates of hypothalamic reward areas. Furthermore, Valenstein, Cox and Kakolewski (1968) have recently shown that behavior elicited by stimulation of the lateral hypothalamus is susceptible to modification by simple training procedures. For example, 'stimulus bound' drinkers exhibit 'stimulus bound' eating upon the omission of the goal object, that is, water, of the initially elicited behavior. Valenstein and his associates thus saw reason to question whether thirst and hunger drives were involved at all in the elicited behaviors. There is also evidence that the reinforcing effect of brain stimulation can be dissociated from other behaviors, such as drinking, eating, etc., which can be elicited by stimulation of the same area. Support for this viewpoint has been presented by Mogenson (1968) who found that Ss that self-administer hypothalamic brain stimulation which also produces drinking will increase self-stimulation but decrease drinking when given amphetamine.

Such considerations support our conclusion that the motivating properties of ESB are inherent in its reinforcement properties in the form of incentive motivation, and that the postulation of ESB-produced drive induction, if present at all, is, at most, superfluous to any explanation of ESB-controlled behavior. While the parsimony of the incentive position may be questioned its value as a model rests in the predictions it generates, as well as in the data it explains. At this particular time, it seems to be successful and fruitful on both counts.

The traditional distinctions between definitions of drive and incentive variables in terms of antecedents and behavioral consequences have recently come under close theoretical and empirical scrutiny. It seems that the favored approach now is that most (Bindra, 1968), if not all (Bolles, 1967; Estes, 1958; Young, 1961), of the data which formerly supported the drive energization notion can be explained in terms of incentive. Hence, Bolles (1967, p. 367) has stated: 'Incentives can explain anything drives can explain, and they can explain a vast number of transient and short-term effects that drives cannot explain.' The last phrase is particularly noteworthy since it seems that much of the mysterious ESB behavior represents 'transient and short-term effects'. And in discussing the relationship between drive and general activity, Bindra (1968, p. 4) has stated: 'These findings raise doubt about the view that a common energizing factor is made operative by all drive manipulations. Rather . . . the relation between each drive manipulation and activity level is a specific one.'

In light of the above, the attempt to formulate and investigate the motivational properties of ESB in terms of incentive, rather than drive, would seem to be not only fruitful but also sensible. Furthermore, the incentive explanation should be appealing not only because it coincides well with the conclusions of general motivational theorists but also because a common language and theoretical system can be used for reinforcing objects and events, regardless of their particular nature.

Given this, it seems that ESB as a reinforcer should be potentially valuable for understanding incentive in general. It is possible to maintain performance for natural rewards of high quality in the absence of deprivation conditions (Panksepp and Trowill, 1967a; Young and Shuford, 1954). ESB, however, provides an effective reward for maintaining behavior in the absence of known deprivation conditions which is independent of post-consummatory effects, such as stomach distension. It also precludes the use of relatively complex preparations such as intraoral fistulation. Therefore, ESB may provide, if it already has not, some of the laws of incentive motivation independent of its interaction with deprivation.

At this time, some speculation about the nature of incentive performance in the absence of deprivation can be derived from brain stimulation behavior. First, the ESB literature suggests that strong reward in the absence of deprivation does serve as a powerful motivator. However, the rapid extinction following prolonged CRF training also suggests that this accumulated motivational effect can be rapidly offset when non-reward is experienced. This strong tendency to 'quit' when expectations are not met interferes with continued performance even in low-PR situations after prolonged CRF training.

The 'extinction without responding' effect (ESB – Howarth and Deutsch, 1962; intraoral injection – Panksepp and Trowill, 1967a), also suggests that this reinforcement-derived motivation, that is, incentive, does decay with time in the absence of responding. However, it should also be noted that training conditions can overcome this motivational decay. Since most studies using natural rewards also use deprivation conditions which would provide a persistent maintenance motivation, this decay tendency is obscured.

The demonstration of both positive and negative contrast effects with ESB intensity shifts may also point out the interfering or modulating effects of deprivation-motivation on performance. With ESB and no deprivation, both effects were observed. However, the positive effect was less durable than the negative effect. Furthermore, shifting ITIs seems to produce an effect on running speeds comparable to incentive shifts. It may be that ITI shifts represent an effect similar to shifting delay of reward, a known antecedent of incentive.

Equally important is the fact that ESB from different anatomical sites seems to covary with specific deprivation conditions. For example, Olds (1958a) has reported separate hypothalamic electrode locations where rate of response varies positively with hunger and negatively with sexual arousal (medial placements) and others (lateral placements) where response rate varies positively with sexual arousal but not at all with hunger. This type of deprivation-specific response-rate covariation should permit an investigation of the 'Drive (deprivation conditions)–Incentive' interaction which is independent of the effects of satiation usually coincident with the consumption of natural rewards.

That deprivation conditions and incentive interact seems conclusive. The further question of 'how' may be answered by using ESB. For example, Bindra (1968) and Young (1961) have essentially suggested that deprivation facilitates behavior not because of drive *per se* but because, 'deprivation increases the incentive value of the goal object' (Young, 1961, p. 180). The fact that stimulation of different sites, all of which yield reward, can also induce, using different parameters of stimulation, consummatory behavior (e.g. eating, drinking, etc.) suggests that ESB as a reward may have specific incentive properties (e.g. related to food or water, etc.) as a function of the electrode location. Hence, strength of performance for ESB as a function of deprivation may reflect changes in specific incentive properties elicited by ESB, rather than a drive-energization reinforcement-incentive interaction.

It is the hope that this particular formulation will provide a bridge in communication between learning theorists interested in motivation-reward processes and physiological psychologists interested in the physiological mechanisms of these processes. The use of a common language by these two groups may accelerate the rate of finding answers to problems of common interest.

References

AMSEL, A. (1958), 'The role of frustrative nonreward in non-continuous reward situation', *Psychol. Bull.*, vol. 55, pp. 102–19.

AMSEL, A. (1962), 'Frustrative nonreward in partial reinforcement and discrimination learning: Some recent history and a theoretical extension', *Psychol. Rev.*, vol. 69, pp. 306–28.

BALAGURA, S., and HOEBEL, B. G. (1967), 'Self-stimulation of the lateral hypothalamus modified by insulin and glucagon', *Physiol. Behav.*, vol. 2, pp. 337–40.

BALL, G. G. (1967), 'Electrical self-stimulation of the brain and sensory inhibition', *Psychonomic Sci.*, vol. 8, pp. 489–90.

BALL, G. G., and ADAMS, D. W. (1965), 'Intracranial stimulation as an avoidance or escape response', *Psychonomic Sci.*, vol. 3, pp. 39–40.

BARRY, H., WAGNER, A. R., and MILLER, N. E. (1962), 'Effects of alcohol and amobarbital on performance inhibited by experimental extinction', *J. compar. physiol. Psychol.*, vol. 55, pp. 464–8.

BINDRA, D. (1968), 'Neuropsychological interpretation of the effects of drive and incentive-motivation on general activity and instrumental behavior' *Psychol. Rev.*, vol. 75, pp. 1–22.

BOLLES, R. C. (1967), *Theory of Motivation*, Harper & Row.

BOYD, E., and GARDNER, L. (1962), 'Positive and negative reinforcement from intracranial self-stimulation in teleosts', *Sci.*, vol. 136, p. 648.

BRADY, J. V. (1957), 'A comparative approach to the experimental analysis of emotional behavior', in P. H. Hock and J. Zubin (eds.), *Exper. Psychopath.*, Grune & Stratton.

BRADY, J. V. (1961), 'Motivational-emotional factors and intracranial self-stimulation', in D. E. Sheer (ed.), *Electrical Stimulation of the Brain*, University of Texas Press.

BRODIE, D. A., MORENO, O. M., MALIS, J. L., and BOREN, J. J. (1960), 'Rewarding properties of intracranial stimulation', *Sci.*, vol. 131, pp. 929–30.

BRUCE, R. H. (1938), 'The effect of lessening the drive upon performance of white rats in a maze', *J. compar. physiol. Psychol.*, vol. 25, pp. 225–48.

BRUNER, A. (1966), 'Facilitation of classical conditioning in rabbits by reinforcing brain stimulation', *Psychonomic Sci.*, vol. 6, pp. 211–12.

BULLOCK, P. H., and SMITH, W. C. (1953), 'An effect of repeated conditioning-extinction upon operant strength', *J. exper. Psychol.*, vol. 46, pp. 349–52.

CAGGIULA, O. R., and HOEBEL, B. G. (1966), '"Copulation-reward site", in the posterior hypothalamus', *Sci.*, vol. 153, pp. 1284–5.

CLARK, F. C., and TAYLOR, B. W. (1960), 'Effects of repeated extinctions of an operant on characteristics of extinction curves', *Psychol. Reports*, vol. 6, p. 226.

CONANT, J. B. (1947), *On Understanding Science*, Yale University Press.

COONS, E. E., and CRUCE, J. A. F. (1968), 'Lateral hypothalamus: Food current intensity in maintaining self-stimulation of hunger', *Sci.*, vol. 159, pp. 1117–19.

CRESPI, L. P. (1942), 'Quantitative variation of incentive and performance in the white rat', *Amer. J. Psychol.*, vol. 55, pp. 467–515.

CULBERTSON, J. L., KLING, J. W., and BERKLEY, M. A. (1966), 'Extinction responding following ICS and food reinforcement', *Psychonomic Sci.*, vol. 5, pp. 127–8.

DEUTSCH, J. A. (1963), 'Learning and electrical self-stimulation of the brain', *J. theoretical Biol.*, vol. 4, pp. 193–214.

DEUTSCH, J. A. (1964), 'Behavioral measurement of the neural refractory period and its application to intracranial self-stimulation' *J. compar. physiol. Psychol.*, vol. 58, pp. 1–9.

DEUTSCH, J. A., and DEUTSCH, D. (1966), *Physiological Psychology*, Dorsey Press.

DEUTSCH, J. A., and DiCARA, L. V. (1967), 'Hunger and extinction in intracranial self-stimulation', *J. compar. physiol. Psychol.*, vol. 63, pp. 344–7.

DEUTSCH, J. A., and HOWARTH, C. I. (1963), 'Some tests of a theory of intracranial self-stimulation', *Psychol. Rev.*, vol. 70, pp. 444–60.

DEUTSCH, J. A., HOWARTH, C. I., BALL, G. G., and DEUTSCH, D. (1962), 'Threshold differentiation of drive and reward in the Olds effect', *Nature*, vol. 196, pp. 699–700.

DICARA, L. V. (1966), 'Brain stimulation and secondary reinforcement' *Dissertation Abstracts*, vol. 27, p. 2157-B.

ELDER, T. S., MONTGOMERY, N. P., and RYE, M. M. (1965), 'Effects of food deprivation and methamphetamine on fixed-ratio schedules of intracranial self-stimulation', *Psychol. Reports*, vol. 16, pp. 1225–37.

ESTES, W. K. (1968), 'Stimulus-response theory of drive', *Nebraska Symposium on Motivation*, University of Nebraska Press, vol. 6, pp. 35–69.

FALK, J. (1961), 'Septal stimulation as a reinforcer of and an alternative to consummatory behavior', *J. exper. anal. Behav.*, vol. 4, pp. 213–15.

FERSTER, C. B., and SKINNER, B. F. (1957), *Schedules of Reinforcement*, Appleton-Century-Crofts.

GALLISTEL, C. R. (1964), 'Electrical self-stimulation and its theoretical implications', *Psychol. Bull.*, vol. 61, pp. 23–34.

GALLISTEL, C. R. (1966), 'Motivating effects in self-stimulation', *J. compar. physiol. Psychol.*, vol. 62, pp. 95–101.

GALLISTEL, C. R. (1967), 'Intracranial stimulation and natural reward: Differential effects of trial spacing', *Psychonomic Sci.*, vol. 9, pp. 167–8.

GANDELMAN, R., PANKSEPP, J., and TROWILL, J. A. (1968), 'The effect of lever retraction on resistance to extinction of a response rewarded with electrical stimulation of the brain', *Psychonomic Sci.* vol. 10, pp. 5–6.

GANDELMAN, R., and TROWILL, J. A. (1968), 'The effects of chlordiazepoxide on ESB-reinforced behavior and subsequent extinction', *J. compar. physiol. Psychol.*, vol. 66, pp. 753–5.

GIBSON, W. E., REID, L. D., SAKAI, M., and PORTER, P. B. (1965), 'Intracranial reinforcement compared with sugar-water reinforcement' *Sci.*, vol. 148, pp. 1357–8.

GLICKMAN, S. E., and SCHIFF, B. B. (1967), 'A biological theory of reinforcement', *Psychol. Rev.*, vol. 74, pp. 81–109.

GOODMAN, I. J., and BROWN, J. L. (1966), 'Stimulation of positively and negatively reinforcing sites in the avian brain', *Life Sciences*, vol. 5, pp. 693–704.

GREER, M. A. (1955), 'Suggestive evidence of a primary "drinking centre" in the hypothalamus of the rat', *Proc. Soc. exper. Biol. Med.*, vol. 89, p. 59.

GROSSMAN, S. P. (1967), *A Textbook of Physiological Psychology*, Wiley.

GROVER, F. S. (1966), 'Electrophysiological and behavioral activity accompanying self-stimulation (a comparative study of the hypothalamus and septum)', *Dissertation Abstracts*, vol. 27, p. 350-B.

HEATH, J. (1954), *Studies in Schizophrenia*, Harvard University Press.

HEATH, R. G., and MICKLE, W. A. (1960), 'Evaluation of seven years experience with depth electrode studies in human patients', in E. R. Ramsey and D. S. O'Doherty (eds.), *Electrical Studies on the Unanaesthetized Brain*, Paul B. Hoeber.

HERBERG, L. J. (1963), 'Determinants of extinction in electrical self-stimulation', *J. compar. physiol. Psychol.*, vol. 56, pp. 686–90.

HERBERG, L. J., and BLUNDELL, J. E. (1967), 'Lateral hypothalamus: hoarding behavior elicited by electrical stimulation', *Sci.*, vol. 149, pp. 349–50.

HERBERG, L. J., and WATKINS, J. (1966), 'The effect of overtraining and repeated extinction on speed of extinction in electrical self-stimulation', *Q. J. exper. Psychol.*, vol. 56, pp. 75–7.

HODOS, W., and VALENSTEIN, E. S. (1960), 'Motivational variables affecting the rate of behavior maintained by intracranial stimulation', *J. compar. physiol. Psychol.*, vol. 53, pp. 502–8.

HOEBEL, B. G., and TEITELBAUM, P. (1962), 'Hypothalamic control of feeding and self-stimulation', *Sci.*, vol. 135, pp. 375–7.

HOWARTH, C. I., and DEUTSCH, J. A. (1962), 'Drive decay: the cause of fast "extinction" of habits learned for brain stimulation', *Sci.*, vol. 137, pp. 35–6.

HULL, C. L. (1943), *Principles of Behavior*, Appleton-Century-Crofts.

HUSTON, J. P. (1968), 'Reinforcement reduction: a method for training ratio behavior', *Sci.*, vol. 159, p. 444.

ISON, J. R. (1962), 'Experimental extinction as a function of number of reinforcements', *J. exper. Psychol.*, vol. 64, pp. 314–17.

JENKINS, W. O., and STANLEY, J. C., Jr (1950), 'Partial reinforcement: a review and critique', *Psychol. Bull.*, vol. 47, pp. 193–234.

KENDLER, H. H. (1951), 'Reflections and confessions of a reinforcement theorist', *Psychol. Rev.*, vol. 58, pp. 368–74.

KLING, J. W., and MATSUMIYA, Y. (1962), 'Relative reinforcement values of food and intracranial stimulation', *Sci.*, vol. 135, pp. 668–70.

KNOTT, P. D., and CLAYTON, K. N. (1966), 'Durable secondary reinforcement using brain stimulation as the primary reinforcer', *J. compar. physiol. Psychol.*, vol. 61, pp. 151–3.

LEWIS, E. M., and FELDMAN, R. S. (1964), 'The depressive effect of chlordiazepoxide on a negative incentive', *Psychopharmacologia*, vol. 6, pp. 143–50.

LILLY, J. C. (1960), 'Learning motivated by subcortical stimulation: the "start" and the "stop" patterns of behavior', in E. R. Ramsey and D. S. O'Doherty (eds.), *Electrical Studies on the Unanaesthetized Brain*, Paul B. Hoeber.

LILLY, J. C. (1958), 'Learning motivated by subcortical stimulation: the start and stop patterns of behavior', in H. H. Jasper, L. D. Proctor, R. S. Knighton, W. C. Noshay and R. T. Costello (eds.), *The Reticular Formation of the Brain*, Little, Brown.

LILLY, J. C., and MILLER, A. M. (1962), 'Operant conditioning of the bottlenose dolphin with electrical stimulation of the brain', *J. compar. physiol. Psychol.*, vol. 55, pp. 73–9.

MARX, M. H., TOMBAUGH, J. W., COLE, C., and DOUGHERTY, D. (1963), 'Persistence of nonreinforced responding as a function of the direction of a prior-ordered incentive shift', *J. exper. Psychol.*, vol. 66, pp. 542–6.

MCINTYRE, R. W., and WRIGHT, J. E. (1965), 'Differences in extinction in electrical brain-stimulation under traditional procedures of reward presentation', *Psychol. Reports*, vol. 16, pp. 909–13.

MENDELSON, J. (1967), 'Lateral hypothalamic stimulation in satiated rats: the rewarding effects of self-induced drinking', *Sci.*, vol. 157, pp. 1077–9.

MERRILL, H. K., BROMLEY, B. L., and PORTER, P. B. (1967), '"Frustration" from withholding electrical stimulation of the brain' paper presented at the meeting of the Western Psychol. Assoc., San Francisco.

MILES, R. C. (1956), 'The relative effectiveness of secondary reinforcers throughout deprivation and habit-strength parameters', *J. compar. physiol. Psychol.*, vol. 49, pp. 126–30.

MILLER, N. E. (1960), 'Motivational effects of brain stimulation and drugs', *Federation Proc.*, vol. 19, pp. 846–54.

MOGENSON, G. J. (1965), 'An attempt to establish secondary reinforcement with rewarding brain self-stimulation', *Psychol. Reports*, vol. 16, pp. 163–7.

MOGENSON, G. J., and MORGAN, C. W. (1967), 'Effects of induced drinking on self-stimulation of the lateral hypothalamus', *Exper. Brain Res.*, vol. 3, pp. 111–16.

NIELSON, H. C., DOTY, R. W., and RUTLEDGE, L. T. (1958), 'Motivational and perceptual aspects of subcortical stimulation in cats', *Amer. J. Physiol.*, vol. 192, pp. 427–32.

OLDS, J. (1956), 'Runway and maze behavior controlled by basomedial forebrain stimulation in the rat', *J. compar. physiol. Psychol.*, vol. 49, pp. 507–12.

OLDS, J. (1958a), 'Effects of hunger and male sex hormones on self-stimulation of the brain', *J. compar. physiol. Psychol.*, vol. 51, pp. 320–24.

OLDS, J. (1958b), 'Satiation effects in self-stimulation of the brain', *J. compar. physiol. Psychol.*, vol. 51, pp. 675–8.

OLDS, J. (1958c), 'Self-stimulation experiments and differentiated reward systems', in H. H. Jasper, L. D. Proctor, R. S. Knighton, W. C. Noshay and R. T. Costello (eds.), *The Reticular Formation of the Brain*, Little, Brown.

OLDS, J. (1958d), Self-stimulation of the brain', *Sci.*, vol. 127, pp. 315–24.

OLDS, J., and MILNER, P. (1954), 'Positive reinforcement produced by electrical stimulation of septal area and other regions of rat brain', *J. compar physiol. Psychol.*, vol. 47, pp. 419–27.

OLDS, M. E., and OLDS, J. (1963), 'Approach-avoidance analysis of rat diencephalon', *J. compar. Neurol.*, vol. 120, pp. 259–95.

OLDS, J., TRAVIS, R. P., and SCHWING, R. C. (1960), 'Topographic organization of hypothalamic self-stimulation functions', *J. compar. physiol. Psychol.*, vol. 53, pp. 23–32.

PANKSEPP, J., and TROWILL, J. A. (1967a), 'Intraoral self injection: I. Effects of delay of reinforcement on resistance to extinction and implications for self-stimulation', *Psychonomic Sci.*, vol. 9, pp. 405–6.

PANKSEPP, J., and TROWILL, J. A. (1967b), 'Intraoral self injection: II. The simulation of self-stimulation phenomenon with a conventional reward', *Psychonomic Sci.*, vol. 9, pp. 407–8.

PANKSEPP, J., and TROWILL, J. A. (1968), 'Extinction following intracranial reward: frustration or drive decay?', *Psychonomic Sci.* vol. 12, pp. 173–4.

PANKSEPP, J., GANDELMAN, R., and TROWILL, J. A. (1968), 'The effect of intertrial interval on running performance for ESB', *PsychonomicSci.*, vol. 13, pp. 135–6.

PIEPER, W. A., and MARX, M. H. (1963), 'Effects of within-session incentive contrast on instrumental acquisition and performance', *J. exper. Psychol.*, vol. 65, pp. 568–71.

PLISKOFF, S. S., and HAWKINS, T. D. (1963), 'Test of Deutsch's drive-decay theory of rewarding self-stimulation of the brain', *Sci.*, vol. 141, pp. 823–4.

PLISKOFF, S. S., WRIGHT, J. E., and HAWKINS, D. T. (1965), 'Brain stimulation as a reinforcer: intermittent schedules', *J. exper. Anal. Behav.*, vol. 8, pp. 75–88.

PORTER, R. W., CONRAD, D., and BRADY, J. V. (1958), 'Some electroencephalographic patterns induced by self-stimulation in monkeys', *Federation Proc.*, vol. 17, p. 125.

POSCHEL, B. P. H. (1968), 'Do biological reinforcers act via the self-stimulation areas of the brain?', *Physiol. Behav.*, vol. 3, pp. 53–60.

REID, L. D., GIBSON, W. E., GLEDHILL, S. M., and PORTER, P. B. (1964), 'Anticonvulsant drugs and self-stimulating behavior', *J. compar. physiol. Psychol.*, vol. 57, pp. 353–6.

ROBERTS, W. W. (1958), 'Both rewarding and punishing effects from stimulation of posterior hypothalamus of cat with same electrode at same intensity', *J. compar. physiol. Psychol.*, vol. 51, pp. 400–7.

ROBERTS, W. W., and CAREY, R. J. (1965), 'Rewarding effect of performance of gnawing aroused by hypothalamic stimulation in the rat', *J. compar. physiol. Psychol.*, vol. 59, pp. 317–24.

ROBERTSON, E. G. (1954), 'Photogenic epilepsy: self-precipitated attacks', *Brain*, vol. 77, pp. 232–51.

ROUTTENBERG, A. (1968), 'The two-arousal hypothesis: reticular formation and limbic system', *Psychol. Rev.*, vol. 75, pp. 51–80.

ROUTTENBERG, A., and LINDY, J. (1965), 'Effects of the availability of rewarding septal and hypothalamic stimulation on barpressing for food under conditions of deprivation', *J. compar. physiol. Psychol.*, vol. 60, pp. 158–61.

SCHLOSBERG, H., and PRATT, G. H. (1956), 'The secondary reward value of inaccessible food for hungry and satiated rats', *J. compar. physiol. Psychol.*, vol. 49, pp. 149–52.

SCOTT, J. W. (1967), 'Brain stimulation reinforcement with distributed practice: effects of electrode locus, previous experience, and stimulus intensity', *J. compar. physiol. Psychol.*, vol. 63, pp. 175–83.

SEWARD, J. P., UYEDA, A. A., and OLDS, J. (1959), 'Resistance to extinction following intracranial self-stimulation', *J. compar. physiol. Psychol.*, vol. 52, pp. 294–9.

SEWARD, J. P., UYEDA, A. A., and OLDS, J. (1960), 'Reinforcing effect of brain stimulation on runway performance as a function of interval between trials', *J. compar. physiol. Psychol.*, vol. 53, pp. 224–7.

SIDMAN, M., BRADY, J. V., CONRAD, D. G., and SCHULMAN, A. (1955), 'Reward schedules and behavior maintained by intracranial self-stimulation', *Sci.*, vol. 122, pp. 830–31.

SIEGEL, S., and WAGNER, A. R. (1963), 'Extended acquisition training and resistance to extinction', *J. exper. Psychol.*, vol. 66, pp. 308–10.

SPEAR, N. E. (1962), 'Comparison of the reinforcing effect of brain stimulation on Skinner box, runway, and maze performance', *J. compar. physiol. Psychol.*, vol. 55, pp. 679–84.

SPENCE, K. W. (1956), *Behavior Theory and Conditioning*, Yale University Press.

STARK, P., and BOYD, E. S. (1961), 'Electrical self-stimulation by dogs, through chronically implanted electrodes in the hypothalamus', *Federation Proc.*, vol. 20, p. 328.

STEIN, L. (1958), 'Secondary reinforcement established with subcortical stimulation', *Sci.*, vol. 127, pp. 466–7.

STUTZ, R. M., LEWIN, I., and ROCKLIN, K. W. (1965), 'Generality of "drive-decay" as an explanatory concept', *Psychonomic Sci.*, vol. 2, pp. 127–8.

TERMAN, M., and KLING, J. W. (1968), 'Discrimination of brightness differences by rats with food or brain-stimulation reinforcement', *J. exper. Anal. Behav.*, vol. 11, pp. 29–37.

VALENSTEIN, E. S. (1964), 'Problems of measurement and interpretation with reinforcing brain stimulation', *Psychol. Rev.*, vol. 71, pp. 415–37.

VALENSTEIN, E. S., COX, V. C., and KAKOLEWSKI, J. W. (1968), 'Modification of motivated behavior elicited by electrical stimulation of the hypothalamus', *Sci.*, vol. 159, pp. 1119–21.

WAGNER, A. R. (1961), 'Effects of amount and percentage of reinforcement and number of acquisition trials on conditioning and extinction', *J. exper. Psychol.*, vol. 62, pp. 234–42.

WAGNER, A. R. (1963), 'Conditional frustration as a learned drive', *J. exper. Psychol.*, vol. 66, pp. 142–8.

WASDEN, R. E., and REID, L. D. (1968), 'Intracranial stimulation: performance decrements and a fear-reducing drug', *Psychonomic Sci.*, vol. 12, pp. 117–18.

WASDEN, R. E., REID, L. D., and PORTER, P. B. (1965), 'Overnight performance decrement with intracranial reinforcement', *Psychol. Reports*, vol. 16, pp. 654–8.

WEINSTOCK, S. (1958), 'Acquisition and extinction of a partially reinforced running response at a 24-hour intertrial interval', *J. exper. Psychol.*, vol. 56, pp. 151–8.

YOUNG, P. T. (1961), *Motivation and Emotion*, Wiley.

YOUNG, P. T., and SHUFORD, E. H. (1954), 'Intensity, duration, and repetition of hedonic processes as related to acquisition of motivation', *J. compar. physiol. Psychol.*, vol. 47, pp. 298–305.

ZARETSKY, H. H. (1965), 'Runway performance during extinction as a function of drive and incentive' *J. compar. physiol. Psychol.*, vol. 60, pp. 463–4.

ZEAMAN, D. (1949), 'Response latency as a function of the amount of reinforcement', *J. exper. Psychol.*, vol. 39, pp. 466–83.

30 D. Bindra

The Interrelated Mechanisms of Reinforcement and
Motivation, and the Nature of their Influence on Response[1]

D. Bindra, 'The interrelated mechanisms of reinforcement and
motivation, and the nature of their influence on response', in
W. J. Arnold and D. Levine (eds.), *Nebraska Symposium on Motivation*,
University of Nebraska Press, 1969, pp. 1–33.

The hypothesis I want to propose in this paper is that the effects
on behavior produced by reinforcement and motivation arise from
a common set of neuropsychological mechanisms, and that the
principle of reinforcement is a special case of the more fundamental principle of motivation.

Reinforcing events that follow a response influence the subsequent probability of occurrence of that response in that situation; this is the principle of reinforcement. The probability of
occurrence of the response can also be influenced by motivating
events present at the time of testing; this is the principle of motivation. It is customary to say that reinforcing events affect (increase
or decrease) future response probability by the process of *response
reinforcement*, that is, the strengthening or weakening of specific
response tendencies, and that motivating events affect future
response probability by the process of *response instigation*, that is,
the activation or energizing of existing response tendencies. Is
only one of these two hypothetical explanatory ideas, response
reinforcement or response instigation, adequate to deal with the
types of influences on response probability traditionally considered under the two separate headings of reinforcement and
motivation?

There is a conceptual difficulty in approaching this question.
The difficulty arises from the common assumption that the process
of response reinforcement works 'backward' on responses that
precede the reinforcing event, and that the process of response
instigation works 'forward' on responses that are to follow the
motivating event. It should be noted, however, that in both cases

1. I thank J. F. Campbell, M. Corcoran, C. Malsbury, Jane Stewart and
I. Szabo for their critical comments on earlier drafts of this paper.

the test of a change in response probability involves a before-and-after comparison. As shown in Table 1, what is actually observed in both cases is that the behavior following the experimental event (reinforcing or motivating) is different from the behavior preceding the experimental event. The fact that in the reinforcement paradigm the investigator specifies a particular response-reinforcement contingency, and may call the successive observation period a trial, is of no consequence so far as the logic of before-and-after comparison is concerned. Both the reinforcement

Table 1 *Experimental Paradigms for Determining Reinforcement and Motivational Effects on Response Probability*

Antecedent behavior	Experimental event	Subsequent behavior
A: Response X	Motivating event	B: Test response*
Trial 1: Response X	Reinforcing event	Trial 2: Test response†

* Comparison of A and B yields the motivational effect.
† Comparison of Trial 1 and Trial 2 yields the reinforcement effect.

and the motivational effects on response probability are *observed after* the reinforcing and motivating events respectively. Thus, while it remains possible that the response-reinforcement process works backward and the response-instigation process works forward, this may not in fact be so. Both may work forward or backward. My point is that there exists no necessary backward versus forward distinction between reinforcement and motivational effects; the procedures employed by the investigator are different but the comparisons that define the two effects are the same.

Thus there is no *a priori* reason for considering reinforcing and motivational processes to be intrinsically different. However, the argument that they are fundamentally one and the same thing requires a close examination of several questions. I have grouped what appear to me to be the critical questions into three categories: questions concerning reinforcement, questions concerning motivation, and questions concerning response determination.

Questions concerning reinforcement

In this discussion, the term *reinforcing event* refers to the manipulation (e.g. presentation, removal) of an *incentive object*, such as food, sexual partner, an electrified grid, or a threatening opponent; and *reinforcement* refers to the arrangement that a reinforcing event is contingent upon the occurrence of a specified response. The phrase *response reinforcement* is used here to denote a particular hypothesis about the process by which reinforcement affects response probability – the hypothesis that the change in response probability is caused by the process of direct, backward 'strengthening' or 'weakening' of particular response tendencies or stimulus-response associations.

Do changes in response probability reflect response reinforcement ?

According to the response-reinforcement hypothesis a reinforcement-induced change in the probability of occurrence of any specified instrumental response should not be possible without the actual occurrence of that response. But instrumental learning without performance of the response during the reinforced trials is possible. Experiments on 'response substitution' (Lashley and McCarthy, 1926; Macfarlane, 1930, quoted by Munn, 1950) and 'learning without responding' (e.g. Dodwell and Bessant, 1960; Solomon and Turner, 1962) have clearly demonstrated this. In these experiments, the probability of occurrence of a specified instrumental response is increased, but the increase cannot be attributed to the strengthening of that response, because the response is not allowed to occur during the training trials. But since such learning without responding does require the reinforcing event, the increase in response probability must be attributed to some influence of the reinforcing event other than response reinforcement. One possibility is that the reinforcing event creates a motivational influence which facilitates the subsequent emergence of certain types of instrumental responses. Such a motivational influence would be more general and would allow for the observed lack of response-specificity in what the animal learns.

Is response reinforcement the basis of 'motivational excitement' ?

A view held commonly since the publication of Hull's (1943) general behavior theory is that motivational excitement – the 'interest' and 'arousal' that accompany goal-directed, instrumental behavior – does not represent a primary motivational process but is dependent upon response reinforcement. According to this view, the responses that are said to constitute motivational excitement are the responses that have been strengthened by prior reinforcement in the situation. Thus, if the principles of motivation and reinforcement appear to be alike, it is because the motivational characteristics of behavior are themselves produced by prior response reinforcement. Reinforcement is the primary factor; motivation is derivative.

This view is untenable. The responses displayed in the presence of an incentive object are seldom the same as the responses that are said to comprise motivational excitement. In a hungry rat, food elicits sniffing, biting and swallowing, but the typical signs of anticipating food are exploration and searching, consisting of rearing, circling, scratching obstacles, etc. Similarly, the responses elicited by an electrified grid are prancing, jumping, squealing and the like, but responses that usually indicate anticipation of electric shock are freezing and crouching. These common observations suggest that the responses usually considered as indicators of motivational excitement are so different from the responses elicited by the incentives themselves that it is unlikely that the basis of the excitement lies in the increased probability of occurrence of responses elicited by incentive stimuli.

However, these casual observations do not rule out the possibility of response reinforcement of the variety of actions that might precede the presentation of the reinforcing event (i.e. incentive presentation). In order to examine this possibility, Bindra and Palfai (1967) exposed thirsty rats to paired presentations of a conditioned stimulus (metronome) and an incentive (water) while the animals were held in restraining cages. After several conditioning sessions, they measured the effects of the conditioned stimulus on the exploratory activity of the rats in another situation. The types of responses that contributed to exploration scores (e.g. rearing, walking) were such that they could not have been performed in the restraining cages – during conditioning. Nevertheless, in the test situation the animals explored more in the presence of the conditioned stimulus than in its absence. Further, the acts displayed by the rats in the restraining cages were quite different from those that occurred on the presentation of the conditioned stimulus in the test situation. Thus, even if certain acts were conditioned in the restraining cages, they were not the acts that comprised motivational excitement in the test situation.

Clearly, the motivational excitement that may arise as a consequence of experience with an incentive is not crucially dependent upon the strengthening of the specific responses preceding or accompanying the incentive presentation. The motivational factor rather seems to be a general motivational state, not specifically linked to any particular responses. The actual actions displayed in the test situation would appear to arise from an interaction of the motivational state with the total stimulus characteristics of the test situation, and not depend on what the animal did just before or during the presentation of the incentive during conditioning. This points to the conclusion that the critical role of a reinforcing event (i.e. incentive manipulation) is to create a certain motivational state, and that while the motivational excitement is dependent upon the prior occurrence of the reinforcing event, it is not dependent upon response reinforcement.

Do all reinforcing events produce motivation?

Before we can confidently conclude that the primary function of reinforcing events (manipulation of incentives) is not response reinforcement but the creation of a motivational state, we should be reasonably sure that all events said to be reinforcing are also motivating. Casual observation, of course, suggests that this is so. It is a common trick in training hungry animals to 'prime' them by giving them an 'appetizer' pellet of food *before* the training session. And a simple everyday success or failure may change a man's mood and outlook on life for several hours to come.

Bindra and Campbell (1967) have experimentally investigated whether events that are known to be positive reinforcers (that is, which increase response probability) have any measurable (motivational) effects on behavior immediately *following* the (reinforcing) event. In order not to confound any intrinsic motivational effects with the presumed effects of response reinforcement, it was necessary to create an experimental arrangement in which the reinforcing event could not be said to reinforce any responses. We achieved this by using intracranial electrical stimulation in lateral hypothalamic 'reward sites' as the reinforcing event and by stimulating only when the animal was motionless. Since this type of reinforcing event requires no consummatory responses (e.g. eating in the case of food reinforcement), no response could be said to be consistently associated with the reinforcing event. We examined the changes in spontaneous behavior of the rat following intracranial stimulation. The results are shown in Figure 1. In the

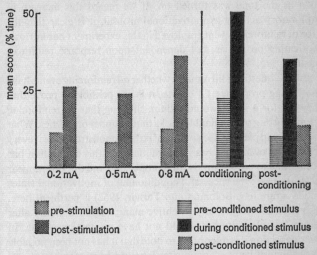

Figure 1 Conditioning of the motivational state produced by intracranial stimulation.
The left part of the figure shows the mean perambulation scores in 3-minute pre- and post-stimulation periods at each of three levels of current applied at a hypothalamic rewarding site. The two sets of bars on the right show the mean perambulation scores obtained during the tests of conditioned motivation: the two final conditioning tests (15-second observation periods) and the two post-conditioning tests (1-minute observation periods) (Bindra and Campbell, 1967)

left part of the figure, the speckled columns represent the pre-stimulation level of general activity. At the end of the prestimulation observation period, a half-second intracranial stimulation was given. Even the first, momentary, response-independent stimulation produced a marked increase in exploratory activity (striped column), which generally lasted for as long as two minutes or more. Since this effect on exploration could have been caused by the novelty of electrical stimulation *per se*, we tried to condition whatever motivational state might have been created by the intracranial stimulation. A conditioned stimulus (metronome) was turned on for fifteen seconds before the onset of a series of pulses of intracranial stimulation lasting for thirty seconds. After several trials of conditioning, the animals started being active as soon as the tone was turned on. If we regard this increase in exploratory activity as motivational arousal, it is clear that the type of reinforcing event employed in this experiment has intrinsic motivating properties, not dependent upon response reinforcement.

But the question still remains whether *all* reinforcing events have motivating properties. Of course, it is not possible to prove that they do, for a proof would require showing that no reinforcing event, existing or imaginable, lacks motivational properties. What must serve in place of decisive proof is the demonstration that every reinforcing event that has been examined in this connection has been found to possess motivating properties. And this does appear to be the case; the successful conditioning of motivational states under curare (e.g. Solomon and Turner, 1962) is pertinent here. It is hard to imagine any incentive manipulation that can alter response probability but would not have motivating effects. In this connection it is interesting to note that it has not been possible to distinguish between brain sites involved in reinforcement and the sites involved in motivation; the same neural systems seem to underlie both (Christopher and Butter, 1968; Glickman and Schiff, 1967; Milner, 1970).

Conclusion

Four summarizing statements can be made on the basis of the above discussion.

1. While reinforcing events obviously are capable of altering response probability, the change in response probability is not produced by 'response reinforcement' – the direct strengthening or weakening influence of the reinforcing event on specific preceding responses.

2. Response reinforcement is not the basis of motivational excitement that accompanies goal-directed, instrumental actions.

3. All reinforcing events (that is, incentive manipulations) that alter response probability also have intrinsic motivating properties not dependent upon response reinforcement.

4. It appears reasonable to proceed on the assumption that the primary effect of a reinforcing event is not response reinforcement, but the creation of a motivational state that influences a wide variety of subsequent behavior of the animal.

Questions concerning motivation

The concept of motivation refers to the fact that animals display particular types of goal-directed actions, such as feeding, copulating and escaping, at certain times but not at others. Typically such actions involve searching or *exploratory responses*, approach-withdrawal or *instrumental responses*, and consummatory or *incentive-related responses*. When habit (i.e. learning or practice) is held constant and the investigator manipulates variables related to incentives, or to bodily changes (e.g. those arising from food deprivation, fatigue, hormonal variations or drugs), or both, the resulting changes in behavior are usually described as 'motivational effects.'

Is motivation equivalent to drive?

Traditionally, motivational effects have been explained mainly with reference to the concept of *drive*, which was introduced into psychology around 1920 (e.g. Richter, 1922; Woodworth, 1918). The drive view of motivation, summarized in Figure 2, holds that particular drive manipulations (e.g. food deprivation, induction of estrus, exposure to painful stimuli) induce particular physiological processes or 'drives' that directly increase the level of general activity of the animal and facilitate the occurrence of particular instrumental and incentive-related responses. Thus, food deprivation is said to produce certain physiological processes, which in turn are thought to make the animal more active and to facilitate the occurrence of food-approach and eating.

For several years the drives were regarded as the primary motivational factors. However, now the developing consensus seems to be that the drive concept in the sense of the physiological consequences of certain drive manipulations, is inadequate for dealing with motivational effects. Some of the reasons are as follows:

1. When precautions are taken to remove from the test situation incentive objects, as well as incentive-related stimuli, drive manipu-

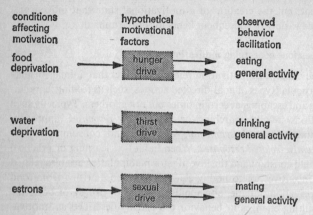

Figure 2 Schematic diagram of the drive view of motivation

lations do not instigate responses that could be described as searching or investigatory. In other words, drive *per se*, in the absence of incentive stimulation, is not sufficient to produce (goal-directed) exploratory responses. The increase in general activity produced by drives lacks the features of excitement and systematic investigation of the environment that characterize exploratory responses. These points have been documented recently by several authors (e.g. Bindra, 1968; Bolles, 1967).

2. The facilitation of instrumental responses by drive manipulations has traditionally been attributed to drive. However, the experiments on which this view was based confounded drive with incentive stimulation. Now it appears that drive *per se*, in the absence of incentive stimulation, is incapable of facilitating instrumental responses (Bindra, 1968). This conclusion can be supported both on the basis of argument (e.g. Black, 1965), and on the results of experiments which separate the effects of drive from those of drive plus incentive stimulation (e.g. Mendelson, 1966).

3. The fact that drive facilitates the occurrence of incentive-related (e.g. consummatory) responses cannot be taken as evidence that drive *per se* is the source of the facilitation, for a test of incentive-related responses cannot be made in the absence of incentive stimulation. However, evidence that, for example, given a certain level of hunger, the readiness with which an animal will eat depends on the palatability of food and other incentive properties (e.g. Young, 1948) indicates that the facilitation of consummatory responses produced by manipulating drive is not independent of incentive stimulation.

4. The concept of drive, as a special physiological process, is not applicable to a wide variety of motivational effects. For example, a normally satiated animal will readily eat a preferred (e.g. sweet) food, and highly novel objects will provoke withdrawal responses without requiring any specific physiological condition. It appears that many goal-directed actions of animals (e.g. grooming, exploring, playing) occur under a wide range of organismic states and do not require any highly specific physiological conditions of the type associated with hunger, thirst, estrus, or pain (Nissen, 1954). Thus, the answer to the question, is motivation equivalent to drive? is *no*.

What, then, is motivation?

Another view of motivation has been gradually emerging over the past couple of decades. Its early beginnings in the concept of 'incentive motivation' (Hull, 1950; Seward, 1951; Spence, 1956) have now led to somewhat clearer formulations that regard environmental incentive stimuli to be a critical factor in goal-directed actions (e.g. Bindra and Palfai, 1967; Bolles, 1967; Black, 1965; Logan, 1960; Sheffield, 1966). The general idea is that motivational processes – that produce the observed motivational effects – are generated by a combination of physiological conditions and incentive stimulation. Within this broad framework, I (Bindra, 1968, 1969) have developed a specific model of motivation (Figure 3). My view is that the processes that produce the observed motivational influences on behavior arise from an interaction between the neural consequences of the prevailing organismic state and the neural consequences of certain types of

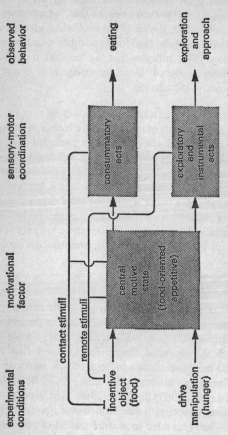

Figure 3 Schematic diagram of the hypothetical interrelations of the central motive state with, on the one hand, organismic state (hunger) and incentive stimulation (food), and, on the other, sensory-motor coordinations underlying the observed behavior

| experimental conditions | motivational factor | sensory-motor coordination | observed behavior |

incentive object (food)

contact stimuli

remote stimuli

central motive state (food-oriented appetitive)

consummatory acts

eating

exploratory and instrumental acts

exploration and approach

drive manipulation (hunger)

environmental incentive stimulation. The particular set of neural processes that arise from any such interaction may be described, following Morgan (1943), as a 'central motive state', or *cms*. The organismic state, which is one of the interacting factors, may be a general state (e.g. being awake, sleepy or sick) or a more specific physiological condition of the type traditionally called a drive (e.g. conditions produced by food deprivation, drug injection or fatigue). The incentive stimulation, which is the other interacting factor, may consist of any stimuli arising from environmental objects that we usually describe as possessing affective properties and label 'incentives', 'reinforcers', or 'emotional stimuli'. The *central motive state*, then, is a functional neural change which is generated by an interaction of the neural representations of organismic state and incentive object, and which, once generated, persists for some time. The reasons for considering the motivational factor as a primary central factor, rather than as dependent upon sensory feedback from visceral or skeletal responses, as suggested by some (e.g. Mowrer, 1947, 1960; Spence, 1956, 1960), have been elaborated elsewhere (e.g. Bindra, 1968; Rescorla and Solomon, 1967).

The generation and persistence of a central motive state is necessary for goal-directed actions: exploratory, instrumental and incentive-linked. While a central motive state persists, it facilitates the occurrence of a certain class of incentive-linked actions (e.g. eating, drinking, copulating); thus central motive states may be classified in terms of the type of incentive objects to which the animal's responses are addressed. Note that the concept of central motive state should not be identified either with organismic state alone or with incentive stimulation alone. It is their interaction that generates the central motive state. Thus, neither hunger nor food can by itself produce a food-directed central motive state, but when the neural consequences of hunger interact with the neural consequences of food-related stimuli (e.g. the smell and sight of food), the central motive state is created and food-oriented behavior ensues.

One advantage of this formulation is that it allows a unified approach to the phenomena of motivation and emotion. The actions we associate with words such as fear, anger, love, joy and depression are usually said to be 'emotional' actions, and the actions we associate with the words such as hunger, thirst, sex and motherhood are generally called 'motivational' actions. My view (Bindra, 1969) is that each of such species-typical actions, whether called emotional or motivational, is crucially dependent on a central motive state, which in turn arises from an interaction of a certain organismic state and a certain class of environmental incentive object. Customarily, we think of emotional actions to be elicited by environmental stimuli and motivational actions to be instigated by internal organismic conditions. But in fact an interaction of internal organismic conditions and environmental factors is involved in both types of actions. While normally emotional actions do appear to be elicitable within a wide range of organismic conditions, it can be demonstrated that, holding environmental conditions constant, organismic conditions do play a part in emotional behavior. Premenstrual depressions, androgen-induced aggression and the use of tranquilizers for reducing anxiety clearly show the role of organismic conditions in emotional behavior. Similarly, while normally motivational actions appear to be instigated in the presence of a wide range of incentive objects, so long as the appropriate organismic state is present, it can be demonstrated that, holding organismic conditions constant, the nature of environmental objects can affect the occurrence of motivational actions. An animal satiated on one food will readily resume eating when offered a preferred food, and a male rat, after copulation with one female, will prefer to copulate with another female than to copulate with the same one (Beach and Ransom, 1967). Even when a species-typical action (e.g. eating or attack) is produced by electrical stimulation of the appropriate hypothalamic site, the precise characteristics of the available incentive object determine the probability that the animal will display the action (Levison and Flynn, 1965; Tenen and Miller, 1964; Roberts, Steinberg and Means, 1967).

What is secondary or learned motivation?

Scores of experiments inspired by the two-process theory of learning have shown that initially neutral stimuli can, through the procedure of classical conditioning, acquire conditioned incentive-motivational properties that resemble some of the properties possessed by the unconditioned (incentive) stimulus. For example, if a hungry animal is exposed to pairings of a tone and food, the tone will acquire some of the motivating properties of hunger-food. These motivating properties can be demonstrated by using the tone to modify a variety of responses in other situations (for recent examinations of this evidence, see Bacon and Bindra, 1967; Bindra, 1968; Bolles, 1967; Rescorla and Solomon, 1967). In terms of the model of motivation presented above, we can say that central motive states are conditionable.

What is the nature of such conditioning of a central motive state? Since a central motive state arises from an interaction of an organismic state and a certain type of incentive stimulation, it is reasonable to ask, what precisely is conditioned? Does the conditioned stimulus – metronome tone, light, etc. – become a conditioned stimulus (or substitute) for the organismic state or for the incentive or for both? Is the basis of secondary or learned motivation the conditioning of the neural consequences of the organismic state or of the neural consequences of the incentive stimulation, or both?

The early concepts of 'secondary drive' and 'secondary reinforcement', advocated in the writings of Hull (1943), Dollard and Miller (1950), and Miller (1951), implied that both organismic state ('drive') and incentive stimulation could be conditioned individually and separately. However, the evidence for the conditioning of organismic state was by no means conclusive. The difficulty, of course, is that of experimentally separating the conditioning of organismic state from the conditioning of incentive stimulation. In the absence of any critical experiments, attempts have been made to settle the issue on the basis of argument. Thus, Brown (1953) has set forth a variety of reasons why the idea of conditioning of an organismic state *per se* – of 'secondary drive' – is untenable.

One of the results of the Bindra and Palfai (1967) experiment described above supports this conclusion. They found that the efficacy of a conditioned incentive-motivational stimulus depends on the actual existence of the appropriate organismic state. They measured the increase in exploratory perambulation produced at various levels of thirst by a conditioned stimulus that had previously been paired with water. As seen in Figure 4, the increase in perambulation produced by the conditioned incentive stimulus

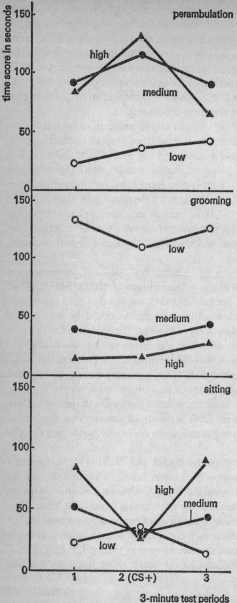

perambulation

Figure 4 Mean time scores for each of three categories of acts obtained by the high, medium, and low-drive groups during the three successive test periods.
The conditioned incentive stimulus (CS+) was presented during the middle test period (Bindra and Palfai, 1967)

was negligible when the animals were not thirsty, but was quite substantial when the animals were thirsty. This means that the efficacy of the conditioned (incentive-motivational) stimulus depended on the existence of a state of thirst. Clearly, if thirst was needed at the time of testing with the conditioned stimulus, then the conditioned stimulus could not have reinstated thirst. Since the actual incentive object (water) was not required at the time of test to produce the increase in perambulation, the conditioned stimulus must have assumed certain properties of the incentive. Thus, the conditioning of a motivational state rests on the conditioning of incentive properties. The conditioned stimuli that can create a central motive state should, therefore, be called *conditioned incentive stimuli*.

Conclusion

The above discussion permits three conclusions.

1. Drive, defined as the direct physiological consequences of certain 'drive' (metabolic) manipulations, is by itself not sufficient for explaining motivational effects on exploratory, instrumental, and consummatory responses.

2. The concept of *central motive state*, defined as a functional neural change which is generated by an interaction of the neural representations of organismic state (including 'drive') and incentive object, appears more suitable for dealing both with naturally occurring species-typical actions and experimentally produced motivational effects.

3. When a central motive state is conditioned to an initially neutral stimulus, the latter serves as a substitute for incentive stimulation, not for organismic state; thus, the basis of secondary or learned motivation is secondary or conditioned incentives, and not secondary or conditioned organismic states (or 'drives').

Questions concerning response determination

The traditional view has been that the motivational factor influences behavior merely by making a response more or less likely to occur, without directly determining *which* response would occur. For example, in Hull's (1943) behavior theory, the motivational factor ('drive') was postulated to explain when or how readily a response would occur, not which one would occur; motivation determines *response occurrence*, not the selection of response. *Response selection* was thought to be determined by the stimuli to which the animal is exposed at the moment and the relative strengths of their associations with different responses in the animal's repertoire. In general, the theorists (e.g. Miller, 1963; Mowrer, 1947; Rescorla and Solomon, 1967; Seward, 1956; Spence, 1956) who have followed the broad framework of Hullian response reinforcement theory have tended not to implicate the motivational factor in response selection.

A different way of conceptualizing the influence of the motivational factor on behavior is to suggest that it determines, in part, both response selection and response occurrence. This is the view taken by Mowrer (1960) in his latest theory, according to which successive acts in a response sequence are determined by moment-to-moment variations in the motivational factor. This appears to me to be a better approach, though Mowrer has made no attempt to outline the exact way in which the motivational factor may contribute to response determination (response selection and response occurrence). In this lack of specification of possible mechanisms, Mowrer's account has the same shortcoming as Tolman's (1948), who failed to specify the type of mechanisms by which cognitive factors ('expectancy', 'cognition', etc.) may determine response.

This section is addressed to the broad question of the way in which the influence of the motivational factor on behavior may be conceptualized. Note that the discussion is not intended to be a full discussion of response determination, but only of the way in which the motivational factor, central motive state, may contribute to response determination. A full account of response determination would also have to include the role of cognitive factors, and this is beyond the scope of this paper.

How does the central motive state influence behavior?

The technique of electrical stimulation of hypothalamic sites involved in various species-typical actions is at present the best way of studying the efferent influences of central motive states. The electrical stimulation of such 'hypothalamic motive sites' produces, not specific motor patterns, but broad response tendencies which, in conjunction with environmental stimuli, determine the exact course of action. For example, the electrical stimulation of hypothalamic 'feeding sites' leads to eating or drinking actions only in the presence of appropriate environmental incentive objects – food or water. Similarly, the stimulation of 'aggression sites' leads to an attacking action only when an attackable incentive object is present in the environment. Thus, such hypothalamic sites are not motor centers, but appear to be parts of a system closely related to the loci at which particular central motive states are generated. It seems reasonable to suppose that the electrical stimulation of, say, a feeding site produces a central motive (feeding) state by bypassing the processes (hunger state and food stimulation) that are normally involved in generating that central motive state. This means that while studies involving electrical stimulation of hypothalamic motive sites cannot tell us anything about the mechanisms by which central motive states are normally produced, they may nevertheless elucidate the way in which central motive states, once generated, influence behavior. Consider some of the results of experiments that have made use of this method.

The first result to note is that though a satiated animal does not display a consummatory response (e.g. eating) in the presence of an incentive object (i.e. food), it begins to display it soon after the electrical stimulation of the appropriate (feeding) site is started. In other words, while in a normally satiated animal the stimulus characteristics of the food incentive are not in themselves sufficient to elicit the response of eating, the electrically induced central motive state renders the food more attractive, leading to appropriate approach and consummatory responses. Thus, it may be said that the central motive state alters the incentive value (attractiveness, repulsiveness) of incentive objects.

The second result of importance is that the electrical stimulation of a hypothalamic motive site is capable of producing exploratory responses even in the absence of any particular incentive object. That is, a stimulation-induced central motive state can render more effective the stimulus characteristics of the experimental chamber, so that they again become capable of eliciting the exploratory responses that presumably had been habituated before. This is consistent with the above suggestion that central motive states alter the incentive value of environmental objects and events.

The third result of interest here is that a stimulation-induced central motive state can be conditioned to an initially neutral stimulus. Thus, a tone paired with electrical stimulation of the hypothalamic feeding site would acquire the capacity of generating the feeding central motive state. But this does not mean that the animal will start to make eating movements on the presentation of the tone alone. The actual responses displayed by the animal will depend on the exact characteristics of the stimulus situation and the strength of the central motive state generated by the conditioned stimulus. In the absence of food, the animal will probably merely explore. If some food-related stimulus objects (e.g. food-delivery tray) are present, the animal is likely, at the presentation of the tone, to display instrumental approach responses to the location of the food-related objects. Finally, if food is present, the animal may, at the onset of the tone, start to eat but (in the absence of electrical stimulation) is not likely to continue to eat. In some observations made in this laboratory (A. Hilton, E. Lewicki and D. Bindra, unpublished experiments), we have found that while conditioned stimuli in the absence of electrical stimulation and food will make the animals (rats) explore and make instrumental approach responses toward the usual location of food, the animals almost never actually eat. Thus the reliable and continuous elicitation of consummatory responses requires the presence of a continuing and strong central motive state, and the central motive states produced by conditioned stimuli (in 'satiated' animals) are not persistent or strong enough to cause animals to display consummatory responses. This is consistent with the observations of Mendelson (1966), and Roberts and Kiess (1964) that while instrumental (approach) responses can be elicited by conditioned incentive stimuli (e.g. alley cues or the sight of a lever in a lever-pressing situation), the actual occurrence of the consummatory responses usually requires both the presence of the incentive object and electrical stimulation. It appears that normally an appropriate organismic state (drive) is required to produce a strong enough central motive state to instigate consummatory behavior. The above analysis also suggests that conditioned stimuli cannot reinstate organismic states, and that while conditioned stimuli acquire some of the properties of remote incentive stimuli (e.g. the smell and sight of food), which attract (or repel) the animal, they do not acquire the properties of contact incentive stimuli, which elicit consummatory responses.

A model that is consistent with the above observations on the way in which a central motive state influences behavior is shown in Figure 5. The basic feature of this model is that it portrays the stimuli arising from the incentive object as having two separate routes to the sensory-motor coordination sites: a direct sensory-motor route and an indirect sensory-motivational-motor route. The fibers in the former, Route X, form direct connections with a variety of efferent coordination systems. The fibers in the latter, Route Y, form connections with central motive sites, where an interaction of the prevailing organismic state and incentive stimulation takes place and a central motive state is generated. The central motive state then selectively modulates (facilitates or inhibits) particular sensory-motor coordinations. The sensory stimulation arising from the other, non-incentive parts of the environment is capable of becoming conditioned stimulation (Route C) for producing the central motive state.

How is a response determined?

Assuming that the general mechanism of motivational influence on behavior is one of selective facilitation and inhibition of particular sensory-motor coordinations, we may next ask precisely how the sensory-motor coordinations corresponding to a particular response are 'selected' and 'activated'? My general approach to this question is that both so-called response selection and response occurrence are aspects of a single set of mechanisms of *response determination*. A response is not first selected and then made to occur; 'selection' and 'occurrence' go hand in hand. A response does not exist prior to its occurrence; it attains a reality only by occurrence. Any defined response is organized afresh each time it occurs. From this point of view, the problem of response determination is simply that of the organized excitation of a sequence of sensory-motor coordinations that corresponds to the behavioral definition of the response.

Following Schneirla (1959), I assume that there exist largely innate sensory-motor coordinations that make animals move

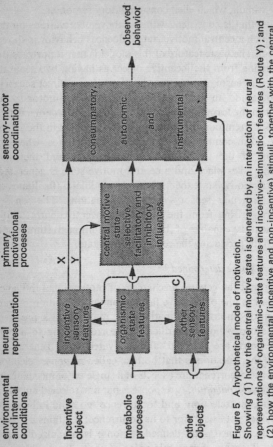

Figure 5 A hypothetical model of motivation.
Showing (1) how the central motive state is generated by an interaction of neural representations of organismic-state features and incentive-stimulation features (Route Y); and (2) how the environmental (incentive and non-incentive) stimuli, together with the central motive state, influence response determination by selective effects (facilitation or inhibition) on sensory-motor coordination. The stimulation arising from non-incentive environmental stimulation can, through conditioning (Route C), acquire the same properties as Route Y

toward certain (appetitive) incentive objects and away from other (aversive) incentive objects. The incentive value of the stimuli from incentive objects depends upon the central motive state created by an interaction of the prevailing organismic state and the remote (olfactory, visual, auditory) stimuli arising from the incentive objects. Inasmuch as certain nonincentive stimuli occur in close temporal and spatial contiguity with the incentive object, they – the initially neutral stimuli – acquire some of the properties of remote incentive stimuli. Thus, goal-directed instrumental approach and withdrawal responses may be attributed to the direct excitation by conditioned and remote incentive stimuli of certain sensory-motor coordinations, which are selectively facilitated by the influence of central motive states. While this formulation is readily applicable to instrumental responses that involve direct approach or withdrawal, its application to the more complicated instrumental responses (e.g. lever pressing) is not obvious. A discussion of the whole problem of 'response shaping' and other aspects of instrumental learning lies outside the scope of this paper.

Note that, according to this view, the occurrence of the successive acts comprising approach or withdrawal does not depend on the sensory feedback from visceral or other 'emotional' responses produced by incentive stimuli – a proposition suggested by Mowrer (1960). As Miller (1963) has pointed out, the dependence of each successive act on sensory feedback would make the response completion much slower than it usually is. According to the present view the excitation of the appropriate sensory-motor coordinations, facilitated by the central motive state, is achieved directly by incentive stimuli, remote or conditioned. The exact neural mechanisms that link particular classes of incentive stimuli to certain sensory-motor coordinations representing approach and withdrawal emerges as an important problem for investigation (Milner, 1970, ch. 19; Schneirla, 1965).

How do reinforcement and motivation affect the probability of particular responses?

As we have seen, the role of reinforcing events (incentive manipulations) is not the strengthening or weakening of preceding responses but the creation of central motive states that affect the subsequent behavior of the animal. This means that the effects on response probability of both reinforcing and motivating events arise from a common source – the central motive state. If the central motive state constitutes a fairly general facilitatory or inhibitory influence not specifically linked to any response, how can we explain the specificity of the influence on response probability obtained in experiments with reinforcement and motivation paradigms?

It should be noted in passing that this question of the specificity of the influences of reinforcing and motivating factors on response probability has not received the attention it deserves. Hullian theorists (e.g. Hull, 1943; Spence, 1956), arguing that reinforcement affects the strength of specific stimulus-response connections $(_sH_R)$, had no difficulty accounting for the specificity of the effects of reinforcing events, but they could not adequately explain the effects of motivating events (e.g. drive). For example, if drive is increased, why does it affect the probability of occurrence of a given response more than of all the other responses in the animal's repertoire that could occur in the given situation? In other words, why does drive interact with a specific habit (SH_R) tendency and not with other habit tendencies in the animal's repertoire? Two-process theorists (e.g. Mowrer, 1947, 1960; Rescorla and Solomon, 1967), who have demonstrated the importance of a learned incentive-motivational factor in determining response probability, have also so far not directed their attention to the problem of how the motivational factor affects the occurrence of any particular instrumental response. In fact, they seem to have so completely separated the motivational factor from the (instrumental) response that it is difficult to foresee how they would conceive of an interaction of these two. In general, the difficulty with all these theoretical formulations, with the possible exception of Mowrer's (1960), is that the motivational factor is regarded primarily as a contributor to response occurrence (Figure 6, A and B) rather than to response selection. The general approach I have outlined above regards response selection and response occurrence to be the two aspects of the same process of excitation of particular sensory-motor coordinations by the joint action of environmental stimuli and the prevailing central motive state (Figure 6C). The neural events by which the motivational factor

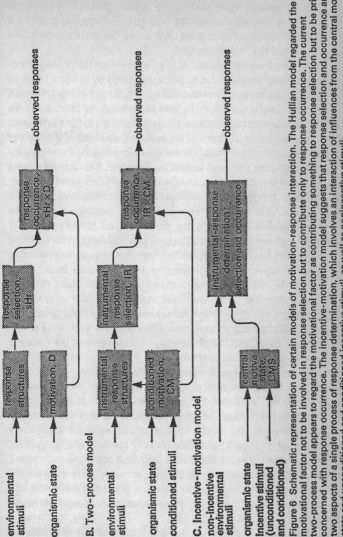

Figure 6 Schematic representation of certain models of motivation-response interaction. The Hullian model regarded the motivational factor not to be involved in response selection but to contribute only to response occurrence. The current two-process model appears to regard the motivational factor as contributing something to response selection but to be primarily concerned with response occurrence. The incentive-motivation model suggests that response selection and occurrence are two aspects of a single process of response determination, which involves an interaction of influences from the central motive state and unconditioned and conditioned incentive stimuli, as well as nonincentive stimuli

influences behavior (i.e. affects response occurrence) are an inherent part of the process of response selection as well. Within this framework, then, there is no special problem of the interaction of response tendencies with the motivational factor, for the motivational factor itself determines the particular response tendencies that will be excited.

Consider now the details of the way in which the probability of a particular instrumental response is altered by the procedure of reinforcement. Imagine the training of a hungry rat to traverse a runway from a start box to a goal box containing food. After the rat, through exploration, has discovered and eaten food in the goal box, the stimulus features of the goal box, and later of the runway and the start box, would become conditioned stimuli and capable of creating the (feeding) central motive state. This central motive state and conditioned incentive stimuli would then jointly produce response tendencies of approaching the conditioned incentive stimuli. As the animal approaches one conditioned incentive stimulus after another (in the different parts of the runway), it will get closer and closer to the goal box and food. With repeated trials, the level of conditioning, that is, the acquired incentive characteristics of the conditioned stimuli, would increase, as would the strength of the central motive state. These developments, together with the habituation of initial exploratory responses, would make the rat approach the goal box faster, and the usual measures of 'response strength', such as starting speed, running speed, and the probability of occurrence of the response (within a given time interval) would show improvement. As the response is performed repeatedly, its successive motor components would become organized into long chains, thereby making the response less dependent on the presence of runway incentive stimuli; at this stage, blinding the animal or any other sensory interference is not likely to disrupt the response completely (DeFeudis, 1968). Thus, while initially the response is 'guided' in the sense that each successive approach component is elicited by a particular conditioned incentive stimulus in the runway, the final response is 'ballistic' in the sense that once initiated it can be completed with a minimum of dependence on environmental stimuli.

The above account of the acquisition of an instrumental

approach response clearly does not attribute any response-strengthening role to reinforcement, but rests on the assumption that a central motive state, together with the related incentive stimuli, guides the animal to the incentive object. The conditioned incentive stimuli, since their incentive properties depend on their proximity to the incentive object, increase the probability of occurrence of those very acts which the experimenter has chosen to 'reinforce' (i.e. the acts on which the incentive is contingent). Thus, though the influence of a central motive state and incentive stimuli is, in principle, non-specific, the influence will be specific to the reinforced response so long as the experimental arrangements remain unaltered (that is, so long as the location of the incentive object in the experimental environment remains the same). A similar interpretation of instrumental behavior has been proposed by Grastyán, Czopf, Ángyán and Szabó (1965) on the basis of their neurophysiological experiments.

The general analysis of the reinforcement paradigm that I have outlined above indicates a way of accounting for several experimental findings that otherwise require *ad hoc* explanations. Consider two of these.

1. In demonstrating the acquisition of an instrumental response, it is customary to make the reward – say, water – contingent upon the response – say, lever pressing – *and* to create the appropriate organismic state, that is, thirst. At the time of training, the animal is thirsty and each lever press delivers a few drops of water, which the animal quickly drinks. If, as I have suggested, the increase in response probability is dependent upon the motivational factor and the motivational factor is dependent upon an interaction of organismic state and incentive stimulation, then it should also be possible to train animals by manipulating organismic state rather than incentive. That is, the probability of occurrence of a response could be increased by making the organismic state (thirst) contingent upon the response and making the reward (water) available all the time. In other words, a non-thirsty animal, with water continuously available, should be able to learn to press a lever that would make it thirsty and make it drink water. This kind of experiment is difficult to do, for organismic states cannot be changed quickly enough to make them contingent upon a response.

But by the use of electrical stimulation of the drinking hypothalamic motive site, it is possible to make the drinking central motive state contingent upon lever pressing. Mendelson (1967) has done this very experiment, and has found that, indeed, a non-thirsty rat will learn to press a lever that would electrically generate the drinking central motive state and make the animal drink for the duration of the stimulation. While this finding completely contradicts the Hullian drive-reduction hypothesis of instrumental learning, it can be readily accounted for in terms of the incentive-motivational view of learning. What probably happens is this. The electrical stimulation leads to drinking (for water is continuously available), and this provides the conditions for the environmental stimuli (lever, water receptacle) to acquire some of the properties of the incentive (water). In the absence of the electrical stimulation, these conditioned incentive stimuli would generate a weak central motive state which would be sufficient for eliciting the (approach) instrumental response, but not for the consummatory response of drinking. However, as soon as the instrumental response (lever press) leads to electrical stimulation, the central motive state would become strong enough to induce drinking (for the duration of the electrical stimulation), thereby providing the conditions for the association of the environmental stimuli with the (unconditioned) incentive object (water). Thus, while a non-thirsty animal would not drink the available water, the conditioned environmental stimuli would become capable of instigating the instrumental response – and this in turn would create the conditions (electrical stimulation) for drinking.

2. If the above account of response determination in terms of unconditioned and conditioned incentive stimuli is correct, it should be possible to obtain increases in the probability of certain approach and withdrawal responses even if these responses are not specifically reinforced in an instrumental reinforcement paradigm. That is, so long as the defined 'instrumental' response involves only approach or withdrawal (rather than any complicated refined sequences of acts requiring special 'response shaping'), a *classical* conditioning procedure may be sufficient for increasing the probability of occurrence of the instrumental response. That this is so is shown by the phenomenon of 'auto-

shaping', recently described by Brown and Jenkins (1968). They showed that a pigeon would reliably increase its rate of key pecking following a classical conditioning procedure, which consisted of momentarily illuminating a key (conditioned stimulus) followed by presentation of food (unconditioned incentive stimulation). According to the incentive-motivational view of response probability, the illuminated key, which is followed by food, would acquire conditioned incentive-motivational properties of the same type as are possessed by the food tray and other remote food-associated stimuli. These conditioned incentive stimuli would then elicit approach responses in the bird, one of the approach components being pecking. It should be noted that this type of response-independent training would increase the probability of occurrence of only those responses that form a part of the general approach pattern of the species. Also, the fact that in the Brown and Jenkins experiment the food tray was located directly below the key may have contributed to the concentration of the approach responses in the general key-tray area.[2]

Conclusion

Five working assumptions appear to be justified on the basis of the discussion in this section.

1. In general, the central motive state influences behavior by facilitating and inhibiting a certain set of sensory-motor co-ordinations.

2. The strength of the central motive state required for the occurrence of exploratory and instrumental responses is less than the strength required for the occurrence of consummatory responses.

3. The processes of response selection and response occurrence are aspects of the common set of mechanisms of *response determination*; the organized excitation of a certain set of sensory-motor coordinations is the basis of response determination.

2. After sending this paper to press I learned that B. R. Moore of the Department of Psychology, Dalhousie University, Halifax, N.S., has independently developed a similar interpretation of auto-shaping, and has extended this kind of incentive interpretation to a wide variety of other learning phenomena.

4. The organized excitation of sensory-motor coordinations corresponding to a particular response depends upon the stability of the spatial arrangement of the incentive stimuli (unconditioned and conditioned) in relation to the incentive object.

5. A change in the probability of occurrence of a particular instrumental response is possible with a reinforcement paradigm because the generation of a central motive state and the related conditioned incentive stimuli depends upon the incentive object in relation to which the response is defined (that is, the acts elicited by the incentive stimuli comprise the defined instrumental response).

Summary

The probability of occurrence of a response can be altered by linking it to a reinforcing event (principle of reinforcement) or by manipulating the prevailing incentive and organismic conditions (principle of motivation). It is customary to attribute these two means of altering response probability to the hypothetical processes of 'response reinforcement' and 'response instigation', respectively. This paper presents evidence and argument in support of the hypothesis that response reinforcement and response instigation arise from a common set of neuropsychological mechanisms, and that the principle of reinforcement is a special case of the more primary principle of motivation. Three sets of questions are discussed and the main conclusions are enumerated at the end of each of the three main sections of this paper.

A reinforcing event is essentially the manipulation of an incentive object in the presence of an appropriate organismic state (e.g. 'drive'). An interaction of incentive stimuli with the relevant organismic state is also the condition for generating motivation. Both reinforcing events and motivating events are regarded here as events that create 'central motive states', that selectively influence a certain set of sensory-motor coordinations. A particular response is organized through an interaction of the prevailing central motive state with unconditioned and conditioned incentive stimuli and other, non-incentive stimuli.

It is argued that the so-called backward-acting response-reinforcement influence of reinforcing events is illusory, and that reinforcing events, like motivating events, create central motive states that influence subsequent behavior. The specificity of this influence on a *particular* instrumental response is explained in terms of the assumption that the generation of a central motive state and the related conditioned incentive stimuli depends upon the incentive object in relation to which the response is defined.

References

BACON, W. E., and BINDRA, D. (1967), 'The generality of the incentive-motivational effects of classically conditioned stimuli in instrumental learning', *Acta biol. exp.*, vol. 27. pp. 185–97.

BEACH F. A., and RANSOM, T. W. (1967), 'Effects of environmental variation on ejaculatory frequency in male rats', *J. compar. physiol. Psychol.*, vol. 64, pp. 384–7.

BINDRA, D. (1968), 'Neuropsychological interpretation of the effects of drive and incentive-motivation on general activity and instrumental behavior', *Psychol. Rev.*, vol. 75, pp. 1–22.

BINDRA, D. (1969), 'A unified interpretation of emotion and motivation', *Ann. N.Y. Acad. Sci.*, vol. 159, pp. 1071–83.

BINDRA, D., and CAMPBELL, J. F. (1967), 'Motivational effects of rewarding intracranial stimulation', *Nature*, vol. 215, pp. 375–6.

BINDRA, D., and PALFAI, T. (1967), 'Nature of positive and negative incentive-motivational effects on general activity', *J. compar. physiol. Psychol.*, vol. 63, pp. 288–97.

BLACK, R. W. (1965), 'On the combination of drive and incentive motivation', *Psychol. Rev.*, vol. 72, pp. 310–17.

BOLLES, R. C. (1967), *Theory of Motivation*, Harper & Row.

BROWN, J. S. (1953), 'Problems presented by the concept of acquired drives', *Nebraska Symposium on Motivation*, University of Nebraska Press, pp. 1–21.

BROWN, P. L., and JENKINS, H. M. (1968), 'Auto-shaping of the pigeon's key-peck', *J. exp. Anal. Behav.*, vol. 11, pp. 1–8.

CHRISTOPHER, SISTER MARY, and BUTTER, C. M. (1968), 'Consummatory behaviors and locomotor exploration evoked from self-stimulation sites in rats', *J. compar. physiol. Psychol.*, vol. 66, pp. 335–9.

DEFEUDIS, P. A. (1968), 'The role of sensory factors in the organization of the instrumental response', unpublished M.A. thesis, McGill University.

DODWELL, P. C., and BESSANT, D. E. (1960), 'Learning without swimming in a water maze', *J. compar. physiol. Psychol.*, vol. 53, pp. 422–5.

DOLLARD, J., and MILLER, N. E. (1950), *Personality and Psychotherapy*, McGraw-Hill.

GLICKMAN, S. E., and SCHIFF, B. B. (1967), 'A biological theory of reinforcement', *Psychol. Rev.*, vol. 74, pp. 81–109.

GRASTYÁN, E., CZOPF J., ÁNGYÁN, L., and SZABÓ, I. (1965), 'The significance of subcortical motivational mechanisms in the organization of conditional connections', *Acta Physiol. Acad. Sci.*, vol. 26, pp. 9–46.

HULL, C. L. (1943), *Principles of Behavior*, Appleton-Century-Crofts.

HULL, C. L. (1950), 'Behavior postulates and corollaries', *Psychol. Rev.*, vol. 57, pp. 173–180.

LASHLEY, K. S., and MCCARTHY, D. A. (1926), 'The survival of the maze habit after cerebellar injuries', *J. compar. Psychol.*, vol. 6, pp. 423–33.

LEVISON, P. K., and FLYNN, J. P. (1965), 'The objects attacked by cats during stimulation of the hypothalamus', *Animal Behav.*, vol. 13, pp. 217–20.

LOGAN, F. A. (1960), *Incentive*, Yale University Press.

MACFARLANE, D. A. (1930), 'The role of kinaesthesis in maze learning', *Univer. Calif. Pub. Psychol.*, vol. 4, pp. 277–305.

MENDELSON, J. (1966), 'Role of hunger in T-maze learning for food by rats', *J. compar. physiol. Psychol.*, vol. 62, pp. 341–349.

MENDELSON, J. (1967), 'Lateral hypothalamic stimulation in satiated rats: the rewarding effects of self-induced drinking', *Sci.*, vol. 157, pp. 1077–9.

MILLER, N. E. (1951), 'Learnable drives and rewards', in S. S. Stevens (ed.), *Handbook of Experimental Psychology*, Wiley, pp. 435–72.

MILLER, N. E. (1963), 'Some reflections on the law of effect produce a new alternative to drive reduction', *Nebraska Symposium on Motivation*, pp. 65–112.

MILNER, P. M. (1970), *Physiological Psychology*, Holt, Rinehart & Winston.

MORGAN, C. T. (1943), *Physiological Psychology*, McGraw-Hill.

MOWRER, O. H. (1947), 'On the dual nature of learning – a re-interpretation of "conditioning" and "problem-solving"', *Harvard educ. Rev.*, vol. 17, pp. 102–48.

MOWRER, O. H. (1960), *Learning Theory and Behavior*, Wiley.

MUNN, N. L. (1950), *Handbook of Psychological Research on the Rat*, Houghton Mifflin.

NISSEN, H. W. (1954), 'The nature of the drive as innate determinant of behavioral organization', *Nebraska Symposium on Motivation*, pp. 281–321.

RESCORLA., R. A., and SOLOMON, R. L. (1967), 'Two-process learning theory: relationships between Pavlovian conditioning and instrumental learning', *Psychol. Rev.*, vol. 74, pp. 151–82.

RICHTER, C. P. (1922), 'A behavioristic study of the activity of the rat', *Compar. psychol. Monogr.*, vol. 1, no. 2.

ROBERTS, W. W., and KIESS, H. O. (1964), 'Motivational properties of hypothalamic aggression in cats', *J. compar. physiol. Psychol.*, vol. 58, pp. 187–93.

ROBERTS, W. W., STEINBERG, M. L., and MEANS, L. W. (1967),
'Hypothalamic mechanisms for sexual aggressive, and other
motivational behaviors in the opossum Didelphis Virginiana',
J. compar. physiol. Psychol., vol. 64, pp. 1–15.

SCHNEIRLA, T. C. (1959), 'An evolutionary and developmental theory of
biphasic processes underlying approach and withdrawal', *Nebraska
Symposium on Motivation*, University of Nebraska Press, vol. 7,
pp. 1–42.

SEWARD, J. P. (1951), 'Experimental evidence for the motivating
function of reward', *Psychol. Bull.*, vol. 48, pp. 130–49.

SEWARD, J. P. (1956). 'Drive, incentive and reinforcement', *Psychol.
Rev.*, vol. 63, pp. 195–203.

SHEFFIELD, F. D. (1966), 'New evidence on the drive-reduction theory
of reinforcement', in R. N. Haber (ed.), *Current Research in
Motivation*, Holt, Rinehart & Winston, pp. 111–22.

SOLOMON, R. L., and TURNER, L. H. (1962), 'Discriminative classical
conditioning in dogs paralyzed by Curare can later control
discriminative avoidance responses in the normal state', *Psychol. Rev.*
vol. 69, pp. 202–19.

SPENCE, K. W. (1956), *Behavior Theory and Conditioning*, Yale
University Press.

SPENCE, K. W. (1960), *Behavior Theory and Learning*, Prentice-Hall.

TENEN, S. S., and MILLER, N. E. (1964), 'Strength of electrical
stimulation of lateral hypothalamus, food deprivation, and tolerance
for quinine in food', *J. compar. physiol. Psychol.*, vol. 58, pp. 55–62.

TOLMAN, E. C. (1948), 'Cognitive maps in rats and men', *Psychol. Rev.*
vol. 55, pp. 189–208.

WOODWORTH, R. S. (1918), *Dynamic Psychology*, Columbia
University Press.

YOUNG, P. T. (1948), 'Studies of food preference, appetite and dietary
habit. VIII. Food-seeking drives, palatability and the law of effect'
J. compar. physiol. Psychol., vol. 41, pp. 269–300.

Part Six
Neural Mechanisms of Motivation and Reinforcement

Studies of the neural mechanism of motivation have naturally been influenced by the general ideas about the nature of motivational processes current at the time of study. Earlier investigations were concerned with isolating the peripheral visceral-homeostatic conditions produced by various experimental manipulations, such as food or water deprivation. When Lashley and Morgan (see Part Two) proposed that motivational effects on behaviour were not fully correlated with visceral changes but involved persisting neural activity that was largely independent of concurrent visceral events, the emphasis shifted to the study of 'motivational brain structures'. Presently a number of investigators demonstrated experimentally that electrical or chemical stimulation of certain hypothalamic sites leads to the facilitation of particular motivational actions (e.g. eating, drinking, copulating). The hypothalamus was thus the obvious choice as a possible centre of motivational processes, and it was around this structure that Stellar formulated the first explicit theory of the neural mechanisms of motivation.

The shift in emphasis from drive to incentive stimulation as the primary basis of motivation was paralleled by increased interest in the characteristics of the consummatory objects to which the animal directs its actions when its hypothalamus is being stimulated. Flynn's work has been especially important in defining the role of environmental incentive stimulation in determining what the effects of hypothalamic electrical stimulation will be.

More recently, the study of the neural mechanisms of motivation seems to have turned to the elucidation of pathways or circuits involved in different types of species-typical motivational actions. How do the neural events at hypothalamic sites influence response output, that is, activate particular sensory-motor coordinations underlying certain consummatory and instrumental actions? How specific or general are these influences? These questions have only begun to be studied. One idea being actively discussed is that of 'chemical coding' of motivational actions. The essence of this idea, here presented in an article by Miller, is that neurons involved in different types of actions have distinctive or coded chemical properties, such that transmission is facilitated along pathways made up by those types of neurons.

Discussions about the degree of specificity of motivational influences is presented here by three papers, one by Valenstein and his colleagues, one by Hoebel and his co-workers, and one by Roberts.

31 E. Stellar

The Physiology of Motivation

E. Stellar, 'The physiology of motivation', *Psychological Review*,
volume 61 1954, pp. 5–22.

In the last twenty years motivation has become a central concept in
psychology. Indeed, it is fair to say that today it is one of the basic
ingredients of most modern theories of learning, personality and
social behavior. There is one stumbling block in this noteworthy
development, however, for the particular conception of motivation which most psychologists employ is based upon the outmoded model implied by Cannon in his classical statement of the
local theories of hunger and thirst (1934). Cannon's theories were
good in their day, but the new facts available on the physiological
basis of motivation demand that we abandon the older concep-
tualizations and follow new theories, not only in the study of
motivation itself, but also in the application of motivational concepts to other areas of psychology.

This argument for a new theory of motivation has been made
before by Lashley (1938) and Morgan (1943). But it is more im-
pelling than ever today because so much of the recent evidence is
beginning to fit into the general theoretical framework which
these men suggested. Both Lashley and Morgan pointed out that
the local factors proposed by Cannon (e.g. stomach contractions
or dryness of the throat) are not necessary conditions for the
arousal of motivated behavior. Instead, they offered the more
inclusive view that a number of sensory, chemical and neural
factors cooperate in a complicated physiological mechanism that
regulates motivation. The crux of their theory was described most
recently by Morgan as a *central motive state* (*c.m.s.*) built up in
the organism by the combined influences of the sensory, humoral
and neural factors. Presumably, the amount of motivated behavior
is determined by the level of the *c.m.s.*

Beach (1942; 1947), in his extensive work on the specific case of sexual motivation, has amply supported the views of Lashley and Morgan. But the important question still remains: Do other kinds of motivated behavior fit the same general theory? As you will see shortly, a review of the literature makes it clear that they do. As a matter of fact, there is enough evidence today to confirm and extend the views of Lashley, Morgan and Beach and to propose, in some detail, a more complete physiological theory of motivation.

There are a number of ways to present a theoretical physiological mechanism like the one offered here. Perhaps the best approach is to start with an overview and summarize, in a schematic way, the major factors at work in the mechanism. Then we can fill in the details by reviewing the literature relevant to the operation of each factor. Some advantage is lost by not taking up the literature according to behavioral topics, that is, different kinds of motivation. But the procedure adopted here lets us focus attention directly on the theory itself and permits us to make some very useful comparisons among the various kinds of motivation. Once the theoretical mechanism and the evidence bearing on it are presented, the final step will be to evaluate the theory and show what experiments must be done to check it and extend it.

Theoretical scheme

A schematic diagram of the physiological mechanism believed to be in control of motivated behavior is shown in Figure 1. The basic assumption in this scheme is that *the amount of motivated behavior is a direct function of the amount of activity in certain excitatory centers of the hypothalamus*. The activity of these excitatory centers, in turn, is determined by a large number of factors which can be grouped in four general classes: (1) *inhibitory hypothalamic centers* which serve only to depress the activity of the excitatory centers; (2) *sensory stimuli* which control hypothalamic activity through the afferent impulses they can set up; (3) *the internal environment* which can influence the hypothalamus through its rich vascular supply and the cerebro-spinal fluid; and (4) *cortical and thalamic centers* which can exert excitatory and inhibitory influences on the hypothalamus.

As can be seen, the present theory holds that the hypothalamus is the seat of Morgan's *c.m.s.* and is the 'central nervous mechanism' Lashley claimed was responsible for 'drive'. Identifying the hypothalamus as the main integrating mechanism in motivation makes the experimental problem we face more specific and more concrete than ever before. But it also makes it more complicated,

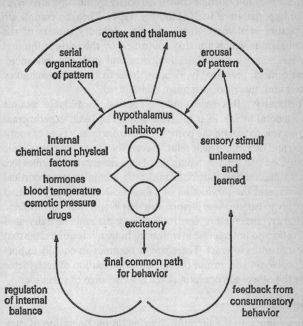

Figure 1 Scheme of the physiological factors contributing to the control of motivated behavior

for the physiological control of the hypothalamus is exceedingly complex. The influence of the internal environment on the hypothalamus is changing continuously according to natural physiological cycles, and of course it may often be changed directly by the chemical and physical consequences of consummatory behavior (see Figure 1). Sensory stimuli may also have varied effects on the hypothalamic mechanism, depending upon their particular pattern, previous stimulation, previous learning, sensory feedback from the consummatory behavior itself, and the influence the internal environment has already exerted on the hypothalamus. Similarly, the influence of the cortex and thalamus will add to the hypothalamic activity already produced by sensory stimuli and the internal environment. Presumably, these cortical and thalamic influences may result directly or indirectly from sensory stimulation, but they may also be controlled partly by the 'upward drive' of the hypothalamus itself (Lindsley, 1951). Then, to complicate the picture even more, there are the inhibitory centers of the hypothalamus which are also controlled by the various internal changes, sensory stimuli, and cortical and thalamic influences. These centers, presumably, depress the activity of the excitatory centers and, therefore, attenuate their output.

Fortunately, this mechanism is not as formidable against experimental attack as it might appear. The basic experimental approach is to isolate the controlling factors in any type of motivation and determine their relative contributions to hypothalamic activity. As you will see, a number of experimental techniques like sensory deprivation, hormone and drug administration, cortical ablation, and the production of subcortical lesions may be used fruitfully to isolate these factors. But that is only half the problem. Obviously, the factors controlling hypothalamic activity and motivation do not operate in isolation. In fact, it is quite clear that their influences interact. Therefore, it becomes an equally important problem to determine the relative contribution of each factor while the others are operating over a wide range of variation.

Experimental evidence

Before going into the literature bearing on the operation of each of these factors in control of motivated behavior, it will help to raise a few questions that ought to be kept in mind while considering the experimental evidence. Are there different hypothalamic centers controlling each kind of motivation? Does the hypothalamus exert its influence through direct control of the final effector pathways or does it simply have a 'priming' effect on effector paths controlled by other parts of the nervous system? Do all these factors operate in the control of each type of motivation or are there cases where sensory stimuli, for example, may not be important or where changes in the internal environment do not contribute? Can the same mechanism describe the control of motivation measured by simple consummatory behavior, preference and learning? Are the same mechanisms involved in the control of simple, biological motives and complex, learned motives?

Hypothalamic centers

Review of the literature on the role of the hypothalamus in motivation brings out three general conclusions.

1. Damage to restricted regions of the hypothalamus leads to striking changes in certain kinds of motivated behavior.

2. Different parts of the hypothalamus are critical in different kinds of motivation.

3. There are both excitatory and inhibitory centers controlling motivation in the hypothalamus; that is, damage to the hypothalamus can sometimes lead to an increase in motivation and sometimes a marked decrease.

The evidence bearing on these three points can be summarized briefly. Many experiments have shown that restricted bilateral lesions of the hypothalamus will make tremendous changes in basic biological motivations like hunger (Brobeck, Tepperman and Long, 1943; Brooks, 1947), sleep (Nauta, 1946; Ranson, 1939; Ranström, 1947), and sex (Bard, 1940; Brookhart and Dey, 1941; Brookhart, Dey and Ranson, 1941). Less complete evidence strongly suggests that the same kinds of hypothalamic integration is also true in the cases of thirst (Verney, 1947), activity (Hetherington and Ranson, 1932), and emotions (Bard, 1939; Wheatley, 1944). We have only suggestive evidence in the case of specific hungers (Soulairac, 1947).

It is clear that there is some kind of localization of function within the hypothalamus although it is not always possible to specify precisely the anatomical nuclei subserving these functions. The centers for hunger are in the region of the ventromedial nucleus which lies in the middle third of the ventral hypothalamus, in the tuberal region (Brobeck, Tepperman and Long, 1943) (see Figure 2). Sleep is controlled by centers in the extreme posterior (mammillary bodies) and extreme anterior parts of the hypothalamus (Nauta, 1946; Ranson, 1939). The critical region for sexual behavior is in the anterior hypothalamus, between the optic chiasm and the stalk of the pituitary gland (Brookhart and Dey,

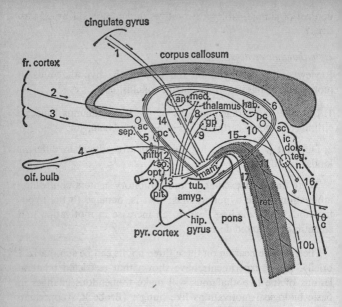

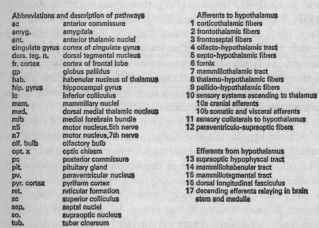

Abbreviations and description of pathways		Afferents to hypothalamus
ac	anterior commissure	**1** corticothalamic fibers
amyg.	amygdala	**2** frontothalamic fibers
ant.	anterior thalamic nuclei	**3** frontoseptal fibers
cingulate gyrus	cortex of cingulate gyrus	**4** olfacto-hypothalamic tract
dors. teg. n.	dorsal tegmental nucleus	**5** septo-hypothalamic fibers
fr. cortex	cortex of frontal lobe	**6** fornix
gp	globus pallidus	**7** mammillothalamic tract
hab.	habenular nucleus of thalamus	**8** thalamo-hypothalamic fibers
hip. gyrus	hippocampal gyrus	**9** pallido-hypothalamic fibers
ic	inferior colliculus	**10** sensory systems ascending to thalamus
mam.	mammillary nuclei	**10a** cranial afferents
med.	dorsal medial thalamic nucleus	**10b** somatic and visceral afferents
mfb	medial forebrain bundle	**11** sensory collaterals to hypothalamus
n5	motor nucleus, 5th nerve	**12** paraventriculo-supraoptic fibers
n7	motor nucleus, 7th nerve	
olf. bulb	olfactory bulb	
opt. x	optic chiasm	Efferents from hypothalamus
pc	posterior commissure	**13** supraoptic hypophyseal tract
pit.	pituitary gland	**14** mammillohabenular tract
pv.	paraventricular nucleus	**15** mammillotegmental tract
pyr. cortex	pyriform cortex	**16** dorsal longitudinal fasciculus
ret.	reticular formation	**17** decending efferents relaying in brain
sc	superior colliculus	stem and medulla
sep.	septal nuclei	
so.	supraoptic nucleus	
tub.	tuber cinereum	

Figure 2 Schematic drawing of the hypothalamus and its major neural connections. Adapted from W. R. Ingram's diagram in Gellhorn (1943) and D. B. Lindsley's Figure 9 (1951)

1941; Brookhart, Dey and Ranson, 1941). The center for activity is not clearly established, but seems to be adjacent with or overlapping the centers for hunger (Hetherington and Ranson, 1942). Finally, the centers for emotion are also in the vicinity of the ventromedial nucleus, perhaps somewhat posterior to the hunger centers and overlapping the posterior sleep center (Ranson, 1939; Wheatley, 1944).

In at least two cases it is clear that there must be both excitatory and inhibitory centers controlling motivated behavior. In the case of hunger, bilateral lesions in the ventromedial nucleus near the midline produce a tremendous amount of overeating (Anand and Brobeck, 1951a; Brobeck, Tepperman and Long, 1943). Such a center is presumably an inhibitory one since removing it leads directly to an increase in eating behavior. On the other hand, lesions 1·5 to 2 millimeters off the midline at the level of the ventromedial nucleus completely eliminate hunger behavior (Anand and Brobeck, 1951 a and b). After such lesions animals never eat again, so we can call such centers excitatory centers. Supporting this interpretation is the fact, recently reported, that stimulating these lateral centers in the waking cat through implanted electrodes results in vast overeating (Delgado and Anand, 1953). The same sort of mechanism turns up in the case of sleep. In the posterior hypothalamus, in the region of the mammillary bodies, there are excitatory centers or 'waking' centers which operate to keep the organism awake (Nauta, 1946; Ranson, 1939). When they are removed, the animal becomes somnolent and cannot stay awake. In the anterior hypothalamus, around the preoptic nucleus, there is an inhibitory center (Nauta, 1946). When that is removed, the animal is constantly wakeful.

So far, only an excitatory center has been found in the case of sexual behavior. Bilateral lesions anterior to the pituitary stalk eliminate all mating behavior (Brookhart and Dey, 1941; Brookhart, Dey and Ranson, 1941), but no lesion of the hypothalamus has ever been reported that resulted in an exaggeration of sexual motivation. What little we know about the center for activity near the ventromedial nucleus suggests that it is also an excitatory center since lesions there produce only inactivity and not hyperactivity (Hetherington and Ranson, 1942). In the case of emotions, the picture is not yet clear. Lesions near the ventromedial nucleus make cats highly emotional (Wheatley, 1944), and therefore this center must be inhibitory. But the lateral regions of the posterior hypothalamus seem to be excitatory, for lesions there make animals placid (Ranson, 1939). Furthermore, direct stimulation of these posterior regions produces many of the signs of rage reactions (Ranson, Kabat and Magoun, 1935).

There is some evidence that sheds light on how the excitatory and inhibitory hypothalamic centers may cooperate in the regulation of motivation. In the clear-cut cases of sleep and hunger it appears that the inhibitory centers operate mainly through their effects on the excitatory centers. At least we know that when both centers are removed simultaneously the effect is indistinguishable from what happens when only the excitatory centers are removed (Anand and Brobeck, 1951a; Nauta, 1946). So it is convenient for present theoretical purposes to think of the inhibitory center as one of the factors which influences the level of activity of the excitatory center. In fact, to speculate one step further, it is worth suggesting that the inhibitory centers may constitute the primary neural mechanism regulating the satiation of motivation.

Sensory stimuli

What effects do sensory stimuli have upon the hypothalamus and how important are such stimuli in the control of motivation? Some answer to the first part of this question is given by the schematic outline of hypothalamic connections shown in Figure 2. Clearly the hypothalamus has a rich supply of afferents coming directly or indirectly from all the various sense organs. In fact the diagram is really an understatement of hypothalamic connections because it is an oversimplified and conservative representation. Physiological evidence shows, for example, that there must be connections from the taste receptors via the solitary nucleus of the medulla (Ingram, 1940). Also there is evidence of rich connections from the visual system via the lateral geniculate of the thalamus (Ingram, 1940). There is no doubt about the fact that the hypothalamus is under very extensive sensory control.

As to the sensory control of motivation, there is excellent reason to believe that the stimuli which can set up impulses in these pathways to the hypothalamus are of particular importance.

Perhaps the best example comes from the study of sexual behavior (Beach, 1947a). The consensus of a group of studies on different mammals is as follows. Sexual behavior is not dependent upon any single sensory system. Extirpation of any one peripheral sense organ has no appreciable influence on the arousal and execution of sexual behavior. If two sensory avenues are destroyed, however, sexual behavior may be eliminated, especially in the case of the naïve animal. With experienced animals, interestingly enough, it may take destruction of three sensory systems. But in neither case does it matter what combination of sensory systems is eliminated. We can conclude, therefore, that it is the sum total of relevant sensory impulses arriving at the central nervous system (hypothalamus) that is important in setting off sexual behavior.

Kleitman's analysis of sleep and wakefulness shows that the same kind of sensory control operates in this case (1939). Wakefulness seems to be dependent upon the sum total of sensory impulses arriving at the waking center in the posterior hypothalamus, regardless of the particular sensory systems involved. Direct support of this kind of view is offered by Bremer's (1937) physiological data which showed that maintenance of the waking rhythm of the brain is less a matter of any particular sensory input and more a matter of the amount of sensory input.

What we know about hunger and thirst suggests that the amount of motivated behavior in these cases should be a joint function of sensory impulses arising from gastric contractions or dryness of the throat and taste, tactile and temperature receptors in the mouth. Unfortunately we have no sensory deprivation experiments that are a good test of this point. But all the evidence on the acceptability of foods and fluids of different temperatures, consistencies and flavoring suggests the joint operation of many stimuli in the control of these types of motivation.

So far, we have mentioned only stimuli which arouse motivation. What stimulus changes could reduce motivation and perhaps lead to satiation? There are three general possibilities: (1) a reduction in excitatory stimuli; (2) interfering or distracting stimuli that elicit competing behavior; and (3) 'inhibitory' stimuli. It is easy to find examples of the first two types of stimulus changes and to guess their mechanisms of operation in terms of the present theory. In the case of 'inhibitory' stimuli, however, all we have is suggestive evidence. For example, the fact that dogs with esophageal fistulas eat (Janowitz and Grossman, 1949) and drink (Adolph, 1941; Bellows, 1939) amounts proportional to the severity of deprivation suggests that the stimuli which feed back from consummatory behavior might have a net inhibitory effect on motivation (see Figure 1). Furthermore, some of the experiments on artificially loading the stomach suggest that a full gut may result in stimuli which inhibit further eating (Janowitz and Grossman, 1949) or drinking (Adolph, 1950; Bellows, 1939) over and above the possibility that there might be no room left in the stomach or that gastric contractions are reduced.

In summary, we can state the following working hypotheses about the sensory factors which operate in the control of motivation.

1. No one sensory avenue is indispensable in the arousal of motivated behavior. Instead, sensory stimuli have an additive effect on the excitability of the hypothalamus so that it is the sum total of relevant impulses arriving at the excitatory centers of the hypothalamus that determine the amount of motivated behavior.

2. Judging from the resistance of experienced animals to the effects of sensory deprivation in the case of sexual motivation, it seems clear that excitatory influences in the hypothalamus may be exerted by learned as well as unlearned stimuli.

3. There are afferent impulses to the hypothalamus which have a net inhibitory effect on the excitatory centers and thus serve to reduce motivation or produce satiation. The best guess at present is that these 'inhibitory' stimuli operate by exerting an excitatory influence on the inhibitory centers of the hypothalamus. Presumably, impulses to inhibitory centers have the same kind of additive properties as impulses to the excitatory centers.

Internal environment

That the internal environment plays an important role in certain kinds of motivated behavior is a well-established fact. Two basic questions must be asked, however, before we can understand much about how the internal environment does its work. What kinds of changes that can occur in the internal environment are the important ones in motivation? How do changes in the internal environment influence the nervous system and, therefore, motivated behavior?

In terms of the present theory, we would expect the internal environment to operate in motivation by changing the excitability of hypothalamic centers. This is a reasonable expectation, for the hypothalamus is the most richly vascularized region of the central nervous system (Craigie, 1940). Not only that, but the hypothalamus is also in direct contact with the cerebrospinal fluid in the third ventricle.

The case of sexual behavior again makes an excellent example. Experiments on the spayed, female cat (Bard, 1940; Bromiley and Bard, 1940) and spayed, female guinea pig (Dempsey and Rioch, 1939) have shown that hypothalamic regions must be intact and functioning if injected sex hormones are to arouse estrous behavior. If a section is made through the spinal cord only rudimentary fragments of sexual behavior can be elicited by appropriate stimulation, and injected sex hormones make no contribution to the response. Essentially the same thing is true if the section is made high in the hind brain but excludes the hypothalamus. When the decerebration is just above the hypothalamus, full estrous reactions can be aroused by appropriate stimulation, but only if sex hormones have been administered. It is clear, then, that not only is the hypothalamus the main integrating center for sexual reactions, but it is also most likely the main site of action of the sex hormones. This point is further supported by studies of female guinea pigs with pinpoint lesions of the anterior hypothalamus. These animals fail to show sexual behavior even under the influence of massive doses of sex hormones (Brookhart, Dey and Ranson, 1940).

A very similar mechanism seems to be involved in the case of motivated behavior dependent upon the organism's defenses against temperature extremes (activity, nesting, hoarding, selection of high-calorie diets). We know, for example, that reactions regulating body temperature in the face of heat and cold are integrated in two separate centers in the hypothalamus (Brobeck, 1950; Ranson, 1940). Lesions in the anterior hypothalamus destroy the ability to lose heat and, therefore, to survive in high temperatures. Posterior hypothalamic lesions, conversely, result in a loss of heat production mechanisms so that the animal succumbs to cold. Furthermore, artificially raising the temperature of the anterior hypothalamus will quickly induce heat loss, suggesting that normally the temperature of the blood may be important in activating the hypothalamic mechanisms (Brobeck, 1950; Magoun *et al.*, 1938). Unfortunately our information stops here. There are no direct physiological studies on the role of these temperature-regulating mechanisms in the control of motivated behavior like activity, hoarding, nesting or food selection. But it seems clear that the temperature of the blood may be one of the kinds of changes in the internal environment that can affect the hypothalamus, and it may be important in motivated behavior.

Ample evidence demonstrates that there are important changes in the internal environment involved in other kinds of motivated behavior. In hunger it has been shown that chemicals like insulin (Grossman, Cummins and Ivy, 1947; Grossman and Stein, 1948; Morgan and Morgan, 1940) and d-amphetamine (Sangster, Grossman and Ivy, 1948) influence the rate of eating. It is clear that these chemicals do not operate primarily through their effects on gastric contractions, but it is only by a process of elimination that we can guess that their sites of action are in the hypothalamus. Supporting this possibility is the evidence that there are chemoreceptors in the hypothalamus which are sensitive to variations in blood sugar and important in the regulation of hunger (Mayer, Vitale and Bates, 1951). In the case of specific hungers, much evidence shows that food preference and diet selection depend upon changes in the internal environment produced by such things as pregnancy, dietary deficiencies or disturbances of endocrine glands (Richter, 1942–3). Furthermore there are some preliminary experimental data, in the case of salt and sugar appetites, to suggest that there are separate regulatory centers in the hypothalamus which are responsive to changes in salt and sugar balance (Soulairac, 1947). Finally, in the case of thirst we know that a change in osmotic pressure, resulting from cellular dehydration, is the important internal change leading to drinking behavior (Gilman, 1937). We know further that in the hypothalamus there are nerve cells, called 'osmoreceptors', which are extremely sensitive to minute changes in osmotic pressure (Verney, 1947). But the direct experiment has not been done to check whether or not it is these nerve cells which are mainly responsible for the control of thirst.[1]

Obviously the experimental evidence on hunger, specific hunger and thirst is incomplete. But enough of it fits into the scheme of the theoretical mechanism proposed here to suggest the real possibility that the internal changes important in these cases operate largely through their effects on the hypothalamus.

One question still remains. What role does the internal environment play in the mechanism of satiation? About all we have to go on at present is the very striking fact from the case of specific hungers that vastly different amounts of consummatory behavior are needed to bring about satiation for different food substances. In vitamin deficiencies only a few milligrams of substance need be consumed to produce satiation, whereas in caloric deficiencies many grams of carbohydrate, fat or protein must be ingested. Presumably, it is not the sensory feedback from consummatory behavior that is important in these cases, but rather some inhibitory effects produced by what is consumed (Figure 1). Within the present theoretical framework, such inhibitory effects could be produced either by depression of excitatory centers of the hypothalamus or by arousal of activity in inhibitory centers. The problem is an important one and it is wide open for study.

It is clear from the foregoing that many types of motivated behavior are dependent upon changes in the internal environment. Several points are worth emphasizing. A variety of kinds of changes in the internal environment can play a role in the regulation of motivation: variation in the concentration of certain chemicals, especially hormones, changes in osmotic pressure and changes in blood temperature. The best hypothesis at present is that these internal changes operate by contributing to the activity of excitatory hypothalamic centers controlling motivation. An equally important but less well-supported hypothesis is that internal changes, normally produced by consummatory behavior, operate in the production of satiation by depressing excitatory centers or arousing inhibitory centers of the hypothalamus.

1. In a recent publication, Andersson of Stockholm (1953) has shown that injection of small quantities of hypertonic NaCl directly into restricted regions along the midline of the hypothalamus produces immediate and extensive drinking in water-satiated goats.

Cortical and thalamic centers

Despite the heavy emphasis laid upon the hypothalamus in this discussion, it is obvious that it is not the only neural center operating in the control of motivated behavior. In the first place, some of the sensory, motor, and associative functions of the cortex and thalamus are directly important in motivation quite apart from any influence they have on the hypothalamus. Secondly, even though the hypothalamus may be the main integrating center in motivation, it does not operate in isolation. There is much evidence that the hypothalamus is under the direct control of a number of different cortical and thalamic centers (Figure 2).

The case of emotions offers the best example of how the cortex may operate in motivation. According to the early work of Bard and his co-workers on the production of 'sham rage' by decortication, it looked as though the entire cortex might normally play an inhibitory role in emotions (1939). More recent work, however, shows that cortical control of emotion is more complicated than this. Bard and Mountcastle (1947), for example, have found that removal of certain parts of the old cortex (particularly amygdala and transitional cortex of the midline) produced a tremendous increase in rage reactions in cats. On the other hand, removing only new cortex resulted in extremely placid cats. Results of work with monkeys (Klüver and Bucy, 1939) and some very recent experiments with cats disagree somewhat with these findings in showing that similar old cortex removals lead to placidity rather than ferocity. The disagreement is yet to be resolved, but at least it is clear that different parts of the cortex may play different roles in the control of emotion, certain parts being inhibitory and others excitatory.

In the case of sleep, it appears so far that the cortex and thalamus play excitatory roles, perhaps having the effect of maintaining the activity of the waking center in the posterior hypothalamus. Decortication in dogs, for example, results in an inability to postpone sleep and remain awake for very long, or, as Kleitman puts it, a return to polyphasic sleep and waking rhythms (1939; Kleitman and Camille, 1932). Studies of humans, moreover, show that even restricted lesions of the cortex or thalamus alone can result in an inability to stay awake normally (Davison and

Demuth, 1945 a and b). But no inhibitory effects of the cortex in sleep have yet been uncovered.

In sexual behavior it has been found that lesions of the new cortex may interfere directly with the arousal of sexual behavior (Beach, 1942; Beach, 1947a). Large lesions are much more effective than small lesions, as you might expect. Furthermore, cortical damage is much more serious in male animals than in females and is much more important in the sexual behavior of primates than it is in the case of lower mammals. On the other hand, in connection with studies of the cortex in emotions, it has been found that lesions of the amygdala and transitional cortex of the midline can lead to heightened sexuality in cats and monkeys (Bard and Mountcastle, 1947; Klüver and Bucy, 1939). So it looks as though the cortex may exert both excitatory and inhibitory influences in sexual motivation.

Evidence from other types of motivated behavior is only fragmentary, but it fits into the same general picture. In the case of hunger, it has been reported that certain lesions of the frontal lobes will lead to exaggerated eating behavior (Langworthy and Richter, 1939; Richter and Hawkes, 1939). Hyperactivity may follow similar frontal lobe lesions and is particularly marked after damage to the orbital surface of the frontal lobe (Ruch and Shenkin, 1943). The frontal areas may also be involved in what might be called pain avoidance. Clinical studies of man show that lobotomies may be used for the relief of intractable pain (Freeman and Watts, 1950). The curious thing about these cases is that they still report the same amount of pain after operation but they say that it no longer bothers them. Presumably the frontal cortex normally plays an excitatory role in the motivation to avoid pain.

In all the cases cited so far, the anatomical and physiological evidence available suggests strongly that the main influence of the cortex and thalamus in motivation is mediated by the hypothalamus. But we do not yet have direct proof of this point and need experiments to check it.

Interaction of factors

Up to now, we have treated the various factors that can operate in the control of motivated behavior singly. However, one of the main points of the theory proposed here is that the various factors operate together in the control of motivation. Presumably this interaction of factors occurs in the hypothalamus and takes the form of the 'addition' of all excitatory influences and the 'subtraction' of all inhibitory influences. Some experimental evidence bears directly on this point.

In the case of sexual behavior, for example, it is clear that excitatory influences of the cortex and hormones are additive. After sexual motivation is eliminated by cortical damage it may be restored by the administration of large doses of sex hormones (Beach, 1944). Since the hypothalamus is the site of action of the sex hormones, it seems likely that it is also the site of interaction of the influences of the hormones and cortex.

In a similar way, it looks as though the contributions of sensory stimulation and sex hormones add in the hypothalamus. Neither hormones nor stimulation alone is sufficient to elicit sexual reactions in most mammals, but the right combination of the two will. Still another example of the addition of excitatory influences is seen in the study of the sexual behavior of the male rabbit. In this case neither destruction of the olfactory bulbs nor decortication will eliminate mating behavior, but a combination of the two operations will (Brooks, 1937).

It is very important to know whether excitatory, and perhaps also inhibitory, influences in other kinds of motivation have the same sort of additive properties as in sexual behavior. Indirect evidence suggests they do, but direct experiments of the sort described here are needed to check the possibility.

Most encouraging in this connection is that students of instinctive behavior in inframammalian vertebrates and invertebrates have presented considerable evidence showing that sensory, chemical and neural influences contribute jointly to the arousal of many kinds of motivated behavior (Tinbergen, 1951). For example, in a number of cases it has been shown that the threshold for arousing behavior by various stimuli is lowered considerably by appropriate changes in the internal environment. In fact, in the extreme case, when internal changes are maximal, the behavior may occur in the absence of any obvious stimulation. Presumably in these cases, as in the examples of mammalian motivation, chemical and neural influences contribute to the arousal of some central response mechanism in an additive way.

The role of learning

It is obvious to every student of mammalian motivation that learning and experience may play extremely important roles in the regulation of motivated behavior. What does this mean in terms of the present physiological theory? Unfortunately, we cannot specify the mechanisms through which learning enters into the control of motivation because we are ignorant of the basic physiology of learning. But we can make some helpful inferences.

The basic hypothesis in the present theoretical framework is that learning contributes to hypothalamic activity along with influences from unlearned afferent impulses, internal changes and cortical activity. In the case of sexual behavior we know that many animals learn to be aroused sexually by stimuli which were not previously adequate. Further, we know that in such experienced animals it is difficult to reduce sexual motivation by eliminating avenues of sensory stimulation, presumably because the extra excitatory effects produced by learned stimuli contribute to hypothalamic activity along with the impulses from unlearned stimuli. Along the same lines, it is known that sex hormones are relatively unimportant in man and in certain of the sub-human primates that have learned to be aroused by a wide variety of stimuli (Beach, 1947b). Again, this may mean that the excitatory effects from the learned stimuli have added enough to the effects of unlearned stimuli to make it possible to dispense with the contribution of the sex hormones in arousing hypothalamic activity.

The evidence available on learning in other types of motivation fits in with this general theoretical picture, but direct physiological experiments have not yet carried us beyond the stage of inference. We know, for example, that vitamin-deficient rats can learn to show motivated behavior in response to certain flavors that have been associated with the vitamin in the past (Harris *et al.*, 1933; Scott and Verney, 1947). In fact, for a short while they will even pass up food containing the vitamin to eat vitamin-deficient food containing the flavor. Again, it looks as though flavor has become empowered by a process of learning to contribute to the excitability of the neural centers controlling motivation.

Limitations of the theory

Like any theoretical approach, the physiological mechanism proposed here has many limitations. Fortunately none of them need be too serious as long as it is recognized that the theory is set up as a general guide for experiments and a framework for further theorizing. Obviously the theory is going to have to be changed and improved many times before it is free of limitations. In this spirit it might be said that the limitations of the theory are not much more than those aspects of motivation which need research the most. But whether we label them limitations or urgent areas of research, they deserve explicit attention.

The concept of 'center'

Throughout this discussion the terms 'neural center' and 'hypothalamic center' have been used. 'Center' is a useful and convenient term but it is also a dangerous one, for it may carry with it the implication of strict localization of function within isolated anatomical entities. Actually this implication is not intended, for it is recognized that localization is a relative matter and that no neural mechanism operates in isolation. Furthermore, it is also possible that there may be no discoverable localization of the neural mechanisms governing some types of motivated behavior. The theory simply states at the moment that the best general hypothesis is that some degree of localization of the mechanisms controlling motivation can be found in the hypothalamus.

Execution of motivated behavior

No attempt has been made in this discussion to describe the details of the efferent pathways or effector mechanisms responsible for the execution of motivated behavior. Discussion of the pathways has been omitted because we know very little about them. About all we can do at present is to guess, from anatomical and physiological studies of hypothalamic function, that the hypothalamus exerts some kind of 'priming' effect on effector pathways controlled by other parts of the nervous system. Perhaps after the relationship of the hypothalamus to motivated behavior has been more firmly established we can profitably turn to the question of how the hypothalamus does its work.

A second aspect of the execution of motivated behavior has been omitted for the sake of brevity. We all recognize that an animal with certain kinds of cortical lesions, or deprived of certain sensory capacities, may be handicapped in executing motivated behavior quite aside from any effects these operations may have on the arousal of motivation. Fortunately most investigators have been aware of this problem and have taken pains to distinguish these two effects, focusing their attention mainly on the arousal of motivation. Some day, however, this theory should address the question of what neural mechanisms govern the execution of motivated behavior.

General nature of the mechanism

For theoretical purposes it has been assumed that essentially the same mechanism controls all types of motivated behavior. Obviously this is not likely to be the case, nor is it an essential assumption. In some types of motivation only parts of this mechanism may be involved, or factors not included in the present scheme may operate. For example, in some cases the hypothalamus may not be involved at all, or it may turn out that there are no inhibitory centers at work, or that internal chemical factors do not contribute significantly. There is no reason why we should not be prepared for these eventualities. But until specific experimental evidence to the contrary is forthcoming, the general mechanism proposed here still remains as the best working hypothesis for any particular type of biological motivation.

Inadequacy of behavioral measures

To a large degree the present discussion is based upon measures of consummatory behavior. We all know that the various measures of motivation are not always in good agreement, so there is good possibility that what we say about consummatory behavior may not apply to motivation measured by other methods. In fact, Miller, Bailey and Stevenson (1950) have recently shown that whereas rats with hypothalamic lesions overeat in the free-feeding situation, they do not show a high degree of motivation when required to overcome some barrier to obtain food.

Confining the present discussion mainly to consummatory behavior is clearly a weakness. But the logic behind this limited approach is to work out the physiological mechanisms in the simplest case first, and then to see how they must be revised to fit the more complicated cases.

Complex motivation

It can also be argued, of course, that the present theory is confined to the simple, biological motives. Again, it seems eminently advisable to keep the theory relatively narrow in scope until it is developed well enough to permit attack on the more complicated, learned motives.

Comparative approach

No attempt has been made here to make it explicit how the proposed theory applies to organisms representative of different phylogenetic levels. There are many obvious advantages to the comparative approach, but unfortunately, except for the case of sexual motivation, the information we have on different species is too scattered to be useful. Judging from what we have learned from the comparative study of sexual motivation, however, we can expect the various factors governing other types of motivation to contribute somewhat differently in animals at different phylogenetic levels. Certainly learning should be more important in primates than in subprimates, and the contributions of the cortex and thalamus should be greater. Much will be gained if future research in motivation follows the excellent example set in the study of sexual behavior and provides the much needed comparative data.

Advantages of the theory

On the assumption that none of these limitations of the theory are critical, it is appropriate to ask: what is gained by proposing an explicit theory of the physiological mechanisms underlying motivated behavior? There are many positive answers to this question, and we can list some of them briefly.

Simplification of the problem

One of the main advantages of the theoretical mechanism proposed here is that it brings together, into one general framework, a number of different kinds of motivation that have been studied separately in the past. Certainly the theory encompasses the basic facts available on sex, hunger, specific hunger, thirst, sleep and emotion. And it may also be able to handle the facts of pain avoidance, hoarding, nesting, maternal behavior and other types of so-called instinctive behavior. As you have seen, one of the benefits deriving from this kind of simplification of the problem of motivation is the possibility of speeding up progress by applying what has been learned about physiological mechanisms from the study of one kind of motivation to the study of other kinds of motivation. Not only that, but the assumption that the hypothalamus is central in the control of all types of motivation may make it easier to explain the various types of interaction among motivations that have shown up in many studies of behavior.

Multifactor approach

Another advantage of the present theory is that it gives strong emphasis to the view that motivation is under multifactor control. Single-factor theories, so prevalent since the days of Cannon, can only lead to useless controversies over which factor is the 'right' one and must always be guilty of omission in trying to account for the control of motivation. Of course, it must be stressed that the aim of the multifactor approach is not simply to list the many possible factors operating in motivation, but rather to get down to the concrete experimental task of determining the relevant factors which control motivation and the relative contribution of each.

Satiation of motivation

Unlike most previous theories of motivation, the mechanism proposed here attempts to account for the satiation of motivation as well as its arousal. In terms of the present theory satiation is determined by the reduction of activity in the main excitatory centers of the hypothalamus. More specifically, it looks as though the inhibitory centers of the hypothalamus may constitute a separate 'satiation mechanism' which is the most important influence in the reduction of the activity of the excitatory centers. The possibility is an intriguing one, and it can be directly explored by experiment.

Peripheral and central control

In the past the study of motivation has been hampered by the controversy over whether behavior is centrally or peripherally controlled. The controversy is nonsense. The only meaningful experimental problem is to determine how the central and peripheral, or sensory, factors operate together in the control of behavior. It is this problem which the present theory addresses directly and this is one of its greatest strengths.

Learned and innate control

The present theory avoids another knotty controversy by directly addressing experimental problems. Much time has been lost in psychology, and particularly in the study of motivation, in arguments over whether behavior is primarily innate or instinctive or whether it is primarily learned or acquired. The answer is obviously that it is both, and again the only meaningful experimental problem is to determine the relative contribution of each type of control. As far as the mechanism proposed here is concerned, both innate and learned factors make their contributions to the control of the same hypothalamic centers. There is still much work needed to determine the details of the mechanisms of operation, particularly of the learned factors, but some headway has been made and the problem is clearly set.

Explicit nature of the theory

Finally, a number of advantages derives simply from having an explicit statement of an up-to-date, physiological theory of motivation. In the first place, an explicit theory can serve as a convenient framework within which to organize the physiological facts we already have at our disposal. Second, the systematic organization of the facts sharply points up many of the gaps in our knowledge and suggests direct experiments that should be done in the investigation of motivated behavior. Third, an up-to-date, systematic theory provides a useful and reasonably clear conceptualization of motivation for psychologists working in other areas of research.

Summary and conclusions

A physiological theory of motivated behavior is presented. The basic assumption in this theory is that the amount of motivated behavior is a function of the amount of activity in certain excitatory centers of the hypothalamus. The level of activity of the critical hypothalamic centers, in turn, is governed by the operation of four factors.

1. Inhibitory centers in the hypothalamus directly depress the activity of the excitatory centers and may be responsible for the production of satiation.

2. Sensory stimuli set up afferent impulses which naturally contribute to the excitability of the hypothalamus or come to do so through a process of learning.

3. Changes in the internal environment exert both excitatory and inhibitory effects on the hypothalamus.

4. Cortical and thalamic influences increase and decrease the excitability of hypothalamic centers.

Detailed experimental evidence is brought forward to show how these various factors operate in the management of different kinds of motivated behavior. The over-all scheme is shown diagrammatically in Figure 1.

Out of consideration of this evidence a number of hypotheses are generated to fill in the gaps in experimental knowledge. All these hypotheses are experimentally testable. The ones of major importance can be given here as a summary of what the theory states and a partial list of the experiments it suggests.

1. There are different centers in the hypothalamus responsible for the control of different kinds of basic motivation.

2. In each case of motivation, there is one main excitatory center and one inhibitory center which operates to depress the activity of the excitatory center.

There is already much experimental evidence supporting these two general hypotheses, but it is not certain that they apply fully to all types of basic biological motivation. The hypotheses should be checked further by determining whether changes in all types of motivation can be produced by local hypothalamic lesions and whether both increases and decreases in motivation can always be produced.

3. The activity of hypothalamic centers is, in part, controlled by the excitatory effects of afferent impulses generated by internal and external stimuli.

4. Different stimuli contribute different relative amounts to hypothalamic activity but no one avenue of sensory stimulation is indispensable.

5. It is the sum total of afferent impulses arriving at the hypothalamus that determines the level of excitability and, therefore, the amount of motivation.

The neuroanatomical and neurophysiological evidence shows that the hypothalamus is richly supplied with afferents coming directly and indirectly from all the sense organs (Figure 2). The behavioral evidence, furthermore, strongly suggests that motivation is never controlled, in mammals at least, by one sensory system, but rather is the combination of contributions of several sensory systems. Sensory control and sensory deprivation experiments are needed to check this point in the case of most kinds of biological motivation, particularly hunger, thirst, and specific hungers.

6. A variety of kinds of physical and chemical changes in the internal environment influences the excitability of hypothalamic centers and, therefore, contributes to the control of motivation. The evidence shows that the hypothalamus is the most richly vascularized region of the central nervous system and is most directly under the influence of the cerebrospinal fluid. Furthermore, it is clear that changes in the internal environment produced by temperature of the blood, osmotic pressure, hormones and a variety of other chemicals are important in motivation and most likely operate through their influence on the hypothalamus. Direct studies are still needed in many cases, however, to show that the particular change that is important in motivation actually does operate through the hypothalamus and vice versa.

7. The cerebral cortex and thalamus are directly important in the temporal and spatial organization of motivated behavior.

8. Different parts of the cortex and thalamus also operate selec-

tively in the control of motivation by exerting excitatory or inhibitory influences on the hypothalamus.

Tests of these hypotheses can be carried out by total decortication, partial cortical ablations, and local thalamic lesions. It should be especially instructive to see what effects cortical and thalamic lesions have after significant changes in motivation have been produced by hypothalamic lesions.

9. Learning contributes along with other factors to the control of motivation, probably through direct influence on the hypothalamus.

10. The relative contribution of learning should increase in animals higher and higher on the phylogenetic scale.

A whole series of experiments is needed here. Particularly, there should be comparisons of naïve and experienced animals to determine the relative effects of sensory deprivation, cortical and thalamic damage and hypothalamic lesions. Presumably animals that have learned to be aroused to motivated behavior by previously inadequate stimuli should require more sensory deprivation but less cortical and thalamic damage than naïve animals before motivation is significantly impaired.

11. The various factors controlling motivation combine their influences at the hypothalamus by the addition of all excitatory influences and the subtraction of all inhibitory influences.

Some experiments have already been done in the study of sexual motivation to show that motivation reduced by the elimination of one factor (cortical lesions) can be restored by increasing the contribution of other factors (hormone therapy). Many combinations of this kind of experiment should be carried out with different kinds of motivated behavior.

A number of the limitations and some of the advantages of the present theoretical approach to the physiology of motivation are discussed.

References

ADOLPH, E. F. (1941), 'The internal environment and behavior. Part III. Water content', *Amer. J. Psychiat.*, vol. 97, pp. 1365–73.
ADOLPH, E. F. (1950), 'Thirst and its inhibition in the stomach', *Amer. J. Physiol.*, vol. 161, pp. 374–86.

ANAND, B. K., and BROBECK, J. R. (1951a), 'Hypothalamic control of food intake in rats and cats', *Yale J. biol. Med.*, vol. 24, pp. 123–40.

ANAND, B. K., and BROBECK, J. R. (1951b), 'Localization of a "feeding center" in the hypothalamus of the rat', *Proc. Soc. Exp. Biol. Med.*, vol. 77, pp. 323–324.

ANDERSSON, B. (1953), 'The effect of injections of hypertonic NaCl-solutions into different parts of the hypothalamus of goats', *Acta Physiol. Scand.*, vol. 28, pp. 188–201.

BARD, P. (1939), 'Central nervous mechanisms for emotional behavior patterns in animals', *Res. Publ. Ass. nervous mental Diseases*, vol. 19, pp. 190–218.

BARD, P. (1940), 'The hypothalamus and sexual behavior', *Res. Publ. Ass. nervous mental Diseases*, vol. 20, pp. 551–79.

BARD, P., and MOUNTCASTLE, V. B. (1947), 'Some forebrain mechanisms involved in the expression of rage with special reference to the suppression of angry behavior', *Res. Publ. Ass. nervous mental Diseases*, vol. 27, pp. 362–404.

BEACH F. A. (1942), 'Analysis of factors involved in the arousal, maintenance and manifestation of sexual excitement in male animals', *Psychosom. Med.*, vol. 4, pp. 173–198.

BEACH, F. A. (1942), 'Central nervous mechanisms involved in the reproductive behavior of vertebrates', *Psychol. Bull.*, vol. 39, pp. 200–206.

BEACH, F. A. (1944), 'Relative effect of androgen upon the mating behavior of male rats subjected to forebrain injury or castration' *J. exper. Zool.*, vol. 97, pp. 249–95.

BEACH, F. A. (1947a), 'A review of physiological and psychological studies of sexual behavior in mammals', *Physiol. Rev.*, vol. 27, pp. 240–307.

BEACH, F. A. (1947b), 'Evolutionary changes in the physiological control of mating behavior in mammals', *Psychol. Rev.*, vol. 54, pp. 297–315.

BELLOWS, R. T. (1939), 'Time factors in water drinking in dogs', *Amer. J. Physiol.*, vol. 125, pp. 87–97.

BREMER, F. (1937), 'Étude oscillographique des activités sensorielles du cortex cérébral', *C. r. Soc. Biol.*, vol. 124, pp. 842–6.

BROBECK, J. R. (1950), 'Regulation of energy exchange', in J. F. Fulton (ed.), *A Textbook of Physiology*, Saunders, pp. 1069–90.

BROBECK, J. R., TEPPERMAN, J., and LONG, C. N. H. (1943), 'Experimental hypothalamic hyperphagia in the albino rat', *Yale J. Biol. Med.*, vol. 15, pp. 831–53.

BROMILEY, R. B., and BARD, P. (1940), 'A study of the effect of estrin on the responses to genital stimulation shown by decapitate and decerebrate female cats', *Amer. J. Physiol.*, vol. 129, pp. 318–19.

BROOKHART, J. M., and DEY, F. L. (1941), 'Reduction of sexual behavior in male guinea pigs by hypothalamic lesions', *Amer. J. Physiol.*, vol. 133, pp. 551–4.

BROOKHART, J. M., DEY, F. L., and RANSON, S. W. (1940), 'Failure of ovarian hormones to cause mating reactions in spayed guinea pigs with hypothalamic lesions', *Proc. Soc. exper. biol. Med.*, vol. 44, pp. 61–4.

BROOKHART, J. M., DEY, F. L., and RANSON, S. W. (1941), 'The abolition of mating behavior by hypothalamic lesions in guinea pigs' *Endocrinology*, vol. 28, pp. 561–5.

BROOKS, C. M. (1937), 'The role of the cerebral cortex and of various sense organs in the excitation and execution of mating activity in the rabbit', *Amer. J. Physiol.*, vol. 120, pp. 544–53.

BROOKS, C. M. (1947), 'Appetite and obesity', *N. Z. med. J.*, vol. 46, pp. 243–54.

CANNON, W. B. (1934), 'Hunger and thirst', in C. Murchison (ed.), *A Handbook of General Experimental Psychology*, Clark University Press pp. 247–63.

CRAIGIE, E. H. (1940), 'Measurements of vascularity in some hypothalamic nuclei of the albino rat', *Res. Publ. Ass. nervous mental Diseases* vol. 20, pp. 310–19.

DAVISON, C., and DEMUTH, E. L. (1945a), 'Disturbances in sleep mechanism: a clinico-pathologic study. I. Lesions at the cortical level', *Arch. Neurol. Psychiat.*, vol. 53, pp. 399–406.

DAVISON, C., and DEMUTH, E. L. (1945b), 'Disturbances in sleep mechanism: a clinico-pathologic study. II. Lesions at the corticodiencephalic level', *Arch. Neurol. Psychiat.*, vol. 54, pp. 241–55.

DELGADO, J. M. R., and ANAND, B. K. (1953), 'Increase of food intake induced by electrical stimulation of the lateral hypothalamus', *Amer. J. Physiol.*, vol. 172, pp. 162–8.

DEMPSEY, E. W., and RIOCH, D. McK. (1939), 'The localization in the brain stem of the oestrous responses of the female guinea pig, *J. Neurophysiol.*, vol. 2, pp. 9–18.

FREEMAN, W., and WATTS, J. W. (1950), *Psychosurgery*, Charles C. Thomas, 2nd ed.

GELLHORN, E. (1943), *Automatic Regulations*, Interscience.

GILMAN, A. (1937), 'The relation between blood osmotic pressure, fluid distribution and voluntary water intake', *Amer. J. Physiol.*, vol. 120, pp. 323–8.

GROSSMAN, M. I., CUMMINS, G. M., and IVY, A. C. (1947), 'The effect of insulin on food intake after vagotony and sympathectomy', *Amer. J. Physiol.*, vol. 149, pp. 100–102.

GROSSMAN, M. I., and STEIN, I. F. (1948), 'Vagotomy and the hunger producing action of insulin in man', *J. appl. Physiol.*, vol. 1, 263–9.

HARRIS, L. J., CLAY, J., HARGREAVES, F. J., and WARD, A. (1933), 'Appetite and choice of diet. The ability of the Vitamin B deficient rat to discriminate between diets containing and lacking the vitamin', *Proc. royal Soc.*, vol. 113, pp. 161–90.

HETHERINGTON, A. W., and RANSON, S. W. (1942), 'The spontaneous activity and food intake of rats with hypothalamic lesions', *Amer. J. Physiol.*, vol. 136, pp. 609–17.

INGRAM, W. R. (1940), 'Nuclear organization and chief connections of the primate hypothalamus', *Res. Publ. Ass. nervous mental Diseases*, vol. 20, pp. 195–244.

JANOWITZ, H. D., and GROSSMAN, M. I. (1949), 'Some factors affecting the food intake of normal dogs and dogs with esophagostomy and gastric fistula', *Amer. J. Physiol.*, vol. 159, pp. 143–8.

KLEITMAN, N. (1939), *Sleep and Wakefulness*, University of Chicago Press.

KLEITMAN, N., and CAMILLE, N. (1932), 'Studies on the physiology of sleep. VI. Behavior of decorticated dogs', *Amer. J. Physiol.*, vol. 100, pp. 474–80.

KLÜVER, H., and BUCY, P. C. (1939), 'Preliminary analysis of functions of the temporal lobes in monkeys', *Arch. Neurol. Psychiat.*, vol. 42, pp. 979–1000.

LANGWORTHY, O. R., and RICHTER, C. P. (1939), 'Increased spontaneous activity produced by frontal lobe lesions in cats', *Amer. J. Physiol.*, vol. 126, pp. 158–61.

LASHLEY, K. S. (1938), 'Experimental analysis of instinctive behavior', *Psychol. Rev.*, vol. 45, pp. 445–71.

LINDSLEY, D. B. (1951), 'Emotion', in S. S. Stevens (ed.), *Handbook of Experimental Psychology*, Wiley, pp. 473–516.

MAGOUN, H. W., HARRISON, F., BROBECK, J. R., and RANSON, S. W. (1938), 'Activation of heat loss mechanisms by local heating of the brain', *J. Neurophysiol.*, vol. 1, pp. 101–14.

MAYER, J., VITALE, J. J., and BATES, M. W. (1951), 'Mechanism of the regulation of food intake', *Nature*, vol. 167, pp. 562–3.

MILLER, N. E., BAILEY, C. J., and STEVENSON, J. A. F. (1950), 'Decreased "hunger" but increased food intake resulting from hypothalamic lesions', *Sci.*, vol. 112, pp. 256–9.

MORGAN, C. T. (1943) *Physiological Psychology*, McGraw-Hill, 1st ed.

MORGAN, C. T., and MORGAN, J. D. (1940), 'Studies in hunger. 1. The effects of insulin upon the rat's rate of eating', *J. genet. Psychol.*, vol. 56, pp. 137–47.

NAUTA, W. J. H. (1946), 'Hypothalamic regulation of sleep in rats; an experimental study', *J. Neurophysiol.*, vol. 9, pp. 285–316.

RANSON, S. W. (1939), 'Somnolence caused by hypothalamic lesions in the monkey', *Arch. Neurol. Psychiat.*, vol. 41, pp. 1–23.

RANSON, S. W. (1940), 'Regulation of body temperature', *Res. Publ. Ass. nervous. mental. Diseases.*, vol. 20, pp. 342–99.

RANSON, S. W., KABAT, H., and MAGOUN, H. W. (1935), 'Autonomic responses to electrical stimulation of hypothalamus, preoptic region and septum', *Arch. Neurol. Psychiat.*, vol. 33, pp. 467–77.

RANSTRÖM, S. (1947), *The Hypothalamus and Sleep Regulation*, Almquist and Wicksells.

RICHTER, C. P. (1942–3), 'Total self regulatory function in animals and human beings', *Harvey Lect.*, vol. 38, pp. 63–103.

RICHTER, C. P., and HAWKES, C. D. (1939), 'Increased spontaneous activity and food intake produced in rats by removal of the frontal poles of the brain', *J. Neurol. Psychiat.*, vol. 2, pp. 231–42.

RUCH. T. C., and SHENKIN, H. A. (1943), 'The relation of area 13 of the orbital surface of the frontal lobe to hyperactivity and hyperphagia in monkeys', *J. Neurophysiol.*, vol. 6, pp. 349–60.

SANGSTER, W., GROSSMAN, M. I., and IVY, A. C. (1948), 'Effect of d-amphetamine on gastric hunger contractions and food intake in the dog', *Amer. J. Physiol.*, vol. 153, pp. 259–63.

SCOTT, E. M., and VERNEY, E. L. (1947), 'Self selection of diet. VI. The nature of appetites for B vitamins', *J. Nutrit.*, vol. 34, pp. 471–80.

SOULAIRAC, A. (1947), 'La physiologie d'un comportement: L'appétit glucidique et sa régulation neuro-endocrinienne chez les rongeurs', *Bull. Biol.*, vol. 81, pp. 1–160.

TINBERGEN, N. (1951), *The Study of Instinct*, Oxford University Press.

VERNEY, E. B. (1947), 'The antidiuretic hormone and the factors which determine its release', *Proc. roy. Soc.*, vol. 135, pp. 24–106.

WHEATLEY, M. D. (1944), 'The hypothalamus and affective behavior in cats', *Arch. Neurol. Psychiat.*, vol. 52, pp. 296–316.

32 J. P. Flynn

Neural Aspects of Attack Behaviour in Cats

J. P. Flynn, 'Neural aspects of attack behavior in cats', in 'Experimental Approaches to the Study of Emotional Behavior', *Annals of the New York Academy of Sciences*, volume 159, 1969, article 3, pp. 1008–12.

The behavior the neural basis of which my colleagues and I have been attempting to outline is that of a cat attacking a rat. If one uses cats that do not spontaneously attack rats, one can obtain a highly repeatable attack of the cat on a rat by electrically stimulating appropriate sites within the cat's brain. The primary point that I wish to make is that the electrical stimulation that elicits attack has an effect on the sensory systems.

In the course of our experiments, we observed that stimulation of certain sites gave rise not to an attack on the rat, but to an attack on the experimenter. One and the same cat would show these two different forms of behavior, depending upon the site stimulated. Hess had earlier found that his cats would sometimes leap at the experimenter, particularly if provoked.

Since attack is guided by vision in many instances, we tried to find out if stimulation of the hypothalamus at sites that elicited attack on the experimenter, as opposed to attack on the rat, would have a differential effect on potentials in the visual system (Chi and Flynn, 1968). Potentials were evoked in the visual system by stimulating the optic tract. The effect of stimulating the hypothalamus or the midbrain for a hundred milliseconds prior to stimulating the optic tract was observed. No differential effect from stimulating the two sites in the hypothalamus was found, but stimulation of the hypothalamus did produce quite different results from those consequent to stimulation of the midbrain reticular formation. Some of the results are shown in Figure 1. The difference between stimulation of the hypothalamus and stimulation of the midbrain reticular formation is revealed primarily at the level of the visual cortex when these two subcortical structures are stimulated at high intensities. Stimulation of the

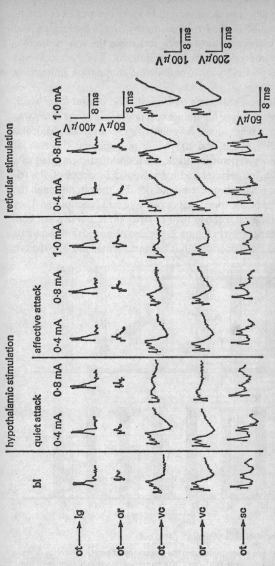

Figure 1 Stimulation of the hypothalamus at high intensities prior to stimulating the optic tract or optic radiations decreased the size of the potentials evoked in the visual cortex, while similar stimulation of the midbrain reticular system leads to an increase in the magnitude of the evoked response. Abbreviations on the left indicate stimulation of optic tract (ot) or optic radiations (or). Abbreviations indicated by the arrow are sites from which recordings were made: lg, lateral geniculate; or, optic radiation; vc, visual cortex; sc, superior colliculus. The responses when not preceded by conditioning stimuli are listed under bl (base line)

midbrain results in an increased amplitude of the evoked potential, while stimulation of the hypothalamus results in a decrease. The differential influence is most clearly seen when the optic radiation, rather than the optic tract, is stimulated. These experiments indicate the possibility of hypothalamic stimulation influencing the visual system.

Other evidence, indicating that stimulation of sites from which attack is elicited has an influence upon sensory systems, was obtained in studies done in collaboration with Dr Malcolm MacDonnell (1966 a and b). While investigating the role of various sensory systems in attack, we found that stimulated cats in which the infraorbital and infraalveolar branches of the trigeminal nerve had been severed did not bite the rat, although the motor nerves of the trigeminal nerve were still functioning. They approached the rat, rubbed their muzzles on it, but did not bite. These data are shown in Figure 2. We also observed that some cats in which the same operation has been performed did bite the rat,

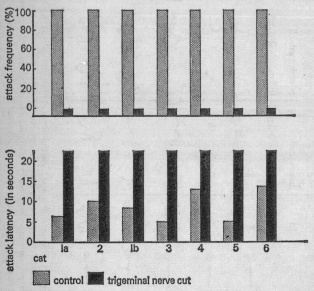

Figure 2 In these seven instances, the frequency of attack, which is defined as biting or striking a rat, fell from 100% to zero when two branches of the trigeminal nerve were cut

but took only one bite, and not repeated ones as an otherwise intact animal would do. We found, however, that when these last animals were blindfolded, they behaved the same way as others did – they did not bite. The data are shown in Figure 3. The stimu-

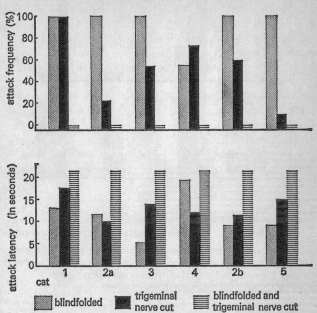

Figure 3 In these six instances, cutting the trigeminal nerves did not abolish attack. Blindfolding alone did not abolish it, either. When the nerves had been cut and the cats were then blindfolded, attack dropped to zero

lation had a differential influence in these two cases. It either blocked the functioning of the visual system in the first group of animals, or it permitted its functioning in the second set. Whatever the case, the visual system was being influenced by the stimulation of the hypothalamus. This interpretation is strengthened by the fact that in two animals either result could be obtained, depending upon which electrode was stimulated. The data from these two cats are shown in Figure 4.

The clearest demonstration of the influence of stimulation of 'attack' sites on sensory systems comes from a study of the region

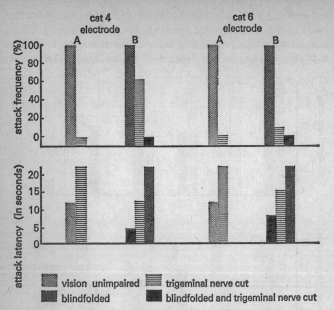

Figure 4 In these two cats, cutting the trigeminal branches abolished the attack if the stimulation was through electrode A. If stimulation was through electrode B, the cats had to be blindfolded as well as having their trigeminal branches cut before attack was abolished

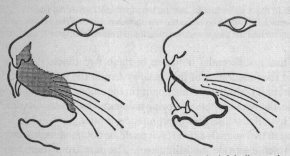

Figure 5 The crosshatched area on the head at the left indicates the region that, on being touched, elicits movement of the head to bring the tactile stimulus to the lips. The heavy line on the head at the right indicates the region that, on being touched, elicits opening of the jaw. Both areas appear during stimulation of sites from which attack is elicited

innervated by the trigeminal nerve. In brief, during stimulation, two receptive fields appear that are not present in the absence of stimulation (Figure 5). One of these is a receptive field that, on being touched, elicits a response of head turning. The cat moves its head to bring the tactile stimulus to the cat's lip. The second receptive field is the lip. When it is touched while the hypothalamus is being stimulated, the mouth snaps open. The more sensi-

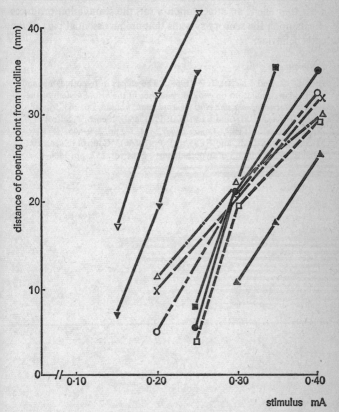

Figure 6 The region on the lip from which opening of the jaw can be elicited during stimulation increases with increasing stimulation to the hypothalamus. The region extends from the midline to a point on the lip. The point at which opening first occurred was determined by moving a probe from the corner of the cat's mouth toward the midline

tive region is contralateral to the side of the hypothalamus stimulated, and the most responsive part of the lip is from the midline to the region of the canine tooth. The size of the receptive field increases with increasing intensity of the stimulus to the appropriate site within the hypothalamus. The data are shown in Figure 6.

In summary, when one stimulates a site in the hypothalamus of a cat that elicits an attack upon a rat, the stimulation produces effects upon the sensory systems that are an essential part of the cat's behavior.

References

CHI, C. C., and FLYNN, J. P. (1968), 'The effects of hypothalamic and reticular stimulation on evoked responses in the visual system of the cat', *Electroenceph. and clin. Neurophysiol.*, vol. 24, pp. 343–56.

MACDONNELL, M., and FLYNN, J. P. (1966a), 'Sensory control of hypothalamic attack', *Animal Behav.*, vol. 14, pp. 399–405.

MACDONNELL, M., and FLYNN, J. P. (1966b), 'Control of sensory fields by stimulation of hypothalamus', *Sci.*, vol. 152, pp. 1406–8.

33 N. E. Miller

Chemical Coding of Behaviour in the Brain

N. E. Miller, 'Chemical coding of behavior in the brain', *Science*, volume 148, 1965, pp. 328–38.

Two classical methods for studying how the brain controls behavior have been to study the effects of destroying specified areas and to study the effects of stimulating specific sites. These methods, which have led to a great increase in our knowledge, can be illustrated by work on the hypothalamus. This is a primitive structure deep in the base of the brain, which first appears in vertebrates, such as primitive fish, and has quite similar structure in mammals from the rat to man.

If a certain small area is destroyed on both sides of the hypothalamus, the animal will stop eating and will starve to death (Anand and Brobeck, 1951). Conversely, electrical stimulation in this same lateral area will cause an animal which has just eaten to satiation to eat voraciously (Hess, 1949). Various studies have shown that such stimulation does not elicit mere reflex gnawing, but that it also can elicit learned food-seeking habits, and that it has many, and perhaps all, of the properties of the strong hunger that normally develops during a fast (Miller, 1964). The results of destruction and of stimulation agree in showing that the lateral hypothalamus is significantly involved in food-seeking behavior.

Additional studies, however, have shown that the effects of lesions and of stimulation in the lateral hypothalamus are not as simple as was originally supposed. Lesions in this area cause animals to stop drinking water as well as to stop eating food. Tests in which water is tubed directly into the stomach show that the interference with eating is not secondary to dehydration produced by failure to drink (Teitelbaum and Epstein, 1962). Furthermore, electrical stimulation of certain sites in the lateral hypothalamus will cause animals which have just drunk water to satiation to resume drinking. Also, stimulation of this area can evoke sexual responses, such as penile erection and ejaculation (Miller, 1961, p. 387). It can serve, also, as a reward: animals learn to press a bar to get a few moments of electrical stimulation in this area (Olds, 1962); yet, paradoxically, if exactly the same stimulation is provided for too long, the same animals learn to press a bar to turn it off (Roberts, 1958; Bower and Miller, 1958, p. 669). Lesions in the lateral hypothalamus will abolish the rewarding effect of electrical stimulation in another region of the brain, and will abolish the appetitive response to a deficiency of salt (Miller, 1963; Wolf, 1964). Thus, it becomes painfully obvious that a number of diverse motivational and emotional functions all involve this tiny area of the brain, and that the techniques of making lesions or of providing electrical stimulation are relatively crude and indiscriminate in that they are likely to affect all of these diverse functions.

When diverse effects are produced from the same site, one may obscure the other. For example, stimulating the lateral hypothalamus with electric current at higher voltages produces frantic, escape-like activity which precludes the possibility of observing anything else. Perhaps we are observing only a few of the most dominant functions.

We first attempted to deal with these difficulties by using electrodes with tinier bare tips for stimulating smaller regions of the lateral hypothalamus of rats. Instead of getting more specific, better effects, we got almost none at all, and we tentatively concluded that one must stimulate a fairly large population of cells or fibers in order to produce observable behavioral effects.

Other investigators have thought it might be easier to isolate functions in the larger brain of the monkey. However, it appears that the probability of getting a given specific effect from electrical stimulation via an electrode in the hypothalamus is lower in the monkey than it is in the rat. Furthermore, stimulation of a site in the hypothalamus may elicit several effects in relatively unpredictable combinations (Robinson, 1964, p. 411). The picture is one of networks that are spread out and interlaced, rather than of functions that are completely separated into distinctive areas. While this diffusion of function is adaptive in preventing a small lesion produced by a tiny blood clot or infection from completely interrupting any vital function, it necessarily makes investigation of the organization of the brain more difficult.

Yet another difficulty arises from the fact that lesions and electrical stimulation both affect fibers that are merely passing through an area, as well as the synapses of neurons, at which information from various fibers is brought together and processed. To use a loose analogy, they affect the telephone cables as well as the switchboard.

The foregoing difficulties have caused workers at our laboratory, among others, recently to explore the possibility that chemical stimulation may produce effects which are more specific to given functional systems than effects produced by electrical stimulation, and may act on synapses or cells without affecting fibers of passage.

Early evidence for chemical specificity

Some early behavioral evidence for 'chemical' specificity came from the work of Andersson, who anesthetized goats and cemented needles into place through their skulls, by means of which minute injections could later be made into the brain of the recovered, normal, unanesthetized animal (1953). He found that injection into the medial anterior region of the hypothalamus of goats of a solution of sodium chloride which had slightly higher osmotic pressure than body fluids have would cause an animal that had just drunk to satiation to resume drinking. We obtained similar results with cats; we showed that such an injection would elicit not only drinking but also the performance of a learned response of working for water, and that an injection of pure water would have the opposite effect, that of stopping either drinking or working for water (Miller, 1961, p. 387). These specific behavioral effects, which are not elicited from other regions of the brain, presumably are due to the osmotic, rather than the chemical, action of the solution and are mediated by specialized sense organs or osmoreceptors in the brain.

Alan Fisher used a similar technique to test the effects of a soluble form of a male hormone, sodium testosterone sulfate, on different parts of the rat's brain (1956). He thought that this hormone might elicit male sexual behavior. What he first observed, however, in both male and female rats, was the maternal behavior of nest-building and retrieving infant rats, activities that male rats ordinarily do not engage in. In an extensive series of subsequent investigations he has found that when this hormone is applied to the medial preoptic region of the hypothalamus it can elicit the maternal-like behavior of nest-building and of carrying infants to the nest in either male or female rats (in press). When the same hormone is applied to a slightly different area, the lateral preoptic region, it can elicit male sexual behavior in either male or female rats. Such injections can cause male rats to mount non-receptive females and even other males or infant rats, going through as much as is physically possible of the complete sex pattern, including ejaculation. It can cause similar behavior in female rats, with the exception, of course, of intromission and ejaculation.

When the needle delivers the hormone to a site between these two areas, mixed behavior may result; a male, for example, may alternately mate with a female and carry strips of paper to build a nest, his responses apparently being determined by the type of object that happens to fall in his sensory field.

These effects occur within from twenty seconds to five minutes after injection of the hormone. They are not produced by injections in other parts of the brain. Interestingly enough, the female hormone, estrogen, which has a related chemical structure, produces similar effects but is apparently less potent. These effects are produced by from one to four micrograms of either hormone, irrespective of whether it is administered in the form of crystals or as a liquid in one-microliter amounts.

Many other chemical substances, ranging widely in osmotic pressure and pH, have been tried, with negative results. So far, the only substance that has been found to produce similar behavior is the chelating agent sodium versenate. The behavioral effects of this agent are highly similar to those of sex hormones and occur after approximately the same delay. In line with previous notions about the normal action of endogenous sex hormones, Fisher interprets their effect as being that of lowering thresholds, so that external cues will be more likely to elicit sexual responses. He does not believe that the hormone is itself a direct excitant of the brain. He advances the tentative hypothesis that a chelating agent may produce its effect of lowering threshold, or reducing inhibition, by removing calcium ions from the nerve cells.

One perplexing aspect of these experiments is the fact that in only about 10 per cent of the implants does Fisher get any effect. Once he finds an animal which shows an effect, however, he often is able to reproduce this effect many times, sometimes over a period of weeks. Thus far he has been unable to determine the cause of this low percentage of effective placements – to learn whether it is due to individual differences in the degree to which cells responsible for such behavior are concentrated in one location or to other factors. The very rareness of the effect has prevented detailed analysis.

Fisher's experiments have shown that the neural circuits necessary for complex patterns of distinctively male or female behavior are present in the brains of both male and female rats. He has also shown that these patterns can be activated by the presence of sex hormones. But the fact that both of these distinctively different types of behavior can be activated by the same hormone is puzzling. What, under normal circumstances, causes activation of characteristically male responses in the brain of the male and of characteristically maternal responses in the brain of the female? It may be that the threshold is lower for the pattern appropriate to the sex of the animal in question, or that two different hormones are normally involved. In either case, since hormones, especially the steroids, frequently are not completely specific, it is entirely possible that a local application of an abnormally high dose activates a response not normally governed by the particular hormone applied. Thus, testosterone might be the normal hormone for eliciting male sexual behavior and some other, as yet untested, hormone might change the normal one for eliciting maternal behavior.

Somewhat similar experiments have been performed by Harris and Michael on cats previously subjected to ovariectomy and hence not sexually receptive (1964). These workers made up a tiny pellet of paraffin containing a synthetic female hormone, stilbestrol; when this was implanted in the hypothalamus the stilbestrol would slowly diffuse into the body. They found that when large pellets were implanted outside the brain or in inactive sites in the brain, changes in vaginal cells always occurred at doses smaller than those required to restore sexual receptivity.

When pellets were implanted in the hypothalamus, however,

doses too small to produce changes in vaginal cells restored complete receptivity. In fact, the cats could be described as hypersexual; they would repeatedly accept successive males at any time of the day or night, without showing any signs of the refractoriness which normally follows mating. These effects first appeared only several days after implantation of the pellets containing the slowly diffusing form of the hormone. However, the proportion of cases in which the effects occurred was much higher than the proportion of cases in which the male sexual behavior or the maternal behavior was elicited in rats by the soluble hormones which Fisher used.

Differential effects of presumptive transmitter agents

The results just described show that specific forms of behavior can be produced by applying directly to the proper part of the brain certain chemical substances that are normally found in the body. The experiments described below differ in that they involve use of a special class of substances believed to act as transmitters in the synapses of the more readily accessible and more thoroughly studied peripheral nerves. Transmission in the synapses of the parasympathetic nervous system is via acetylcholine. Chemicals having this effect are called cholinergic. Similarly, norepinephrine seems to be the transmitter for at least some of the synapses in the sympathetic nervous system. Chemicals having this effect are called adrenergic. Does similar chemical coding of transmission occur in the brain, and if it does, is it related to specific forms of behavior? Biochemists have shown that the hypothalamus is especially rich in both acetylcholine and norepinephrine. What are they doing there?

Effects of same agent in different sites

Investigators have shown that injection of acetylcholine into the brain of a cat can evoke a variety of responses (Delgado, 1955; Feldberg, 1958; MacLean, 1957). When injected at one site it produced motor responses such as circling. When injected at another it produced catatonic-like postures, at another, rage, and at yet another, convulsions, followed by purring and other apparent manifestations of pleasure. In addition to the naturally occurring substance acetylcholine, these investigators used a synthetic substance, carbachol, which is similar in structure and in cholinergic effects. Because of a slight difference in its molecule, carbachol is not disposed of by the deactivating enzymes as rapidly as acetylcholine is, hence its effects last longer.

Effects of different agents in the same site

Encouraged by these results, Grossman, in our laboratory, tried implanting, in the 'feeding-drinking' area of the lateral hypothalamus, minute crystals (weighing from one to four μg) of various substances thought likely to act as transmitter agents (1960, 1962). An anesthetized rat was placed in a stereotaxic instrument with its head at the proper angle for insertion of a tiny cannula through a hole drilled in the skull. When the tip of this cannula was in the desired location the cannula was cemented into place and the skin was sewed together; the rat recovered and appeared perfectly normal and healthy. Plate 10 (left) shows photographs of the cannula. It consisted of a tiny hypodermic needle fitting snugly inside a slightly larger one; the two tips were cut off flush and the hubs were machined down so that the inner needle could screw into the outer one. After the rat had completely recovered, the inner cannula was withdrawn, tiny crystals were tapped into the tip, and the cannula was reinserted.

By this means Grossman found that either acetylcholine (mixed with eserine to delay its destruction by enzymes in the brain) or carbachol would cause rats that had just eaten or drunk to satiation to start drinking again within five to ten minutes after implantation of the cholinergic agent and to consume an average of twelve milliliters of water during the next hour. These cholinergic agents would also cause satiated rats to work at the learned response of pressing a bar to get water. Subsequent implantation of tiny crystals of the adrenergic substances epinephrine or norepinephrine into the brains of the same satiated rats, at exactly the site where the cholinergic agent had been implanted, via the same cannulas, elicited a different response – eating, or pressing a different bar – one that delivered food.

When carbachol was implanted in the brains of thirsty rats, the amount of water drunk was increased and the amount of food eaten was decreased, relative to the results for non-thirsty rats. Implantation of norepinephrine in the brains of hungry rats had the opposite effect, that of decreasing water consumption and increasing food consumption.

Whereas in previous studies different types of behavior were induced by implanting the same substance at different sites, in Grossman's study different types of behavior were induced by implanting different substances at the same site. These results clearly showed that systems located in the same region of the brain but controlling different types of behavior can be selectively affected by cholinergic or adrenergic substances.

Effects of blocking agents

It is conceivable that the different behaviors induced by the administration of different transmitter agents to the brain could be due to some differential side effects, rather than to the transmitter, or even due to a disinhibitory or modulating effect in the brain. Therefore, a number of control studies were made; these ruled out osmotic pressure, pH, and vasoconstriction or vasodilation as factors in the behavioral effects observed.

The most convincing control studies, however, were of a different nature. Studies on more easily isolated and manipulated peripheral nerves have shown that atropine blocks only the transmitting effect of carbachol or acetylcholine in such nerves, and fails to block that of norepinephrine; conversely, ethomoxane blocks the effect of epinephrine or norepinephrine without affecting that of acetylcholine or carbachol. Therefore, Grossman investigated the effects of these blocking agents on the behavioral effects of chemostimulation in the brain (1962). He injected the blocking agent into the peritoneal cavity so that it was circulating throughout the body before the crystals were applied to the brain.

He found that either blocking agent, if administered at sufficiently high dosage would prostrate the rat and eliminate all behavior. But at an intermediate dose, results were differential. Results for such a dose are summarized in Figure 1. It may be seen that the cholinergic blocking agent atropine produced little reduction in the eating elicited by norepinephrine, while completely eliminating the drinking elicited by carbachol. Conversely, the adrenergic blocking agent ethomoxane produced only a moderate reduction in the drinking elicited by carbachol but a much larger reduction in the eating elicited by norepinephrine.

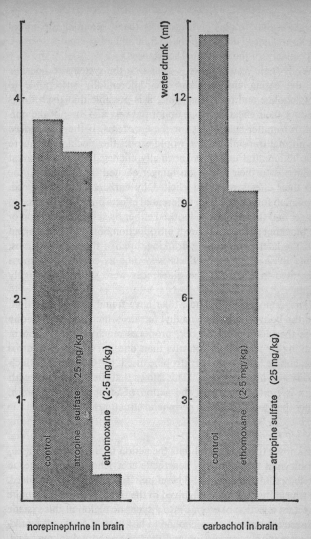

norepinephrine in brain   carbachol in brain

Figure 1 Differential effects of blocking agents on eating and drinking elicited by application of norepinephrine and carbachol, respectively, in the internal hypothalamus of the rat. First, blocking agent is injected systemically, then crystals of norepinephrine or carbachol are implanted in the brain. (Data from Grossman, 1962)

These results strongly indicate that the differential behavioral effects are indeed due to the cholinergic and adrenergic properties, respectively, of the implanted substances.

While these results make it clear that the systems responsible for the eating and drinking are differentially susceptible to acetylcholine and norepinephrine, it is possible that these drugs produce their effects in some abnormal way and are not the normal transmitter substances for these systems. If they are indeed the normal transmitters, we would expect the blocking agents to have differential effects on normally elicited hunger and thirst analogous to their effects on hunger elicited by norepinephrine and their effects on thirst elicited by carbachol. And, indeed, Grossman found that such differential effects on normally elicited hunger and thirst could be induced either by systemic injection of the blocking agent or by direct introduction of the blocking agent into the lateral, or feeding-drinking, area of the hypothalamus. While these differential effects were not as complete as those illustrated in Figure 2, the differences were statistically highly reliable.

Furthermore, Coons and Miller have found that an injection, into the body, of atropine methyl nitrate, which does not readily cross the blood-brain barrier, produces much less reduction in drinking by water-deprived rats than does an injection of atropine sulfate, the form of atropine used by Grossman, which readily gets into the brain.[1] This shows that the interference with thirst is primarily due to the action of atropine in the brain, rather than to its action on peripheral structures.

Effect of enzyme inhibitor

It is known that eserine inhibits the action of the cholinesterases, the enzymes that normally deactivate acetylcholine soon after it is released at the synapse. Therefore, if acetylcholine is indeed the transmitter normally involved in the thirst system, one would expect an injection of eserine into a synaptic region of this system to cause the normal acetylcholine to last longer, so that it would stimulate more transmission and thus cause more drinking. And

1. Where names but no references are given, the results are from recent unpublished studies in this laboratory (Department of Psychology, Yale University, Connecticut).

indeed Chun-Wuei Chien and Miller have recently found that an injection of 3×10^{-8} mole of eserine into the preoptic area of the brain of a rat very slightly deprived of water will increase the amount it drinks during the next 30 minutes from an average of 0·3 milliliter to 10·5 milliliters. In addition to being an independent test of our conclusions, this is a more powerful test than that of injecting a cholinergic substance for demonstrating the normal participation of such a substance in thirst.

Dose-response curves

A dose-response curve is useful in determining whether an apparent differential effect is an artifact of a particular dose-threshold interaction and whether the amount of substance needed to produce an effect is of the order of magnitude one might reasonably expect for the normal process.

While Grossman's use of crystals prevents spread up the needle shaft, with crystals the concentration is highly abnormal and it is impossible accurately to control the dose. Therefore, in the dose-response study performed in our laboratory, aqueous solutions were used (Miller, 1964). The results are presented in Figures 2 and 3. It may be seen that there is a marked differential effect of all active doses of the carbachol and norepinephrine. Increasing the dose of carbachol produces marked increases in drinking but not in eating, while increasing the dose of norepinephrine produces marked increases in eating but not in drinking. With either substance, the highest doses produce side effects, such as convulsions, which interfere with eating and drinking.

The carbachol elicits drinking at doses as low as $2·7 \times 10^{-10}$ mole (0·047 μg); the smallest dose of norepinephrine that elicits eating is 24×10^{-10} mole (0·8 μg). The effective dose for carbachol seems to be somewhere near the content of the normal substance, acetylcholine, in the volume of tissue probably reached by our injections. The norepinephrine content of this part of the brain probably is no higher (in micrograms) than the acetylcholine content, but our effective dose of norepinephrine is approximately twenty times as high. This seems to be a high dose, but in our present state of considerable ignorance we cannot be sure that more of the norepinephrine reaches the receptor sites after an injection than is involved in normal transmission.

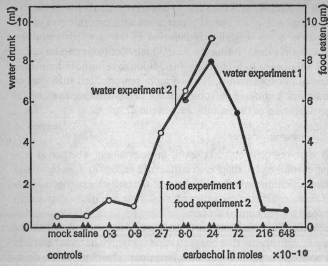

Figure 2 Dose-response curve for drinking elicited by injections of carbachol into the lateral hypothalamus of rats that had eaten and drunk to satiation. No eating is elicited. (From Miller, Gottesman and Emery 1964)

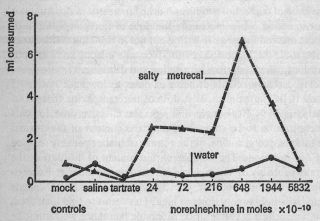

Figure 3 Dose-response curve for consumption of a liquid food (salty Metrecal) elicited by injection of norepinephrine into the lateral hypothalamus of rats that had eaten and drunk to satiation. Negligible amounts of water are consumed. (From Miller, Gottesman and Emery 1964)

It should be noted that both dose-response curves cover the whole range, from the dose producing no effect to that producing prostrating side effects. In neither case is there any suggestion that low doses activate one behavioral system while higher doses cause the other system to be dominant. Thus, these results agree with those of the previous experiments in indicating that the difference between the systems is indeed a qualitative one, rather than the product of a mere quantitative interaction of the thresholds and the dominance of the systems with a non-specific difference in the potency of the cholinergic and adrenergic compounds used.

Central versus peripheral effects

Dextroamphetamine is a compound closely resembling norepinephrine in its general structure and many of its physiological effects. But extensive clinical experience with people and careful experimental work with animals consistently show that dextroamphetamine lessens appetite. Why should these effects be opposite to those just described for norepinephrine?

There are two plausible possibilities. One is that the dextroamphetamine molecule is similar enough to the norepinephrine molecule to attach itself to the same receptor sites in the brain, but not similar enough to excite them. According to this hypothesis, dextroamphetamine acts like a bad key which jams in a lock without opening it. The fact that dextroamphetamine is administered peripherally, either by mouth or by injection, suggests the other major possibility: the peripheral action of substances of this class may be opposite to, and may occur at lower thresholds or be stronger than, their action in the feeding-drinking area of the brain; thus, when the substance is administered to the whole body, the peripheral effects may override the effects of the substance diffusing from the blood to the brain.

In order to test these hypotheses, Coons, Quartermain and Miller used the dose of norepinephrine ($22\,\mu$g) that had been shown by the dose-response study to be optimum for eliciting eating when injected into the lateral hypothalamus. We injected exactly this dose into the jugular vein, via a permanently implanted catheter, and washed it down with isotonic saline. This injection caused hungry rats to stop eating, or to stop pressing a bar for food. These results demonstrate that the central and the peripheral effects of the same dose of norepinephrine are indeed antagonistic. They fit in with previous unpublished results, obtained by Coons in our laboratory, which show that peripheral administration of another adrenergic compound, epinephrine, raises the threshold for eating elicited by electrical stimulation of the lateral hypothalamus, and with results of Russek and Pina which show that peripheral administration of epinephrine will stop eating (1962). Since we found that the same peripheral dose of norepinephrine stopped drinking as well as eating, it seems likely that it produces some general disturbance, perhaps as a result of a sudden increase in blood pressure, rather than a specific inhibition of a drive.

The norepinephrine injected into the blood stream becomes vastly more diluted than that affecting the cells adjacent to the cannula in the brain. Thus, the fact that the same dose is quite effective by either route is surprising. Perhaps the peripheral receptors are much more sensitive than the central ones, or the central receptors may be so well protected that only a minute fraction of the chemicals in the surrounding tissue reaches them. We must also consider the possibility that the consistent pattern of central-nervous-system results we have described is only an effect of a dose that is abnormally high, and thus does not necessarily mean that norepinephrine is involved in normal transmission in this part of the brain.

If norepinephrine does indeed act as a normal neural transmitter in the brain, its natural release should be limited to the active sites and not be diffused wisely. Some of the norepinephrine which we inject into the lateral hypothalamus must diffuse into the bloodstream, where, presumably, it produces appetite-inhibiting peripheral effects. These effects may well mask some of the central hunger-arousing effects of the norepinephrine injected into the brain. If we could eliminate the peripheral effects by administering to the body a blocking agent for norepinephrine that would have difficulty in getting into the brain across the blood-brain barrier, we could eliminate or greatly reduce the antagonistic peripheral effects and might get a clearer picture of how norepinephrine works in the brain. To date, we have been unable to find such an agent, but it seems likely that side chains could be attached to the molecule of a suitable adrenergic blocking agent to produce a drug that would have difficulty in diffusing through the blood-brain barrier.

Activating various elements of a general homeostatic system

Although carbachol in the brain elicits drinking and norepinephrine elicits eating, it is conceivable that these drugs do not directly stimulate thirst and hunger systems in the brain but, instead, produce their effects indirectly. For example, carbachol could stimulate nuclei in the brain which, in turn, stimulate a sudden water loss via the kidney, the subsequent thirst and drinking being a by-product of the normal reaction of the body to the rapid dehydration. Similarly, norepinephrine could stimulate nuclei to send neural impulses that would cause the pancreas to secrete insulin; this would produce a drop in blood sugar and elicit eating. It is known that a peripheral injection of insulin can cause rats just fed to satiation to eat. Thus, it is possible that the thirst and hunger mechanisms are not themselves chemically coded, but that the differential effect of these chemicals is on some completely different systems which activate the thirst and hunger mechanisms in some indirect way. In the examples cited, which are the most plausible ones, we would expect the carbachol in the brain to produce a sudden excessive secretion of urine (in other words, diuresis), and the norepinephrine to produce a drop in the blood sugar, or glucose.

There is another possibility, however, from which one would predict the opposite results. Perhaps we are activating general homeostatic systems, which regulate food and water balance by activating a variety of mechanisms, some physiological and some behavioral, to deal with any deficit. If we are activating the entire system that normally responds to water deficit, we would expect one corrective measure to be stimulation of the secretion of the antidiuretic hormone which causes the kidney to reabsorb water from the urine, so that a smaller volume of more concentrated urine is lost. While thus conserving water, the animal would also go out looking for water to drink to replenish its supply. Similarly, the activation of an entire system for responding to a nutritional deficit would mobilize stores, such as those in the liver and fat, pouring them out as glucose into the blood, and at the same time would elicit hunger which would motivate the animal to find and

N. E. Miller 425

eat food as a new source of nutrition. While the hypothesis given in the preceding paragraph predicts increased secretion of urine and a drop in blood sugar in response to stimulation of the brain by carbachol and norepinephrine, respectively, this second hypothesis predicts the opposite results.

Effects on secretion of urine

Chun-Wuei Chien and Miller have recently tested the effects on urine secretion of injecting into the lateral hypothalamus the optimum dose of carbachol ($0.43 \mu g$) for eliciting drinking. First, we briefly anesthetized water-satiated rats with ether and gently squeezed them to remove the residual urine from their bladders; we then administered, via stomach tube, fifteen milliliters of water and injected into the hypothalamus either one microliter of carbachol solution or, as a control, the isotonic saline used as the vehicle. After this the rats were put in metabolism cages without food or water, and the urine was collected via stainless steel funnels underneath the cages.

We found that the carbachol greatly reduced the volume of urine. It also increased the concentration, as measured by the freezing-point-depression test of osmolarity; this increase in turn showed that the decrease in volume was caused by reabsorption stimulated by the secretion of the antidiuretic hormone normally released in response to water deprivation.[2] If the carbachol had merely caused some interference with kidney function – for example, by producing a drop in blood pressure that interfered with the initial secretion by the kidneys – the decrease in volume would not have been accompanied by an increase in concentration.

Similar results were obtained from another part of the brain, the preoptic area; carbachol in this area, too, elicits drinking. Injection into the jugular vein (via an implanted cannula) of exactly the same dose as that given in the earlier studies (the optimum dose for eliciting drinking when injected into the brain) neither appreciably elicited drinking in water-satiated rats nor decreased the volume and increased the concentration of urine of water-satiated rats that had been given additional water by stom-

2. I wish to thank Dr Howard Levitin and Mrs Nadia T. Myketey of the Yale School of Medicine for supplying the measures of osmolarity.

ach tube. Administration of this same dose to thirsty rats produced no obvious lessening of drinking. Thus, with carbachol, at least at this dose level, we do not find the marked differences in the behavioral effects of central and peripheral administration that we observed with norepinephrine.

To return to the antidiuretic effect of carbachol injected into the brain, if this is indeed a cholinergic effect, it should be blocked by atropine but not by ethomoxane. Chun-Wuei Chien and Miller tested these expectations. First we injected intraperitoneally either the blocking agent or isotonic saline as a control. We used the doses that had produced the greatest differential effects on drinking and eating. Then, twenty minutes later, after the agent had had time to diffuse through the body, we gave the water-satiated rats additional water by stomach tube and injected into the lateral hypothalamus either the optimum dose of carbachol or a control dose of the isotonic saline used as the vehicle.

The results are shown in Figure 4. It may be seen that, as compared with the injection of saline, both intraperitoneally and into the brain, injection of carbachol into the brain (preceded by a control injection of saline) greatly reduced the volume and increased the concentration of the urine. Previous injection of the adrenergic blocking agent ethomoxane did not interfere with this antidiuretic effect, but previous injection of the cholinergic blocking agent atropine markedly reduced it. In another experiment we injected these two agents into water-satiated rats given additional water by stomach tube but not injected with carbachol. Neither agent produced a marked effect. Thus, the effects observed in the preceding experiment presumably were due to differential blocking of the effects of carbachol rather than to any other direct effects of these agents.

Our results confirm those of previous investigators who have concluded, from work on anesthetized dogs, that secretion of the antidiuretic hormone is mediated by a cholinergic link in the preoptic area (Pickford, 1947). Our results show that such links exist in at least two areas – the lateral hypothalamus and the preoptic area – in which carbachol can elicit drinking and that they are strongly stimulated by the dose that elicits the most drinking. The results show that the carbachol does not produce behavioral manifestations of thirst in some indirect way, but that

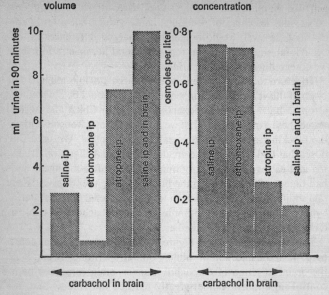

Figure 4 Effects of injecting carbachol into the lateral hypothalamus of unanesthetized rats. Such injection reduces the volume and increases the concentration of urine. Prior intraperitoneal (ip) injection of the cholinergic blocker atropine reduces these effects, but injection of the adrenergic blocker ethomoxane does not. Injections of the isotonic saline used as the vehicle serve as controls. (Unpublished recent data of Miller and Chien)

it activates a general water-conserving mechanism, one aspect of which is conservation of water by reabsorption in the kidneys and another aspect of which is motivation of animals to perform learned water-seeking habits.

As an extension of the foregoing study we injected norepinephrine into the lateral hypothalamus of a number of rats at the dosage (22 µg) that we had found optimum for producing eating. While the major response of the rats was eating, to our surprise some of them drank a few milliliters of water before starting to eat. When we investigated the effects of norepinephrine on the secretion of urine, we found in general little, if any, effect in the animals whose first response had been eating but some reduction in the volume, and some increase in the concentration, of urine in the rats which had done a little preliminary drinking. These antidiuretic effects observed to date have been considerably less than those elicited in our experiments with carbachol, but we cannot draw any definitive conclusions until we have completed dose-response studies. We must also determine the action of blocking agents on these effects. When stained slides of these rats' brains are completed, it will be interesting to see whether or not the location of the implants differs slightly for the animals which showed only an eating effect and for those which showed also a slight drinking effect.

Effects on blood sugar

Coons, Booth, Pitt and Miller have shown recently that the same electrical stimulation in the hypothalamus that causes satiated rats to eat produces a marked elevation in blood sugar during tests in which no food is present. This result suggests that stimulation in that area of the brain activates a general homeostatic mechanism which deals with a nutritional deficit both by increasing blood sugar and by motivating the animal to get food to replenish the deficit.

We are using chemostimulation to further investigate this problem. Some recent results are shown in Figure 5. In these tests, no food is present. Samples of blood are taken from the tip of the animal's tail at specified intervals and analysed by the glucose oxidase method. The portions of the curve for time prior to injection of substances into the lateral hypothalamus show a gradual rise; this rise continues with negative acceleration following the injection of isotonic saline into the brain, suggesting that the stress of handling and the taking of successive samples of blood produces some increase in the level of blood glucose. This increase, however, is definitely less than that which follows injection of the norepinephrine into the brain, a finding which shows that the mechanism by which the norepinephrine injection elicits eating is not that of stimulating insulin secretion and thus producing a drop in blood sugar. The results obtained thus far are symmetrical and esthetically satisfying and favor the hypothesis that norepinephrine activates a general mechanism for correcting nutritional deficits.

From such an hypothesis, one would not expect carbachol to produce an increase in blood sugar. But, as Figure 6 clearly shows,

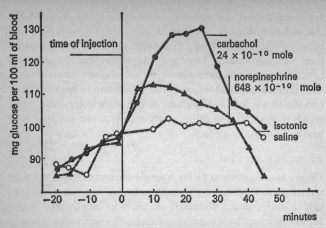

Figure 5 Effects on blood glucose of injecting norepinephrine and carbachol into the lateral hypothalamus of rats. As compared with an injection of isotonic saline, an injection of the dose of norepinephrine that is optimum for eliciting eating produces an increase in blood glucose, but an injection of the dose of carbachol that is optimum for eliciting drinking produces an even greater increase. No food and water are given during these tests. (Unpublished recent data of Coons, Booth, Pitt and Miller)

the carbachol produces a considerably greater increase than the norepinephrine does. This unexpected result shows that our understanding of what is going on is still far from complete; it presents us with a puzzle that we would not have discovered had we confined our studies to electrical stimulation.

When the same dose of carbachol or of norepinephrine that was injected into the brain is injected into the jugular vein by means of an implanted cannula, the carbachol has no measurable effect, but the norepinephrine has approximately the same effect that it has when injected into the brain; the latter result suggests that at least some of the increase in blood sugar following the injection of norepinephrine into the brain could be caused by peripheral effects after it has been absorbed into the blood.

Effects on shivering and temperature

Feldberg and Myers recently have shown that both shivering and an increase in body temperature are elicited by the injection into the anterior hypothalamus of a cat of a few micrograms of serotonin, an amine normally found in this area. Conversely, injections of either epinephrine or norepinephrine inhibit such shivering and reduce the fever. They also cause a drop in the temperature of normal cats. Injections outside this general area of the brain do not produce such effects.

Evidence that serotonin is indeed involved in normal temperature regulation comes from a study in which Canal and Ornesi showed that cyproheptadine, an agent that blocks serotonin, inhibits a fever induced by injecting typhoid vaccine into the ventricles of the brain (1961). These studies suggest that the central mechanisms controlling shivering and temperature regulation may be chemically coded, and the results add a new substance, serotonin, to the list of substances known to produce differential effects.

But there is an intimate relationship between temperature, on the one hand, and food and water regulation on the other. For example, Andersson and Larsson found in the goat that local cooling in the preoptic area, which is adjacent to the anterior hypothalamus, will elicit eating and shivering, while heating will stop eating and elicit panting and drinking (1961).

These facts suggested to us the desirability of studying, in the rat, the effects on body temperature of injecting carbachol and norepinephrine into the lateral hypothalamus in the doses that are optimum for eliciting drinking and eating, respectively. Coons, Levak, Wechsler and Miller found that the norepinephrine produces a drop in temperature of approximately $0.5°$ C., while the carbachol produces approximately twice this drop in temperature. Except for the fact that the effect is a drop instead of a rise, the curves look strikingly like those of Figure 6. Furthermore, as was found for blood sugar, the effects of this dose of norepinephrine are much the same regardless of whether it is injected in the vein or in the brain, but injection of this dose of carbachol by vein has no measurable effect.

To summarize, the effects on body temperature of injecting norepinephrine in the vein, norepinephrine in the brain, and carbachol in the brain are similar to each other and opposite to those of injecting serotonin in the brain. The effects on blood sugar of injecting carbachol in the brain and norepinephrine in the brain and in the vein are also similar to each other. But the effects on food intake of injecting norepinephrine in the vein and in the brain are opposite. Injection of norepinephrine in the lateral hypothalamus typically increases food intake and decreases water intake, while such injection of carbachol typically has the opposite effects.

It seems unlikely that the drinking elicited by injection of carbachol in the lateral hypothalamus and the eating elicited by injection of norepinephrine are secondary to temperature changes, since these two substances change temperature in the same direction, while a given change in temperature has opposite effects on eating and drinking. The fact that norepinephrine in the central system and norepinephrine in the peripheral system produce similar effects on body temperature but opposite ones on eating also argues against the hypothesis that the effect of this substance on temperature produces its effect on eating.

Use of chemostimulation for tracing neural circuits

Since Grossman's initial demonstration, a number of investigators have been using the selectivity of chemostimulation to trace the circuits involved in various behavioral effects.

The thirst system

Fisher and Coury have found that injection of carbachol into any of the ten different structures they have investigated throughout the limbic system will elicit drinking (1962). This is a system that extends beyond the hypothalamus and is characterized by a number of closed loops and other intricate interconnections which seem to provide the anatomical basis for sustaining activity by central positive feedback, as well as providing alternate pathways and intimate intercorrelations between various functions. They have also found that carbachol in any of ten nearby areas outside this circuit does not elicit appreciable drinking.

While Fisher and Coury found that the relationship between cholinergic stimulation and drinking throughout the limbic system was remarkably specific, they did find a few cases in which carbachol increased both eating and drinking. And we have noted instances in which norepinephrine elicited some slight drinking. Myers has noted even more drinking elicited by norepinephrine (1964). Also, as discussed earlier, the effects of carbachol and norepinephrine on blood sugar are similar. These exceptions are puzzling. The effects of blocking agents on these exceptional effects have not yet been investigated. These exceptions may indicate that the same system changes its chemical coding in different parts of the brain; they could be produced by interactions between different systems that are differently coded, or they might have still other implications. We do not yet know the answer.

The reward system

It has long been known that the limbic system is involved in emotional behavior. As Fisher and Coury point out (1964, p. 515), there is a remarkable parallelism between the brain structures from which they can elicit drinking by injection of carbachol and those from which MacLean and Ploog, by electrical stimulation, have elicited penile erection (1962). Furthermore, these are the same structures in which electrical stimulation has been shown, by Olds, to act as a reward to reinforce learning and maintain the performance of learned habits (1962).

In addition to investigating the rewarding effects of electrical stimulation of the brain, Olds has recently tested the rewarding effects of various chemicals applied in minute amounts to different sites in the brain (1964). In these studies the rat is in a small cage containing a bar. Every time the rat presses the bar he activates a device which injects approximately three millimicroliters of solution via a thin polyethylene tube leading to a special needle permanently implanted in the skull. If the injection is rewarding, the rat learns to press the bar and works to give itself injections. Olds gets rewarding effects from injecting acetylcholine or carbachol in certain brain areas, while norepinephrine, epinephrine, and serotonin have the opposite effect of reducing the rewarding effect of another solution. He also gets good rewarding effects with chelating agents, and the best of all with testosterone sulfate. It is interesting to note that these two latter agents are the only ones with which Fisher could elicit either male sexual or maternal nest-building and infant-retrieving behavior in the rat.

Specificity of responsiveness of overlapping systems

As further evidence for the specificity of response to chemostimulation of overlapping systems, Fisher and Coury have found one animal that consistently responded to injections of carbachol by drinking, to injections of norepinephrine by eating, and to injection of a soluble sex hormone by building nests (1962). All three chemicals were applied to the same site at the junction of the area of the diagonal band of Broca and the medial preoptic region, and all three effects were specific.

Variety of tests required

Certain studies which Grossman has made since he left our laboratory have indicated further lines of fruitful work on chemical stimulation and, at the same time, the difficulty of the survey that is needed to give us a more adequate picture of the brain (1964b). He found that carbachol in the medial septal area elicited drinking in water-satiated rats and increased the water consumption of thirsty ones. It also depressed the food intake of hungry rats and impaired the learning and the performance of responses which allowed the rat to avoid electric shocks.

Implantation of the cholinergic blocking agent atropine into this area of the brain reduced the water consumption of thirsty rats and improved the performance of a previously acquired avoidance response. Implantation of noradrenaline had no effect on intake of food or water but improved the avoidance response; hence, in this respect, noradrenaline acted oppositely to carbachol. Thus the inclusion of an avoidance-learning situation, presumably measuring fear-motivated behavior, proved to be a useful addition to the tests.

Grossman observed no marked or consistent effects of chemostimulation of the ventral amygdala of satiated rats (1964a). From this one might conclude that there were little, if any, effects of chemostimulation in this area on hunger or thirst. But when he tested animals that had been deprived of food and water, he found that norepinephrine increased the food intake and decreased the water intake, while administration of an adrenergic blocking agent, dibenzyline, in the same area of the brain had the opposite effect of decreasing food intake and increasing water intake.

Cholinergic agents produced symmetrically opposite results; carbachol decreased food intake and increased water intake, while the blocking agent atropine tended to increase food intake but decrease water intake.

A number of other agents and control substances had no observable effects. Gamma-amino butyric acid, however, produced results similar to those produced by carbachol. This substance, which is normally found in the brain, is believed not to have any cholinergic effect. Thus, it is possible that it acted by blocking an inhibitory system. Recent results by Booth at Yale fit in with such an interpretation of the effects of gamma-amino butyric acid. Booth injected this substance into the ventromedial nucleus of the hypothalamus, an area known to exert an inhibitory effect on hunger. He found that such injections markedly increased the rate at which rats pressed a bar to get food without producing comparable increases in rates of pressing other bars to get water or to avoid an electric shock.

To return to Grossman's experiments on the amygdala, the fact that the effective chemicals did not elicit any appreciable results with satiated animals, but only with animals deprived of food and water, suggests that the function of the sites he stimulated is to modulate ongoing activity rather than to initiate activity.

Even when one is investigating a limited aspect of behavior, such as motivation, there are various different types of tests which are needed in initial screening investigations. Such tests should be made not only when the appropriate motive is initially absent but also when it is present. After an effect is discovered, additional tests are often needed to check alternative interpretations of the results. We have illustrated in detail elsewhere (Miller and Barry, 1960; Miller, 1964, p. 1) the desirability of using a variety of behavioral tests to cross-check all conclusions.

In each of these behavioral tests one must try the effects of a number of different presumptive transmitters, and also blocking agents. Each of these must be tested at a number of dosages, since our inverted U-shaped dose-response curves in Figures 3 and 4 show that one can fail to get results by using either too high or too low a dose. Furthermore, this process must be carried out for a great number of different points in the brain, sometimes separated by as little as one millimeter. It is obvious that a thorough survey will involve an enormous amount of work, and also that there are many opportunities for significant discoveries.

Combination of classical and chemostimulation techniques

The classical technique of destroying a certain part of a pathway can be combined with the technique of chemostimulation to determine the direction of the pathway, or to indicate what are the most critical parts of the system. Thus, Wolf and Miller have shown (1964) that a lesion in the feeding-drinking area of the lateral hypothalamus eliminates drinking elicited by chemostimulation at sites anterior or posterior to this location, while lesions in the anterior or posterior sites do not eliminate drinking elicited by chemostimulation in the lateral hypothalamus. Such results show the special importance of the lateral hypothalamic area.

Similarly, Paolino and Miller are combining the technique of electrical stimulation of brain areas in reward and punishment experiments with the use of reversible biochemical lesions. When a general blocking agent, such as the local anesthetic xylocaine, is used to make such a lesion in the lateral hypothalamus, it greatly reduces the rewarding effects of electrically stimulating the anterior part of the medial forebrain bundle but seems to have less effect on the punishing effects. Having used a general blockade by a local anesthetic to confirm the location of a crucial point in the system, we are now exploring the effects of specific blocking agents to produce biochemical lesions that are not only reversible but also selective, and to throw light on the chemical coding of the system.

Additional combinations of classical and chemostimulation techniques are used in studies of the sleep and arousal systems.

Sleep versus arousal in the cat

Hernandez-Peon *et al.* (1963) have demonstrated the usefulness of chemostimulation for dissecting out, in more detail than had been possible in work with electrical stimulation, the brain circuits involved in sleep and in arousal (see also Hernandez-Peon, 1965). At the same time his work demonstrates a puzzling species difference between effects on the rat, the animal used for most of the studies so far described, and the cat, which he used. Thus, these results provide still further evidence for both the fruitfulness of work with chemostimulation and the magnitude of the task.

Hernandez-Peon and his co-workers found that the sleep system involves a number of pathways descending from the cortex through the limbic midbrain circuit, and also an ascending component coming up from the spinal cord through the medulla and pons to the midbrain. Along the pathways of this circuit, stimulation with acetylcholine or carbachol elicits sleep. As might be expected, if the normal transmitter is cholinergic, injection into this system of eserine, which is known to inhibit the enzymes that destroy natural acetylcholine, will elicit sleep. By preventing the destruction of the transmitter, presumably the eserine potentiates impulses that are a part of the normal background activity of this system, and thus tips in the direction of sleep the balance between such impulses and those of arousal.

Additional evidence that the chemostimulation is indeed cholinergic comes from the finding that it can be blocked by atropine. If one point in a circuit is stimulated by an injection of acetylcholine and a crystal of atropine is placed downstream, the atropine blocks the induction of sleep. But if the location of the injections of the two substances is reversed, no blockade occurs. Tests involving the use of atropine, production of temporary chemical lesions by a local anesthetic, or permanent destruction of the path by an electrolytic lesion have yielded similar results, confirming earlier findings concerning the direction of the pathways.

An arousal system that runs roughly parallel to the sleep system at some levels and overlaps it at others responds to injections of norepinephrine. At some levels of the brain, acetylcholine and norepinephrine elicit their effects from different sites. At these sites, presumably, the two systems do not overlap. At other brain levels both substances produce an effect from the same site; the nature of the effect is determined by the type of substance. Here, presumably, the two systems overlap. One such point of overlap is the preoptic area, where the application of noradrenaline elicits alertness, while application of acetylcholine via the same cannula into the same site elicits sleep. Another site where injection of one and then the other substance via the same cannula produces opposite results is the central gray matter of the spinal cord at the level of the eighth cervical vertebra.

A number of investigators have elicited sleep through electrical stimulation of some of these same parts of the brain (Hess, 1949; Magoun, 1963, p. 161). In some sites, long slow pulses have elicited sleep while short rapid ones have produced arousal. In other sites, Hernandez-Peon and his collaborators have found it easy to elicit sleep by chemostimulation but difficult or perhaps impossible to do so by electrical stimulation. Furthermore, while studies with electrical stimulation have seemed to indicate that there is an anterior center for light sleep and a posterior one for deep sleep (Jouvet, 1961, p. 188), Hernandez-Peon and his colleagues have found it possible to elicit light sleep from either location by weak doses of acetylcholine or carbachol, and deep sleep from either location by stronger doses. Thus, it appears that the depth of sleep is a function of the strength of stimulation of the sleep system, and that the earlier apparent finding of two different centers for these two types of sleep probably was an artifact of a difference in the degree of separation of the sleep system and the arousal system, which allowed electrical stimulation to produce a stronger differential effect in one case than in the other.

Although cholinergic stimulation of certain brain areas in the cat produces sleep, stimulation of other areas, some of them quite close to the sleep circuits, elicits a spectacular attack response: the cat growls, hisses, flattens back its ears, arches its back, raises its hair, strikes out with its claws and bites. Similar manifestations of rage had previously been elicited by electrical stimulation of these areas. These results further illustrate that the response elicited depends on the area stimulated as well as on the 'transmitter' used.

Species differences

Some of the sites at which injection of carbachol or acetylcholine elicits either sleep or rage in the cat correspond to sites at which injection of these substances elicits drinking in the rat. Nevertheless, in investigating these and many other sites in the cat's brain, Hernandez-Peon (1965) and Fisher and Coury (1962) have not observed a single instance of elicited drinking. The fact that drinking can be elicited easily by application of cholinergic substances at any of a wide variety of brain sites in the rat but has not yet been elicited by these substances in the cat is puzzling. It could be that carbachol and acetylcholine, although somewhat more differential in their effects than electrical stimulation, nevertheless stimulate a number of overlapping systems, the effect on thirst being dominant in the highly domesticated albino rat and effects on rage, sleep and other systems being dominant in the cat. Perhaps stimulation of the remnants of the rage system in the domesticated rat was the basis for the unexpected rise in blood sugar that accompanied the dominant drinking elicited by carbachol. If species differences are merely a matter of the relative dominance of systems in different animals, one might expect different results from the wild cousins of laboratory rats, which show much more fear and aggression, or from certain desert rats that apparently can get along without any water. On the other hand, it is conceivable that there are genuine differences in the chemical coding of the brains of different species of mammals, or that we are not yet using quite the right substances in the right way to exploit the subtleties of the chemical code.

Summary

Distinctive patterns of behavior can be elicited by directly stimulating the brain with substances that are normally found in it, or with synthetic compounds resembling these substances. Recent research shows that the response elicited depends on both the site stimulated and the type of chemical used. Compounds of different classes, applied via the same cannula to exactly the same site in the brain, can elicit different kinds of behavior, or opposite effects on the same kind of behavior. This differential sensitivity is useful in tracing the circuits in the brain that control different types of behavior, especially since some of these circuits are intimately interlaced in certain places. A better understanding of the chemical coding of behavioral systems in the brain may also help ultimately to provide a more rational foundation for the discovery of new drugs to treat certain forms of mental disorder.

Evidence is accumulating that a general homeostatic system, with both overt behavioral and internal physiological components, may use neural circuits that are chemically coded in the same way in at least certain different regions of the brain. Stimulation of any of a number of areas of the rat brain by the cholinergic substances acetylcholine or carbachol causes water-satiated rats to drink and to perform thirst-motivated learned behavior, at the same time conserving water by stimulating the reabsorption of water by the kidneys. Cholinergic stimulation also causes water- and food-deprived rats to drink more and to eat less. On the other hand, stimulation of some of these sites by the adrenergic substances epinephrine and norepinephrine has the opposite effect of causing rats that have eaten and drunk to satiation to eat, or rats that have been deprived of food and water to eat more and to drink less.

In the cat a similar antagonism has been found between the effects of cholinergic and adrenergic substances, only in this case the cholinergic effect is sleep and the adrenergic one arousal. While cholinergic stimulation of certain areas of the cat brain elicits sleep, cholinergic stimulation of other areas elicits a spectacular rage response: the cat hisses, arches its back, raises its hair, flattens its ears and makes an accurately directed attack.

The finding that some of the brain structures in which cholinergic stimulation elicits drinking in the rat are analogous to structures in which it elicits sleep or attack in the cat is an unsolved puzzle.

Agents that are known to block the effects of certain transmitter substances, or to have the opposite effect of inhibiting the enzymes that destroy these substances, provide a means of rigorously cross-checking conclusions. Such cross checks have provided data that are consistent with, and strongly support, the conclusions drawn from the studies described.

Although the new method of chemostimulation has revealed some esthetically satisfying symmetrical patterns of lawful relationships, it has also turned up some unexpected, apparently discordant, and tantalizing results. It is becoming increasingly clear that we need to use a variety of behavioral tests to determine the effects of different doses of a considerable number of possible transmitting, inhibitory, modulating or blocking agents at a vast number of different sites in the brain. The chemical methods should be combined, also, with other approaches, such as electrical stimulation, the recording of evoked potentials, and the destroying of discrete pathways or nuclei by lesions. The task before us is enormous, but, by the same token, so is the opportunity for making new discoveries about one of the most miraculous products of nature – the brain.

References

ANAND, B. K., and BROBECK, J. R. (1951), 'Hypothalamic control of food intake in rats and cats', *Yale J. biol. Med.*, vol. 24, pp. 123–40.

ANDERSSON, B. (1953), 'The effect of injections of hypertonic NaCl-solutions into different parts of the hypothalamus of goats', *Acta Physiol. Scand.*, vol. 28, pp. 188–201.

ANDERSSON, B., and LARSSON, B. (1961), 'Influence of local temperature changes in the preoptic area and rostral hypothalamus on the regulation of food and water intake', *Acta Physiol. Scand.*, vol. 52, pp. 75–89.

BOWER, G. H., and MILLER, N. E. (1958), 'Rewarding and punishing effects from stimulating the same place in the rat's brain', *J. compar. physiol. Psychol.*, vol. 51, pp. 669–74.

CANAL, N., and ORNESI, A. (1961), 'Serotonina encefalica e ipertermia da vaccino', *Atti Accad. Med. Lombarda*, vol. 16, pp. 69–74.

DELGADO, J. M. R. (1955), 'Cerebral structures involved in transmission and elaboration of noxious stimulation', *J. Neurophysiol.*, vol. 18, pp. 261–75.

FELDBERG, W. S. (1958), 'Behavioral changes in the cat after injection of drugs into the cerebral ventricle: A contribution to the study of subcortical convulsions and impairment of consciousness', *Proc. Assoc. Res. nervous mental Diseases*, vol. 36, pp. 401–423.

FELDBERG, W. S., and MYERS, R. D. (1965), 'Changes in temperature produced by microinjections of amines into the anterior hypothalamus of cats', *J. Physiol. London*, vol. 177, pp. 239–245.

FISHER, A. E. (1956), 'Maternal and sexual behavior induced by intracranial chemical stimulation', *Sci.*, vol. 124, pp. 228–9.

FISHER, A. E. (1966), 'Chemical and electrical stimulation of the brain in the male rat', in R. A. Gorski, and R. E. Whalen (eds.), *Brain and Behavior*; vol. 3, *The Brain and Gonadal Function*, University of California Press.

FISHER, A. E., and COURY, J. N. (1962), 'Cholinergic tracing of a central neural circuit underlying the thirst drive', *Sci.*, vol. 138, pp. 691–3.

FISHER, A. E., and COURY, J. N. (1964), 'Chemical tracing of neural pathways mediating the thirst drive', in M. J. Wayner (ed.) *Thirst*, Pergamon, pp. 515–31.

GROSSMAN, S. P. (1960), 'Eating or drinking elicited by direct adrenergic or cholinergic stimulation of hypothalamus', *Sci.*, vol. 132, pp. 301–2.

GROSSMAN, S. P. (1961), 'Behavioral effects of direct adrenergic and cholinergic stimulation of the hypothalamic mechanisms regulating food and water intake', doctoral thesis, Yale University.

GROSSMAN, S. P. (1962a), 'Direct adrenergic and cholinergic
stimulation of hypothalamic mechanisms', *Amer. J. Physiol.*, vol. 202,
pp. 872–82.

GROSSMAN, S. P. (1962b), 'Effects of adrenergic and cholinergic
blocking agents on hypothalamic mechanisms', *Amer. J. Physiol.*,
vol. 202, pp. 1230–6.

GROSSMAN, S. P. (1964a), 'Behavioral effects of chemical stimulation of
the ventral amygdala', *J. compar. physiol. Psychol.*, vol. 57, pp. 29–36.

GROSSMAN, S. P. (1964b), 'Effects of chemical stimulation of the septal
area on motivation', *J. compar. physiol. Psychol.*, vol. 58, pp. 194–200.

HARRIS, G. W., and MICHAEL, R. P. (1964), 'The activation of sexual
behaviour by hypothalamic implants of oestrogen', *J. Physiol. London*,
vol. 171, pp. 275–301.

HERNANDEZ-PEON, R. (1965), 'Central neuro-humoral transmission in
sleep and wakefulness', in K. Akert, C. Bally and J. P. Schadé, (eds.),
Progress in Brain Research, Elsevier.

HERNANDEZ-PEON, R., CHÁVEZ-IBARRA, G., MORGANE, P. J., and
TIMO-IARIA, C. (1963), 'Limbic cholinergic pathways involved in
sleep and emotional behavior', *Exper. Neurol.*, vol. 8, pp. 93–111.

HESS, W. R. (1949), *Das Zwischenhirn: Syndrome, Localisationen
Functionen*, Schwabe.

JOUVET, M. (1961), 'Telencephalic and Rhombencephalic sleep in the
cat', in G. E. W. Wolstenholme and C. M. O'Connor (eds.), *The
Nature of Sleep*, Churchill, pp. 188–208.

MACLEAN, P. D. (1957), 'Chemical and electrical stimulation of
hippocampus in unrestrained animals', *Arch. Neurol. Psychiat.*, vol. 78,
pp. 128–42.

MACLEAN, P. D., and PLOOG, D. W. (1962), 'Cerebral representation
of penile erection', *J. Neurophysiol.*, vol. 25, pp. 29–55.

MAGOUN, H. W. (1963), 'Central neural inhibition', in M. R. Jones (ed.)
Nebraska Symposium on Motivation, University of Nebraska Press,
pp. 161–193.

MILLER, N. E. (1961), 'Learning and performance motivated by direct
stimulation of the brain', in D. Sheer (ed.), *Electrical stimulation of the
Brain*, University of Texas Press, pp. 387–96.

MILLER, N. E. (1963), 'Some motivational effects of electrical and
chemical stimulation of the brain' *Electroencephalog. clin. Neurophysiol.*,
suppl. 24, pp. 247–59.

MILLER, N. E. (1964), 'Some psychophysiological studies of motivation
and of the behavioral effects of illness', *Bull. Brit. psychol. Soc.*, vol. 17
no. 55, pp. 1–20.

MILLER, N. E. (1964), 'The analysis of motivational effects illustrated
by experiments on amylobathibitone', in H. Steinberg (ed.) *Symposium
Animal behaviour and drug action*, Churchill, pp. 1–18.

MILLER, N. E., and BARRY, H. (1960), 'Motivational effects of drugs:
Methods which illustrate some general problems in
psychopharmacology', *Psychopharmacologia*, vol. 1, pp. 169–99.

MILLER, N E, GOTTESMAN, K S., and EMERY, N. (1964), 'Dose response to carbachol and norepinephrine in rat hypothalamus', *Amer. J. Physiol.*, vol. 206, pp. 1384–8.

MYERS, R. D. (1964), 'Modification of drinking patterns by chronic intracranial chemical infusion', in M. J. Wayner (ed.) *Thirst*, Pergamon, pp. 533–51.

OLDS, J. (1962), 'Hypothalamic substrates of reward', *Physiol. Rev.*, vol. 42, pp. 554–604.

OLDS, J. (1964), 'The induction and suppression of hypothalamic self-stimulation behavior by micro-injection of endogenous substances at the self-stimulation site', *Proc. internat. cong. Endocrinol.*, London. Also in *Excerpta Med. internat. cong.*, no. 83, pp. 426–34.

PICKFORD, M. (1947), 'The action of acetylcholine in the supraoptic nucleus of the chloralozed dog', *J. Physiol.*, *London*, vol. 106, pp. 264–70.

ROBERTS, W. M. (1958), 'Both rewarding and punishing effects from stimulation of posterior hypothalamus of cat in the same electrode at same intensity', *J. compar. physiol. Psychol.*, vol. 51, pp. 400–7.

ROBINSON, B. W. (1964), 'Forebrain alimentary responses: some organizational principles', in M. J. Wayner (ed.) *Thirst*, Pergamon, pp. 411–27.

RUSSEK, M., and PINA, S. (1962), 'Conditioning of adrenalin anorexia', *Nature*, vol. 193, pp. 1296–7.

TEITELBAUM, P., and EPSTEIN, A. N. (1962), 'The lateral hypothalamic syndrome: Recovery of feeding and drinking after lateral hypothalamic lesions', *Psychol. Rev.*, vol. 69, pp. 74–90.

WOLF, G. (1964), 'Sodium appetite elicited by aldosterone', *Psychonomic Sci.*, vol. 1, pp. 211–12.

WOLF, G., and MILLER, N. E. (1964), 'Lateral hypothalamic lesions: Effects on drinking elicited by carbachol in preoptic area and posterior hypothalamus', *Sci.*, vol. 143, pp. 585–7.

34 E. S. Valenstein, V. C. Cox and J. W. Kakolewski

Reexamination of the Role of the Hypothalamus in Motivation

E. S. Valenstein, V. C. Cox and J. W. Kakolewski, 'Reexamination of the role of the hypothalamus in motivation', *Psychological Review*, vol. 77, 1970, pp. 16–31.

During the past fifteen years, a great number of studies using electrical stimulation techniques have investigated consummatory behavior that could be elicited by hypothalamic stimulation. The behavior described has included, among others, eating, drinking, gnawing, hoarding, stalking-attack and sexual behavior (cf. review by Valenstein, Cox, and Kakolewski, 1969b). These responses elicited by hypothalamic stimulation have been referred to as 'stimulus-bound'[1] behavior. Stimulus-bound behavior has generally been considered to reflect motivational states rather than a stereotyped motor act because animals will not exhibit the behavior unless appropriate goal objects are present. Also, during stimulation, animals will perform some learned task in order to obtain access to the relevant goal object (Coons, Levak and Miller, 1965) and will tolerate aversive stimulation, such as shock (Morgane, 1961) or quinine additives (Tenen and Miller, 1964) to obtain relevant goal objects. There exists a wide-spread acceptance of the idea that stimulus-bound eating is elicited by activation of specific neural circuits underlying 'hunger' and that drinking is elicited from activation of specific 'thirst' circuits. Similar conclusions have been drawn with regard to the other elicited behavior that has been studied. Distinguishable from the issue of specific neural circuits is the view, held by some investigators, that relatively discrete hypothalamic regions are involved in the regulation of behavior related to specific biological needs. There can be little doubt that contemporary concepts of hypo-

1. It might have been less confusing to have used the term 'stimulation bound' to denote the behavior which is temporally linked to the electrical stimulus and 'stimulus bound' if the association with a particular goal object was to be stressed.

thalamic function and organization have been greatly influenced by the fact that stimulation of the hypothalamus can elicit a wide variety of biologically important behaviors.

During the past two years, the authors have conducted a series of studies directed toward modification of the behavior elicited by hypothalamic stimulation and toward examination of the nature of the motivation underlying these behaviors. These studies have led to an alternative interpretation of hypothalamic function and organization in the regulation of behavior. We began our studies of stimulus-bound behavior following a review of the literature, which indicated that there was an impressive amount of overlap of the anatomical sites yielding different behaviors. It was difficult to justify the impression given by many investigators who had restricted their observations to one behavior, that there were discrete areas associated with a specific behavior. Indeed, it seemed more than possible that the behavior observed in many studies was determined by the experimenters' interest and the consequent limitations of the testing situation.

Modification of stimulus-bound behavior

The initial report stressed the fact that if ample opportunity was provided, the behavior elicited by hypothalamic stimulation was subject to change without any modification of stimulus parameters (Valenstein, Cox and Kakolewski, 1968a, 1969b). For example, if a rat ate in response to stimulation, removal of food resulted in the gradual emergence of another behavior such as drinking or wood gnawing. When the food was again inserted into the test chamber, the new behavior was elicited as frequently as eating. Table 1 illustrates these data, which have subsequently been replicated in several hundred animals. These results suggested that the relationship between a specific hypothalamic site activated by electrical stimulation and the resultant behavior pattern was not fixed.

In our experience with the elicitation of eating, drinking and wood gnawing there have been only a few instances in which it was not possible to add at least one of these stimulus-bound patterns to that initially elicited by the hypothalamic stimulation. Even in those cases there may have been an explanation for the failure. It was observed that in some instances the stimulation

Table 1 Eating (E), Drinking (D) and Gnawing (G) Behavior
Elicited during Hypothalamic Stimulation

| Animal | Behavior | Test series | | | | | Competition | Stimulus parameters (μa.) |
| | | First series | | | Second series | | | |
		1	2	3	1	2		
	E	0	0	0	15	17	11	RP, 80
60S	D	20	20	20	—	—	14	RP, 80
	G	0	0	0	0	0	0	RP, 80
	E	0	0	0	20	20	15	RP, 120
61S	D	20	20	20	—	—	12	RP, 120
	G	0	0	0	0	0	0	RP, 120
	E	0	0	0	0	0	0	RP, 500
63S	D	0	0	0	20	20	12	RP, 500
	G	20	20	20	—	—	8	RP, 500
	E	0	0	0	20	20	12	SW, 20
74S	D	20	20	20	—	—	13	SW, 20
	G	0	0	0	0	0	0	SW, 20
	E	19	16	12	—	—	10	RP, 120
80S	D	1	5	8	19	16	10	RP, 120
	G	0	0	0	2	2	6	RP, 120
	E	0	0	0	18	20	16	SW, 24
89S	D	19	19	20	—	—	4	SW, 24
	G	0	0	0	0	0	0	SW, 24

Each test had 20 stimulation periods. Maximum score for any one behavior
is 20, but the animal could exhibit different behaviors during each period.
The dash (—) in the second series of tests indicates which goal object had
been removed. RP = rectangular pulses; SW = sine wave. All animals
except 80S were males. (Reprinted with permission from an article by E. S.
Valenstein, V. C. Cox, and J. W. Kakolewski published in *Science* (1968),
vol. 159.)

elicited behavior that was directed toward the animal's own body,
but this had not been scored as stimulus-bound behavior because
at that time it did not conform to our arbitrarily chosen classification system. It was conceivable that such behavior could have
interfered with the development of an alternative and 'scoreable'

stimulus-bound behavior. A striking case arose, which illustrates the relevance of this interpretation. In one animal, hypothalamic stimulation always elicited a response consisting of picking up the end of the tail and moving it laterally in the mouth, seemingly as a form of preening. It was not possible to modify this behavior until it occurred to us to fasten the tail to the animal's back with adhesive tape. After being stimulated with identical current parameters, but without access to the initially preferred goal object (its tail), the animal gradually started drinking in response to stimulation and this response was later displayed as frequently as the 'tail preening' when both tail and water were available. This result raised the possibility, presently being tested in our laboratory, that in many cases in which stimulation does not elicit a 'scoreable' stimulus-bound behavior, the 'locomotor exploratory behavior' may represent an interference similar to that of tail preening.

The conclusion that the relation between a specific hypothalamic site and a given response is subject to modification has been subsequently strengthened by several sources of new evidence. In the first place, the changes in behavior were not restricted to oral behavior such as eating, drinking and gnawing, for it was subsequently found that many of these electrodes could also elicit various preening activities, shuffling of food with the forepaws and sand digging. Others displayed very stereotyped motor patterns which seemed to be as important a component of stimulus-bound behavior as the eating or drinking. In several instances, whether an animal ate or drank in response to stimulation seemed to depend on whether the food or water was placed in a particular corner. In addition, Caggiula (1970) and Gallistel (1970) both have noted that male sexual behavior and eating could be elicited from the same electrode at the same current parameters, while earlier von Holst and von Saint Paul (1963) noted that in the fowl, behavior as different as clucking, fluffing of feathers, or preening (or nothing at all) could be obtained from the same electrode at different times without altering the stimulus parameters.

Wise (1968) has recently offered an alternative explanation of our data based on his observation that once an initial behavior was elicited by hypothalamic stimulation, a second behavior could be elicited by simply increasing stimulation intensity to a sufficiently high level. This evidence led to the assumption that interdigitated neural circuits mediating different behaviors have different stimulation thresholds and that the emergence of a second behavior was not due to environmental manipulation but to a gradual increase in the sensitivity of the separate neural system responsible for the new behavior.

As has been pointed out in a reply (Valenstein, Cox and Kakolewski, 1969a), Wise's procedure confounded the effects produced by increasing the stimulation intensity with those resulting from removal of the initially preferred object. We have determined that in the majority of cases in which stimulation elicited only one behavior, even high-intensity stimulation does not elicit a new behavior if the initially preferred goal object was not removed (Cox and Valenstein, 1969). Furthermore, after the removal of the initially preferred goal object, a new behavior emerged gradually, whereas its immediate display would have been expected if the behavior was mediated by an independent neural substrate with a high threshold.

It has also been suggested that smaller electrodes would make it possible to elicit one behavior exclusively. We have explored this possibility and found that the likelihood of obtaining a specific stimulus-bound behavior is radically decreased with small diameter electrodes, but if a response was elicited, a second response could be obtained (Valenstein, Cox and Kakolewski, 1969b). Bengt Andersson noted, when he reduced the size of his electrodes, that drinking could no longer be elicited in goats.[2] Miller (1965) reported similar results in the rat.

Motivation underlying elicited behavior

The fact that stimulation elicited several different behaviors led us to question whether specific motivational states were involved at all. Several situations were found where animals displaying eating or drinking in response to hypothalamic stimulation do not respond as hungry or thirsty animals. For example, animals eating in response to stimulation did not readily switch to another familiar food when the first food was removed from the test chamber. In fact, many switched eventually to stimulus-bound drinking (see Table 2); nor did they switch to the same food when

2. Personal communication, September 1968.

Table 2 Eating of a Cat-Dog Food (c/d), Food Pellets (FP) and Drinking of Water (W) during Standard and Switch Tests

| | Tests | | | | | |
| Animal | Standard | | | Switch | | |
	1	2	3	1	2	3
94U						
c/d	20	19	20	—	—	—
FP	0	0	0	2	7	4
W	0	0	0	16	14	16
95U						
c/d	18	18	19	—	—	—
FP	0	0	0	1	1	2
W	0	0	0	15	19	18
97U						
c/d	18	16	17	—	—	—
FP	0	0	0	0	0	0
W	0	0	0	15	12	11
39T						
c/d	20	18	19	—	—	—
FP	0	0	0	0	0	0
W	0	0	4	19	20	19
7V						
c/d	12	10	12	—	—	—
FP	0	2	0	0	1	1
W	0	0	0	13	12	18

Each test had 20 stimulation periods. Maximum score for any one behavior is 20. The dash (—) in the switch tests indicates that the cat-dog food was omitted. (Reprinted with permission from an article by E. S. Valenstein, V. C. Cox, and J. W. Kakolewski published in *Physiology and Behaviour* (1968), vol. 3.)

it was changed in shape, as when food pellets were ground to a powder (Valenstein, Cox and Kakolewski, 1968b). More recently, it was observed that animals reared from infancy on a liquid diet displayed stimulus-bound eating of food pellets, when mature, but if deprived of the pellets they did not eat the familiar liquid diet in response to stimulation (Valenstein and Phillips, 1970). Similarly, as illustrated in Table 3, animals displaying stimulation-

Table 3 Stimulus-Bound Drinking from a Water Bottle (WB) and Water Dish (WD) and Eating (E) during Standard, Pseudo and Switch Tests

Animal	Standard			Pseudo	Switch			Current
	1	2	3	1	1	2	3	
31X								
WB	15	18	17	—	—	—	—	
E	0	0	0	0	1	19	6	60 μa., R
WD	—	—	—	9	0	2	12	
48X								
WB	20	20	20	—	—	—	—	
E	0	0	0	2	15	14	6	20μa., S
WD	—	—	—	8	2	6	14	
24X								
WB	18	20	19	—	—	—	—	
E	2	1	2	0	14	18	19	9 μa., S
WD	—	—	—	11	5	0	0	
26X								
WB	16	13	16	—	—	—	—	
E	3	2	0	6	11	15	6	16 μa., S
WD	—	—	—	7	1	0	5	
45W								
WB	20	18	19	—	—	—	—	
E	0	0	0	0	0	0	0	150 μa., R
WD	—	—	—	8	0	0	0	

The standard and switch tests consisted of 20 stimulations. The maximum score for any one behavior on a single test was 20, but animals could exhibit more than one behavior during a single stimulation. The dash (—) indicates which goal object was removed. No stimulation was presented during the pseudo test, but animals, water-deprived for 24 hours, were scored for drinking during comparable periods. The pseudo test demonstrated the animals' familiarity with the water dish. The stimulating current was either a 60-cycle sine wave (S) or a biphasic, rectangular pulse (R) as produced by the Grass S6 stimulator. (Reprinted with permission from an article by E. S. Valenstein, J. W. Kakowlewski, and V. C. Cox published in *Communications in Behavioral Biology* (1968), vol. 2.)

induced drinking did not switch to drinking from another, although familiar, container. Also, the taste preferences of animals exhibiting stimulus-bound drinking and those drinking when thirst has been induced by water deprivation are quite different. Water-deprived animals always prefer water to a glucose solution while the converse is true in the case of stimulus-bound drinking. Furthermore, animals exhibiting stimulus-bound drinking often continued to lap at the water tube even after the water had been removed, suggesting that the ingestion of water was not essential to the maintenance of the elicited lapping behavior (Valenstein, Kakolewski and Cox, 1968).

Conclusions

Several important conclusions that are suggested by these results warrant serious consideration.

1. Animals displaying stimulus-bound eating or drinking do not exhibit response or stimulus generalization gradients similar to those of known hungry or thirsty animals. If deprived of the opportunity to engage in the initial behavior, the selection of a new goal object is not dictated by its capacity to satisfy the same presumed drive state.

2. The behavior elicited by hypothalamic stimulation may be maintained by some variable other than the satisfaction of a simulated need state such as hunger or thirst.

If stimulation does not evoke specific drive states such as hunger or thirst, then it is less paradoxical that a new behavior oriented to a very different goal object can become associated with the stimulus. Furthermore, the problems raised by the fact that animals will self-stimulate at electrode sites that are presumed to evoke drives such as hunger can be eliminated. The paradox of why an animal should stimulate itself and thereby produce a hunger drive state is created by the assumption that the animal is hungry.[3] It is true the stimulated animal is motivated to eat in

3. The paradox simply takes a different form if we assume that stimulation produces a state similar to that experienced by the animal while eating (Wyrwicka, 1966), as we must then be equally puzzled over the fact that the stimulus elicits eating.

the operational sense that an opportunity to engage in this act will maintain instrumental behavior, but the assumption that the animal is experiencing the aversive consequences specifically associated with hunger has produced confusion. The awkwardness of this conception of the problem becomes more apparent when it is appreciated that we have also to postulate that hypothalamic stimulation evokes specific aversive states associated with gnawing, food shuffling, tail preening, etc., and, as will be described subsequently, object carrying.

Anatomical correlates

With respect to the anatomical correlation between hypothalamic region and elicited behavior, our results confirm the initial impression of overlap gained from the authors' survey of the literature. Figures 1 and 2 summarize the results obtained from over three hundred rats and four hundred electrode placements in which both the histological and behavioral data were judged to be reliable by a set of explicit criteria.

Even a casual inspection of the figures reveals that with the exception of the anterior and ventromedial hypothalamic nuclei, the sites eliciting eating, drinking and gnawing coexist with the sites that elicit only non-specific exploratory behavior. It should also be indicated that many of these latter electrodes were found to support high rates of self-stimulation and in some instances higher rates than electrodes (in the same animal) that did elicit specific stimulus-bound behavior. Furthermore, it was not possible to distinguish the sites that elicited eating from those eliciting drinking or gnawing. Feeding and drinking points were found in the posterior hypothalamic region previously associated with the elicitation of male copulatory behavior (Caggiula, 1970; Caggiula and Hoebel, 1966). The converse is also true as Caggiula (1970) has noted that hypothalamic electrodes located rostral to the posterior hypothalamus can elicit sexual behavior. Also, elicitation of sexual behavior reported earlier by Vaughan and Fisher (1962) was attributed to the 'anterior dorsolateral hypothalamus'. Although the present investigators have not explored extensively beyond the limits of the hypothalamus, stimulus-bound eating and drinking have been elicited from the medial portions of the ventral thalamic nucleus. Other investigators have also reported

Figure 1 The location of electrodes which elicited eating, drinking or gnawing behavior. (Except in a few instances in which no attempt was made to modify the behavior, each electrode elicited at least two of these behaviors)

numerous extrahypothalamic sites capable of eliciting eating (cf. review by Morgane and Jacobs, 1969, pp. 153–71). The data have forced us to conclude that within the hypothalamus, discrete anatomical regions cannot be found to correlate with the elicitation of any of the behaviors studied.

We have made electrolytic lesions at critical regions which would disrupt pathways to the brain stem from the hypothalamic

E. S. Valenstein, V. C. Cox and J. W. Kakolewski 453

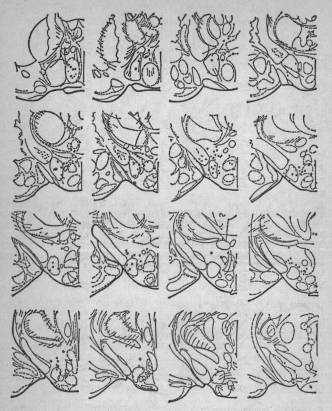

Figure 2 The location of electrodes which did not elicit eating, drinking, or gnawing. (Stimulation at these sites evoked 'Locomotor exploratory behavior' and, in the majority of cases tested, animals self-stimulated)

electrode sites. This work is only in the preliminary stages, but it appears that lesions in the ventral tegmental area of Tsai can significantly reduce stimulus-bound eating and drinking. It is important to note that these lesions may not interfere with normal eating or drinking and in those cases in which two bilaterally placed electrodes both elicited stimulus-bound behavior, unilateral midbrain lesions may disrupt behavior produced by only one of the electrodes. Figure 3 depicts an electrode site and the lesions that disrupted the stimulus-bound eating and drinking it elicited. The fact that such lesions are effective suggests, at the very least, that brain stem structures are participating in the process. Most interesting are the cases of the unilateral disruption of stimulus-bound eating and drinking. In these instances the animals are not in a state of general debilitation (their appearance, general behavior and growth curves confirm this), and the eating and drinking responses have not been impaired. It is important to consider the implications of why these animals do not eat or drink in response to hypothalamic stimulation. Among the interpretations available is the possibility that stimulation of hypothalamic sites produces hunger only in concert with brain stem structures (in which case brain stem structures may prove to be equally effective for producing these effects) or that hypothalamic stimulation achieves its results because it has the capability of activating brain stem motor pathways. The second possibility will be considered further at a later point in this discussion.

It is possible that functionally discrete systems may be inter-digitated in the hypothalamus, but the electrical stimulation evidence does not provide strong support for this view (Valenstein, Cox and Kakolewski, 1969b). An argument often mustered in support of interdigitation of functionally specific systems is based on the elicitation of eating and drinking by chemical stimulation of the hypothalamus (Grossman, 1962a, 1962b; Miller, 1965). The fact that adrenergic substances elicit eating and cholinergic[4] compounds elicit drinking when administered via the same hypothalamic cannula has been viewed as strong presumptive evidence for the existence of pharmacologically coded discrete systems that are in close proximity. However, a great deal of controversy surrounds the interpretation of these effects. The evidence is not clear, for example, that the site of application is the site of action of these chemicals. The cannula sites that yield drinking in response

4. Most studies have used Carbachol (carbamylcholine) as a cholino-mimetic substance, but this presents several problems. The cholinomimetic action of this substance occurs at very low dose levels, larger doses have other effects including changes in membrane permeability, elevation of adrenalin and noradrenalin levels, changes in blood vessel size, nicotinic action and nonspecific changes resulting from local irritation (cf. reviews by Krnjevic, 1965; Rand and Stafford, 1967).

to cholinomimetic stimulation are widespread (Fisher and Coury, 1964) and the possibility of diffusion from the brain to the ventricles or vice versa remains unresolved (Chiaraviglio and Taleisnik, 1969; Fisher and Levitt, 1967; Gloor, 1969; Routtenberg, 1967). The delay in the initiation of drinking and eating following application of cholinomimetic and adrenergic compounds suggests the possibility of secondary effects because it is known that these compounds diffuse very rapidly. Furthermore, a subsequent report by Booth (1967) claimed that adrenergic stimulation is most effective in the preoptic and lateral septal areas. It is not apparent at this time, therefore, whether the chemical stimulation evidence supports a position of anatomically discrete or interdigitated areas.

Work in our laboratory further complicates interpretation of chemical stimulation effects. It was observed that picking up rats and replacing them in their home cages elicits a high incidence of preening, drinking and eating, usually in that order. While the quantities of food and water consumed are considerably less, the latencies to drinking and eating are comparable to those observed with chemical stimulation. In this context it may be important to note that in the rat, where chemical stimulation is most effective, non-specific activation has a high probability of producing eating and drinking. Consequently the possibility must be considered that adrenergic and cholinergic stimulation may exert their influence by selectively sustaining eating or drinking rather than eliciting these responses.

In other species eating and drinking appear to be difficult to elicit with chemical stimulation, and cholinergic compounds may induce quite different responses. For example, Glickman[5] has not observed any drinking in the gerbil following carbachol administration, but the prepotent 'foot thumping' response can be elicited frequently. Many similar examples could be provided which suggest that the cholinergic compounds may elicit prepotent responses in a given species rather than drinking (cf. Myers and Sharpe, 1968, p. 988). Cholinergic stimulation has even been reported to inhibit drinking in monkeys (Sharpe and Myers, 1969). While it is necessary to be cautious in interpreting such results because of the probability of dose-specific responses, it is

5. S. E. Glickman, personal communication, September 1969.

a distinct possibility that 'cholinergic drinking' is induced by a motivation state other than thirst. Supporting this possibility are the reports (Cicero and Myers, 1969; Gandelman, Panksepp and Trowill, 1968) that the fluid preferences of water-deprived animals and the animals exhibiting 'cholinergic drinking' may be quite different. It should be emphasized that the concept of a pharmacological coding of functionally discrete systems has been supported primarily by data restricted to eating and drinking in the rat. No one has been bold enough to extend these results, by analogy, to include a similar coding of the neural circuits underlying gnawing, copulation, grooming, stalking-attack, hoarding, tail preening and the numerous other elicited behaviors that have been reported.

Response determinants

Although anatomical location does not provide a good indication of the behavior which will be elicited, an examination of the data obtained from a large number of animals suggests an alternative hypothesis. The authors have observed that in those cases in which two electrodes in one animal both elicit stimulus-bound behavior, it is highly probable that the behavior will be the same in quality even though the anatomical location of the electrodes may be widely disparate. This was true of animals that exhibited only one behavior initially, such as drinking, eating, or wood gnawing, as well as animals that exhibited two or more behaviors from the same electrode. On occasion animals exhibited uncommon stimulus-bound behavior as, for example, food shuffling with the forepaws or preening of the tail, and these relatively rare behaviors also tended to be displayed from both electrodes even though their hypothalamic location was quite different. Figure 3 depicts several such cases. We would not argue that this is always the case, but it does appear that the stimulus-bound behavior expressed is determined, in part, by some characteristic of an animal which makes that particular response prepotent, rather than by specific anatomic site.

Valenstein, Cox and Kakolewski (1969b) and others have observed instances where two electrodes in a given animal may elicit different behaviors, but it is possible that at least some of these may result from the testing methods employed. A study,

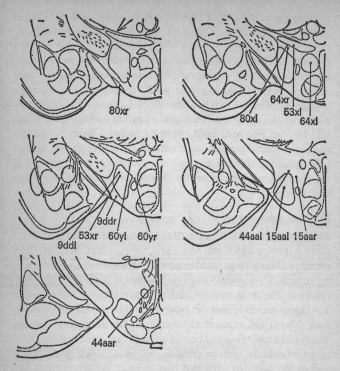

behavior: eating (e), drinking (d), gnawing (g), and tail preening (t)

animal	left (l) electrode	right (r) electrode
53x	strong d	strong d
60y	intermediate e+d	intermediate e+d
15aa	intermediate e	intermediate e
80x	strong d	strong d
44aa	intermediate g	strong g
64x	strong d	strong d
9dd	strong t	intermediate t

Figure 3 Examples of cases in which different electrode sites in the same animal elicited the same behavior

still in progress, illustrates the possible relevance of special 'training'. Animals which initially exhibited only one stimulus-bound behavior have been compared following two different training procedures. Half of the animals received a large number of tests with only the one relevant goal object present, while the other animals were placed in the test chamber an equivalent period of time, but received no additional stimulation experience. Both groups were then stimulated in the absence of their preferred goal object until a second stimulus-bound behavior pattern emerged. Following the appearance of a second behavior, the animals were tested in a competitive situation with both goal objects present. The animals that had received the additional stimulation experience with only the preferred goal object available exhibited a stronger preference for the first behavior and displayed the second behavior relatively infrequently. It would appear, therefore, that the estimate of specificity of a stimulus-bound behavior pattern may be influenced by the amount of restricted experience provided prior to competitive tests with multiple goal objects.

Ethological considerations

The behaviors elicited by hypothalamic stimulation appear to be well-established motor responses that are especially significant to the animal and are often species-specific. This has become even more evident as a result of some recent collaborative work with A. G. Phillips (Phillips, Cox, Kakolewski and Valenstein, 1969). The subjects were rats with implanted electrodes located at different sites throughout the hypothalamus (see Figure 4). These animals were tested in a Plexiglas chamber in which photocells were located close to either end of the chamber. If the animal activated the photocells on one end (*on* side), it received continuous hypothalamic stimulation until the photocell beam on the other end (*off* side) was interrupted and the stimulus was terminated. The animals learned rapidly to self-stimulate and control the duration of stimulation by running back and forth. After they had learned to self-stimulate, a pile of assorted objects, consisting of food pellets, rubber erasers, wooden dowel sticks and molding strips, was placed in the *on* side of the chamber. In a short time, all the animals that had self-stimulated reliably (nineteen out of twenty-two) regularly picked up both the edible and inedible objects and carried them to the opposite side where they were deposited as soon as the stimulus terminated. The behavior was clearly stimulus-bound as animals never carried objects when they

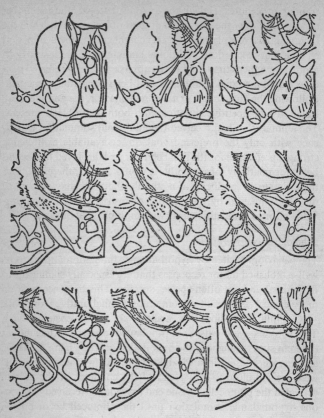

Figure 4 The location of electrodes which elicited carrying behavior (filled circles) and the three placements which did not support reliable self-stimulation or object carrying (filled triangles). (Reprinted with permission from an article by A. G. Phillips, V. C. Cox, J. W. Kakolewski and E. S. Valenstein published in *Science*, 1969, vol. 166.)

were not stimulated. Animals that had never exhibited any specific stimulus-bound behavior, such as gnawing or eating, carried objects as frequently as those that had, and they did not differ in their choice of objects. Animals deprived of food and tested when hungry self-stimulated at higher rates and consequently carried back more objects per unit of time, but they did not increase the relative preference for edible items.

Important points are illustrated by several extensions of the study of elicited object carrying. We divided the *on* side of the chamber in half, lengthwise, with a Plexiglas partition (illustrated in Figure 5). The animals were tested first without objects and could self-stimulate by entering the *on* side of the chamber either to the right or left of the partition. Objects were then placed in the less preferred side, and the data, which are depicted in Figure 6, indicate that all the animals significantly increased their preference for the side providing an opportunity to carry back objects. Therefore, object carrying is another behavior which can be elicited from widely distributed hypothalamic sites, and, in common with stimulus-bound eating, drinking, gnawing, sexual behavior, etc. the performance of object carrying during stimulation is reinforcing. Should we now add another specific drive system to our hypothalamic lists?

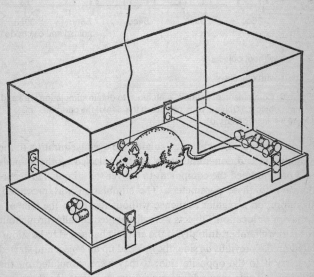

Figure 5 Illustration of rat carrying a wooden dowel stick from stimulation (right) to non-stimulation (left) side of test chamber. (Animal had choice of receiving hypothalamic stimulation with or without an opportunity to carry objects)

E. S. Valenstein, V. C. Cox and J. W. Kakolewski 461

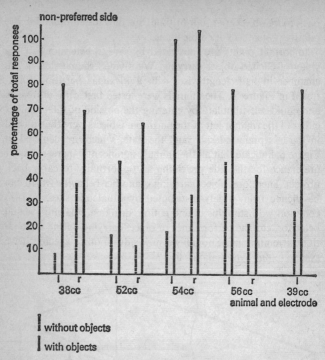

Figure 6 Comparison of animals' preference to obtain stimulation with and without objects. (Objects were placed on the side of the partition – cf. Figure 5 – least preferred)

In a subsequent study we calculated the average duration of the stimulation and non-stimulation periods selected by the animals and programmed the equipment to deliver the stimulus in accordance with these parameters. The stimulation was presented, therefore, on a regular sequence without regard to the animal's behavior or location. Objects were distributed equally throughout the entire chamber. Initially, if the animals happened to be stimulated on the previous *on* side, they picked up an object and started to carry it to the opposite side; if they were stimulated on the previous *off* side they seldom picked up an object. As there was no consistent relationship between the animal's location and the stimulus onsets and offsets, the carrying of objects was terminated within several minutes. It was clear that stimulation by itself was not sufficient to elicit object carrying. Only when the stimulation had some regular relation to the animal's behavior and/or the spatial arrangement of the environment was object carrying observed.

Two other facets of this study should be mentioned to complete the picture. A group of rats were reared in the authors' laboratory on a liquid diet from birth. Hypothalamic electrodes were implanted in the mature animals and tests with wooden objects in the Plexiglas chamber were administered. These animals, which had had no contact with manipulable objects other than their own bodies and feces, carried objects as efficiently as did the normally reared animals. It would appear that very little, if any, specific experience with manipulable objects is required for the display of this behavior when the stimulus conditions are appropriate. Roberts and Bergquist (1968) arrived at a similar conclusion with respect to the elicitation of attack behavior by cats, which had been reared without contact with other cats. Glickman and Schiff (1967) have reviewed other evidence that some responses may be organized in a 'preformed' state. In contrast, guinea pigs, which we have reared under normal laboratory conditions with food pellets available, self-stimulated by running back and forth in the test chamber, but they never carried objects although they were observed eating while being stimulated.

It is well known that rats carry objects in situations related to hoarding, nest building and retrieving of young. They also carry objects that have no obvious utility at all. The 'pack' or 'trade' rat (*Neotoma cinerea occidentalis*), for example, may even leave behind an object it had been carrying in favor of a more desirable shiny object. Under natural conditions, whether engaged in food hoarding or various aspects of maternal behavior, the transporting of objects is invariably from a more open and vulnerable location to one that is relatively familiar and protected. Eibl-Eibesfeldt (1961) has stressed the fact that establishment of a home or sleeping site in a new environment was necessary before carrying behavior was displayed.

Object carrying by the rat may be incorporated into more complicated behavior patterns that serve the purposes of specific motivational states, but it can be studied as a basic response unit divorced from other biological need states. In contrast, the guinea pig does not possess a basic carrying pattern, probably because it uses natural burrows rather than building nests and does not carry its young, which are born very mature. Object carrying can be elicited by stimulation of widely disparate hypothalamic sites in the rat, but not unless the stimulation is presented under spatial conditions which are consistent with the natural environmental relations that elicit carrying. Taken together, these results stress the importance of viewing the behavior elicited by hypothalamic stimulation in terms of biologically essential behavior, species-specific response patterns, and the environmental conditions which normally elicit them in an aroused animal. At this juncture, the collection of relevant ethological information pertinent to the species-specific responses elicited by stimulation is likely to prove more fruitful than restricting our interpretation to presumed motivational states related to biological needs.

A new look at the hypothalamus

In the cases of stimulus-bound eating, drinking, or gnawing, we have argued that hypothalamic stimulation does not create hunger, thirst, or gnawing drives, but seems to create conditions which excite the neural substrate underlying well-established response patterns ('fixed action patterns'). Discharging this sensitized or excited substrate is reinforcing and it can provide the motivation to engage in instrumental behavior which is rewarded by the opportunity to make the response. When contact with an external goal object such as food or water is necessary to make the response, the behavior was classified as stimulus bound, but, as was indicated, locomotion and bodily oriented activities in response to stimulation could just as appropriately be considered stimulus bound. Furthermore, the feedback associated with the execution of this consummatory response is reinforcing in addition to any reinforcement produced directly by the stimulation. Our data obtained from the study of object carrying are similar to the earlier report by Mendelson (1966) that rats which display stimulus-bound eating prefer the combination of food and brain stimulation to brain stimulation alone. It is concluded, therefore, that the brain stimulation does not fully activate all the neural circuits underlying reinforcement. It is clear that the feedback, which is a concomitant of the response, adds to the strength of the reinforcement. It is maintained that the execution of the elicited response is reinforcing, not because it decreases some 'hypothalamic drive state' but rather as a consequence of the discharge of the excited substrate underlying the response. A similar concept was advanced earlier by Craig (1918) and Glickman and Schiff (1967). Preliminary lesion data have suggested that the neural substrate for these prepotent responses is likely to be in the brain stem, as disruption of descending pathways from the hypothalamus interferes with the elicitation of stimulus-bound eating and drinking.

Hypothalamic stimulation does not activate only one specific behavior pattern. The stimulation seems to excite the substrate for a group of responses that in a given species are related to a common state. We are not suggesting that any elicited consummatory response may substitute for any other, but rather that the states induced by hypothalamic stimulation are not sufficiently specified to exclude the possibility of response substitution. Von Holst and Von Saint Paul (1963), for example, referred to these general states elicited by stimulation as 'moods' and reported:

With a single mood are associated several behavioral elements, which thus reveal an internal relationship. Thus, spontaneous crowing, a general expression of masculine self-confidence, very often follows stimulus-bound 'wing scratching' (Kratzfuss), or calling a hen to the nest, or threatening a rival or pecking (p. 10).

It should be noted that these behaviors do not involve the same motor elements. We have commented extensively about the possibility of a wide variety of appetitive behaviors, not just oral responses, being elicited from the same electrode. The response that is elicited first appears to reflect a prepotency characteristic of the individual animal and species. Our evidence suggests that perhaps as a result of the reinforcement accompanying the execution of the response, the association between the stimulation and the response may be strengthened as a by-product of repetition.

The present interpretation of elicited behavior emphasizes the motor system and reinforcement produced by the execution of a consummatory response. We are suggesting that the performance of a consummatory act, during hypothalamic stimulation or natural motivational state, is reinforcing quite apart from its subsequent biological consequences or the incentive properties of the goal object. In an earlier publication (Valenstein, 1966), the 'immediate reinforcement' produced by afferent neural patterns resulting from external stimulation was stressed. This 'direct' activation of the reinforcing brain area was postulated as a mechanism for the fact that the motivational consequences of stimuli (e.g. food) do not always depend on feedback from the biological consequences of interaction with the stimulus (e.g. digestion and utilization). At that time, it was suggested that the main function of 'drive states' was to act as 'gating mechanisms' which direct afferent neural impulses and thereby determine their ability to activate reinforcing neural areas. The present position, which stresses feedback accompanying the execution of responses, is meant to supplement rather than replace this view.

References

BOOTH, D. A. (1967), 'Localization of the adrenegic feeding system in the rat diencephalon', *Sci.*, vol. 158, pp. 515–16.

CAGGIULA, A. R., and HOEBEL, B. G. (1966), '"Copulation-reward site" in the posterior hypothalamus', *Sci.*, vol. 153, pp. 1284–5.

CAGGIULA, A. R. (1970), 'Analysis of the copulation-reward properties of posterior hypothalamic stimulation in rats', *J. compar. physiol. Psychol.*, vol. 70, pp. 399–412.

CHIARAVIGLIO, E., and TALEISNIK, S. (1969), 'Water and salt intake induced by hypothalamic implants of cholinergic and adrenergic agents', *Amer. J. Physiol.*, vol. 216, pp. 1418–22.

CICERO, T. J., and MYERS, R. D. (1969), 'Preference-aversion functions for alcohol after cholinergic stimulation of the brain and fluid deprivation', *Physiol. Behav.*, vol. 4, pp. 559–62.

COONS, E. E., LEVAK, M., and MILLER, N. E. (1965), 'Lateral hypothalamus: Learning of food-seeking response motivated by electrical stimulation', *Sci.*, vol. 150, pp. 1320–21.

COX, V. C., and VALENSTEIN, E. S. (1969), 'Effects of stimulation intensity on behavior elicited by hypothalamic stimulation', *J. compar. physiol. Psychol.*, vol. 69, pp. 730–33.

CRAIG, W. (1918), 'Appetites and aversions as constituents of instincts', *Biol. Bull.*, vol. 34, pp. 91–107.

EIBL-EIBESFELDT, I. (1961), 'The interactions of unlearned behavior patterns and learning in mammals', in J. F. Delafresnaye (ed.), *Brain Mechanisms and Learning*, Charles C. Thomas.

FISHER, A. E., and COURY, J. N. (1964), 'Chemical tracing of neural pathways mediating the thirst drive', in M. J. Wayner (ed.), *Thirst*, Macmillan.

FISHER, A. E., and LEVITT, R. A. (1967), 'A reply to Routtenberg', *Sci.* vol. 157. pp. 839–41.

GALLISTEL, C. R. (1969), 'Self-stimulation: failure of pretrial stimulation to affect rats' electrode preference', *J. compar. physiol. Psychol.*, vol. 69, pp. 722–9.

GANDELMAN, R., PANKSEPP, J., and TROWILL, J. (1968), 'Preference behavior differences between water deprivation-induced and carbachol-induced drinkers', *Communc. behav. Biol.*, vol. 1, pp. 341–6.

GLICKMAN, S. E., and SCHIFF, B. B. (1967), 'A biological theory of reinforcement', *Psychol. Rev.*, vol. 74, pp. 81–109.

GLOOR, P. (1969), 'Chemical mechanisms in the hypothalamus mediating eating and drinking in the monkey', *Ann. New York Acad. Sci.*, vol. 157, pp. 918–33.

GROSSMAN, S. P. (1962a), 'Direct adrenergic and cholinergic stimulation of hypothalamic mechanisms', *Amer. J. Physiol.*, vol. 202, pp. 872–82.

GROSSMAN, S. P. (1962b), 'Effects of adrenergic and cholinergic blocking agents on hypothalamic mechanisms', *Amer. J. Physiol.*, vol. 202, pp. 1230–36.

HOLST, E., VON, and SAINT PAUL, U., VON (1963), 'On the functional organization of drives', *Animal Behav.*, vol. 11, pp. 1–20.

KRNJEVIC, K. (1965), 'Actions of drugs on single neurons in the cerebral cortex', *Brit. med. Bull.*, vol. 21, pp. 10–14.

MENDELSON, J. (1966), 'Role of hunger in T-maze learning for food by rats', *J. compar. physiol. Psychol.*, vol. 62, pp. 341–9.

MILLER, N. E. (1965), 'Chemical coding of behavior in the brain', *Sci.*, vol. 148, pp. 328–38.

MORGANE, P. J. (1961), 'Distinct "feeding" and "hunger" motivating systems in the lateral hypothalamus of the rat', *Sci.*, vol. 133, pp. 887–8.

MORGANE, P. J., and JACOBS, H. L. (1969), 'Hunger and satiety', in G. H. Bourne (ed.), *World Review of Nutrition and Dietetics*, S. Karger.

MYERS, R. D., and SHARPE, L. G. (1968), 'Chemical activation of ingestive and other hypothalamic regulatory mechanisms', *Physiol. behav.*, vol. 3, pp. 987–95.

PHILLIPS, A. G., COX, V. C., KAKOLEWSKI, J. W., and VALENSTEIN, E. S. (1969), 'Object carrying by rats: an approach to the behavior produced by stimulation', *Sci.*, vol. 166, pp. 903–905.

RAND, M. J., and STAFFORD, A. (1967), 'Cholinergic drugs: a cardiovascular effect of choline esters', in W. S. Root and F. G. Hofmann (eds.), *Physiological Pharmacology* vol. 3, (part C), Academic Press.

ROBERTS, W. W., and BERGQUIST, E. H. (1968), 'Attack elicited by hypothalamic stimulation in cats raised in social isolation', *J. compar. physiol. Psychol.*, vol. 66, pp. 590–95.

ROUTTENBERG, A. (1967), 'Drinking induced by carbachol thirst circuit or ventricular modification?', *Sci.*, vol. 157, pp. 838–9.

SHARPE, L. G., and MYERS, R. D. (1969), 'Feeding and drinking following stimulation of the diencephalon of the monkey with amines and other substances', *Exper. Brain Res.*, vol. 8, pp. 295–310.

TENEN, S. S., and MILLER, N. E. (1964), 'Strength of electrical stimulation of lateral hypothalamus, food deprivation, and tolerance for quinine in food', *J. compar. physiol. Psychol.*, vol. 58, pp. 55–62.

VALENSTEIN, E. S. (1966), 'The anatomical locus of reinforcement', in E. Stellar and U. Sprague (eds.), *Progress in Physiological Psychology*, vol. 1, Academic Press.

VALENSTEIN, E. S., COX, V. C., and KAKOLEWSKI, J. W. (1968a), 'Modification of motivated behaviour elicited by electrical stimulation of the hypothalamus', *Sci.*, vol. 159, pp. 1119–21.

VALENSTEIN, E. S., COX, V. C., and KAKOLEWSKI, J. W. (1968b), 'The motivation underlying eating elicited by lateral hypothalamic stimulation', *Physiol. behav.*, vol. 3, pp. 969–71.

VALENSTEIN, E. S., COX, V. C., and KAKOLEWSKI, J. W. (1969a), 'Hypothalamic motivational systems: Fixed or plastic neural circuits?', *Sci.*, vol. 163, p. 1084.

VALENSTEIN, E. S., COX, V. C., and KAKOLEWSKI, J. W. (1969b), 'The hypothalamus and motivated behavior', in J. Tapp (ed.), *Reinforcement*, Academic Press.

VALENSTEIN, E. S., KAKOLEWSKI, J. W., and COX, V. C. (1968), 'A comparison of stimulus-bound drinking and drinking induced by water deprivation', *Communc. behav. Biol.*, vol. 2, pp. 227–33.

VALENSTEIN, E. S., and PHILLIPS, A. G. (1970), 'Stimulus-bound eating and deprivation from prior contact with food pellets', *Physiol. behav.*, vol. 5, pp. 279–82.

VAUGHAN, E., and FISHER, A. E. (1962), 'Male sexual behavior induced by intracranial electrical stimulation', *Sci.*, vol. 137, pp. 758–60.

WISE, R. A. (1968), 'Hypothalamic motivational systems: fixed or plastic neural circuits?', *Sci.*, vol. 162, pp. 377–9.

35 M. Devor, R. Wise, N. W. Milgram and B. G. Hoebel

Physiological Control of Hypothalamically Elicited
Feeding and Drinking

M. Devor, R. Wise, N. W. Milgram and B. G. Hoebel, 'Physiological
control of hypothalamically elicited feeding and drinking', *Journal of
Comparative and Physiological Psychology*, vol. 73, 1970, pp, 226–32.

Hess demonstrated in cats that electrical stimulation of the brain
through implanted electrodes could elicit a variety of behavior
patterns. One example described was bulemia in which the cat
sniffed, searched and upon finding food, ate voraciously (Hess,
1957). Other investigators adopted the stimulation technique as
a means of experimentally exciting the lateral hypothalamus in
rats, a region where stereotaxic lesions had been found to disrupt
feeding. Stimulation of this region in the presence of food induced
feeding behavior that was not reflexive. Stimulated rats would
perform learned responses to obtain food (Coons, Levak and
Miller, 1965), and expressed normal taste preferences (Tenen and
Miller, 1964). It appeared that lateral hypothalamic stimulation
activated the neural substrate controlling natural hunger.

Two sets of recent experiments raise new questions about
hypothalamically elicited behaviors. First, chronic stimulation
experiments have shown that rats can be made to eat three times
their normal daily intake leading to obesity (Hoebel and Thompson, 1969; Steinbaum and Miller, 1965). This calls for experiments to determine whether hypothalamic stimulation bypasses
satiety controls or whether electrically induced behavior is subject
to such factors. Second, elicited eating, although powerful, seems
to be labile; other elicited behaviors such as drinking or gnawing
can emerge in the course of repeated testing with the same
electrode (Valenstein, Cox and Kakolewski, 1968). Will all these
behaviors respond alike to physiological changes or will each
behavior respond in a manner which is physiologically appropriate?

The present experiments dealt with animals that exhibited both
eating and drinking during stimulation through a single electrode.

This made it possible to determine, first whether or not homeo-static mechanisms can inhibit elicited feeding or drinking, and second whether such an effect is specific to the appropriate behavior. If inhibition is specific, then food intake should reduce elicited eating, but not drinking, and water intake should have the converse effect, inhibiting drinking but not eating.

Experiment 1

This experiment examined the effects of food and water intake on the threshold for eliciting eating or drinking.

Method

Subjects. These were seven, male adult Wistar rats, individually housed with food and water present in their home cages at all times. A monopolar electrode made from 0·01 inch diameter, stainless steel wire was implanted into the lateral hypothalamus of each rat. The stereotaxic coordinates used were 1·5 millimeters lateral to the midline, 8·2 millimeters below the superior surface of the skull and 0·8 millimeters posterior to bregma with the incisor bar 3·2 millimeters above the intraural line. A screw in the anterior region of the skull served as the indifferent electrode.

Procedure. All testing was done in a 20 × 10 × 16 inch box with one-way vision glass as the front wall and a mirror as the back wall. Water, when available, was in bottles mounted on each end of the box, and Purina food pellets, when available, were scattered on the floor of the box. Electrical stimulation was delivered by a 60 Hz sinewave stimulator programmed to turn on and off for 20 seconds in alternation.

During preliminary testing, the approximate intensity of stimu-lation necessary to elicit feeding and drinking was determined for each rat by taking daily threshold measurements for both be-haviors. An ascending and descending method of limits technique was used to determine the thresholds while the animals had access to either food or water (Wise, 1968). With this technique, if a rat ate during a train of stimulation, then the current was lowered for the next train. If the animal failed to eat during a train of stimula-tion, then the current was raised for the next train.

During the experimental phase only one elicited behavior was studied on a given day. Each day's test had three parts, initial threshold measurement, intervening stimulation, and final threshold determination, scheduled as shown in Table 1.

Table 1 *Order of Testing in Experiment*

Day	First threshold measurement	Intervening behavior	Second threshold measurement
1	Eating	Eating	Eating
2	Drinking	Drinking	Drinking
3	Eating	Control (Stimulation alone)	Eating
4	Drinking	Control (Stimulation alone)	Drinking
5	Eating	Drinking	Eating
6	Drinking	Eating	Drinking

The initial threshold for a given behavior was measured during ten trains of stimulation. Then fifty trains of stimulation were delivered according to the same procedure in order to maintain ingestion of food or water. As indicated in Table 1, on some days neither food nor water was available as a control for the effects of stimulation alone. On these days stimulation intensity was set at the average of its value on the previous days of eating or drinking tests. Finally, the animal received ten trains of stimulation in a second threshold test exactly like the first in order to determine the effects of the intervening behavior.

Results and discussion

Inhibition of elicited behaviors. Food or water intake raised the thresholds for eliciting the corresponding behavior as summarized in Figure 1. In every rat food ingestion caused an increase in the threshold for eating, and similarly water increased the threshold for drinking. The control procedure of stimulating the rat without food or water had no effect on the threshold; therefore threshold changes after elicited feeding and drinking were caused by intake between the two threshold tests, not by any artifact of stimulation itself. Table 2 presents the data for individual rats.

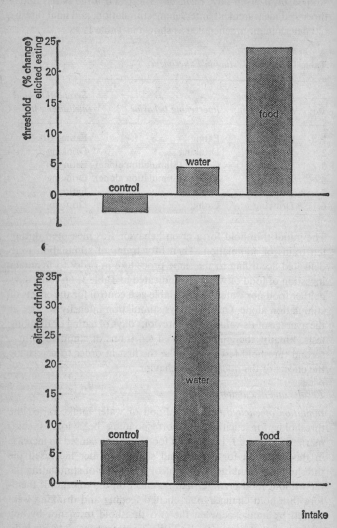

Figure 1 Mean changes in electrical thresholds for eliciting eating (top) and drinking (bottom) after intake of food, water or neither as a control. (Food intake affects elicited eating; water intake affects elicited drinking.)

Table 2 *Percentage Change in Threshold for Eliciting Eating and Drinking*

Rat No.	After water intake	After food intake	After stimulation alone (Control)
Per cent change in eating threshold			
1	− 1·9	+26·0	+0·4
2	+11·3	+22·1	−4·5
3	0·0	+ 8·3	−4·2
4	+ 8·8	+27·3	−3·0
5	+17·1	+26·4	+1·0
6	− 1·1	+13·3	−6·1
7	− 2·0	+47·3	−2·1
Per cent change in drinking threshold			
1	+25·2	+ 7·3	+16·1
2	+44·3	+ 8·1	+15·4
3	+23·8	+ 9·4	− 5·0
4	+32·5	− 1·6	+ 4·9
5	+18·6	− 6·1	0·0
6	+42·1	+20·8	+ 1·1
7	+56·6	+ 5·0	+12·7

Specific inhibition. Water intake during the time between threshold tests had no consistent effect on the threshold for elicited eating, and similarly food intake did not affect the drinking threshold (Figure 1). Thus the inhibition of elicited behavior was specific to the appropriate consummatory response. It appears that the neural mechanisms which elicit feeding or drinking in response to stimulation are subject to the same specific inhibitory factors that control normal ingestion.

Experiment 2

Instead of examining thresholds, this experiment was designed to measure changes in the amount of elicited feeding and drinking following food and water intake. The experimental design is built on the finding that stimulation which initially elicits just feeding or just drinking will usually elicit both behaviors at the same current intensity if testing is continued daily. The emergence of a second behavior occurs even though the initially preferred stimulus object is not removed (Milgram, Devor and Hoebel, 1970). After several days of testing, the amounts of eating and drinking that are elicited become consistent in each rat. These stable levels of intake provide a baseline for studying manipulations of both behaviors elicited from a single electrode at a single current level.

Method

Subjects. The subjects were six Sherman albino female rats and four Long-Evans hooded females with lateral hypothalamic electrodes. Electrodes were 0·009 in platinum 20 per cent iridium wire insulated except for about 0·5 millimeters of the sharpened tip. They were implanted 6·0 millimeters anterior to the intraural line, 1·75 millimeters lateral to the midsagittal sinus and 7·3 millimeters below the dural surface with the surface of the skull perpendicular to the electrode path. Following surgery, the animals lived in individual cages with food, water and a block of wood continually present.

Procedure. In the testing apparatus food pellets, water and wood were placed at the opposite end from a lever which triggered in individual cages with food, water and a block of wood con-stimulation. The rat initiated the current by pressing the lever. This arrangement insured that the animal was always equidistant from each of the stimulus objects whenever the current came on. Stimulation consisted of 0·1 millisecond pulses at 100 Hz delivered through an isolation transformer at intensities between 0·1 and 0·4 mA.

Five days or more after surgery the animals were trained to press the lever for self-stimulation. Each daily test began with 15 minutes of self-stimulation for 0·5 second stimulation trains which was done as part of another experiment. For the remainder of the test the food, water and wood were introduced and each bar press delivered 20-second non-overlapping stimulation trains. A session ended when the rat had initiated 60 trains. A practice session was given to each rat daily until there was relatively little day to day variation in the amount of feeding and drinking during the session. In the subsequent experimental tests, measurements were made of food intake, water intake and weight of chewed-off wood after the first 30 stimulations and then again after the last 30. Each animal was tested on at least 4 days. The purpose was to determine whether intake during the first half of the session influenced the amount of intake during the second half.

Results

Stabilization of elicited behaviors. The animals readily learned to press for 20-second trains of pulses. After initial training they consistently pressed, within 5 seconds after termination of a train so that the requisite 60 stimulations occurred within 25 minutes. The responses to food, water and wood changed greatly during the first several sessions. By the time of final testing, all of the animals both ate and drank during hypothalamic stimulation at a given current, even though often only one behavior was apparent initially. The stabilized ratio of eating to drinking was very different from animal to animal. Gnawing, unlike feeding and drinking, gradually disappeared in the two cases in which it was initially seen, therefore only feeding and drinking were involved in the tests which followed.

Inhibition of elicited behavior. In general, eating reduced subsequent elicited eating, and drinking reduced elicited drinking (Figure 2). All animals that averaged at least 1 gram food intake during the first half of the session ate less during the second half. This is most clearly illustrated on the left hand side of Figure 2 by the rat represented with black triangles. Similarly, whenever the animals drank more than 2 cc of water in the first half of the session, their water intake decreased during the second half as illustrated by the rat with open squares on the right side of Figure 2.

As would be expected if it is actually food and water that is causing the inhibition of subsequent intake, the inhibitory effect is lost at low levels of initial intake. In the cases of very light eating or drinking during the first half of the session, some animals showed a decrease, some an increase, and in others intake remained unchanged. Thus, the strength of the satiety effect was roughly related to the amount ingested. Strongest inhibition of

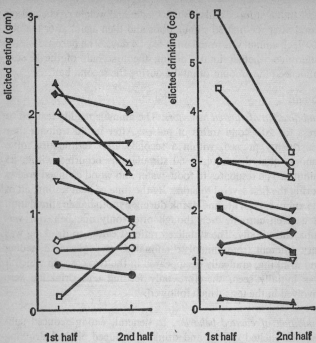

Figure 2 Mean amounts of elicited eating (left) and drinking (right) during the first and second halves of the stimulation session. Each symbol represents an individual rat

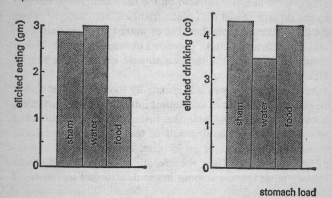

stomach load

Figure 3 The mean effects of sham, water and food loads on elicited eating (top) and drinking (bottom). (Intragastric food loads depress elicited eating but not drinking in animals that do both; water loads depress drinking as opposed to eating)

eating occurred in the animals that ate the most, while strongest inhibition of drinking occurred in the animals that drank the most.

Discussion

In showing that animals that initially only performed one of the behaviors during stimulation would eventually perform the other as well, these experiments confirm the finding of Valenstein, Cox and Kakolewski (1968) that changes can be produced in the behaviors elicited by hypothalamic stimulation. They also confirm the finding of Milgram, Devor and Hoebel (1970) that changes can occur without altering the available stimulus objects. The responses to electrical stimulation of the lateral hypothalamus are not fixed. The present experiment demonstrates that even after stabilization this remains true. The degree to which a rat will display stimulation-elicited eating or drinking depends in part on physiological factors normally controlling hunger and thirst.

Experiment 3

The present authors now ask whether oral factors are necessary for inhibition of elicited intake, or whether food and water administered intragastrically can satiate elicited behaviors.

Method

The procedure was a continuation of Experiment 2, using nine of the same animals. The rats were manually intubed with a French 8 rubber catheter at the beginning of each daily test. On alternate days the rats were sham fed by inserting and withdrawing the empty intragastric tube. On the days of actual loading, 6 rats received 8 cc of egg-milk-sugar diet (Teitelbaum and Campbell, 1968) on two days, and 8 cc of tap water on two days. Three rats were tested in the reverse order with water loads given first and food second. Results were evaluated by comparing the mean elicited intake on days when an animal was stomach loaded with intake on the immediately preceding and following sham days.

Results and discussion

Specific inhibition. Food loads reduced eating in all the rats, but had no consistent effect on drinking. Water loads reduced elicited

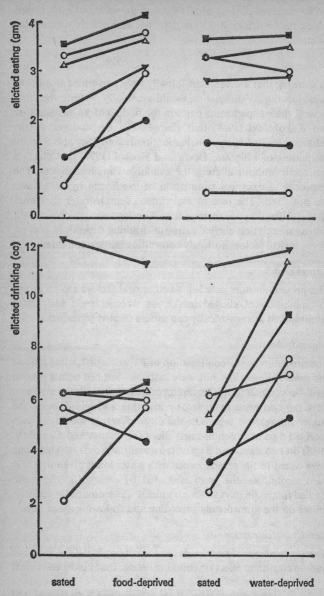

Figure 4 Effects of food or water deprivation on elicited eating and drinking. (Each symbol represents the mean amount of intake for an individual rat that both ate and drank during stimulation)

drinking in all but one rat, without significant effects on eating. Mean results are shown in Figure 4. Inhibition resulting from water was smaller on the average than the food effect, due largely to the one rat which failed to reduce drinking after being water loaded. When this rat was retested with two 8 cc water loads instead of one, it too showed the typical inhibition of elicited drinking.

It is evident that post-ingestional factors were sufficient to inhibit elicited consummatory behavior in the absence of prolonged oral contact with food or water. Even though the rat lacked taste or motor feedback associated with ingestion, the inhibition from food was specific to elicited feeding, and water to drinking.

Experiment 4

The previous experiments have shown that it is possible to selectively inhibit elicited feeding and drinking by food and water intake. This experiment investigated the effect of food and water deprivation.

Method

The subjects were six female rats, five of which had been used in Experiments 2 and 3. The apparatus was modified in that wood was unavailable and the food and water were placed immediately next to the lever which initiated stimulation. The testing procedure was the same as that followed in Experiment 2 except that 23 hours of food or water deprivation preceded half of the sessions. Following a week of daily practice sessions, each animal was tested on nine days of alternating deprivation and ad lib conditions. On the first two deprivation days 3 rats were 23 hours food-deprived and on the other two, 23 hours water-deprived. Three rats were tested in the reverse order.

Results

Food deprivation produced a consistent increase in eating in every animal, but it did not affect elicited drinking in any consistent manner (Figure 4). Similarly water deprivation increased drinking during the session without affecting elicitation of eating. Just as Experiments 1 and 3 demonstrated that elicited eating and drinking can be inhibited selectively, this experiment shows they can be facilitated selectively.

Histological verification

To determine the location of electrode tips, the brains were perfused with physiological saline followed by formalin, cut in frozen sections and stained with cresyl violet. Electrode placements were located in 16 of the 18 rats used in the four experiments. Electrode tips were located in the lateral hypothalamus, lateral to the fornix at the level of the ventromedial nucleus, the same region as shown in a previously published photomicrograph (Hoebel, 1969).

General discussion

The present experiments demonstrate that electrically elicited feeding and drinking are neither immutable nor capricious consequences of brain stimulation but are modified by internal physiological conditions according to homeostatic principles. There were two main results. First, hypothalamical elicited eating, like natural eating, was inhibited by food intake, and elicited drinking, like normal thirst, was reduced by water intake. Second, these effects of ingestion were specific to the appropriate behavior. Excessive food intake or deprivation substantially affected elicited eating without altering drinking; water specifically modified elicited drinking. Apparently the behavior systems excited by hypothalamic activation are under separate physiological control. These results demonstrate a basic similarity between the electrically and the naturally induced behaviors, thereby further supporting the idea that hypothalamic stimulation can trigger neural substrates which regulate normal feeding and drinking.

The findings complement earlier studies showing that chronic stimulation can elicit feeding leading to obesity (Steinbaum and Miller, 1965; Hoebel and Thompson, 1969) or chronic excessive drinking (Mogenson and Stevenson, 1967). It is clear from such studies that hypothalamic stimulation can supersede the level of normal homeostatic control. The present results indicate, however, that stimulation does not bypass such controls, but that satiety factors are manifest at a higher level of intake. The experiments have demonstrated that the particular behavior expressed during stimulation depends in part on the animal's internal state.

It is unlikely that food and water intake simply inhibited a generalized drive or arousal mechanism, for if such were the case then both feeding and drinking would have been depressed simultaneously. The authors conclude instead that food and water exert specific, homeostatically appropriate inhibitory control over hypothalamically elicited food and water intake.

References

COONS, E. E., LEVAK, M., and MILLER, N. E. (1965), 'Lateral hypothalamus: Learning of food-seeking response motivated by electrical stimulation', *Sci.*, vol. 150, pp. 130–21.

HESS, W. R. (1957), *The Functional Organization of the Diencephalon*, J. R. Hughes (ed.), Grune & Stratton.

HOEBEL, B. G. (1969), 'Feeding and self-stimulation', *Ann. New York Acad. Sci.*, vol. 157, pp. 758–78.

HOEBEL, B. G., and THOMPSON, R. D. (1969), 'Aversion to lateral hypothalamic stimulation caused by intragastric feeding or obesity', *J. compar. physiol. Psychol.*, vol. 68, pp. 536–43.

MILGRAM, N. W., DEVOR, M. G., and HOEBEL, B. G. (1970), 'Separate systems controlling hypothalamic elicitation of eating and drinking from the same hypothalamic electrode', paper presented at meeting of the Eastern Psychological Association, April 1970.

MOGENSON, G. J., and STEVENSON, J. A. F. (1967), 'Drinking induced by electrical stimulation of the hypothalamus', *Exper. Neurol.*, vol. 17, pp. 119–27.

STEINBAUM, E. A., and MILLER, N. E. (1965), 'Obesity from eating elicited by daily stimulation of the hypothalamus', *Amer. J, Physiol.*, vol. 208, pp. 1–5.

TEITELBAUM, P., and CAMPBELL, B. A. (1958), 'Ingestion patterns in hyperphagic and normal rats', *J. compar. physiol. Psychol.*, vol. 51, pp. 135–41.

TENEN, S. S., and MILLER, N. E. (1964), 'Strength of electrical stimulation of lateral hypothalamus, food deprivation, and tolerance for quinine in food', *J. compar. physiol. Psychol.*, vol. 58, pp. 55–62.

VALENSTEIN, E. S., COX, V. C., and KAKOWLEWSKI, J. W. (1968), 'Modification of motivated behavior by electrical stimulation of the hypothalamus', *Sci.*, vol. 159, 1119–21.

WISE, R. A. (1968), 'Hypothalamic motivational systems: Fixed or plastic neural circuits?', *Sci.*, vol. 162, pp. 377–9.

36 W. W. Roberts

Are Hypothalamically Motivational Mechanisms Functionally
and Anatomically Specific?

W. W. Roberts, 'Are hypothalamically motivational mechanisms
functionally and anatomically specific?', *Brain, Behavior and
Evolution*, volume, 2, 1969, pp. 317–42.

Introduction

The common assumption that motivational responses elicited by
hypothalamic stimulation are produced by relatively specific and
differentiated neural mechanisms has been severely questioned by
Valenstein, Cox and Kakolewski (1968, 1969, 1970). In its place,
they have marshalled evidence favoring a single non-specific
plastic mechanism capable of producing different and normally
independent responses through learning processes. Their principal evidence has been their finding that performance of eating,
gnawing and drinking induced by electrical stimulation of the
hypothalamus of rats is 'modifiable' by experience under certain
conditions. They have also reported that mixtures of two or
three responses are much more frequently elicited than pure
responses after 'training', and that the anatomical zones where
the three responses are elicited are not differentiated from each
other. While the latter findings are consistent with their position,
they do not rule out the alternative possibility of separate but
spatially intermeshed mechanisms.

Although Valenstein's *et al.* data bear directly on only three
responses in one species, they and others (e.g. Doty, 1969; Stutz,
Butcher and Rossi, 1969; Wise, 1968) have often interpreted it in
much broader and less specific terms, and their 1969 and 1970
papers cited anecdotal evidence from other laboratories suggesting that the hypothalamic mechanisms for male copulation and
other centrally induced behaviors may similarly lack functional

1. The assistance of Andrew P. Phalen and Eunice K. Roberts is grate-
fully acknowledged.

or anatomical specificity. They have also argued strongly against alternative explanations of their findings in terms of overlapping or intermeshed mechanisms that normally function independently, but are artificially excited together by the nonspecific action of electrical stimulation.

The question of the specificity of hypothalamic behavior mechanisms enters importantly into the planning of experimental strategy and tactics, the interpretation of research data, and the formulation of general theories of hypothalamic functions in motivation. The present writer's bias favors the presumption of neural specificity in the absence of unequivocal contrary evidence, partly because of the unfortunate consequences of Lashley's law of equipotentiality, which discouraged many researchers from investigating functional specificity and localization in the cortex for a couple of decades (Milner, 1969), and partly because of the powerful analyses that have often resulted when research has been strongly influenced by assumptions of functional and anatomical specificity, as in Hubel and Wiesel's remarkable analysis of hierarchical detection mechanisms in the visual cortex (Hubel, 1967). Improved anatomical specification is needed in neurobehavioral studies to link them more tightly to neurophysiological and neurochemical studies at the cellular level and to resolve contradictions in the swelling literature, but this is likely to be discouraged by neo-Lashleyan views of hypothalamic specificity.

The purposes of the present paper are to discuss some of the special characteristics of electrical stimulation that must be borne in mind in interpreting Valenstein's *et al.* findings, to review some of the clearcut evidence for hypothalamic specificity in species other than the rat, and to present some data from an experimental reexamination of the 'modifiability' phenomenon reported by Valenstein *et al.*

Special properties of electrical stimulation

The initiation of neural activity with localized electrical stimulation differs from normal synaptic excitation in several important respects. Some of these differences limit the inferences that can be drawn, others can cause irrelevant artifacts or side-effects, while still others give stimulation special advantages in the study of certain problems.

Functional nonspecificity

Within the small zone of direct electrical excitation surrounding an electrode tip, the current acts indiscriminately on afferent axons, short-axon interneurons and efferent neurons projecting to other brain areas. Some of these neurons may exert excitatory synaptic effects, others inhibitory effects. A partial degree of specificity is indicated by Porter's (1963) finding that gross electrode current thresholds for axons are lower than for their somas or dendrites, but the thresholds for both effects were close enough so that most supra-threshold stimulation probably produces combined effects. Because of the abnormal mixture of activity within the zone of direct electrical excitation, it is likely that its normal information processing functions are considerably distorted or impaired, but this is probably irrelevant for the relayed effects of the stimulation on the rest of the brain and on behavior, since the direct action of the stimulation on the low threshold efferent axons would produce a strong non-specific efferent discharge regardless of other events within the directly excited zone. This means that electrical stimulation can tell us nothing about the nature of the normal input to the stimulated zone or the information processing that takes place there. It can only disclose the effects of a *general* increase in the output of the zone (Doty, 1969). If the output of the stimulated zone is normally heterogeneous and finely differentiated, a general increase in efferent activity would produce abnormal effects, as humans have reported when stimulated electrically in the sensory systems (Penfield and Jasper, 1954). On the other hand, when the stimulation induces complex responses that closely resemble adaptive species-typical behaviors such as mating, attack, sleep, grooming, or feeding, it is likely that the normal output of the stimulated zone is similar to that induced by the stimulation, and exerts a relatively simple quantitative control over the sensory-motor mechanisms for the behaviors.

Mixed responses. Since independent brain mechanisms often overlap or are closely adjacent, especially in structures as densely packed as the hypothalamus, non-specific electrical stimulation may elicit mixtures of responses that are normally uncorrelated, such as eating and circling to the right, or attacking and grooming, or threatening and mating behavior. There are probably significant species differences in the frequency of such mixtures, since they are appreciably less frequent in the opossum (Roberts, Steinberg and Means, 1967) than they appear to be in the rat (Valenstein, Cox and Kakolewski, 1969; Roberts and Phelan, in preparation). Von Holst and Von Saint Paul (1963) attempted to explain one such mixture in terms of a higher level of brain organization, when they attributed a combination of centrally elicited attack and fleeing in chickens to a superordinate 'enemy response mood'. However, until the possibility of non-specific excitation of independent mechanisms can be ruled out, such broad constructs must remain speculative.

One of the most effective ways to separate multiple responses is to apply a more specific type of stimulation. In our laboratory, we have been using localized radio-frequency diathermic warming because it acts selectively on thermoreceptor neurons in the preoptic and anterior hypothalamic region (Roberts, Bergquist and Robinson, 1969; Roberts and Robinson, 1969). Conventional 60 Hz electrical stimulation of different parts of this region in opossums elicits grooming, male mating behavior, attack, eating, exploration, and escape-like activity, while thermal stimulation applied through the same electrodes induces grooming, a normal heat dissipation response of the opossum, without any of the other responses that are elicited by electrical stimulation. The two response patterns that have the greatest amount of functional and anatomical overlap when stimulation is used, grooming and male mating behavior (Roberts, Steinberg and Means, 1967), can be thus completely dissociated by more specific stimulation. It may be concluded that electrical stimulation gives a false indication of the degree of unity or functional interconnections between mechanisms that are spatially intermeshed or closely adjacent, especially when large bipolar electrodes like those in the diathermic warming experiment are used.

Another method for dissociating multiple unrelated responses elicited by electrical stimulation is the local application of neurohumors and other neurochemicals having relatively specific effects. The eating and drinking that Valenstein, Cox and Kakolewski (1968) and others (Miller, 1960) have often elicited together by electrical stimulation in the hypothalamus of the rat have been experimentally separated by Grossman (1960, 1964), who found that application of cholinergic drugs in the hypothalamus induced drinking and decreased normal hunger, while adrenergic substances applied through the same cannulae induced eating and reduced normal thirst. Further evidence that the hypothalamic mechanisms for hunger and thirst are different is Grossman's finding (1962) that hypothalamic application of cholinergic and adrenergic blocking agents selectively reduced normal thirst and hunger, respectively. Valenstein, Cox and Kakolewski (1970) have expressed a number of reservations regarding this research, but have not offered an explanation of how the several types of double dissociation of eating and drinking could be produced by a single non-specific mechanism.

Blocking or masking of responses. Another consequence of the non-specificity of electrical stimulation is that some elicited responses can be so strong that they prevent or mask the performance of other responses. When the preoptic area and anterior hypothalamus of opossums were warmed, the animals not only increased their grooming, but they also evidenced drowsy relaxation and panting. When 60 Hz electrical stimulation was applied through the same electrodes, neither of the last two responses was ever detected, probably because the relaxation was incompatible with the increased activity and arousal that accompanied all of the electrically induced responses, and because the panting was prevented or undetectable in the presence of the rapid respiration and sniffing that accompanied the increased activity.

Analogous findings have been obtained with diathermic warming of the preoptic and anterior hypothalamic region in cats (Roberts and Robinson, 1969). Electrical stimulation of the region in this species elicited various combinations of locomotion, sniffing, looking around, piloerection, hissing, growling, attack on a rat, jumping, and circling. When diathermic warming was applied through the same electrodes, it produced none of these excited responses, only the behavioral and EEG signs of sleep and, at higher temperatures, panting. Figure 1 compares the location of warming electrodes that were effective and ineffective

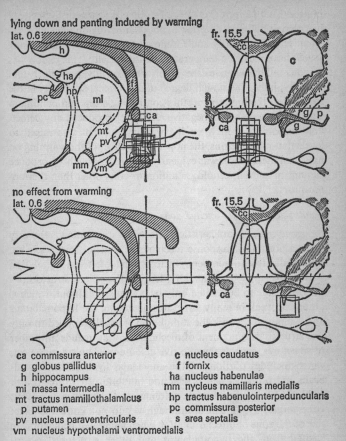

lying down and panting induced by warming

no effect from warming

ca commissura anterior
g globus pallidus
h hippocampus
mi massa intermedia
mt tractus mamillothalamicus
p putamen
pv nucleus paraventricularis
vm nucleus hypothalami ventromedialis

c nucleus caudatus
f fornix
ha nucleus habenulae
mm nycleus mamillaris medialis
hp tractus habenulointerpeduncularis
pc commissura posterior
s area septalis

Figure 1 Location of warming electrodes that caused cats to lie down, fall asleep and pant (at higher temperatures) compared with location of ineffective electrodes. Left diagrams show sagittal section 0·6 mm from midline. Right diagrams show frontal section through plane indicated by dashed line in sagittal diagram, located 15·5 mm anterior to interaural axis. Region of maximal warming enclosed by each electrode shown by 2 x 2 mm squares. For positive cases, electrodes with lowest thresholds denoted by heavy lines, those with medium thresholds by medium lines, and those with highest thresholds by light lines. In the sagittal diagram of ineffective electrodes, the two cases indicated by dotted lines were located 3 mm lateral to the midline. (From Roberts and Robinson, 1969)

in producing panting and sleep. The effective cases were clustered in the preoptic and anterior hypothalamic region where Naka-yana, Hammel, Hardy and Eisenman (1963) and Wit and Wang (1968) have localized temperature-sensitive cells. This region was surrounded by negative cases anteriorly, dorsally, posteriorly and laterally, indicating a high degree of anatomical specificity in the location of the thermoreceptors controlling sleep and panting in cats. Since none of the negative electrodes produced any detect-able responses, even when the warming current was raised to levels that made lesions, the non-specific effect of the warming on neuronal metabolism was evidently not great enough to produce significant suprathreshold excitation in units other than thermo-receptors.

Small size of directly excited zone

A second major characteristic of electrical stimulation is the very limited portion of response mechanisms that it directly excites. This results from a number of factors. First, electrical stimulation is typically applied unilaterally, leaving the paired structure on the other side to be excited only by commissural input, which is absent or weak in many structures, including the hypothalamus and thalamus. Second, the stimulation is usually applied to only one structural component of mechanisms that include a number of structures, such as the affective defense mechanism in the cat, which includes portions of the amygdala, hypothalamus, mid-brain and probably neocortical and hindbrain structures (Bard, 1928, 1950; Fernandez de Molina and Hunsperger, 1959; Hunsperger, 1956). Third, although we do not know the exact size of the zone of direct excitation when integrated behaviors are elicited from the hypothalamus and other structures, neuro-physiological studies of cortical and subcortical stimulation (Schlag and Villablanca, 1968; Stoney, Thompson and Asanuma, 1968) and indirect evidence from elicited behavior studies (Roberts, Steinberg and Means, 1967) suggest that it is usually small enough that it excites only a fraction of the neurons in a given component of a behavior mechanism. Not only is the zone of electrical excitation small, but the current density within the zone decreases relatively rapidly as a function of distance from the electrode. For a near-spherical monopolar electrode, current density declines inversely as the square of the distance from the center of the pole, and for bipolar stimulation, current density at a distance much greater than the interpolar distance declines inversely as the cube of the distance, while at closer distances (which are more relevant for the zone of direct electrical excitation), the function approaches the inverse square law. Thus, within the small zone of direct electrical excitation surrounding either monopolar or bipolar electrodes, the neurons closest to the electrode probably contribute much more to the output to other brain areas than the neurons on the fringe.

Incomplete responses. The smallness of the zone of direct electrical excitation has a number of special consequences that must be taken into consideration in the interpretation of stimulation data. One of these effects is wide variation between electrodes in the completeness of elicited response patterns. This is illustrated in Figure 2, which is based on our own data from the opossum (Roberts, Steinberg and Means, 1967) and Hess and Brugger's (1943) data from the cat. Each response pattern includes 3–5 different response elements that were elicited in different combinations by different electrodes. Some electrodes produced complete patterns, but the majority evoked different incomplete combinations that are indicated by the placement of Xs beneath the bar graphs. The combinations shown in this figure include almost all possible subsets, except for those that are physically impossible or difficult. This inter-electrode variation cannot be attributed to individual differences between animals because different combinations of elements were often obtained from different electrodes in the same animal, and because a statistical analysis showed that the inter-electrode variation within animals did not differ appreciably from the variation between animals.

The high frequency of incomplete patterns gives additional support to the conclusion that stimulation in the hypothalamus usually excites only a small fraction of the neurons in a given mechanism. It also indicates that there are relatively few if any interconnections between the neurons controlling the different elements of these responses within the hypothalamus or in its efferent pathways. Thus, the tendency of these elements to occur

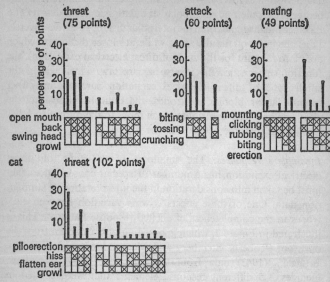

Figure 2 Percentage of electrode points that elicited different combinations of elements of the mating, threat and attack patterns in the opossum (Roberts, Steinberg and Means, 1967) and of the threat pattern in the cat (Hess and Brugger, 1943). Response elements are listed in descending order of frequency

together in normal behavior must result from some other mode of integration, such as a common physical stimulus, as may be the case with the thermoregulatory behaviors (Roberts, Bergquist and Robinson, 1969) or a common neuronal input from other central structures or peripheral receptors.

The more sequentially organized responses of eating and drinking have not been tested in sufficient detail to determine whether they are ever elicited in incomplete form. However, we have had a number of rats that did not gnaw on wooden boards, but gnawed persistently on food pellets and allowed most of the crumbs to fall out of their mouths, suggesting that perhaps the initial biting component was induced without the later elements of mastication and swallowing. If later components of sequentially organized responses and their rewarding properties can be potentiated without a change in initial components, it could explain why occasional responses are very slow to emerge, even in the apparent absence of interfering responses. In such cases, the development of consistent performance of the response sequence would be delayed until the animals happened to experience the later components of the sequence during stimulation (perhaps in the course of oral investigatory responses or normal eating and drinking), which would then reinforce the full consummatory sequence and preceding instrumental responses.

Unilateral responses. Another possible effect of the limited area excited by the stimulation is some degree of unilateral dominance in the response or in the goal object stimuli controlling it, as in Macdonnell and Flynn's (1966) study of reflex biting components in hypothalamic attack in cats. They found that unilateral hypothalamic stimulation that elicited integrated biting attack also potentiated mouth orientation and opening reflexes that could not be elicited in the absence of stimulation. The specific sensory fields on the lip where the reflexes were elicited were much larger and more sensitive on the side contralateral to the stimulation, indicating that the neural mechanisms for these components of the biting attack pattern were more strongly excited on one side of the brain than on the other side. This evidence also argues strongly against the possibility that the basic elements of biting attack are learned (Hutchinson and Renfrew, 1966), since such unilaterality and precise differentiation of reflexes is a far more common characteristic of innately organized neurological mechanisms than of learned habits. Our finding that the biting attack response can be elicited in cats raised in isolation from prey objects and other cats (Roberts and Bergquist, 1968) also supports the existence of an innately organized core in biting attack. Valenstein, Cox and Kakolewski (1970) have subsequently obtained similar evidence for object-carrying evoked by hypothalamic stimulation in rats raised on a fluid diet from birth.

Advantage of localized stimulation. Although the relatively localized action of electrical stimulation cannot be expected to mimic precisely the patterns of excitation produced by natural inputs to behavior mechanisms, this need not be viewed as a drawback for all purposes. Analysis of complex brain mechanisms requires that they be broken down into separate components and subcomponents, and the different functions of the individual parts identified. For this purpose, the anatomical specificity of electrical stimulation, which lies intermediate between gross lesion methods and single unit recording, is an advantage. For example, Asanuma and Sakata (1967) have been able to use stimulation of cat's motor cortex with microelectrodes to map specific and differentiated areas only 1·0 mm in diameter controlling stretch reflexes for different foreleg muscles. Another example of the usefulness of electrical stimulation in fractionating behavior mechanisms is the previously discussed incompleteness of many hypothalamic responses, which is significant for concepts of their integrative organization.

Other properties

Two related characteristics of electrical stimulation that often create obvious differences between centrally and normally induced behavior are the abnormally strong activation that higher current levels produce in brain mechanisms (despite the smallness of the directly excited zone), and the suddenness of the onset and termination of stimulation. When we compared normal and centrally elicited mating and attack in opossums (Roberts, Steinberg and Means, 1967), the principal difference was that the centrally induced responses were much stronger, as indicated by shorter latencies, higher intensity, and greater persistence in the face of threat or counter-attack. We have elicited gnawing in some rats that was so intense that the teeth were loosened and the gums bled (Roberts and Carey, 1965). Andersson and McCann (1955) have described centrally elicited drinking in goats that continued until the animals' body weight had increased by 40 per cent, which would be equivalent to 29 quarts for a 150 lb man. Vaughan and Fisher (1962) have reported a similar intensification and reduced satiation of male mating behavior in rats. Against this background of uncommonly strong performance, the sudden onset and offset of stimulation cause centrally induced behavior to be initiated and terminated much more percipitously than normal behavior. This was particularly striking in a study of centrally induced biting attack (Roberts and Kiess, 1964), in which we observed that the stimulated cats stopped attacking rats immediately after the end of the stimulation, while the rats' squealing, struggling, pawing, and occasional biting continued and only gradually diminished in the face of the passivity of the cats.

Conclusions

1. Electrical stimulation of a structure discloses primarily the effects of a non-specific increase in the output from the structure to other brain areas. It tells nothing about the normal input to the structure, and yields only very limited information regarding the organization within the structure.

2. When complex responses that resemble normal species-typical behaviors are induced by electrical stimulation, it may be concluded that efferents from the stimulated zone exert an eliciting or modulating control over the responses. However, when a behavior is not elicited from a structure, it does not necessarily mean that the structure has nothing to do with the behavior. The stimulation may also evoke interfering responses that block performance of the behavior, or, as is probably the case in most parts of sensory and motor systems, a recognizable or 'normal' response may require a differentiated and finely timed pattern of discharge that cannot be produced by electrical stimulation.

3. Because of the special characteristics of electrical stimulation, motivational responses induced by it must unavoidably differ in at least some respects from natural motivational behaviors. It is therefore an oversimplification to ask whether the centrally induced states are or are not 'natural drives'. Instead, the functional properties of centrally and normally induced motivational responses need to be compared in detail to determine where the two are similar and where they differ. When similarities are found, as in the ability to modulate reinforcer effectiveness and the probability of performance of consummatory and instrumental responses (Miller, 1960; Roberts, in press), it may be concluded that efferents of the stimulated structures can act on other parts of the brain to produce those components of natural motivational states, and probably play an important if not exclusive

role in normal temporal modulation of those components. When differences are found, care must be taken to distinguish differences that have a possible functional significance from trivial or artifactual differences that result from the special properties of electrical stimulation. Careful analysis of the former may yield some of our best clues regarding the functions that are not performed by structures efferent to the zone of direct excitation, and therefore may be performed by the structure stimulated (which is 'jammed' or abnormally activated by the stimulation) or by other structures acting in series or parallel with the stimulated region.

Anatomical specificity

Since Dr Valenstein and his coworkers have recently questioned the anatomical specificity of hypothalamic motivational mechanisms in the rat (Valenstein, Cox and Kakolewski, 1968, 1969, 1970), I would like next to review briefly some of the evidence for anatomical specificity in some other species. First, however, it should be pointed out that topographical specificity within the brain is always a matter of relative density, rather than abrupt mosaic-like compartmentalization. In mapping the motor cortex, Woolsey *et al.* (1952) used deep anesthesia to minimize intracortical spread of excitation, but nevertheless found considerable successive overlap between the areas controlling different muscles or muscle groups. In a mapping study more similar to current stimulation research with conscious animals, Penfield and Boldrey (1937) found much more extensive overlap when they stimulated the motor and somatosensory cortex in conscious humans. For example, in their Figure 25, which is a composite of data from a group of patients, 27 per cent of the area for finger movements overlapped with the area for mouth movements, 85 per cent overlapped with the area for arm movements, and 53 per cent overlapped with the area for leg movements. Similar overlap was obtained between other areas in both motor and sensory cortex. Despite this considerable overlap, the classical sequence of motor and sensory representation found in anesthetized animals was generally clear in these conscious humans. In view of the appreciable amount of gross anatomical overlap in the classical motor system, we should take care not to set such unrealistically high standards for topographical differentiation in the small and densely packed hypothalamus that we overlook useful evidence for functional specificity.

In addition, it should be pointed out that the massing of data from different brains, as in Penfield and Boldrey's study and current animal studies of central motivational mechanisms, systematically overestimates the amount of overlap in individual brains, because the variance between brains in morphology and functional organization and the error variance of localization are unavoidably added to the intrinsic scatter present in the individual case. A particularly striking example is Asanuma and Sakata's (1967) fine-grain microelectrode study of the cat's motor cortex, in which individual differences were so large in the location of areas controlling different muscles that composite diagrams would have overestimated the size of the areas 8–10 times, increasing their apparent overlap proportionately. If individual differences in the locations of neuron concentrations controlling several responses are appreciable within a given region, the degree of actual overlap in individual cases could fall considerably below 100 per cent and still yield apparent coextensive overlap in massed group data.

Hypothalamic motivational mechanisms in opossum

The lack of anatomical specificity reported by Valenstein, Cox and Kakolewski (1968, 1969, 1970) for eating, drinking and gnawing in the rat contrasts with numerous earlier studies in the opossum and cat. Figure 3 shows the location of electrodes in the opossum hypothalamus and preoptic region that elicited male mating behavior, biting attack, defensive threat, eating, grooming, exploration and escape-like activity (Roberts, Steinberg and Means, 1967). In the top row, the points that evoked mating are represented by circles of different degrees of complexity, corresponding to the completeness of the response. Negative points are indicated by black dots. The great majority of positive mating points were concentrated in the medial preoptic region shown in the second diagram from the right. The other five planes were almost entirely negative, with only a few scattered points that elicited responses that tended to be weaker or less complete than those obtained in the main cluster. If the second column is

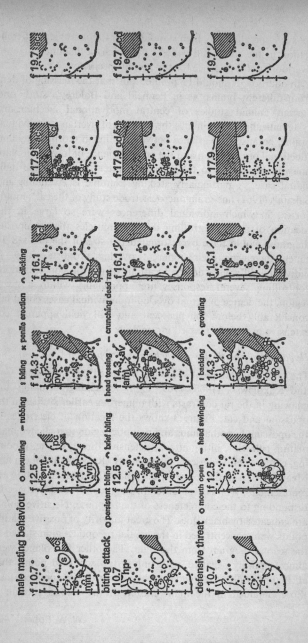

Figure 3 Location of electrodes that elicited motivational and species-typical behaviors in opossum. Plotted on frontal plane diagrams of the hypothalamus and preoptic area located 10·7–19·7 mm anterior to the interaural axis. Negative points are indicated by small, solid circles. (From Roberts, Steinberg and Means, 1967)

○ locomotion, sniffing and looking ✶ sniffing and looking ↟ upward looking and climbing ⇒ pressing against glass cage front

ac commissura anterior
am nucleus anterior medialis thalami
av nucleus anterior ventralis thalami
c nucleus centralis
cd nucleus caudatus
ci capsula interna
d nucleus dorsalis hypothalami
f columa fornicis

ha nucleus habenularis
h hippocampus
hc commissura hippocampi
hp tractus habenulopeduncularis
lh nucleus lateralis hypothalami
mm corpus mamillare
oc chiasma opticum
mt tractus mammillothalamicus

ot tractus opticus
pc pedunculus cerebri
pv nucleus filiformis pars paraventricularis
r nucleus reticularis
s nucleus subthalamicus
sm stria medullaris
th thalmus
vm nucleus ventromedialis hypothalami

se area septalis

followed from top to bottom, it will be seen that different response patterns have different distributions. In this plane, there are almost no mating points, a cluster of attack points is located dorsally, a cluster of threat points is located ventrally in the vicinity of the ventromedial nucleus, a narrow group of eating points is located dorsally in the same region as attack, grooming points are absent, and locomotion is elicited from almost all regions with the exception of the ventromedial nucleus and thalamus. In the diagram as a whole, the zones for different responses overlap to different degrees, but all of the zones differ appreciably from each other in at least some portion of their distribution, and the two responses that overlapped the most, grooming and mating, were dissociated in a later study in which localized warming of the zone of overlap induced grooming without mating (Roberts, Bergquist and Robinson, 1969).

Bergquist (1968, 1970) has shown that the output pathways for eating, male sexual behavior, biting attack, grooming and investigatory behavior descend in the medial forebrain bundle to the midbrain, while those for defensive threat descend through a dorsomedial path, probably the periventricular system. Elicitation of the first group of responses by hypothalamic stimulation was blocked by lateral posterior hypothalamic lesions in the vicinity of the medial forebrain bundle, but not by medial posterior lesions. The defensive threat response was blocked by medial or dorsomedial posterior lesions, but not by lateral lesions. The lesions blocked responses evoked by ipsilateral electrodes, but not those induced by contralateral electrodes, which rules out the possibility that the blockage might have been caused by lethargy or other general impairment. Larger lesions that interrupted the anterior medial forebrain bundle in the preoptic region or severed the lateral connections of the hypothalamus with the amygdala and basal ganglia had no effect, indicating that the paths to the midbrain are not only necessary for hypothalamic elicitation of the responses, but are also sufficient in the absence of the anterior or lateral connections. Valenstein, Cox and Kakolewski (1970) have reported preliminary evidence confirming these findings for eating and drinking elicited from the hypothalamus of the rat.

Hypothalamic specificity in other species

Unfortunately, none of the stimulation studies of hypothalamic motivational mechanisms in the cat have combined maximally broad behavioral testing with a systematic distribution of electrodes throughout the hypothalamus and preoptic region. Despite incompleteness with respect to behavioral or anatomical coverage or both, an appreciable degree of anatomical differentiation is discernable in the studies of Hess (1957), Hunsperger (1956), Flynn (1967), Roberts and Kiess (1964) and Roberts and Robinson (1969). The components of affective defense are most consistently elicited by electrical stimulation in the medial hypothalamus, silent biting attack is most consistently evoked from the lateral and part of the dorsomedial hypothalamus, and bodily relaxation going over into sleep is induced by diathermic warming of the medial preoptic and anterior hypothalamic region (Figure 1).

Because of the considerable evidence for specificity in the hypothalamus of the opossum and the cat, I feel that we must take a skeptical attitude toward conclusions that the rat's hypothalamus is organized differently until more complete data is available on a wide variety of behaviors and a relatively thorough anatomical exploration of the hypothalamus and preoptic region. This conclusion is reinforced by a study of centrally elicited attack in rats by one of my students, Mrs Carrol Woodworth (1970), in which she also tested for a number of other oral and locomotor responses. Although the study was not designed to be a complete mapping of the hypothalamus, clear evidence was obtained for a significant degree of anatomical differentiation among at least three groups of responses. As the second row of Figure 4 shows, a group of oral responses that included eating, gnawing, carrying objects, licking, and mouthing of objects were elicited predominantly from the dorsal two-thirds of the lateral hypothalamus. Attack responses, shown in the top row, were evoked predominantly from a smaller region located ventral and lateral to the fornix. A third pattern, termed 'alarm' by Woodworth, which consisted of crouching, intermittent bursts of rapid locomotion and jumping, was elicited from the largest zone, including all levels of the medial hypothalamus and part of the

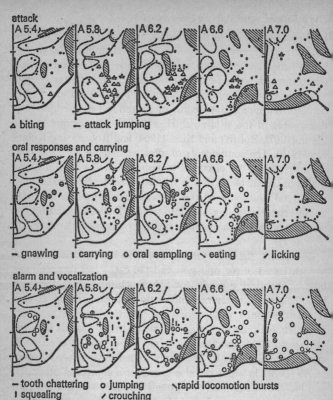

attack

A 5.4 A 5.8 A 6.2 A 6.6 A 7.0

△ biting   — attack jumping

oral responses and carrying

A 5.4 A 5.8 A 6.2 A 6.6 A 7.0

— gnawing   ı carrying   o oral sampling   ↘ eating   ⁄ licking

alarm and vocalization

A 5.4 A 5.8 A 6.2 A 6.6 A 7.0

— tooth chattering   o jumping   ↘ rapid locomotion bursts
ı squealing   ⁄ crouching

Figure 4 Location of electrodes that elicited biting attack, a group of oral responses and an 'alarm' response pattern plotted on frontal plane diagrams of the middle and anterior hypothalamus (after de Groot, 1959). Negative points are indicated by small, solid circles
(courtesy of Carrol H. Woodworth)

anterior lateral hypothalamus. Exploratory locomotion accompanied by sniffing and looking around was induced to a varying degree by almost all hypothalamic electrodes and so was not plotted in the figure.

Woodworth's finding that the oral response group was elicited predominantly from the dorsolateral hypothalamus is confirmed by a detailed examination of Figures 1 and 2 in Valenstein, Cox and Kakolewski (1970). In addition to the anterior and ventromedial nuclei mentioned as negative areas by the authors, the great majority of points in the dorsomedial hypothalamus and the ventral third of the lateral hypothalamus were also negative. Thus, 89 per cent of the positive points in the first eight diagrams (which correspond to the region covered in Woodworth's study) were located lateral to the medial edge of the fornix and dorsal to the ventral edge of the fornix. Of the 168 points in this dorsolateral zone, 53 per cent elicited eating, gnawing, or drinking, and 47 per cent did not, while only 12 per cent of the 91 points located ventral or medial to this zone were positive, and 88 per cent were negative. This difference in the anatomical distribution of positive and negative cases was significant beyond the 0·001 level (chi square = 41·6). Woodworth's finding regarding the predominantly ventrolateral location of the biting attack is also in good agreement with the descriptions of King and Hoebel (1968), Panksepp and Trowill (1969), and Vergnes and Karli (1969). In diagrams 1–8 of Valenstein, Cox and Kakolewski (1970) Figures 1 and 2, this region (defined as ventral to the edge of the fornix and 0·3 mm or more lateral to the anterior and ventromedial nuclei) contained only 4 points that elicited eating, gnawing, or drinking out of a total of 28, which differed from the proportion of positive points in the dorsolateral region at the 0·001 level (chi square = 14·4). Similar results were obtained when the analysis was limited to diagrams 5–8.

Thus, Woodworth has shown that the apparently coextensive overlap of eating, drinking, and gnawing reported by Valenstein, Cox and Kakolewski (1969, 1970) is a special characteristic of certain oral responses, and that if a wider range of behaviors is examined, significant evidence for anatomical differentiation, and therefore functional specificity, can be found in the hypothalamus of the rat. Clearly, the attack response was produced by different hypothalamic neurons than the oral responses, and although the alarm pattern overlapped appreciably with the other two patterns in the rostral hypothalamus, its distribution was too disparate in the medial hypothalamus and in the lateral hypothalamus in planes 5·4 and 5·8 to be attributed to the same mechanism as attack or the oral responses.

The apparently coextensive overlap of the oral responses cannot be taken as conclusive evidence that they were all produced by a single undifferentiated mechanism, because of the alternative possibility that the non-specific stimulation was exciting separate but overlapping mechanisms. Although anatomical data are unable to resolve the question of the specificity of the substrates for the oral responses, further evidence regarding the functional specificity of eating, gnawing and drinking is available from an experiment that tested whether the 'modifiability' phenomenon reported by Valenstein and his co-workers is sufficiently broad to be consistent with a single underlying mechanism.

An experimental reexamination of 'modifiability' of hypothalamic responses

Valenstein's *et al.* (1968, 1969) principal basis for questioning the specificity of the mechanisms for motivational responses elicited from the hypothalamus was their finding that in initial tests most electrodes elicited only one of the three responses that they studied, but a second response could be 'trained' by removing the goal object for the first response and giving a large number of stimulation trials in the presence of the goal objects for both missing responses.

After reading this report, we felt that the crucial aspect for the issue of specificity versus plasticity was not the evidence that practice strengthened the performance of responses, but rather the implication that experience was the *sole* determinant of which of the three responses would be obtained. The increased performance of responses with practice (which has a counterpart in normal consummatory behavior (e.g. Bolles, 1967, pp. 190–91, 206–10) could be explained by the rewarding effect of performance of centrally induced responses (or their sensory feedback), which has been demonstrated in a number of studies from our own and other laboratories (Andersson, Larsson, and Persson, 1960; Coons, Levak and Miller, 1965; Roberts and Carey, 1965; Roberts and Kiess, 1964; Roberts, Steinberg and Means, 1967). Such reward effects are not incompatible with specific unlearned stimulus-response mechanisms, which they would supplement under natural conditions by training instrumental approach responses toward goal objects, specific incentive motivation, and other adaptive habits (Roberts and Carey, 1965). The failure of

Valenstein's *et al.* rats to show more than one response during the first phase of their experiment, and the delayed emergence of a second response after the removal of the initially preferred object can both be explained in terms of learning of approach habits and incentive motivation toward specific goal objects which would interfere with experience with other objects. Also, the early development of a single object preference in the first phase of Valenstein's *et al.* experiment was probably facilitated by their failure to interchange systematically the location of the goal objects, as is usually done in choice experiments.

The critical question is whether this learning process is the sole determinant of which components of the eating-drinking group are obtained, or whether the learning only supplements and reinforces the contributions of separate but spatially overlapping mechanisms controlling specific sensorimotor circuits and associated reinforcement mechanisms. Valenstein, Cox and Kakolewski (1968, 1969, 1970) have argued forcefully against the possibility of separate overlapping mechanisms, and instead have proposed that all three responses have a single substrate similar to that proposed by Von Holst and Von Saint Paul (1963) for their higher order 'moods'.

If it is true that eating, gnawing and drinking evoked by hypothalamic stimulation are produced by the same undifferentiated mechanism under the influence of learning, it follows that any electrode capable of exciting the mechanism, as indicated by elicitation of one of the three responses, should be trainable to elicit either of the other two responses equally well. This crucial property was not really demonstrated in Valenstein's *et al.* experiment, in which most animals displayed only two responses at the end of training, and the few who did display three responses did not perform them equally. Andrew P. Phelan and I therefore decided to test the hypothesis of non-specific plasticity by using non-competitive single-object tests to detect as many responses as possible in the initial phase, followed by overnight training with the one type of object that was most ignored in the pretests. If the missing responses appeared and grew as strong as the initially dominant response, the data would be consistent with non-specific plasticity. If an appreciable number of missing responses could not be trained, or if trainable, were markedly weaker than the initially prefered response, non-specific plasticity would be ruled out, and the alternative hypothesis of overlapping specific mechanisms supported. Because of the appreciable individual differences in detailed anatomical localization discussed earlier, we felt that we might find less than complete overlap in individual animals, in spite of the apparently coextensive overlap of massed group data.

Figure 5 shows the relative frequency with which one, two and

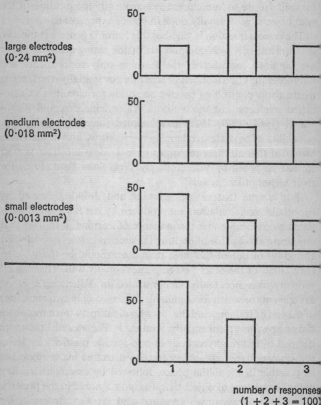

Figure 5 Relative frequency of electrodes that elicited one, two, or three responses of the eating-gnawing-drinking group in preliminary tests. For comparison, the data of Table 1 of Valenstein, Cox and Kakolewski (1969) is summarized in the bottom line

three oral responses were obtained in the initial tests from positive electrodes (i.e. electrodes that elicited at least one of the three responses). The electrodes were located in the same dorsolateral hypothalamic region as those of Valenstein *et al.* Because such a high proportion of electrodes in the first group elicited two or three responses, we reduced the scraped area on the electrodes of the second group to $\frac{1}{4}$ of the area of the first electrodes, and for the third group, it was reduced further to $\frac{1}{185}$ of the initial area. Despite this wide variation in tip size, a large proportion of positive electrodes in each group (55–75 per cent) elicited two or three responses. This contrasts with the experiment of Valenstein, Cox and Kakolewski (1969), shown in the bottom line, in which only 36 per cent of the positive electrodes elicited more than one response, and none evoked three responses. This difference strongly suggests that the competitive multiple-object pretests used by Valenstein *et al.* tended to focus the animal's behavior on a single response to the exclusion of other responses that could have been detected in the pretests if only one type of object had been presented at a time.

Next, 12 rats having electrodes that elicited one or two oral responses were given seven nights of training with one type of ignored object. They received an average total of 1,051 stimulation trials that were 30 sec long and were separated by $4\frac{1}{2}$-minute rest periods. This was about three times the average amount of training given by Valenstein *et al.* Competitive choice tests were given at the beginning, in the middle, and at the end of the seven nights.

Figure 6 shows the frequency and duration of the preferred and the trained responses in the competitive tests. Six rats, indicated by the solid line, showed absolutely no evidence of new responses, although they continued to perform their preferred responses vigorously, indicating that the effectiveness of the electrodes and current levels had not deteriorated. All three responses were represented in this group. The other 6 rats, indicated by the dashed line, developed weak responses that in no case reached the performance level of the initially dominant response. The differences between the preferred and trained responses in both frequency and duration were significant beyond the 0·0001 level. In the group that displayed some overnight acquisition, the weak-

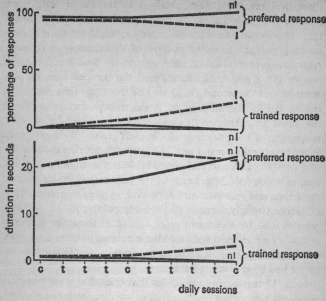

Figure 6 Average percentage and duration of initially preferred and trained responses in choice tests before, in the middle and after seven nights of intermittent stimulation in the presence of initially ignored goal objects. Six rats that evidenced no learning of the trained response are represented by the solid lines, six that evidenced weak learning by the dashed lines

ness of the trained responses was evident even in post-training single-object tests, where they did not have to compete with the initially preferred response. The difference between the mean duration of the trained response, 15·6 sec, and the initially preferred response, 26·4 sec, was significant at the 0·02 level. Since all of the acquired responses were evidenced in the midtraining tests, which were followed by 606 training trials, their weakness cannot be attributed to insufficient practice.

Valenstein, Cox and Kakolewski (1969, 1970) have suggested that failure to train responses in overnight sessions may sometimes be due to extended practice on the first appearing responses or to acquisition of interfering responses outside of the eating-gnawing-drinking group, such as grooming the tail or other parts of the body. However, in the present experiment, the amount of experience with the initial responses was limited to the minimum necessary to verify their presence and to measure their strength during training, which was of the same order as the amount of experience given in Valenstein's *et al.* tests. While we have occasionally observed interfering responses like those described by Valenstein *et al.* in other experiments, they were not apparent in the animals of the present experiment except for one rat who displayed weak tail biting on 25 per cent of the final single-object test trials with the training object, but not in the competitive choice tests. The fact that the rats who evidenced weak learning performed the acquired responses for 15·6 sec in the final single-object tests also argues against strong unidentified interfering responses.

In summary, this evidence indicates that many electrodes that elicit eating, drinking, or gnawing cannot be trained to elicit all three responses equally. If single-object tests are used at the beginning to detect as many responses as possible, the remainder are either untrainable or only weakly trainable despite a very large number of trials. This evidence is incompatible with the hypothesis of a single non-specific plastic substrate, but is consistent with the alternative hypothesis of overlapping but specific mechanisms. It appears that the circuits for eating, drinking, and gnawing intermesh considerably in the hypothalamus of rats, but not so much that they are excited equally by all electrodes located within their zones.

Valenstein's *et al.* demonstration of the strong capacity of practiced responses to interfere with unpracticed responses in competitive choice tests with fixed goal objects is a striking example of the reinforcing property associated with the performance or sensory feedback of many hypothalamic motivational responses. In competitive tests, the development of approach habits and incentive motivation for a particular goal object evidently depends not only on the availability of the object, but also on sufficient 'free time' from interfering behaviors to investigate and practice consummatory responses with the object. Even when only one object is available, there is occasionally a brief initial period of improvement in the latency and duration of responses. It appears that the stimulation potentiates the capacity of rather specific proximal cues to elicit specific consummatory responses (MacDonnell and Flynn, 1966), but approach responses toward many distal cues of goal objects or toward associated environmental cues must be learned through consummatory reinforcement.

References

ANDERSSON, B., LARSSON, S., and PERSSON, N. (1960), 'Some characteristics of the hypothalamic "drinking centre" in the goat as shown by the use of permanent electrodes', *Acta physiol. scand.*, vol. 50, pp. 140–52.

ANDERSSON, B., and McCANN, S. M. (1955), 'Drinking antidiuresis, and milk ejection from electrical stimulation within the hypothalamus of the goat', *Acta physiol. scand.*, vol. 35, pp. 191–201.

ASANUMA, H., and SAKATA, H. (1967), 'Functional organization of a cortical efferent system examined with focal depth stimulation in cats', *J. Neurophysiol.*, vol. 30, pp. 35–54.

BARD, P. (1928), 'A diencephalic mechanism for the expression of rage with special reference to the sympathetic nervous system', *Amer. J. Physiol.*, vol. 84, pp. 490–515.

BARD, P. (1950), 'Central nervous mechanisms for the expression of anger in animals', in M. L. Reymert, *Feelings and Emotions*, McGraw-Hill, pp. 211–37.

BERGQUIST, E. H. (1968), 'Output pathways of hypothalamic mechanisms for sexual, aggressive, and other motivational behaviors in opossum', doctoral dissertation, University of Minnesota.

BERGQUIST, E. H. (1970), 'Output pathways of hypothalamic mechanisms for sexual, aggressive and other motivational behaviors in opossum', *J. compar. Psychol.*, vol. 70 pp. 389–98.

BOLLES, R. C. (1967), *Theory of Motivation*, Harper & Row.

COONS, E. E., LEVAK, M., and MILLER, N. E. (1965), 'Lateral hypothalamus: learning of food-seeking response motivated by electrical stimulation', *Sci.*, vol. 150, pp. 1320–1.

DOTY, R. W. (1969), 'Electrical stimulation of the brain in behavioral context', *Ann. Rev. Psychol.*, vol. 20, pp. 289–320.

FERNANDEZ DE MOLINA, A., and HUNSPERGER, R. W. (1959), 'Central representation of affective reactions in forebrain and brain stem: electrical stimulation of amygdala, stria terminalis, and adjacent structures', *J. Physiol.*, vol. 145, pp. 251–65.

FLYNN, J. P. (1967), 'The neural basis of aggression in cats', in D.C. Glass, *Neurophysiology and Emotion*, Rockefeller University Press, pp. 40–60.

GROSSMAN, S. P. (1960), 'Eating or drinking elicited by direct adrenergic or cholinergic stimulation of hypothalamus', *Sci.*, vol. 132, pp. 301–2.

GROSSMAN, S. P. (1962), 'Effects of adrenergic and cholinergic blocking agents on hypothalamic mechanisms', *Amer. J. Physiol.*, vol. 202, pp. 1230–6.

GROSSMAN, S. P. (1964), 'Some neurochemical aspects of the central regulation of thirst', in M. J. Wayner, *Thirst*, Pergamon, pp. 487–510.

HESS, W. R. (1957), *The Functional Organization of the Diencephalon*, Grune & Stratton.

HESS, W. R., and BRUGGER, M. (1943), 'Das subkortikale Zentrum der affektiven Abwehr-Reaktion', *Helv. physiol. pharmacol. Acta* 1, pp. 33–52.

HOLST, E. VON, and SAINT PAUL, U. VON (1963), 'On the functional organization of drives', *Anim. Behav.*, vol. 11, pp. 1–20.

HUBEL, D. H. (1967), 'Effects of distortion of sensory input on the visual system of kittens', *Physiologist*, vol. 10, pp. 17–45.

HUNSPERGER, R. W. (1956), 'Affektreaktionen auf elektrische Reizung in Hirnstamm der Katz', *Helv. physiol. pharmacol. Acta*, vol. 14, pp. 70–92.

HUTCHINSON, R. R., and RENFREW, J. W. (1966), 'Stalking attack and eating behaviors elicited from the same sites in the hypothalamus', *J. compar. physiol. Psychol.*, vol. 61, pp. 360–7.

KING, M. B., and HOEBEL, B. G. (1968), 'Killing elicited by brain stimulation in rats', *Comm. Behav. Biol.* Part A2, pp. 173–7.

LASHLEY, K. S. (1929), *Brain Mechanisms and Intelligence*, University of Chicago Press.

MACDONNELL, M. F., and FLYNN, J. P. (1966), 'Control of sensory fields by stimulation of hypothalamus', *Sci.*, vol. 152, pp. 1406–8.

MILLER, N. E. (1960), 'Motivational effects of brain stimulation and drugs', *Fed. Proc.*, vol. 19, pp. 846–54.

MILNER, P. M. (1969), 'Do behaviorists really need a brain drain?', in R. B. Macleod, *William James: Unfinished Business*, American Psychological Association, Washington, D.C., pp. 17–19.

NAKAYAMA, T., HAMMEL, H. T., HARDY, J. D., and EISENMAN, J. S. (1963), 'Thermal stimulation of electrical activity of single units of the preoptic region', *Amer. J. Physiol.*, vol. 204, pp. 1122–6.

PANKSEPP, J., and TROWILL, J. (1969), 'Electrically induced affective attack from the hypothalamus of the albino rat', *Psychon. Sci.*, vol. 16, pp. 118–9.

PENFIELD, W., and BOLDREY, E. (1937), 'Somatic motor and sensory representation in the cerebral cortex of man as studied by electrical stimulation', *Brain*, vol. 60, pp. 389–443.

PENFIELD, W., and JASPER, H. (1954), *Epilepsy and the Functional Anatomy of the Human Brain*, Little, Brown.

PORTER, R. (1963), 'Focal stimulation of hypoglossal neurones in the cat', *J. Physiol.*, vol. 169, pp. 630–40.

ROBERTS, W. W. (in press), 'Hypothalamic mechanisms for motivational and species-typical behavior', in N. Whalen, B. Thompson, F. Verzeano and R. Weinberger, *The Neural Control of Behavior*, Academic Press.

ROBERTS, W. W., and BERGQUIST, E. H. (1968), 'Attack elicited by hypothalamic stimulation in cats raised in social isolation', *J. compar. physiol. Psychol.*, vol. 66, pp. 590–5.

ROBERTS, W. W., BERGQUIST, E. H., and ROBINSON, T. C. L. (1968), 'Thermoregulatory grooming and sleep-like relaxation induced by local warming of preoptic area and anterior hypothalamus in opossum', *J. compar. physiol. Psychol.*, vol. 67, pp. 182–8.

ROBERTS, W. W., and CAREY, R. J. (1965), 'Rewarding effect of performance of gnawing aroused by hypothalamic stimulation in the rat', *J. compar. physiol. Psychol.*, vol. 59, pp. 317–24.

ROBERTS, W. W., and KIESS, H. O. (1964), 'Motivational properties of hypothalamic aggression in cats', *J. compar. physiol. Psychol.*, vol. 58, 187–93.

ROBERTS, W. W., and ROBINSON, T. C. L. (1969), 'Relaxation and sleep induced by warming of preoptic region and anterior hypothalamus in cats', *Exper. Neurol.*, vol. 25, pp. 282–94.

ROBERTS, W. W., STEINBERG, M. L., and MEANS, L. W. (1967), 'Hypothalamic mechanisms for sexual, aggressive, and other motivational behaviors in the opossum. Didelphis virginiana', *J. compar. physiol. Psychol.*, vol. 64, pp. 1–15.

SCHLAG, J., and VILLABLANCA, J. (1968), 'A study of temporal and spatial response patterns in a thalamic cell population electrically stimulated', *Brain Res.*, vol. 8, pp. 255–70.

STONEY, S. D., THOMPSON, W. O., and ASANUMA, H. (1968), 'Excitation of pyramidal tract cells by intracortical microstimulation; effective extent of stimulating current', *J. Neurophysiol.*, vol. 31, pp. 659–69.

STUTZ, R. M., BUTCHER, R. E., and ROSSI, R. (1969), 'Stimulus properties of reinforcing brain shock', *Sci.*, vol. 163, pp. 1081–2.

VALENSTEIN, E. S., COX, V. C., and KAKOLEWSKI, J. W. (1968), 'Modification of motivated behavior elicited by electrical stimulation of the hypothalamus', *Sci.*, vol. 159, pp. 1119–21.

VALENSTEIN, E. S., COX, V. C., and KAKOLEWSKI, J. W. (1969), 'The hypothalamus and motivated behavior', in R. Tapp, *Reinforcement*, Academic Press.

VALENSTEIN, E. S., COX, V. C., and KAKOLEWSKI, J. W. (1970), 'Reexamination of the role of the hypothalamus in motivation', *Psychol. Rev.*, vol. 77, pp. 16–31.

VAUGHAN, E., and FISHER, A. E. (1962), 'Male sexual behavior induced by intracranial electrical stimulation', *Sci.*, vol. 137, pp. 758–60.

VERGNES, M., and KARLI, P. (1969), 'Effects of stimulation of the laterial hypothalamus, amygdala and hippocampus on interspecific rat-mouse aggressive behavior', *Physiol. Behav.*, vol. 4, pp. 889–94.

WISE, R. A. (1968), 'Hypothalamic motivational systems: fixed or plastic neural circuits?', *Sci.*, vol. 162, pp. 377–9.

WIT, A., and WANG, S. C. (1968), 'Temperature-sensitive neurons in preoptic/anterior hypothalamic region: effects of increasing ambient temperature', *Amer. J. Physiol.*, vol. 215, pp. 1151–9.

WOODWORTH, C. H. (1970), 'Attack elicited in rats by electrical stimulation of the lateral hypothalamus', doctoral dissertation, University of Minnesota.

WOOLSEY, C. N., SETTLAGE, P. H., MEYER, D. R., SENCER, W., HAMUY, T. P., and TRAVIS, A. M. (1952), 'Patterns of localization in precentral and "supplementary" motor areas and their relation to the concept of a permotor area', *Res. Publ. Ass. nerv. ment. Diseases*, vol. 30, pp. 238–64.

Further Reading

Berlyne, D. E. (1960), *Conflict, Arousal and Curiosity*, McGraw-Hill, chs 4, 5, and 6. (For Part Two.)

Bindra, D. *Motivation: A Systematic Reinterpretation*, Ronald Press. (For Parts One and Two.)

Bindra, D. (1969), 'A unified interpretation of emotion and motivation', *Ann. of New York Acad. Sci.*, vol. 159, pp. 1079–83. (For Part Four.)

Bindra, D. (1968), 'Neuropsychological interpretation of the effects of drive and incentive-motivation on general activity and instrumental behavior', *Psychol. Rev.*, vol. 75, pp. 1–22. (For Parts Three and Four.)

Bolles, R. C. (1967), *Theory of Motivation*, Harper Row. (For Parts One and Two.)

Bowlby, J. (1969), *Attachment and Loss*, vol. 1, *Attachment*, Hogarth Press. (For Part Four.)

Cofer, C. N., and Appley, M. H. (1964), *Motivation: Theory and Research*, Wiley, ch. 10. (For Part Two.)

Harlow, H. F. (1962), 'The heterosexual affectional system in monkeys', *Amer. Psychol.*, vol. 17, pp. 1–9. (For Part Four.)

Kent, E., and Grossman, S. P. (1969), 'Evidence for a conflict interpretation of anomalous effects of rewarding brain stimulation', *J. compar. physiol. Psychol.*, vol. 69, pp. 381–90. (For Part Five.)

Landauer, T. K. (1969), 'Reinforcement as consolidation', *Psychol. Rev.*, vol. 76, pp. 82–96. (For Part Six.)

Lehrman, D. S. (1953), 'A critique of Konrad Lorenz's theory of instinctive behavior', *Q. Rev. Biol.*, vol. 38, pp. 337–63. (For Part One.)

Malmo, R. B. (1958), 'Measurement of drive: an unsolved problem in psychology', in M. R. Jones (ed.), *Nebraska Symposium on Motivation*, University of Nebraska Press, pp. 229–65. (For Part Two.)

Mayner, M. J. (1970), 'Motor control functions of the lateral hypothalamus and adjunctive behavior', *Physiol. Behav.*, vol. 5, pp. 1319–25. (For Part Six.)

Nissen, H. W. (1954), 'The nature of the drive as innate determinant of behavioral organization', in M. R. Jones (ed.), *Nebraska Symposium on Motivation*, University of Nebraska Press, pp. 281–321. (For Parts One and Two.)

Olds, J. (1969), 'The central nervous system and the reinforcement of behavior', *Amer. Psychol.*, vol. 24, pp. 114–32. (For Part Five.)

Roberts, W. W., and Kiess, H. O. (1964), 'Motivational properties of hypothalamic aggression in cats', *J. compar. physiol. Psychol.*, vol. 58, pp. 187–93. (For Part Two.)

Roberts, W. W., Steinberg, M. L., and Means, L. W. (1967), 'Hypothalamic mechanisms for sexual, aggressive, and other motivational behaviors in the opossum, Didelphis Virginian A', *J. compar. physiol. Psychol.*, vol. 64, pp. 1–15. (For Parts Five and Six.)

Routtenberg, A. (1968), 'The two-arousal hypothesis: Reticular formation and limbic system', *Psychol. Rev.*, vol. 75, pp. 51–79. (For Part Six.)

Schneirla, T. C. (1959), 'An evolutionary and developmental theory of biphasic processes underlying approach and withdrawal', in M.R. Jones (ed.), *Nebraska Symposium on Motivation*, University of Nebraska Press, pp. 1–42. (For Part Four.)

Seward, J. P. (1956), 'Drive, incentive and reinforcement', *Psychol. Rev.*, vol. 63, pp. 195–203. (For Part Four.)

Stein, L. (1968), 'Chemistry of reward and punishment', in D. H. Efron (ed.), *Proceedings* (1968) *American College of Neuropsychopharmacology*, United States Government Printing Office, Washington, D.C. (For Part Six.)

Stewart, J. (1960), 'Reinforcing effects of light as a function of intensity and reinforcement schedule', *J. compar. physiol. Psychol.*, vol 53, pp. 187–93. (For Part Four.)

Thorpe, W. H. (1963), *Learning and Instinct in Animals*, (2nd edn.), Methuen. (For Part One.)

Tinbergen, N. (1963), 'On aims and methods of ethology', *Zs. Tierpsychol.*, vol. 20, pp. 410–33. (For Part One.)

Young, P. T. (1961), *Motivation and Emotion*, Wiley. (For Parts One and Two.)

Acknowledgements

Permission to reproduce Readings and Plates in this volume is acknowledged to the following sources:

Readings

1 Methuen & Co.
2 Basic Books Inc. and Hogarth Press
3 Cambridge University Press
4 Clarendon Press
5 Cambridge University Press
6 American Psychological Association and F. A. Beach
7 Columbia University Press
8 American Psychological Association and K. S. Lashley
9 McGraw-Hill
10 Appleton-Century-Crofts
11 McGraw-Hill
12 American Psychological Association and H. F. Harlow
13 American Psychological Association and D. O. Hebb
14 Appleton-Century-Crofts
15 Macmillan Co.
16 Appleton-Century-Crofts
17 Macmillan Co.
18 Yale University Press
19 University of Nebraska Press
20 American Psychological Association and D. Bindra
21 Van Nostrand Co.
22 American Psychological Association and P. T. Young
23 American Psychological Association and C. P. Pfaffman
24 *Animal Behaviour*, P. K. Levinson and J. P. Flynn
25 American Psychological Association, H. F. Harlow and S. J. Suomi
26 Little, Brown & Co.
27 University of Nebraska Press
28 American Psychological Association, S. E. Glickman and B. B. Schiff
29 American Psychological Association, J. A. Trowill, J. Panksepp and R. Gandelman
30 University of Nebraska Press
31 American Psychological Association and E. Stellar
32 The New York Academy of Sciences

33 *Science* and N. E. Miller
34 American Psychological Association, E. S. Valenstein, V. C. Cox and J. W. Kakolewski
35 American Psychological Association, M. Devor, R. Wise, N. W. Milgram and B. G. Hoebel
36 *Brain, Behaviour and Evolution*

Plates

1–9 Wisconsin Regional Private Research Centre
10 Pergamon Press

Author Index

Subject Index

Acetylcholine, 416–17, 437–40

Adrenergic sites or circuits, 416–24, 455

Affective processes (including Hedonic processes), 193–204, 207–208, 214, 219, 221–6

Aggression, *see* Attack

Amygdala, 224, 289, 297–9, 388, 434–5, 488

Anxiety, *see* Fear

Approach (appetitive) behaviour, 25, 30–31, 174, 189, 285–99, 309, 361, 364; *see also* Instrumental response

Arousal (including Activation), 126–31, 206, 225–6

Attack, 175, 182, 232, 236–7, 285–9, 296–9, 357, 404–410, 438, 491, 495

Avoidance (aversion), 182, 196, 212, 219, 223, 280, 297, 299, 309, 361, 434, 485, 495; *se e also* Escape

Blood chemistry, *see* Chemical factor

Caudate nucleus, 253, 268–9

Central motive state (c.m.s), 9, 73, 77–82, 178–80, 183–4, 350–69, 375–6, 464–6

Cerebral cortex, 287, 376, 378, 388, 494

Chemical coding, 374, 411–40, 455
  acetylcholine, 416–17, 437–40
  adrenergic sites or circuits, 416–24, 456
  amphetamine, 423
  atropine, 420, 427, 434
  carbachol, 417–18, 421, 425–40, 456
  cholinergic sites or circuits, 416–24, 432, 455, 457, 486

  cholinesterase, 420
  dibenzyline, 434
  epinephrine, 424, 431, 433, 440
  gamma-amino butyric acid, 435
  norepinephrine, 416, 421–5, 428–40
  reward–punishment systems and, 433, 436
  serotonin, 431
  transmitter agents and, 416, 418–20, 435–7, 440

Chemical factor, 75–6, 290, 393, 398; *see also* Internal environment

Conditioned emotional response (CER), 308

Consummatory activity or response, 25, 30–32, 69–70, 171, 175–7, 180, 182, 208, 215, 219, 222, 224, 226, 251, 277, 287–8, 291, 294, 296, 310, 332, 345, 349, 355, 357–9, 374, 387, 393, 444, 464–5, 479, 491, 493

Copulating (including sexual motivation), 285, 329, 379, 383, 385, 389–90, 412–16, 482, 484–5, 492

Cue function, 128

Curiosity, 111–12, 122, 125, 130 *see also* Exploration

Defensive action, 286–7, 297–9, 495, 498

Displacement activity, 33–4, 41

Drinking (including thirst), 285, 287, 291, 293–5, 328, 357, 379, 411–13, 417, 420–35, 439, 444–60, 469–86, 490, 498, 507

Drive (including *D*), 9, 12, 65–8, 72–4, 85–92, 104, 120, 129, 153–7, 165, 171–9, 181–3, 290, 310–12, 317–18, 326–8, 330–31, 347–9, 353–5, 362, 366, 373, 376, 451, 464

Penguin Modern Psychology Readings

Other titles in this series

Penguin Science of Behaviour

Penguin Modern Psychology Major Texts

Behaviour Therapy in Clinical Psychiatry
V. Meyer and Edward S. Chesser

A thorough, balanced account of the theory, practice and
effectiveness of behaviour therapy. This form of treatment, derived
from experimental psychology, plays a growing role in the treatment
of many illnesses, such as phobic anxieties, alcoholism, sexual
deviations, stammering, tics and eneuresis. Its techniques have at times
also been successfully employed in psychoses, psychosomatic disorders,
obsessional neuroses and childhood behaviour disorders.

Introducing Psychology:
An Experimental Approach
D. S. Wright, Ann Taylor
D. Roy Davies, W. Sluckin, S. G. M. Lee and J. T. Reason

This volume is a general introduction to the study of psychology.
However, it differs in certain respects from the usual introductory
text. Instead of trying to say something about everything, the authors
select a number of the main areas and deal with them in some depth.
These include the biological and structural determinants of behaviour,
the analysis of such functions as perceiving, remembering and thinking,
the structure of intelligence and personality, and the social influences
which shape behaviour. The emphasis is upon the experimental study
of the problems, and the treatment throughout is conceptual and
empirical rather than theoretical.